C000220684

WORK STRESS
AND COPING

I would like to thank all my Ph.D students for the support they have given me over the years in the field of stress and well-being, they are truly 'stars'!

Cary Cooper

To Linda with love and thanks.

Philip

PHILIP J. DEWE   CARY L. COOPER

WORK STRESS AND COPING

FORCES OF CHANGE AND CHALLENGES

Los Angeles | London | New Delhi
Singapore | Washington DC | Melbourne

Los Angeles | London | New Delhi
Singapore | Washington DC | Melbourne

SAGE Publications Ltd
1 Oliver's Yard
55 City Road
London EC1Y 1SP

SAGE Publications Inc.
2455 Teller Road
Thousand Oaks, California 91320

SAGE Publications India Pvt Ltd
B 1/I 1 Mohan Cooperative Industrial Area
Mathura Road
New Delhi 110 044

SAGE Publications Asia-Pacific Pte Ltd
3 Church Street
#10-04 Samsung Hub
Singapore 049483

Editor: Kirsty Smy
Editorial assistant: Lyndsay Aitken
Production editor: Katherine Haw
Proofreader: Christine Bitten
Indexer: Charmian Parkin
Marketing manager: Alison Borg
Cover design: Shaun Mercier
Typeset by: C&M Digitals (P) Ltd, Chennai, India
Printed by CPI Group (UK) Ltd, Croydon, CR0 4YY

© Philip Dewe 2017 and Cary Cooper 2017

First published 2017

Library of Congress Control Number: 2016955193

British Library Cataloguing in Publication data

A catalogue record for this book is available from
the British Library

ISBN 978-1-4739-1569-5
ISBN 978-1-4739-1570-1 (pbk)

At SAGE we take sustainability seriously. Most of our products are printed in the UK using FSC papers and boards.
When we print overseas we ensure sustainable papers are used as measured by the PREPS grading system.
We undertake an annual audit to monitor our sustainability.

CONTENTS

LIST OF TABLES

Note

The tables should be read in conjunction with the text. Each has been constructed from the text and reading them together gives a much richer understanding. Each table is an overview so it is the text that gives them a fuller meaning. Where authors are cited in the table they offer the opportunity to read further around the point being made.

ABOUT THE AUTHORS

Cary L. Cooper, CBE, is the author and editor of more than 150 scholarly books and is one of Britain's most quoted business gurus. He is the 50th Anniversary Professor of Organizational Psychology and Health at Manchester Business School, University of Manchester. He is a founding President of the British Academy of Management, a Companion of the Chartered Management Institute and one of only a few UK Fellows of the (American) Academy of Management, President of the Chartered Institute of Personnel and Development (CIPD), President of RELATE, President of the British Academy of Management and President of the Institute of Welfare. He was the Founding Editor of the *Journal of Organizational Behavior*, former Editor of the scholarly journal *Stress and Health* and is the Editor-in-Chief of the Wiley-Blackwell *Encyclopaedia of Management*, now in its third edition. He has been an advisor to the World Health Organisation, the ILO, and the EU in the field of occupational health and well-being, was Chair of the Global Agenda Council on Chronic Disease of the World Economic Forum (2009-2010) (currently serving on the Global Agenda Council for mental health of the WEF) and was Chair of the Academy of Social Sciences 2009-2015 (comprising 47 learned societies in the social sciences and 90,000 members). He was awarded the CBE by the Queen in 2001 for his contributions to occupational health and safety; and in 2014 he was awarded a Knighthood for his contribution to the social sciences.

Philip Dewe is Emeritus Professor of Organizational Behaviour in the Department of Organizational Psychology, Birkbeck, University of London. He graduated with a Masters degree in management and administration from Victoria University in Wellington, New Zealand and with an MSc and PhD from the London School of Economics. After a period of work in commerce in New Zealand he became a Senior Research Officer in the Work Research Unit, Department of Employment (UK). In 1980 he joined Massey University in New Zealand and headed the Department of Human Resource Management until joining the Department of Organizational Psychology, Birkbeck, University of London in 2000. Research interests include work stress and coping, emotions and human resource accounting. He is a member of the editorial board of *Work & Stress*. He has written widely in the area of work stress and coping.

I

INTRODUCTION

Stress and mental well-being at work

In a World Economic Forum and KPMG report (WEF 2015) on global mental health, it was found that although 'mental health disorders account for 13% of the total global burden of disease, yet receive only 2% of the health spend... and these carry considerable economic costs of some $2.5 trillion annually...', when it comes to the workplace, the common mental disorders of stress, depression and anxiety are enormous in terms of sickness absence and lost productive value. An OECD report of 21 countries found that not only were the incidence of stress-related absence and presenteeism (going to work ill but contributing no added value) significantly rising in these countries, but also that the average duration of the absence days was significantly longer than that for just physical illnesses. In the UK alone, poor mental well-being and stress in the workplace accounts for around £26b per annum in terms of absence, presenteeism and labour turnover, and over £120b for society at large (Cooper, Field, Goswani, Jenkins & Sahakian 2009).

Much of these costs to society and the economy can be attributed to the recession and the changing nature of work. Jobs are no longer for life, there are fewer people with heavier workloads (in order to keep the labour costs down to keep competitive with the emerging economies), people are working longer hours than ever before and many managers from top to shopfloor are managing people more as 'disposable assets'. This is also exacerbated by technology | (e.g. mobile phones, emails, social media) which means that people feel the need to be connected 24/7! Even before these technologies Albert Einstein allegedly once remarked 'I fear the day that technology will surpass our human interaction. The world will have a generation of idiots'. We may not be a generation of idiots yet, but this technology takes us away increasingly from our social relationships and ultimately from a sense of community.

We can see the impact of the recession and the inevitable changing nature of work in the latest Quality of Working Life survey of a cohort of 10,000 managers, from shop to top floor, by Worrall and Cooper (2016):

- 92% of managers work longer than their contracted hours; one more hour per day compared to 2012 or an extra 29 days a year unpaid.

- 78% report that the volume of work has substantially increased and 67% that the pace of work has increased, with 58% saying morale in their workplace has fallen.

- 68% say technology (e.g. emails) has made them stay productive and less job satisfied; 61% say they can't switch off and that this is adversely affecting family life.

- 54% say working longer hours is having a negative effect on their stress levels.

- 97% report their organization has undergone major change, leading to change fatigue.

- Command and control managers generate four times more stress than engaging managers.

In addition, the issue of flexible working arrangements is also significant, and change is needed given the demands of technology, the work–life balance issues and the difficulties experienced by two-earner and single-parent families. In the recent report by The Work Foundation *WorkingAnywhere* (TWF 2016) it was found among a sample of over 500 managers who worked flexibly that 54% said they got more work done, 49% felt 'trusted', 41% empowered and 46% that their work–life balance improved significantly. It is obvious that we need to change dramatically our way of working to accommodate this generation's needs, otherwise as Mark Twain once allegedly put it 'if you always do what you always did, you'll always get what you always got'.

Along with employers and managers being more flexible, managing people by praise and reward rather than faulting, ensuring staff have manageable workloads, realistic deadlines, achievable objectives and feel valued and trusted, we need to help people to become more resilient in coping with environmental and job stresses. Resilience is comprised of four characteristics (Cooper, Flint-Taylor & Pearn 2013):

1. Adaptability is how flexible and adaptable you are to changing situations which are beyond your control, and how you cope with the change. As Winston Churchill once said 'to improve is to change, to be perfect is to change often'.

2. Confidence is about your feelings of competence and effectiveness in coping with stressful situations – whether you have a firm sense of self-esteem.

3. Social support is about building good relationships with others and whether you have the ability to seek social support from others to overcome adverse situations.

4. Purposefulness is having a clear sense of purpose, clear values, drive and direction in the face of setbacks. This means being positive, being a 'glass half full' personality. As Kahlil Gibran the philosopher once wrote 'the optimist sees the rose and not the thorns, the pessimist stares at the thorns, oblivious to the rose'.

This book is about providing an historical account of workplace stress, what the research in the field of occupational stress tells us about the changing nature of work, and what individuals and organizations can do about it to create more liveable environments. Understanding the science of occupational stress and coping literature is the first step, then taking remedial and preventative actions can follow. We need to create more resilient and well-being cultures in workplaces (Chen & Cooper 2014). As John Ruskin, the social reformer, remarked in 1851: 'in order that people may be happy in their work, these three things are needed: they must be fit for it, they must not do too much of it, and they must have a sense of success in it'.

The themes running through the book

This book grew from our Dewe and Cooper (2012) publication. But here we wanted to explore in more depth the forces of change and then assess the ways these forces have changed the direction our research into work stress and coping has taken. As we go on to explain, these forces mark the significance of concepts like context and the explanatory potential that comes from that descriptive knowledge, of refining our approach and measures and the importance of the concept of relevance. Relevance has the power and authority to guide and direct the researcher-practitioner relationship. It gives new meanings to the concept of robustness and how relevance needs to be not just seen as a powerful tool but accepted by researchers as one that rates alongside reliability. It is also crucial to maintaining those moral responsibilities we have to those whose working lives we study. Running through this book are a number of other themes that allow us to assess our progress towards the goals outlined by John Ruskin. Of course the world has dramatically changed since Ruskin outlined his vision of meaningful work but it resonates with, and reflects, contemporary aspirations. These themes stem from the world we live in, the change and challenges of the realities of contemporary work and how they direct us implicitly and explicitly to consider the tools we need when considering the turbulence these forces of change produce.

These forces of change - globalization, advances in technology and the changing nature and structure of work, the type of work and the way we work all present challenges to those concerned with work stress and coping research. What distinguishes the power of these forces is their speed, their reach, both nationally and globally, and the fact that they touch all parts of society leaving all institutions and individuals engulfed in what seems like constant change, at times dramatically conditioned by the inevitable crisis that follows them. These forces test not just the individuals' resilience but that of the researchers as well, in their belief in those systems that once represented stability and certainty (Weinberg & Cooper 2012). It is why our first theme emphasizes getting to know the context within which our research is embedded and the power of the descriptive knowledge that comes from that understanding.

Understanding the context leads to our second theme that touches on the meanings individuals draw from the context and how these meanings represent the personal contexts that offer researchers considerable explanatory power and authority. These personal meanings are embedded in work stress research through the appraisal process (Lazarus 1999, 2001) and should now be given the critical attention they deserve. Our belief is that in work stress and coping research the need to give attention to the subtleties that allow distinguishing between 'describing a relationship and giving that relationship meaning' can only add to our understanding of the stress process (Dewe & Cooper 2012, p. 6), reflecting what Thoits describes as being 'faithful to the dynamic unfolding nature of the phenomena under investigation' (1995, p. 63).

As our themes are not mutually exclusive they lead us to the need to ensure that our work reflects the new realities of contemporary working and to express the nature of the work experience; hence the significance of the process of refining our measures to ensure their relevance. The themes of refinement and relevance are designed to strengthen our discipline and meet our moral responsibilities to those whose working lives we study. These themes are clearly embedded in the nature of our discipline and the relationship we establish with those who are consumers of our research. Refining measures hinges on researchers asking the question 'are our measures measuring what we think they are?' (Dewe & Cooper 2012, p. 93) and how well do they express the work experience? Refining is about ensuring that our measures capture the realities of the work experience giving them their relevance. Relevance is, in our view, a powerful concept ranking as highly as concepts like robustness and reliability. Relevance gives a new meaning to robustness – can research be robust if it is not relevant? Can measures be reliable if they are not relevant? Do we emphasize reliability at the expense of relevance? These themes of context, meaning, refining and relevance all reflect the power of the forces of change and reflect the significance of these themes in reshaping the nature of the empirical and moral responsibilities they impose on us and on our role as researchers.

The structure of the book

Following this introduction, Chapter II (Forces of change) explores each of the forces of change in some detail to provide an overview of their nature, power and authority and a context for much that follows. The chapter opens with a discussion of globalization noting that it is an 'undeniable and inescapable part of contemporary experience' (Bartelson 2000, p. 180), and how it is now so much a part of our everyday language (Therborn 2000). Globalization is generally defined in terms of the movement of 'people, objects, places and information and the structures they encounter and create' that limit or accelerate their movement (Ritzer 2011, p. 22). It is clear that there is still much debate around how globalization should be defined, whether it is a good thing and how it shapes our thinking, our theories and our research. It is also clear how 'globalization pressures' reflect the 'emerging realities of work' for all those working in the global workplace (Bhagat, Segovis & Nelson 2012, pp. 14–16; Noon, Blyton and Morrell 2013) and how 'bubbles and crashes' will be 'part of the future storyline' of globalization (Gratton 2014, pp. 32–33). Yet while globalization is described as multifaceted there is clearly a move to shift our focus towards alternative paths to considering globalization, calling for giving it a more progressive social meaning (Teivainen 2002, p. 628). This perhaps helps to explain the internationalization of well-being, as part of the search for metrics that are socially progressive and measure what matters to individuals - what they value. In this way we are breaking free from the limits that are imposed when GNP is measured in narrow economic terms; how the idea of happiness has assumed an international following and likewise the search for meaningful work. Illustrating globalization's reach, its power and authority provides a context against which we can assess how our measures, our theories and our research express the realities of contemporary work. The chapter then turns to the second of these forces: technology.

We begin our discussion of technology by exploring its transformational properties, the speed with which we have reached an interconnective world best expressed in terms of it being anytime, anyplace and always ready (Kleinrock 2008) and transforming 'from computer to computer, human to human, human to thing, and thing to thing' (Tan & Wang 2010, V5-376). But in addition to its speed and transformational properties (or because of them) technology has transformed behaviour, offering what are now known as cyberbehaviours. These cyberbehaviours may best be described as its legacy, introducing a new branch to our discipline – cyberpsychology – and expressing through behaviours like technostress, problematic internet use (Chiang & Su 2012), cyberslacking and cyberloafing (Lim & Chen 2012) and cyberbullying (Baruch 2005; D'Cruz & Noronha 2013) behaviours that we can use as the lens to best understand technology's impact, offering another opportunity through which we can better understand the realities of contemporary work.

Finally we turn to the third force, the changing nature of the workforce, society and sustainability (Gratton 2014). This is best expressed perhaps as a product of globalization and technology and reflecting their impact on the structure of organizations, the reshaping of work, the ways we work, the skills needed and the way in which contemporary organizations are managed and led, and the blurring of boundaries between work and home. This change to organizations and the type of working leads to the idea of social sustainability because of the 'costs imposed on people' as a result of organizational practices, policies and practices 'that have serious harmful effects on employees' physical and psychological wellbeing' (Pfeffer 2009, p. 5). This chapter focusing on globalization, technology and the changing nature of the workforce sets the scene and provides the context for what follows as we explore how these forces of change have influenced our theory, research and practice making the concepts of refinement and relevance significant tools when assessing our progress.

Chapter III traces the evolution of theory as it is shaped by the forces of change, testing our assumptions and their utility to express the nature of the contemporary experience of work. We begin by exploring how theories we are as familiar with as we are with those names associated with them (scientific management and human relations) are products of their time, emphasizing the importance of the context for understanding why such ideas emerged at the time they did. This theme of understanding theory through the lens of the context is echoed throughout this chapter as we move towards exploring open system thinking, powered by the significant role played by environmental factors and expressed through general system theory and the contingency theme, where behaviour is contingent on the relationship between the person and the environment. We then turn to the work of Lewin and to the ideas of person–environment fit and the fundamental understanding these ideas laid down to give us a context for studying and understanding behaviour of work. This leads on to a discussion of work stress theories and their evolution.

Work stress theory has moved through a number of phases closely reflecting the way work stress was defined. Its structural phase was influenced by the ideas of the person–environment fit approach, giving researchers the building blocks to explore the interactional relationship between a stimulus and a response. It was this phase that allowed researchers, as we have noted before, to engage in 'structural manipulations' that represented its second phase where researchers introduced a third variable to explore its moderating impact on the stimulus–response relationship. While providing much needed information on the causes and consequences of work stress, this phase failed to capture what was a complex relationship or the idea of the nature of the underlying process (Cooper & Dewe 2004; Cooper, Dewe & O'Driscoll 2001; Dewe & Cooper 2012). It was the idea that stress was a transaction between the individual and the environment (Lazarus 1999, 2001) that represented the third phase, and the idea of a transaction rather than an interaction offered researchers the opportunity to focus on the nature of the stress process. The key to the transaction is how it links through the appraisal process the individual and the environment. It is the appraisals process that gives Lazarus's work its authority and explanatory power. This focus through the power of appraisals introduced researchers to the explanatory potential of personal meanings and the context within which a stressful encounter occurred. Although, as Lazarus and Folkman (1991) admitted, while work stress researchers paid attention to process considerations they paid only 'lip service to the most advanced theories about the stress process' (1991, p. 2). To ignore the importance of the role of appraisals in the stress process is to fail to give these meanings the attention they deserved.

The chapter also reviews the widespread use of the person–environment fit framework for understanding work stress because it offers an instinctive appeal as it provides 'a process of adjustment' (Caplan 1987, p. 249), the description of the 'fit' relationship in terms of matching or a sense of congruence (Van Harrison 1978) and what Edwards and Cooper describe as the 'common sense notion' that one person's fit may be another's misfit (1990, p. 293). The notion of balance has also attracted attention (Meurs & Perrewé 2011) allowing researchers the opportunity to explore the adaptive qualities of balance, placing at the centre of their work the transaction between demands and resources (Karasek 1979; Demerouti, Bakker, Nachreiner & Schaufeli 2001), not forgetting Hobfoll's conservation of resources theory and the significance of the role of resource depletion and resource gain in determining stress. Work stress theories now offer frameworks for capturing the nature of the stress process and implicitly and explicitly pointing to adjustment, coping and meanings. Each offers a perspective that is transactional in nature, pointing to the ways in which the encounter is determined as stressful. Each in their way point to a context that allows the nature of the stressful encounter to emerge, giving the opportunity to explore not just personal meanings but to further explore the nature of concepts like resources, coping and demands to ensure that they reflect the contemporary work experience.

Chapter IV is headed 'The new millennium: developments, change and turbulence'. It identifies three waves of developments that welcomed the new millennium. The first wave points to two developments that have shaped our discipline: the positive psychology movement; and the second, that found its voice in the last decades of the twentieth century, saw, as the new century progressed, what was described as 'an affective revolution' (Barsade, Brief & Spataro 2003, p. 3) where the richness of studying discrete emotions at work came of age. The second wave saw individuals engulfed in an economic crisis that soon became described as a human crisis, where what we thought was stable and reliable was torn away with 'a terrible impact on well-being' (Anderson, Jané-Llopis & Cooper 2011, p. 353) where 'two worlds collided in mutual incomprehension' (Clark 2010, p. 6); the economic, financial world colliding with the individuals' world of hopes and aspirations, and wreaking mayhem across all parts of society. This turbulence released a call to consider alternative designs of corporate capitalism (Kasser, Cohn, Kanner & Ryan 2007a), the call for economic metrics like GNP to be recalibrated to represent what it is that people value reflecting the quality of their lives, the global interest in happiness as a measure of value and work that is meaningful. This turbulence also pointed to the way the language of economics had infiltrated management theory, setting in motion a narrow and reductionist view of management and leadership practices with the consequence that 'bad management theories are destroying good management practices' (Ghoshal 2005, p. 75).

The third wave in Chapter IV explores 'what may be' for the theories of organizational psychology and organizational behaviour (OP/OB) (Porter 2008; Porter & Schneider 2014). This involves considering the gap between research and practice (Corley & Gioia 2011), the arrival of the discipline of occupational health psychology and 'what may be' for our disciplines. Porter points to a future where OP/OB engage in what he describes as the two Cs (context and change) giving them 'more concentrated research' (Porter 2008, p. 525). Porter and Schneider (2014) put into question form what they believe are 'at least' some of the challenges that need to be confronted. The first concerns our ability to build 'a robust evidence-based analysis of behaviour in organizational settings'. The second questions whether we can demonstrate an ability to achieve a more meaningful integration of findings across the array of topics researched. The third question considers whether we can, through our research findings, achieve a greater impact on managerial practice and their final question asks about relevance and whether 'our theories [are] up to the task' (2014, pp. 14–18). The new millennium has brought considerable change, crises and turbulence. When there is 'change or the prospect of change there is turbulence in our lives as we try to come to terms with a new reality and prepare to adjust' (Weinberg & Cooper 2012, p. 3).

ChapterV is headed 'The evolving nature of work stressors: a prologue to change'. So this chapter explores how these forces of change have shaped and fashioned the structures of organizations, the direction of work and the nature of work itself and the way of working, setting the context for exploring the evolving nature of work stressors. It is a prologue to change and provides the context for the next chapter, which explores the changing nature of work stressors that express aspects of contemporary work, reflect widespread concern, and have received considerable empirical support. This chapter explores how globalization has been used as a tool through the processes of mergers and acquisitions to reshape and fashion organizations (Cartwright 2008). It looks at how work has been refashioned as we enter an age of information and knowledge, with the economy being described as 'weightless' (Coyle & Quah 2002, p. 8) meaning that the type of work assumes an emotional quality with features that require more collaboration, the skills to facilitate, be flexible and have the ability to boundary span (Dewe & Cooper 2012, pp. 36–37) accompanied by a call for 'what makes good work' and 'why job quality in a changing economy matters' (Coats & Lekhi 2008, p. 11). Researchers need also to be alert to the 'change [that] is clearly afoot' and to consider their assumptions about 'the standard ways of working' in the context of the growing variety of 'non standard ways of working' (Ashford, George & Blatt 2007, p. 67).

Chapter VI follows on from Chapter V and explores in more detail a number of specific work stressors that reflect the realities of contemporary work experiences: job insecurity, the changing meaning of employability and what is described as flexicurity (Ackers & Oliver 2007); technostress and new concerns for health and well-being; technology's new behaviours, including problematic internet use, cyberloafing, cyber incivility and cyberbullying; and work–life balance with its shift in focus from spillover to crossover and the role of individual differences; segmenters and integrators and the growing interest in workaholism. The chapter ends by exploring the challenges facing stressor measurement, picking up on the themes of refinement, relevance, reliability and meaning. Measurement of stressors is about ensuring that they reflect the work experience and the changing context of work. When considering stressor measurement, it is important to be not only conscious of new-evolving stressors but also mindful of how established stressors evolve and how well measures reflect their changing nature that match the contemporary work experiences; hence the importance of refining measures so they have a relevancy to those filling out such measures. So, refinement and relevance should now be given emphasis as techniques of measurement practice, as has traditionally been given to reliability – raising the issue of what does reliability account for if measures are not relevant.

As researchers have illustrated their creativity when identifying new stressors we argue in this chapter that creativity should be applied to how stressor measures are analyzed. We explore, as we have before, under two broad headings within and between relationships to better create the nature of the experience (see Dewe & Cooper 2012, pp. 95–97). Within relationships refer to how the stressor items that make up a measure pattern and relate to one another, offering a context for understanding the roles each stressor item plays. Between relationships explore the relationship between different stressors and the nature of the impact of one stressor on another, reminding us of their cumulative impact and the chain of events, as one stressor may leave individuals vulnerable to another stressor (Dewe & Cooper 2012, p. 97). Finally we discuss the all-important way stressors are appraised and how such a focus would release the explanatory potential that resides in the appraisal process. Ignoring these personal meanings is to overlook the most powerful pathway that the transactional model gives us and support for this need to focus on appraisals should surely be encouraged when the research on exploring stressors as challenges or hindrances is considered (Cavanaugh, Boswell, Roehling & Boudreau 2000). It is this appraisal pathway that should now be given the attention it deserves (Dewe & Cooper 2012, p. 97). Not of course forgetting positive meanings, and what aspects of the experience can be valued (Beehr & Grebner 2009).

Chapter VII (Coping with stress, future directions and challenges) begins by exploring the growing variety of coping strategies (Folkman & Moskowitz 2004) which may reflect the social and economic turmoil that welcomed the new millennium, pointing to how coping strategies are sensitive to the context and the appraisal of events. Two points are clear to researchers as the list of coping strategies grows. It signals that constructing coping scales needs to be done sensitively and with care to ensure participants can express the range of strategies they may use. It also makes the classifying of coping strategies a more complex task as new varieties of strategies emerge putting a responsibility on researchers to consider in more detail an account of how coping strategies are actually being used. It is this type of descriptive knowledge that comes from asking participants how they used a strategy that may offer a more direct initial route to classifying coping strategy as the actual way strategies are being used may be lost when simply relying on where a strategy rests after being factor analyzed. The chapter builds on the work of Folkman and Moskowitz (2004) and comments on and explores the growing variety of coping strategies: religious coping; meaning-focused coping including stress-related growth; proactive coping; culture and collective and collaborate coping; leisure coping; and emotional-approach coping. 'The challenge for coping researchers' is to find a 'common nomenclature for these diverse coping strategies so that findings across studies can be discussed meaningfully' (Folkman & Moskowitz 2004, p. 751).

The sensitive construction of coping measures is as vital as will be deciding on the appropriate framework for classifying them; complex, yet important to ensure our knowledge of the coping process advances. Other challenges also face researchers interested in coping. These include what is meant by coping effectiveness, enhancing our understanding of coping flexibility, coping and ageing, coping and gender, coping and personality. The chapter ends by exploring the future challenges facing coping researchers.

Chapter VIII (Interventions and challenges) takes a creative approach to the question of work stress management and interventions. It begins with a brief historical account of the theory of preventative stress management before moving into a discussion on the role of an applied discipline and the researcher and practitioner divide debate. Our argument is that the area of work stress management and interventions reflects a meeting place – the fertile ground for issues like the responsibilities of an applied discipline, the relationship between the researcher and practitioner, how evidence-based we are and what is meant by good work. To meet these challenges the work stress management and intervention literature has shifted its focus to an examination of the process of evaluation; evaluating how effective stress management interventions are and using that knowledge to enhance working life (Cox, Taris & Nielsen 2010). It is clear from reviews that intervention research needs to move beyond narrowly confining the evaluation of interventions to outcomes and focusing more on 'how and why' an intervention works so as to provide 'sustainable improvements' (Nielsen 2013, p. 1042). This broader view of evaluating 'how and why' interventions work raises the question of what guidance can work stress researchers gain from the field of training and development, particularly from issues around the transfer of training (Baldwin & Ford 1988) and the different levels of evaluation (Kirkpatrick 1994). We then turn to the guidance that may help work stress management and intervention researchers from the literature on accounting for people (Roslender & Fincham 2001; Roslender, Stevenson & Kahn 2006) as a means of expressing the wellness of an organization captured in the ideas of intellectual capital. As Biron and colleagues suggests, 'integrating occupational health with daily business remains a serious issue and one of the most challenging parts of occupational health intervention' (Biron, Hilaire & Brun 2014b, p. 277).

Chapter IX (Conclusions) draws the book to a close. It begins by arguing that the nature and character of the forces of change are changing. Globalization is being challenged with the need to consider an alternative form that is more social sustaining witnessed by the international interest in well-being. Well-being should now be at the heart of economic measures like GNP expressing 'metrics that matter' (OECD 2013), which reflect the quality of life that is valued. International interest in the role happiness can play as a measure of value is also increasing, as is the search for what is meant by meaningful work. Technology as a force is also changing – its speed and transformational properties will still define it, but what may reflect the spirit of the age is how it has changed behaviours, giving us the disciplines of cyberbehaviour and cyberpsychology. The power of these two forces has reshaped organizations and refashioned work, the type of work and how we work. This sets the context for our conclusions and points to the significance of the role that meaning needs to play in work stress research in the future. The importance of and explanatory power of context and the descriptive knowledge it offers is clear, as is the continued importance of processes like refining and the integrating power of relevance. It is relevance that closes the gap between research, researcher and practitioner. It also points to our moral and ethical responsibilities to those whose working lives we study. Meaning, context, refining and relevance are not mutually exclusive but are powerful tools that should reflect the aspirations of those interested in advancing and progressing the quality of working life.

II

FORCES OF CHANGE

We begin this chapter, and indeed this book, sowing the seeds of change for work stress and coping research by exploring how forces like globalization, technology and diversity are themselves in a constant state of change. As they change, so too do they initiate change, shape ideas and stimulate new directions for theory, influence how and what we research, how we use knowledge and how that knowledge should be used, and what responsibilities and what moral obligations we have to those whose working lives we study. In this way, this chapter gives us a context, a history; an anchoring point for understanding why different ideas have emerged at different times, why they become important and how the present can be better understood (Cooper & Dewe 2004, pp.114–115; Fotinatos-Ventouratos & Cooper 2015). It is this context viewed through the lens of globalization, technology and diversity that gives an opportunity to test our assumptions, inform our perspective, evaluate, question and critique the relevance of accepted practice and maintaining the status quo, consider where, what and how much progress has been made, identify new ideas, new opportunities and new ways forward and fully appreciate the richness and complexity of the issues we face. Our knowledge and understanding does not always precisely reflect history (Rose 1988), nor does it occur in some sort of orderly fashion, nor is it free from 'misunderstandings, controversy and intense debate' (Cooper & Dewe 2004, p. 115), nor are the different forces independent of each other as change in one inevitably brings change in another. What cannot be ignored though is that understanding such forces intertwines the contextual with the developmental (Viney 1993), and from one springs the other, and so the opportunity to monitor and assess contemporary ideas, trends and debates against the richness of history provokes a review of progress and the identification of innovative and creative pathways for the future (Saridikis & Cooper 2013).

Globalization

The term globalization defined the 1990s (O'Rourke & Williamson 2002). It soon became regarded as a process of change taking place 'out there' and 'an undeniable and inescapable part of contemporary experience' (Bartelson 2000, p. 180), to the extent that it has now become the buzzword of the last two decades (*The Economist* 2013b) and very much a part of our everyday language in that it now comes attached to varying degrees of meaning and associations (Therborn 2000). Despite its buzzword status the term globalization has been used since 1951 and entered the dictionary in 1961 (Bhagat et al. 2012, p. 1). Nevertheless, defining the term globalization is, as Bartelson suggests, 'never innocent' (2000, p. 182), and while its earliest meaning captured the notion of 'the spread of the global economy to regional economics around the world' (Bhagat et al., p. 1) more recent definitions include not just the notion of multi-directional movement of 'people, objects, places and information' but the 'structures they encounter and create' that limit or accelerate their movement (Ritzer 2011, p. 22). Reviewers still, however, point to why we need to rethink the term (Martens & Zywietz 2006), understand the criteria by which it should be defined (Therborn 2000), and agree when globalization began (O'Rourke & Williamson 2002), as it seems that only by understanding this can we define and understand whether or not it is a good thing (*The Economist* 2013b). Notwithstanding that, at times we may need to separate globalization from global history (Gratton 2014, p. 31) and better understand why it is we are still arguing about globalization (Sumner 2004). So, to better understand the changing nature of globalization, the influence it has in shaping our thinking, our theories and our research and the directions it signals for future research, we begin with a light touch of history.

A light touch of history

Articles with headings like 'When did globalization begin?' (O'Rourke & Williamson 2002), or 'When did globalization start?' (*The Economist* 2013b), or 'A brief history of globalization' (Sheel 2008) all illustrate that outlining the history of globalization 'is no easy matter' (Ritzer 2011, p. 17) simply because the different perspectives offered and the arguments presented reinforce what 'turns out to be a very complex [set] of issues' (Ritzer 2011, p. 17). Beginning with the perspective that globalization may be 'hardwired' into all of us, Ritzer (2011, p. 17) goes on to outline how 'a good sense' of the origins and history of globalization can be captured by thinking in terms of cycles, epochs or waves, and specific momentous events, noting that more recent events suggest something of a 'sea change' in the nature of globalization, its beginnings and its distinctiveness (pp. 17–22). The arguments as to the historical origins and progression of globalization across the centuries are detailed, frequently vigorously expressed, comprehensive in scope and likely to be debated for some time. Questions as to what it is, what it should be, how it has changed, how modern a phenomenon it is, whether it is good or bad, how it is measured, its nature, structure and distinctiveness are all issues that continue to express its complexity. Nevertheless it is taking place (Bartelson 2000), and it has become a defining term of the world we live in (O'Rourke & Williamson 2002).

While not wishing to ignore the complexity of what we are dealing with, or the rich history that accompanies that complexity, it does seem possible to identify the emergence of four themes that help to express the nature of globalization and our contemporary view of it. The first is the significance of the initiatives flowing from the Bretton Woods Conference in 1944 that began to shape our understanding and the meaning of globalization (Gratton 2014, pp. 31–32). The second is the transformational world changes that have occurred in the last 25 years that have come to define globalization as we know it today (Bhagat et al. 2012; Gratton 2014; Ritzer 2011). The third captures the idea that 'what globalization is about' may now be best understood by the discourse that surrounds it (Bartelson 2000; Therborn 2000). The fourth theme turns to the 'darker side' (Gratton 2014, p. 33) of globalization and explores how, in addition to its many positive aspects 'negative global flows and processes' inevitably accompany globalization (Ritzer 2011, p. 230).

Turning to the first theme the most influential effects of Bretton Woods were on trade, monetary and fiscal order, and investment, all enabled through the establishment of 'truly international trade institutions' (Gratton 2014, p. 31; Ritzer 2011). This inspired an atmosphere where innovation, economic cooperation, worldwide capital flows, trade liberalization, consumerism, global marketing and the changing nature of work (Bhagat et al. 2012; Gratton 2014; Ritzer 2011) helped to explain why the term globalization became the popular way of describing the social, political, economic, cultural and organizational changes that were being experienced. Yet the influence of the Bretton Woods system was not to last, not just because of the currency changes initiated by the United States but by 'major forces' that could not have been anticipated or perhaps 'even dreamed of' when the Bretton Woods system was first established (Ritzer 2011, p. 67–68).

Historic changes and influences

Economic turbulence and turmoil, the emerging realities of world order, the growth of the multinational organization and what are described as 'born global' organizations (Gabrielsson & Kirpalani 2004; Bowles & Cooper 2012), issues of sustainability, technological transformation, interconnectedness and cultural awareness all express the transforming nature of world changes, a move towards new understandings of the nature of globalization and reflect the transforming nature of our second theme. This second theme, and these 'historic change[s]' (Bhagat et al. 2012, p. 5) can be explored in terms of three, not mutually exclusive, influences: *world transformation, global organizations and the changing nature of work and economic crisis* (Fotinatos-Ventouratos & Cooper 2015). The first would include, for example, changing 'economic contexts of the world' (Bhagat et al. 2012, p. 6) with the emerging significance of economies in South East Asia, South America and Eastern Europe – the role, importance and influence of the BRIC countries (Brazil, Russia, India, and China), competition built around international, political and geographical linkages, alliances, blocs and networks. All this suggests the arrival of a 'boundaryless world' spurred on by greatly improved transport links, technological innovation, educational opportunities, the role and influence of global institutions, the growing interconnectedness of ideas, concepts, inventions, products, services, transactions, competition, decision making, capital distribution, financial arrangements, markets including labour markets, cultures and cultural understandings. Not to forget the internationalization of innovation, research and development, and the international cooperation required to ensure a 'green agenda' where sustainability, resource maintenance, expenditure, allocation and protection are a significant part of any change (Bhagat et al. 2012; Gratton 2014; Martens & Zywietz 2006; Mullins 2002; Noon et al. 2013; Ritzer 2011; Therborn 2000).

The second influence, multinational and global corporations, 'energized by global competition', a boundaryless world, technological advances, growing new economies and developing markets, have had 'major implications for the structuring of work and work organizations around the world' (Bhagat et al. 2012, p. 10). The different ways through which corporations have grown multinational clearly reflect decades of mergers, acquisitions, strategic collaborations, equity purchasing and Greenfield and market oriented investments (Ritzer 2011, pp. 73-74). The result is complex organizational networks and structures that require different approaches to management, working and employment arrangements, leadership, culture and values, heralding in the resource based strategies (competing through people) and the increasing significance and complexity of human resource strategies including career management, work-life balance, well-being and the ideals of a 'good work agenda' (Coats & Lekhi 2008, p. 6; Dewe & Cooper 2012, p. 37). Add to this the demands for new work designs, redundancies, job insecurity, unremitting change, performance management, job stress and strain, then 'globalization pressures' reflect the 'emerging realities of work' for all those working in this global workplace (Bhagat et al. 2012, pp. 14–16; Noon et al. 2013).

When there is change or even the likelihood of change then 'there is turbulence in our lives as we try to come to terms with a new reality and prepare to adjust' (Weinberg & Cooper 2012, p. 3). Notwithstanding all the change that has accompanied globalization, and all the issues that accompany it, it was the third influence, the economic crisis of 2008, that wreaked havoc across the world rippling out and causing despair in every facet of life. The promise of prosperity 'had been wiped away almost over-night' (Weinberg & Cooper 2012, p. 8), and it was those very same macroeconomic forces designed to provide that prosperity, robustly defended, widely admired, supported and accepted as the pathway to wealth and stability that caused an economic catastrophe of tumultuous proportions, an irrecoverable human cost, a sense of anger, betrayal and unfairness that left no aspect of society untouched, unblighted, or unviolated (Dewe & Cooper 2012, 2014; Weinberg & Cooper 2012). While understanding that continued 'bubbles and crashes' will be 'part of the future storyline' of globalization (Gratton 2014, pp. 32–33) and while it was the interconnectedness between countries that made the economic crisis so overwhelming and so quick to spread (Noon et al. 2013; Ritzer 2011), it was also this interconnectedness aided by established world institutions and regular economic summits that led to the galvanizing of international cooperation and synchronization of actions aimed at combating the crisis (Weinberg & Cooper 2012). Nevertheless there is no doubt that the rise of anti-globalization movements, and the level of feeling they express, indicated that 'there are many alternative viewpoints on what globalization is or what it should be' (Martens & Zywietz 2006, p. 332). It was clear that globalization could no longer be defined in narrow terms that simply focused on economic variables and that a definitional shift was now required that drew attention to, and embraced, the social, cultural and environmental consequences of globalization (Marten & Zywietz 2006).

While we are now used to terms like 'austerity', 'deficit cutting', 'long-term economic decisions', and 'crackdowns', the question remains what happens next? Clearly there is considerable debate not just about how globalization should be defined but its contribution to international development (Huq & Tribe 2004), its pursuit of a 'more human-centred' approach (White, Gaines & Jha 2012, p. 764), and its effectiveness as a solution to developmental issues without the need for other more focused policies or interventions (Jenkins 2004). Whether the time is right to think in terms of global developmentalism as a more 'central organizing principle' (Gore 2010, p. 734) or whether it is now time to lift the limits imposed by the more traditional narrow economic definitions to a more broader definition that embraces a range of other interconnected and interrelated issues that acknowledge 'the pluralistic character of the forces that drive globalization and its consequences' (Martens & Zywietz 2006, pp. 349–350), what emerges from this debate is, at the very least, a genuine call by a growing body of commentators to recalibrate the meaning of globalization to capture the 'challenges of the global' (Therborn 2000, p. 151). So 'what globalization is about' may now best be understood by the discourse that surrounds it (Bartelson 2000, p. 180; Therborn 2000).

Discourse surrounding globalization

While the economic crisis and its consequences may have given a sense of urgency to the drive to become more inclusive when defining the nature of globalization, reviewers have for some time pointed to 'globalization as a plural phenomenon' (Therborn 2000, p. 151) and the need to 'unpack the terms of the conceptual consensus that informs' our understanding of globalization, that is, to find out what is going on in the discourse of globalization (Bartelson 2000, p. 181). If, as it seems, there is now a growing need for change as to how globalization is defined and measured, then what are the drivers that reflect this demand for a greater inclusiveness? Acknowledging the complexity of the arguments for change, the difficulties of agreeing what to include, and the metrics by which they should be measured, a flavour of what emerges from this debate follows. It is, as Sumner (2004) captures in the detail of his argument, that more often than not the impact of 'globalization-led' growth 'seems clear, [however] the quality of the growth is not' (2004, p. 1020). So in pursuit of what is required to achieve this sense of quality of experience, when defining globalization, much can be gained by exploring the discourse that surrounds the term.

'At least' five topics emerge, argues Therborn when you apply such an approach to the discourse that accompanies the term globalization. Predictably the first, which he describes as 'the most widespread', is '*competition economics*', capturing the traditional notion of intense world competition and its consequences. The second captures the '*sociocritical*', which reflects the negative reaction to, and 'a critical concern' for the social consequences of competitive economics. The third '*state (im)potence*' concerns the role of the state and its capacity in the face of global economics to govern and control. While these three all tend to cluster around issues about the global economy and its consequences the final two approach globalization from 'quite different angles' either by pointing to '*cultural*' or 'planetary *ecology*' concerns. The first, Therborn argues, expresses concerns about the impact of globalization on lifestyles, society and national cultures, while the latter he suggests explores environmental, human and organizational actions on global sustainability (Therborn 2000, pp. 151–153). This summary cannot capture the richness or the complexity and detail that accompany Therborn's analysis. But his work signals what has to be done; how this 'plurality of social processes' (2000, p. 154) is brought together, integrated and measured in a way that captures how globalization and its consequences are experienced. This demand to take a more inclusive approach is in itself somewhat of a global phenomenon, as researchers and commentators continue to question how the quality of life, the reality of life experiences, well-being and happiness can continue to be expressed through traditional rather narrowly defined economic indicators.

Writers on globalization continue to point to its multifaceted nature. Bhagat and his colleagues, for example, identify two facets of globalization: economic globalization; and social and cultural globalization. The latter refers to 'the exchange of ideas and information and those people who carry ideas and information with them'. These authors emphasize both the impact of the internet and technology generally on the flow of ideas and their power to change societies, and, whilst acknowledging the arbitrary selection of these two facets, point to how each 'carries with it' the power to influence the other and vice versa (2012, p. 4). Similarly Ritzer when discussing the 'flows' of globalization illustrates its multifaceted meaning by including in his discussion politics, culture, technology, migration and the environment (2011, pp. vi-viii). The debate surrounding what actually constitutes globalization, its impact on economic growth, the distribution of its benefits across society and its role in fostering international development has signalled the need for globalization to adopt a more 'human face' (Huq & Tribe 2004, p. 921), although whether globalization can be entirely relied upon to resolve society's ills remains a moot point (Jenkins 2004). Finally, there is, at the heart of all these arguments, the inescapable issue of measurement. The issue is clear; identifying a way forward that explores a more inclusive approach to measurement does, as Martens and Zywietz (2006) argue, draw attention to those aspects of globalization that go beyond traditional economic indicators, reinforcing its pluralistic nature and providing a crucial step in describing the realities of globalization and its consequences.

The dark side of globalization

The accelerating advances of globalization since the 1980s, and its accompanying doctrine that 'trade liberalization is in itself an effective route to growth' (Huq & Tribe 2004, p. 917), have been made in the face of a growing body of criticism, alternative voices, protests and social movements all calling for alternative forms of globalization (Ayres 2004; Bramble 2006; Buttel & Gould 2004; Huq & Tribe 2004; Teivainen 2002). Criticisms over the conventional economic wisdom surrounding globalization, the role of private ownership, the dependence and emphasis placed on the mechanisms of the market, issues around government intervention and the structural reforms necessary for countries to effectively perform in a globalized economy (Huq & Tribe 2004, pp. 915–918) have shaped 'quite ferocious' debates as to how globalization and its consequences and benefits are interpreted and understood and 'how these conceptual framings coalesce to structure global protest' (Ayres 2004, pp. 11–12). These global protests are driven by the view that neoliberal globalization is not inevitable, that there are alternatives shaped in 2001 in the aims of the World Social Forum, its mission 'Another World is Possible' (Teivainen 2002, p. 629) and its growth into what is 'arguably the most significant global social movement today' (Buttel & Gould 2004, p. 50).

It would be 'politically unwise', as Teivainen suggests, to see the World Social Forum as *against* globalization but 'looking for a *different kind* of globalization' (2002, p. 628), although there is still more debate needed as to what those different kinds of globalization are, how structurally they can be organized and how social, economic, ecologically sustainable processes can be developed and integrated (Ayres 2004, p. 13; Buttel & Gould 2004; Teivainen 2002). Hence, as Bramble suggests, the term '*alter-globalization*' (2006, p. 288) may better describe the movement or 'anti corporate globalization movement' (Buttel & Gould 2004, p. 40), signalling that globalization is multifaceted and there are likely to be different futures for different facets (Ritzer 2011). Whatever the descriptor, if people can work together to give globalization a 'more progressive meaning then the World Social Forum offers many opportunities for this to happen' (Teivainen 2002, p. 628). The protests, collective actions and formation of social movements were all in response to what has become described as the dark side of globalization. While the debate will continue to swirl around conventional economic wisdom, trade liberalization, the role of international financial institutions and the power and behaviour of multinational corporations (Buttel & Gould 2004), these underline and provide the context for other fundamental concerns and passionately held views about global inequality, the distribution of wealth and resources, and other 'negative global flows' that include borderless diseases, crime, terrorism and war, race, ethnicity and gender inequalities, the digital divide, and the rural–urban divide (see Ritzer 2011, Chapters 10-11). Fashioning these issues into a list does not, of course, capture their subtleties, character, complexity, scale and reach, the significance of their impact and their costs and consequences to nations, societies and individuals. Even in this form though, they still illustrate the unavoidable truth that globalization is as much multifaceted in terms of its reach and consequences as it is in terms of its nature and meaning.

Work, of course, is not immune from the tentacles of globalization, and the last 25 years have seen fundamental changes to the nature and structure of work, how people work, where and how they work, the sector they work in, their employment relationship (or psychological contract), the way they develop careers, balance their working lives and achieve satisfaction and well-being. These changes have not been without costs. Stress, depression and anxiety accounts for around 39% (487,000) of all work-related illnesses in Great Britain, reflecting a level that has remained relatively consistent over the last decade (Health & Safety Executive 2014). The main work activities that contribute to stress or make it worse include excessive workload pressures, interpersonal relationships including bullying and harassment, and change including lack of resources and additional responsibilities (Healthy & Safety Executive 2014, p. 2). The 'fact remains', as Bhagat and his colleagues suggest, 'that globalization does have adverse consequences whose implications for work stress and coping need to be carefully analyzed' (Bhagat et al. 2012, p. 44). The different facets of globalization have also, as we shall describe in later chapters, influenced theory development, provided a fertile ground for the emergence of new movements, new disciplines, the internationalization of ideas and concepts, how working lives are expressed, described and given meaning, the way knowledge transfers, the changes to management practices, leadership styles, and the design of work. All these changes emphasize the need to explore where current theories are taking us, what alternative theories can provide, how adequately they express the realities of work and how it is experienced, and how they offer pathways that challenge the status quo, point to future directions and offer researchers and practitioners an opportunity to fulfil their obligations to those whose working lives they study.

Summary

It is clear from this brief review that the term 'globalization', despite its long and rich history of waves, epochs and events, its buzzword status, and the shifting meanings and associations attached to it, needs once more to be redefined and reconstructed to ensure that it continues to express more comprehensively not just its character but the hopes, expectations and values that reflect those experiences that describe the quality of working lives. This is not to say, that author(s) have failed to do this. It is more to ensure that the term continues to express the discourse that surrounds it, how that discourse sharpens our understanding, brings new meanings and gives a sense of how it now captures what exactly is being experienced. In short, the term

globalization should now be as much about the quality of the experience as it has
been about those processes that have described its structures or driven that experience. It is, as we shall encounter with other terms, no longer possible to define it
through traditional economic terms alone. The word needs to become more inclusive in order to capture its pluralistic nature, the breadth and scope of what it involves
and the quality of the experience itself. The word and its meaning will then provide
a context for exploring its reach and how, and just how far, our theories and practices
have been influenced by its nature and express its properties.

TABLE II.1

GROWING THE SEEDS OF CHANGE

GLOBALIZATION

- 'An undeniable and inescapable part of contemporary experience' (Bartelson 2000, p. 180).
- The theme of recent definitions includes the notion of multi-directional movement of 'people, objects, places and information' and 'the structures they encounter and create', that limits or accelerates their movement (Ritzer 2011, p. 22).
- Economic turbulence and turmoil, the emerging realities of world order, the growth of the multinational organization and what has been described as 'born global' organizations (Gabrielsson & Kirpalani 2004), issues of sustainability, technological transformation, interconnectiveness and cultural awareness of the green agenda all express the transforming nature of world changes.
- The result is complex organizational structures and networks that require different approaches to management, working and employment arrangements, leadership, culture and values, resource-based strategies and the increasing significance and complexity of resource-based strategies, including career management and work–life balance, well-being and the ideals of the 'good work agenda' (Coats & Lekhi 2008, p. 6; Dewe & Cooper 2012, pp. 29–32).
- Add to this the demands for new work designs, job insecurity, unremitting change, performance management and job stress, then 'globalization pressures' reflect the 'emerging realities of work' for all those in this global workplace (Bhagat et al. 2012, pp. 14–16; Noon et al. 2013).
- When there is change or the likelihood of change then 'there is turbulence in our lives as we try to come to terms with a new reality and prepare to adjust' (Weinberg & Cooper 2012, p. 3).

Technology

We now turn to the second of those forces that influence the nature of the social context within which work takes place, and explore its role in shaping work and working lives not to mention every other aspect of society. The idea that we now live in an 'information society or an age of information' has become so much a part of our culture that it is simply 'widely taken to characterize our times' (Mahoney 1988, p. 113) – although it may now be more correct to express our times in terms of how fortunate we are to 'live in a very connected world' (Chen 2011, p. 3); or perhaps just as expressive of our times is the quote used by Scoble and Israel when marking the opening chapter of their book: 'computing is not about computing anymore, it is about living' (2014, p. 1). However it may be expressed, the role of the computer has been a central force in the transformation of life (Mahoney 1988), and along with headings like 'the computer is everywhere' (Stewart 2012) or understanding 'how computing has changed the world' (Misa 2007) or 'how networks changed the world' (Chen 2011), the word 'computer', now so ubiquitous and such a part of our everyday language has 'over time generated an entire subfield of the history of technology called "the history of computing"' (Norberg 1984, p. 197).

None of this will come as a surprise but the sheer numbers involved explains why it captures the very nature of the world we live in: 'over 5 billion cell phone users, more than 2 billion internet users, more than 1 billion personal computer users, 800 million active Facebook users and 180 million registered Twitter users' (Chen 2011, p. 3). The speed by which the numbers continue to grow is simply astounding, with the International Telecommunications Union (ITU) predicting that the number of mobile phones is approaching the number of people on earth with 7 billion by the end of 2014, with mobile broadband uptake reaching 2.3 billion 'almost 5 times as many as just six years ago', and 3 billion people using the internet (ITU 2014, p.1). It doesn't stop there of course and, as we endeavour to understand the future and the innovation and developments that will continue then, as Gratton's research suggests, we might expect to see, just to mention a few, 'complex technology available on everyday devices, technological capability to continue to increase exponentially', social participation to increase – predicting and understanding 'what people will actually do with this unprecedented level of connectivity', 'the world's knowledge becoming digitalized, the emergence of mega-companies and micro-entrepreneurs, and the increasing presence of avatars and virtual worlds' (Gratton 2014, pp. 28–29).

This section unfolds by again engaging in a light touch through the history of computing, not to establish if we have witnessed a second Industrial Revolution, although its impact has frequently been described as nothing short of revolutionary, but more as an opportunity to illustrate how this 'rapidly growing economic and social activity' (Norberg 1984, p. 197) has acquired a symbolism of its own; a force offering a vision of a 'society radically altered by this new technology'. It is the computer that 'has directed people's eyes toward the future' (Mahoney 1988, pp. 122, 123) and the power of what may yet be seen. Using this brush with history as a context, we then explore a range of issues that follow in the wake of this exponential growth in product innovation, differentiation, value added design, a growing attention to fashion and a sense of inter-connectiveness that expresses the way we live and the manner in which our lives have changed. We explore, for example, the speed of change in the nature of technology, the role of computers in our lives and the arrival of the internet and social media, before turning our attention to exploring the impact of the internet in terms of its role in aiding or inhibiting community life and social interaction (the internet paradox), problematic internet behaviours, innovations like the internet of things, psychology and the new media, work–life balance and the emergence of technostress.

A brief history of computing

Faced with outlining even the briefest history of computing means confronting 'the daunting complexity' of a field that has not just 'grown exponentially' but become 'a significant presence in science, technology and society' (Mahoney 1988, p. 115). Computing and the computer are many different things rather than just one thing, so that a history could and has involved themes that trace technical developments, hardware and software (Campbell-Kelly 2007; Mahoney 1988; Norberg 1984), and the internet (Kleinrock 2008). Here our aim is to try to trace the speed and direction with which computing has transformed societies, economies, cultures and technology itself (Misa 2007). Even this is no easy task, because innovations shaped by people, cultures and context change, and in the process are changed themselves, but there has long been a call to shift the historical lens from 'an "insider" history full of facts and firsts' (Mahoney 1988, p. 114) to a longer view that reflects on those processes and innovations that shaped such transformations and the countless ways in which our daily life has changed (Misa 2007). It is this latter view that we try and capture here. In trying to understand how computing has changed the world, Misa argues that 'very roughly' computing has passed through 'three distinct thematic traditions' (Misa 2007, p. 52).

The first represents an insider's approach that captures what Misa describes as a *machine-centred* phase where the emphasis was on dates, technical advances, working details and machine histories. This theme, important as it was, is now seen more as a primary data source (Mahoney 1988) offering little in the way of assessing its transformational properties (Mahoney 1988; Misa 2007). The second theme focused on '*the information age*': the processing of information, the embedding and impact of these machines and related technologies in business and government, and how computing advanced this age, made it distinctive and how the computer itself was shaped by this age (Misa 2007, p. 54) and became a 'symbolic force' in 'the business community, [government] and society at large' (Mahoney 1988, p. 119). The third theme reflecting perhaps the '*institutional context*' describes how 'institutions shape[d] computing', accelerated the pace of change and development and ushered in a need to explore what difference this made, why it mattered to society, how it influenced the path of future directions (Misa 2007, p. 55) and what would have happened if 'things had turned out differently' (Edwards 2001, p. 86).

Yet important as these themes are to our understanding of the impact of computing and the computer, there is perhaps 'a tradition to be made', as Misa advocates, for a fourth theme that centres on what needs to be studied if we 'believe that computing has changed the world' (2007, p. 56). By adopting what Misa describes as a 'hybrid' approach that calls on different disciplines and methods then this would give 'vigour' and scope to better understanding how computing evolved, shaped such 'transformations' and was itself shaped by them (2007, pp. 56–57). Yet it is only now, with around 80 years of accumulated history that perhaps such histories are possible (Campbell-Kelly 2007), even though there has always been, underlying all these themes, a strong conviction that the computer has brought about a revolution 'as profound as that triggered by the automobile' (Mahoney 1988, p. 122). While not perhaps fulfilling the intentions of the fourth theme, turning to a timeline nevertheless captures the speed of change and the advent of a revolution. Here we turn to the work of Kleinrock (2008, 2010) and Boyd and Ellison (2008) amongst others to outline, if not the detailed analysis, richness and commentary of their work then at least to draw on their analysis to illustrate the remarkable rate at which innovation, inventiveness and development occurred. The 1960s saw the arrival of mainframe computers, continuing developments that heralded the beginnings of the internet taking its 'first breath of life' in 1969 (Kleinrock 2008, p. 13, 2010). The 1970s saw the arrival of mini and micro computers, the 1980s and 1990s laptops, notebooks, email (see Waterson 2014, p. 224), and mobile phones becoming widely available. 1991 saw the first website available on the internet; 1992 the number of internet hosts passed the million mark; in 1996 more email was sent than postal mail (Kleinrock 2008, p. 14); in 1997 the first social networking site Six Degrees appeared (Boyd & Ellison 2008); 1998 saw the arrival of the blog and Google; 1999 saw the first use of the term 'internet of things'; and by 2001, there were 500 million users on the internet (Kleinrock 2008, p. 14).

Why is the internet so popular? Hershman suggests three reasons: the needs of users are satisfied; the technology used was developed by 'solving real problems'; and its flexibility both technically and organizationally (1992, p. 285). The new millennium continued to usher in innovations including internet-based appliances, advances in mobile technologies and the arrival of 'ubiquitous technologies' (Waterson 2014, p. 224). There was no slowing the speed of change: 2004 saw the arrival of Facebook; by 2005 mobile phone sales exceeded 800 million and laptop sales exceeded 200 million (Kleinrock 2008, p. 14); MySpace arrived in 2005; peer-to-peer networks continued to grow; YouTube made an entry in 2006; and iPhones appeared in 2007 (Boyd & Ellison 2008; Kleinrock 2008). What is it about these social media sites that have not only attracted millions of users, but offered individuals the opportunity to 'openly and freely' express their world through online networks not without, at times, risks to their privacy (O'Brien & Torres 2012, p. 64)? The answer, it seems, rests in their 'unique' ability to offer individuals just that: an opportunity to express and display a profile, and communicate with those who are already part of their extended social network (Boyd & Ellison 2008); hence the 'internet of people'.

The incredible, almost overwhelming level of innovation and invention illustrates just how powerful a tool the internet has become; always there, always available, always ready (Kleinrock 2008). Looking back, Kleinrock describes all these changes, shifts and transformations in terms of a history of first 'the early pioneers, then the implementers, followed by the value adders, the launchers and let us not forget the billionaires' (Kleinrock 2008, p. 15).

It isn't over yet, as wireless capability has already begun to drive the next round of innovations, meaning that we are entering into the age of anytime, anyplace, anywhere (Kleinrock 2008): 'from computer to computer, human to human, human to thing, and thing to thing' (Tan & Wang 2010, p. V5–376). Enter the internet of things: connecting everyday items to the internet so that they become smarter. Often called the 'internet of everything' because 'the Internet is connected to every physical object via ubiquitous sensors' (Shin 2014, p. 519) making them 'more reliable, more resilient, more autonomous and smarter' (Kyriazis & Varvarigou 2013, p. 442), the internet of things can transform daily living, through the seamless interconnectivity where things can exchange information by themselves or with other things on behalf of people or to provide a service to people, ushering in a new era 'where we have connectivity for anything' (Tan & Wang 2010, p. V5–376). Little wonder it is referred to as ubiquitous computing (Rainie & Wellman 2014). The potential is revolutionary as it offers the possibility of things to better serve our needs. Things will help, if of course we allow them to, by telling us we have left the oven on or that we have run out of cereal 'while our bathroom scales messages our GP's computer to let it know that we are not sticking to our diet plan' (Naughton 2014, p. 19). Despite its potential, there are growing concerns about its security and privacy (Tan & Wang 2010; *The Economist* 2014). We will watch and see if promise turns into reality.

We are, it seems, in the age of things and ubiquitous computing best captured by Kleinrock, when he describes 'a person wearing a digital watch and a two way email pager and carrying a cell phone, MP3 player, PDA camera and notebook computer' (2008, p. 16). However, the speed of innovation is so great that it is difficult at times to determine what best describes the age we are in and whether in fact we have ever left the information age. Nevertheless it is the coming together of many of these innovations that herald what Scoble and Israel (2014) describe as the 'age of context'; the working together of what they describe as 'five forces' of contextual technology all currently part of our lives (mobile devices, social media, big data, sensors and location-based services) that will transform the way we live and work. This transformation will come about because 'they are all built on the premise of knowing more about the context' and in this way and with this knowledge offer a better way of serving users (2014, p.xx). Scoble and Israel are acutely aware that the 'controversial and sometimes volatile dark side [of this age] is the issue of user privacy', the importance of trust and transparency and how they are accomplished, integrated and managed, the complexity of the issues involved, what can be controlled and the balances that need to be achieved (2014, p. 161).

This age is also described in terms of the triple revolution (Rainie & Wellman 2014) where social networks, the internet and mobile computing come together and reflect not just the current state of technology but 'make possible' a new social operating system called 'networked individualism' where individuals draw on the resources residing in the triple revolution to 'function more as connected individuals and less as embedded group members' (2014, p. 12). It is this triple interconnectivity that becomes the 'social lubricant', and these networks that become the systems of support (p. 107), reflecting a relational shift as people have 'access to a greater variety of people and to more information from a greater variety of sources' (p. 13). The changes inherent in the triple revolution are, as Rainie and Wellman point out, dependent on personalities and contexts and while noting that their impact is not all good and not all bad, they acknowledge that challenges remain and that capabilities and capacities will be tested. These overviews of the work of Scoble and Israel, and Rainie and Wellman, cannot capture the level of research, the detail and richness of their arguments nor the illustrations, opportunities and challenges they outline. What they do point to though, is the coming together and interconnectivity of the different technologies to illustrate, through either the age of context or the new social operating systems we are now presented with, the potential of a technologically enabled transformation of how we may live, how we may work and how we manage and cope with such change. It is now time to turn to the other side of computing.

Let's not forget in addition to the above the arrival of wearable technology, smart garments and textiles, health and fitness gadgets (*The Guardian* 2015), the commercialization and use of drones (*The Observer* 2015), self-driving cars and advances in home and work robots (*The Press* 2014), and the ever more sophisticated technology that is offered via iwatches and iPhones. It is also interesting to note in terms of the remarkable impact of technology that when investigating the 'greatest 80 moments, discoveries, and people of the last eight decades' (*The Observer* 2014, p. 37) the top 20 included the internet (1st), home computers (2nd), growth of social media (12th), satellite technology (13th) and mobile phones (15th).

The other side of computing and the internet

The term 'internet paradox' was first used by Kraut and his colleagues to question, for better or for worse, the impact of internet use on personal and social life, and led to a debate that has become as much a part of the history of computing as has the speed by which innovations have occurred and lives have been transformed (Kraut, Patterson, Lundmark, Kiesler, Mukopadhyay & Scherlis 1998). Rather than minimize the impact of the internet, this debate has continued to review and research issues around use, choice, storage, security, personal concerns and effective management.

At the same time, whilst acknowledging that constant innovation and development coupled with greater interconnectivity simply reinforces the importance of this debate, it also highlights the demand for more research and for more attention to be given to issues of access, policy, procedures, law, privacy, trust, scope, capability and damage. The impact of this debate can be gauged not just by the new term *cyberpsychology* but by the introduction of two important journals (*CyberPsychology & Behavior* in 1998; *Cyberpsychology, Behavior and Social Networking* in 2003) to aid such research.

It wasn't long before terms like technological addiction (Griffiths 1995), and internet addiction (Young 1996, 2004) began to appear in the literature along with internet abuse (Griffiths 2010) and problematic internet use (Chiang & Su 2012) to capture an addictive disorder, disturbed patterns of behaviour and problematic behaviour associated with internet use. While all these terms are somewhat related they are, as Griffiths suggests, 'not the same thing' and terms like abuse or problematic behaviours may in the long term have more of an impact on the organization than on the individuals themselves (2010, p. 465–466). Researchers have explored not just the culture of the internet and how having this knowledge may help in understanding why this type of behaviour occurs (Beard 2002; Griffiths 2010; Weiser 2001), but also the different types of abuse or problematic behaviours (Chiang & Su 2012; Griffiths 2010), workplace interventions (Beard 2002), characteristics of abusers or problem users (Beard 2002; Huang 2010) and the impact on health and well-being (Chiang & Su 2012; Huang 2010; Shaw & Gant 2002; Weiser 2001).

As an interesting contrast there is also cyberslacking and cyberloafing, terms used to describe employees who voluntarily use the internet to generally engage in non-work related browsing or emailing during work time (Lim & Chen 2012). However, this contrast may not be all that it seems, particularly when it is used as a form of 'production deviance' motivated by a need to compensate for feelings of inequity and unfairness (Lim 2002). On the other hand, there is an upside to cyberslacking and cyberloafing as it may also offer a means of emotion-focused coping when it is used for 'constructive recreation' providing individuals with the opportunity to better equip themselves to face workplace demands, or as an 'escape mechanism' or 'safety value' for those faced with seemingly unrelenting demands (Oravec 2002, p. 61), or as a way of engaging in pro-social behaviours (Stanton 2002). We will return to these ideas in the chapter on work stressors and coping.

The other side of the internet also includes cyber crime (Nykodym, Ariss & Kurtz 2008), cyber bullying (ACAS 2012; Tokunaga 2010), the use and abuse of social media (Jennings, Blount & Weatherly 2014; Tsikerdekis & Zeadally 2014), the rudeness of emails and email management (Giumetti, Hatfield, Scisco, Schroeder, Muth & Kowalski 2013; Gupta, Sharda, Ducheneaut, Zhao & Weber 2006), the impact of the rate of technological change at work (O'Driscoll, Biron & Cooper 2009) and of course technostress (Arnetz & Wiholm 1997; Day, Scott & Kelloway 2010; O'Driscoll, Brough, Timms & Sawang 2010; Salanova, Llorens & Cifre 2013) with its issues of productivity (Tarafdar, Tu, Ragu-Nathan & Ragu-Nathan 2007), well-being (Arnetz & Wiholm 1997) and work-overload, home–work conflict and balance generated by perceptions of 'constant connectivity' and 'simultaneously handling different streams of information' (Ragu-Nathan, Tarafdar, Ragu-Nathan 2008, p. 421; Ayyagari, Grover & Purvis 2011). The arrival of the information age and the growth of knowledge work also creates demands for new ways of working that emphasize collaboration, facilitation and networking, challenging the role and well-being of knowledge workers in a world that is 'even more technologically and socially wired than ever before' (Barjis, Gupta & Sharda 2011, p. 615; Spira & Feintuch 2005). The common theme that runs through much of this work is the idea of balance: the accessibility of knowledge and information, its benefits and rewards, balanced against problematic behaviours, addiction, abuse, crime, and technostress and constant concerns about privacy, security, equity and data sharing.

Summary

More change is to come. In addition to a world of increasing interconnectivity, advances in robotics and artificial intelligence have shifted from the confines of manufacturing, and the realms of speculation, fantasy and science fiction to the realities of a brave new world and what this may mean to the way we live and work. In terms of computer innovation and development, we have arrived at what Brynjofsson and McAfee describe as an 'inflection point', where the forces of 'sustained exponential improvement in most aspects of computing' coupled with huge amounts of digital information and the recombining of innovations that already exist or 'recombinant innovation' heralds in the 'second machine age' (2014, p. 90). These building blocks clear the way for transformational change, this time in the field of robotics and artificial intelligence that will 'convert science fiction into everyday reality, outstripping even our recent expectations and theories' (Brynjofsson & McAfee 2014, p. 90). Giving examples of the progress that has been made and the technology already available, their economic consequences and what may be necessary in terms of policy, procedures and controls, Brynjofsson and McAfee conclude that in the end the choices we make and the values we aspire to will shape the kind of world that emerges.

All these changes and the speed at which they have transformed the way we live and work have also been instrumental in shaping the nature of our economy to such an extent that whether it is now best to describe it as 'post industrial' or 'knowledge based' is perhaps at best a moot point, as we witness a fundamental shift in its nature as it becomes 'increasingly weightless' (Coyle & Quah 2002, p. 8). The idea of 'weightlessness' captures notions of value added, innovation, invention and design 'being much less dependent on physical mass, and more on intangibles, such as human intelligence, creativity and even personal warmth' (Coyle & Quah 2002, p. 8). As Brinkley suggests, these intangibles are 'transforming our economy', to the extent that little by little boundaries between traditional sectors are disappearing, opportunities for investing in intangibles are growing, markets focusing on ideas and knowledge are being created globally, relentlessly driven on by the demand for 'high value added, knowledge intensive goods and services' (2008, p. 9). In this new world managers already experienced in managing relentless demands for change are now faced with the demand for profound changes to 'the very nature of the "business model" which dominates organizational thinking' and researchers are faced with the allied call as to whether organizational behaviour theories actually express these changes, or have the capacity to capture the essence of the experience of work 'in the electronic age' (Gephart 2002, p. 327).

Raising the issue of 'how do people experience, interpret and make sense of the new workplace and new workforce' (Gephart 2002, p. 328) means that it is now time to search for those organizing principles that will help shape our theories to capture the impact of 'electronic work' acknowledging that we have arrived at a defining moment in the way work is experienced. The shadow of interconnectivity is everywhere; creative effort is now the norm in many workplaces, work is embedded in networks of teams reflecting the new structures of organizations that are more organic, flatter, value driven and offering more autonomy and control (Rainie & Wellman 2014). The pressure for change will continue, traditional assumptions about the nature of work will continue to be questioned, the need for transparency and trust will change the way organizations are led (Gratton 2014, p. 41), competing through people will be the new comparative advantage, and collaboration, facilitation and inclusion will be the skills fashioned by social networks and demanded by the thrust of interconnectivity. This new age, irrespective of what we call it, simply challenges all of us to ensure that theoretically, empirically and individually we are ready for the new realities of work.

TABLE II.2

GROWING THE SEEDS OF CHANGE

TECHNOLOGY

- o An age characterized by the remarkable speed at which innovation, intventiveness and creative development have occurred.
- o The new millennium continues to usher in inventions including internet based applications, advances in mobile technologies and the arrival of 'ubiquitous technologies' (Waterson 2014, p. 224).
- o Offering individuals the opportunity to express their world through online networks and connecting with those who are part of their extended social network (Boyd & Ellison 2008); hence the internet of people – always there, always available, always ready (Kleinrock 2008).

o Wireless capability drives the next round of inventions where we are entering the age of anytime, anyplace, anything (Tan & Wang 2010, V5–376). Enter
   the internet of things.

o Not forgetting the age of context – the forces of contextual technology that
   have transformed our lives and the way we live – mobile devices, social media,
   big data sets, sensors and location-based services (Scoble & Israel 2014).

o And new innovations that include wearable technology, smart garments and
   textiles, health and fitness gadgets (*The Guardian* 2015), the commercialization of drones (*The Observer* 2015), self driving cars and advances in home
   and work robots (*The Press* 2015).

o Creating issues of privacy, security and transparency, policy in respect of
   access, law, crime, scope, ownership, capability damage and cyber behaviours and technostress (Ragu-Nathan et al. 2008; Day et al. 2010; O'Driscoll
   et al. 2009).

o 'How do people experience, interpret and make sense of the new workplace and new workforce?' (Gephart 2002, p. 328).

o The new age, irrespective of what we call it, simply challenges all of us to
   ensure that theoretically, empirically and individually we are ready for the
   new realities of work.

Workforce changes, society and sustainability

The title of our third force draws on the work of Gratton (2014), although each is
intimately linked and simply reflects how the rule of interdependence is the underlying theme that binds all themes together. Each is another transforming experience
tempered by the impact of globalization and technology and honed by trends that
influence the behaviours, values and movements of people, the ways lives are viewed,
the choices made, the communities lived in, the interactions made with others,
where and how they work and the ways they want to work, the sustainability of their
actions, of the actions of others and the actions of organizations, the kind of economy they want, the way responsibilities are balanced across society, and the protocols
for policies and practice (Donkin 2010; Gratton 2014; Hirsch 2005; Isles 2008). We
will under each heading explore the changing nature of the workforce including
generational differences, ageing, gender and migration, the changing shape of society and sustainability including building sustainable and greening organizations and
sustainable work. The forces of globalization and technology are ever present, so we
will touch on issues of mobility, the arrival of technology for all and the inclusive
revolution, the new wave in sustainable business and the 'net positive' movement and
communication, culture and change.

Workforce changes

The Chartered Institute of Personnel and Development (CIPD 2013a) points to three trends that have shaped the workforce: ageing, migration and gender, letting the numbers tell the story. By 2013 the proportion of those in employment over the age of 50 reached 29%, an increase of 3.2 million in the last decade (p. 6). As a result of other workforce trends including a greater participation rate of young people in higher education, and more disturbingly by 2011 over a million younger people 'lost in transition' and not in employment, education or training (Sissons & Jones 2012, p.8), those over 50 now represent an even greater proportion of those actively involved in employment (CIPD 2013a). This, as the CIPD goes on to report, raises issues about meeting the demands for and the flow of higher skill levels into the workforce, the need to ensure that retaining and re-skilling the existing workforce is part of any Human Resource strategy, and how the continued provision of welfare support will be influenced in part by the employment opportunities for older workers and those who have caring responsibilities (CIPD 2013a, p. 6).

As those over 50 will become more important in terms of overall workforce performance, Turner and Williams (2005) explore the implications, challenges and policy issues facing employers, government and society. In their comprehensive review they raise the issue of how well the ageing workforce is profiled and understood, the choices for older individuals, the implications for the labour market and social cohesion, how governments, organizations and other agencies have responded and the challenges that management face. For Turner and Williams, the key management challenges, in addition to 'a good deal of organizational analysis', include changing attitudes, understanding what is required by the legislation and evaluating initiatives and monitoring and understanding outcomes (2005, p. 40). At present there are around 8.6 million people over the age of 50 in employment; around 1 million of those are over 65 and this employment rate for those aged 65 and over is the highest since comparable records began in 1992 (ONS 2013, p. 2).

By 2021 the number of those over the age of 50 in employment is expected to rise to 12 million (Turner & Williams 2005, p. 7). Describing the over 50s as the 'new work generation', the Equality and Human Rights Commission's (Maitland 2010, pp. 6–7) research illustrates that the aspirations of this 'new generation' challenges many of the assumptions made about this age group because, in general, they want to keep working, seek promotion, continue to learn and enjoy what they do (pp. 6–7). While of course there are issues and barriers around health, flexibility and choice of work, employment policies, and attitudes and beliefs about older workers (Maitland 2010, pp. 7–9), the evidence is clear that this 'extraordinary increase in productive life' (Gratton 2014, p. 38) should be seized upon and developed. The answer is 'yes' to an age wave and one that deserves and 'demands some forward-thinking policies in employment' (Donkin 2010, p. 47). Now described as 'the silver economy' with 'age-positive practices' (Maitland 2010, p. 6), the number of those aged over 65 will continue to rise in proportion to those in the 15-64 age group ten times faster year on year until 2037 (Roberts 2014, p. 30).

The discussion around age brings us to another age-related aspect of the workforce: generational differences (Field, Burke & Cooper 2015). As each new generation enters the workforce the belief is that important inter-generational differences or gaps will emerge within the workforce that create conflict (O'Bannon 2001, p. 95), present management challenges (Benson & Brown 2011) and where managers 'are encouraged' to deal with these assumed differences (Smola & Sutton 2002, p. 363). How real these differences really are (DiRomualdo 2006), and whether 'the gap' is more of a myth that diverts attention away from more important realities of management (Giancola 2006), demands a more balanced approach when considering any generational gap and the need for systematic research into where inter-generational differences may lie (Benson & Brown 2011; Cogin 2012). Researchers have, of course, identified different generational groups with names that we are all familiar with. While there may be some consistency as to how these different generational groups are named (Baby Boomers, Generation X and the Generation Y or Millennials), inconsistencies still remain as to the years each group represents (Smola & Sutton 2002). The two groups that are most frequently compared because of their established presence in the workforce are the Baby Boomers and Generation X (Smola & Sutton 2002).

The years around 1946 to perhaps 1964 represent the Baby Boomers; a time of economic expansion, social movements and protest and the offer and opportunity of a good life (Smola & Sutton 2002; Fay 1993). The years around the early 1960s to perhaps the early 1980s represent Generation X. This may have been a time of slow economic growth and a sluggish job market, but when asked to describe themselves Generation X pointed to their 'ambition, determination and independence' (O'Bannon 2001, p. 105; Fay 1993). This brief description of these two groups does not capture the detailed work that researchers have done reflecting on, and describing their similarities and differences in terms of belief, attitudes, values, expectations, hopes and desires (Benson & Brown 2011; Cogin 2012; Gratton 2014; Jurkiewicz 2000; O'Bannon 2001; Smola & Sutton 2002). Yet despite the lack of a consensus as to the years that best define a particular generation similarities and differences have been found. While research points, at times, to surprising levels of similarities between Baby Boomers and GenXers, differences are present and have been found around issues of personal growth at work (Jurkiewicz 2000, p. 63), work values (Cogin 2012; Smola & Sutton 2002), job satisfaction, and willingness to quit and the antecedents that led to these attitudes (Benson & Brown 2011).

Looking into the future, Gratton suggests that 'the coming decades' will still be defined by the Baby Boomers and, when by 2025, most have gone from the workforce they will have left behind a huge gap in 'tactical knowledge and knowhow' (p. 35). GenXers will, by 2010 Gratton argues, have reached 'the height of their earning power' (p.35), GenYers will, by 2025, have reached 'a crucial stage' (p. 36) in their working lives – one that is intertwined and interconnected with technology, and by 2020 a new generation (GenZers) will be emerging and will increasingly be exerting its influence on business worldwide (Gratton 2014, pp. 35–36). These differences in work values and personal growth present challenges, and increasingly require management to be more sensitive to 'generational diversity' when design-ing reward and performance structures and work arrangements (Benson & Brown 2011, p. 1860; Cogin 2012), understanding issues that influence their psychological contract (Smola & Sutton 2002), and how differences can complement each other and enhance working together (Jurkiewicz 2000).

Researchers acknowledge the difficulties when engaging in inter-generational research, and all are acutely aware that work needs to continue to question the role of stereotyping, clearly identify what work values and attitudes should be measured, how these work values and attitudes play out in the workplace, whether differ-ences are generational differences or reflect life cycle, social or contextual changes, or reflect the years each generation represents and the different events that have occurred, whether generational groups can and should be further segmented, how generational groups change and will change over time, whether similarities out-weigh differences, the importance and nature of any gap and whether it matters, and the extent of different generational groups within a workforce (see Benson & Brown 2011; Cogin 2012; DiRomualdo 2006; Giancola 2006; Gratton 2014; Jurkiewicz 2000; Smola & Sutton 2002). Perhaps, as Lyons and Kuron conclude, it is time to move away from the 'simple notion of birth cohorts' as a means of exploring differences in the workplace to 'more nuanced approaches' and meth-ods that balance and better capture the ways in which generational differences are actualized and the mechanisms through which attitudes and behaviours emerge (2014, p. S153).

While there may still be debates about what age you become an older worker (Turner & Williams 2005), what ages does a generation cover and how best it is described (Smola & Sutton 2002), the nature of the workforce is not immune from other societal and demographic changes that add to its complexity and diversity, and it to these that we now turn. 'There is no doubt that migration has had a huge impact on the UK labour market over the past decade' (CIPD 2013b, p. 3). In the last decade the proportion of non UK-born people in employment has increased by over 60%, reaching around 4.26 million or 14% of the total workforce (CIPD 2013b; ONS 2013), spurred on somewhat by the expansion of the European Union (EU) in 2004. The issue of immigration is complex and must be considered, for example, in terms of whether workers are from the EU or outside the European Economic Area (EEA), whether the jobs are skilled or non-skilled, the nature of skill shortages, the skill mix required, workforce planning, the impact on different employment sec-tors and employment as a whole, changes to immigration policy and the challenges facing policy implementation, economic prospects, the factors driving the employ-ment of migrant workers, the recruitment market and recruitment market practices and the impact and consequences for recruitment and development of the domestic labour market (CIPD 2013b, pp. 9–18).

The number and importance of women in the workforce can, in part, be illustrated by numbers. The workforce is now almost evenly split by gender with women making up around 47% (13.848 million) of all those in employment, compared with 37% in 1971 (CIPD 2013a). Nevertheless, despite this 'wider talent pool available to employers' stark differences still remain between men and women 'in terms of pay and access to senior positions' (CIPD 2013a, p. 8). The realities of workplace pay equality may have their roots in a part-time versus fulltime work divide with 5.199 million women working part time, compared with 1.514 men (ONS 2013). Although causes for this divide are complex, there may be economic reasons where there is pressure to be in work or return to work, generational reasons with gender segmentation for young men and women entering the workforce (Brinkley, Jones & Lee 2013), legislative reasons encouraging movement into part-time work, and career reasons where guidance offers a greater range of potential work options. Recent attention has been drawn to the number of women holding senior positions, particularly those at boardroom level. Detailed research by Gregory-Smith and his colleagues found evidence of a 'gender bias' in the appointment of women non-executive directors to the boardrooms of large companies, with mixed evidence in terms of discrimination in wages or fees proposing 'greater board diversity may be best structured around the moral value of diversity rather than with reference to an expectation of improved company performance' (Gregory-Smith, Main & O'Reilly 2014, p. F109).

Work environments are already 'complex in terms of human resource legislation, more demanding in terms of equity, fairness and equal opportunities and more responsive in terms of care, support, flexibility' and, 'the ability to make choices, express individual preferences' and to learn and develop (Dewe & Cooper 2012, p. 34). Diversity, inclusion and social justice are now core to organizational life but are challenges still being met and progress being made? Pointing to the creative and strategic work being done, the knowledge gained, and the centrality of diversity and inclusion as essential to the people-policy organizational mix, the CIPD identify a number of implications that emerge from their research that need to be confronted if progress is to continue and momentum sustained. These include, for example, that 'diversity is seen as "a real" business issue rather than something simply managed by HR, that it be clearly and coherently integrated into HR strategies, that there is a transition from a legislative culture towards a inclusive culture, that the need is for a long term commitment,' that a systematic evaluation and development of the strategic case for diversity and inclusion is ongoing and that there is active engagement from the top of the organization (CIPD 2012, pp. 4, 19–20).

Society and sustainability

Change continues to sweep into every corner of society at a rate that sees invention, innovation and products tumbling over themselves and each other to be the next to transform lives. Ravaged by the dogma of the economic imperative, and stunned by its consequences, society seems caught between wondering what the new world will bring and already living it. Change is so rapid that we are bombarded with labels that express the different ages we are, or have been passing through, each illustrating just how fast change is occurring by having a lifespan no longer it seems than the next generation of innovation that overtakes it. New words are now entering our vocabulary that express if not the world we have, then at least the world that is wanted. These include words like inclusiveness, sharing, balance, trust, transparency, connectiveness and sustainability. It is, as Gratton illustrates, a world of paradoxes; we want and are eager to engage with new innovative technology and the connectivity it brings but 'we also yearn to be comforted and crave time on our own'. Similarly we want to be able to express ourselves and enjoy the autonomy of who we are and what we do but 'on the other hand we want also to be part of a regenerative community' (Gratton 2014, p. 39–40). Yet it is here, Gratton argues, that the forces of change can be 'harnessed to create a more crafted outcome'; enter the idea of 'crafted futures', where through choice, personal initiatives and actions coupled with understanding the forces of change come the opportunities to craft a workable future (2014, p. 16).

What if, Gratton (2014) goes on to add, some of these choices – individual, organizational and societal – were to lead to a growing culture of sustainability? There is no doubting the fundamental issue of climate change, the challenges faced and that it is no longer an issue of more proof but more of the need for urgent action. The greater challenge, argues Isles (2008, p. 4), is the balance of responsibilities between individuals, organizations and the state. Yet the voice that has been 'almost completely absent' has been that of organizational researchers (Andersson, Jackson & Russell 2013, p. 151). So what can be done? For organizations there are challenges that include raising awareness, 'recognition and insights,' taking steps to mobilize, 'commit and set directions,' changing design and processes and finally establishing 'continuity' through monitoring, complying and developing trust and transparent relationships (Swedish Council for Working Life and Social Research (SCWLSR) 2009, pp. 19-20). For organizational behaviour researchers, three types of research emerge: at the organizational level, as outlined above; and two at the individual level – one in terms of developing pro-environment behaviours, and the other in sustaining working lives.

If sustainability is to be achieved then it depends on what happens in the workplace. How the 'carbon footprint of work' may be reduced by 'green' organizational practices is well illustrated by Isles (2008, p. 4). However, Isles presents a sense of the challenge faced by, and indeed being met by, some organizations by pointing to four areas where business strategy and green practices can converge. These include by being more efficient and getting the same result by using fewer resources, and by using technology to redesign and reorganize work that is reducing the 'performance gap' between how performance is being managed and how it could be managed. Isles argues that the remaining two require even more fundamental change and require organizations to rethink the notion of 'place' and how and where they do business, embracing issues like working from home, reducing journey times to and from work, and rethinking ideas about mobility, flexibility and location. If the notion of 'place' is challenged then, Isles argues, so must the idea of work, its nature, its meaning and what we understand by it (2008, pp. 10–12). Howard-Grenville and her colleagues also set out the implications of climate change to show how 'this issue poses pressing and important questions for management and organizational scholars' (Howard-Grenville, Buckle, Hoskins & George 2014, p. 618).

Howard-Grenville and her colleagues suggest four issues but add 'they are neither exhaustive nor inclusive' but simply 'ripe for study' (2014, p. 618). These include the 'reshaping of value chains,' the rethinking (because climate change will change 'how we live and work') of how work is arranged, the sorts of skills required, how managers and employees work with one another, are motivated, communicate, identify and relate to the organization. There will be a demand, these authors go on to argue, as responses to 'climate change are truly without precedent', for new processes and structures in terms of how decisions are made, how forecasting is approached and how organizations plan, adapt and remain resilient. They add that climate change will have 'far reaching' effects on how we relate to other societies, 'the burdens we place on them,' the decisions we make and the obligations we impose. It will also challenge how change will be introduced at a societal level, how communities are designed, developed and integrated, how society as a whole is made more resilient, how collaboration and cooperation is achieved and what will be required in terms of changing values, technology, culture and expectations (Howard-Grenville et al. 2014, pp. 618, 619–621).

Researchers are already talking about 'the next chapter of sustainable business' (Haigh & Hoffman 2012, p. 126), and describing the arrival of and benefits that accrue from a new type of organization that they call hybrid organizations. The hybrid model of organization is 'sustainability driven', in that it explores ways to develop and generate 'social and environmental improvements through their practices and products' going that one stage further than simply attempting to reduce the environmental impact side of organizations (Haigh & Hoffman 2012, p. 127). A number of distinctive features separate these organizations from others. They are, argue Haigh and Hoffman, driven by a 'growing demographic'; people who build from the core value of sustainability and place it at the heart of how they conduct their business. Other features include their relationships within and outside the organization and their lifestyles. Sustainability is the singular organizational goal; it creates relationships that are 'mutually enriching' and environmentally progressive in their interactions and connections with others (Haigh & Hoffman 2012, pp. 126, 127).

Also in this 'new wave' of organizations is the idea of the 'net positive' organization where the promise is that in all that they do 'they will leave the world in a better place than they found it' (Balch 2014, p. 3). Here too the idea is to take that next step, and to take actions and move thinking beyond just how organizations can reduce their environmental impact to thinking how they become more regenerative. Perhaps this is why we are seeing the rise of the 'shared economy'. The shared economy involves transactions between peers or peer-to-peer business where, for example, assets, skills, products and much more are shared (e.g. rented) by one person with another; anything from rooms in a house to seats in a car and lots more. There are multiple ways in which exchanges can take place, incentives for doing so and opportunities for creating added value. Online markets offer trading posts, synergies for interactions and hubs that offer a socially relevant economic system (see European Commission: Business Innovation Observatory 2013; *The Economist* 2013a, 2013b). Is this the time to think of the arrival of the regenerative age?

Finally, sustainability at the employee level involves exploring both what encourages pro-environmental behaviours and what sustains working life. Work exploring the promotion of pro-environmental behaviours in the workplace points to how it may be enhanced by developing pro-environmental attitudes and nurturing positive work emotions (Bissing-Olson, Iyer, Fielding & Zacher 2013), transformational leadership (Robertson & Barling 2013) and through understanding the role of 'self-concordance' – that is, the extent to which pro-environmental behaviours are in accord with and express a person's values, interests, and goals (Unsworth, Dmitrieva & Adriasola 2013, p. 214). These brief outlines do not capture either the richness or detail of the work cited but provide an overview of what is a necessary shift in focus, where attention is now being directed towards building a better understanding of 'intra-organizational process and individual behaviour'. In this way they show how greening organizational behaviour research can provide 'unique insights' into why, how and in what ways organizations can work, and are already working, towards the goal of environmental sustainability (Andersson et al. 2013, p. 151).

Sustaining working life takes altogether another focus, but in terms of its values and goals aspires to achieve the same ends by asking how can working lives be made more sustainable (Hirsch 2005; Pfeffer 2009, 2010). Often referred to as 'social sustainability' to distinguish it from 'environmental sustainability', the former's concern is on the costs imposed on people through organizational and management practices, policies and procedures 'that have serious harmful effects on employees' physical and psychological wellbeing' (Pfeffer 2009, p. 5) or what would make working lives more sustainable where individuals play a more productive, rewarding, balanced, fulfilled and satisfying role (Hirsch 2005; Pfeffer 2010; Spreitzer & Porath 2012; Spreitzer, Porath & Gibson 2012). It is, as Pfeffer points out, 'not just the natural world that is at risk from harmful business practices', and so continuing to develop our understanding of the causes and consequences of these practices should also be a priority and focus of our research, our interventions and our actions (Pfeffer 2010, p. 43, 2009).

TABLE II.3

GROWING THE SEEDS OF CHANGE

WORKFORCE CHANGES, SOCIETY AND SUSTAINABILITY (GRATTON 2014)

o   Three trends have shaped the workforce: ageing, migration and gender.
o   While there may be debates about what age you become an older worker
    (Turner & Williams 2005) and what age does a generation cover and how best
    it is described (Smola & Sutton 2002), the workforce is not immune from these
    societal and demographic changes that add to its complexity and diversity.
o   Immigration is complex and should be considered, for example, in terms
    of whether workers are from the EU or outside the European Economic
    Area (EEA), whether jobs are skilled or non-skilled, the nature of skill short-
    ages, the skills that are required, workforce planning, the impact on different
    employment sectors and employment as a whole, changes to immigration
    policy and the challenges facing policy implementation – just to mention a
    few of the complexities (CIPD 2013b, pp. 9–18).
o   The number and importance of women in the workforce can, in part, be
    illustrated by numbers. The workforce is now almost evenly split by gender
    with women making up around 47% (13.848 million) of those in employ-
    ment (CIPD 2013a).
o   Nevertheless despite this 'wider pool available to employers' stark differ-
    ences still remain between men and women 'in terms of pay and access to
    senior positions' (CIPD 2013a, p. 8).
o   'Work environments are already complex in terms of human resource
    legislation, more demanding in terms of equity, fairness and equal oppor-
    tunities and more responsive in terms of care, support, flexibility,' and
    'the ability to make choices, express individual preferences' and learn and
    develop (Dewe & Cooper 2012, p. 34).
o   Diversity, inclusion and social justice are now core to organizational life.
o   What about sustainability? New words are now entering our vocabulary
    that express if not the world we live in but at least the world that is wanted.
    These words include inclusiveness, sharing, balance, trust, transparency, con-
    nectiveness and sustainability.
o   Sustainability is represented in what have been described as hybrid
    'sustainability driven' organizations that explore ways to generate 'social
    and environmental improvements through their practices and products'
    (Haigh & Hoffman 2012, p. 127).

(Continued)

> *(Continued)*
>
> o   Sustainability at the employee level includes exploring what encourages pro-environment behaviour and attitudes (Bissing-Olson et al. 2013).
> o   Social sustainability also concerns how working lives can be made more sustainable (Hirsch 2005; Pfeffer 2009, 2010). Often described as social sustainability to distinguish it from environmental sustainability its focus explores the 'costs imposed on people' through organizational and management practices, policies and procedures 'that have serious harmful effects on employees' physical and psychological wellbeing' (Pfeffer 2009, p. 5) or what would make working lives more sustainable where individuals play a more productive, rewarding, balanced, fulfilled and satisfying role (Hirsh 2005; Pfeffer 2009, 2010; Spreitzer & Porath 2012).

Summary

This chapter is not just about identifying all the many ages that describe a particular phase in our history, and how it has transformed our lives. Its purpose goes beyond just offering a descriptive tour of these forces of change and how each has evolved, developed and changed. Nor is it just an opportunity to discuss directly, or more often indirectly, how each is interdependent and how a change in one changes the others and in this way it itself is changed. For there is underlying these forces two not mutually exclusive themes that are fundamental to our understanding of their impact; these are the themes of 'context' and 'development' (Viney 1993). A sense of context provides a framework for understanding why at a certain time our understanding changes, different issues emerge and why an issue assumes importance. It is from this context we get a sense of place, of time, of explanation and of intervention. Without this context it makes the present more difficult to understand, often giving it a sense of importance that lures us into accepting the status quo, failing to understand or account for or consider contemporary trends, ideas and debates (Cooper & Dewe 2004, p. 114).

Throughout this chapter there is an underlying sense of theoretical progression, adaptation and change, coupled at times with those tipping points that precipitated such change. It is the idea of 'context' that allows us to anchor such points against events and evaluate them in terms of their relevance and explanatory power. Understanding contextual issues has also taught us that there is not some simple linear way in which theories develop by building neatly on one another, how within this turmoil of change comes controversy, criticism and sometimes confusion where our beliefs are tested, where the search is leading us in terms of those organizing concepts around which we can capture meaning and understanding and build for the future. It is the second theme that provides us with a sense of development, providing us with a way of not just identifying new ideas but why some ideas better represent the nature of our concerns. This is what we hope comes from this chapter; a context for exploring the state of our theories, whether, how and in what way they have been influenced, evolved, and developed but more fundamentally their relevance, how readily they capture the work experience, and the challenges they present for the future.

III

THE EVOLUTION OF THEORY AND THEORIES OF WORK STRESS

The transformational nature of change leaves no part of society untouched; it reaches into every corner, obligating us as researchers and practitioners to engage in a process of continuous evaluation that assesses and tests the relevance of our theories, the ideas and assumptions that shape them, and their utility in expressing contemporary work experiences. It also requires us, as we have noted before, to distinguish between 'developing knowledge and applying it', understanding the difference between 'describing a relationship' and 'giving that relationship meaning', questioning whose reality we are measuring by asking 'where are current methodologies taking us', what can alternative methodologies provide and how the 'creative tension' that accompanies change allows us to accept the critical debate that must follow, requires us to avoid the convenience of maintaining established practices and protocols and frees us to acknowledge the responsibilities we have to those whose working lives we study (Dewe & Cooper 2012, pp. 6, 7, 8; van Maanen 1979). It is against this backdrop of transformational change, and the need for critical debate, that we set the context for exploration in this chapter – first the evolution and utility of organizational behaviour theory, and then more specifically the evolution of theories of work stress. We begin our examination of theory with a touch of history exploring through the tradition of a 'thematic approach' how terms that are entirely familiar to us, like scientific management, human relations and contingency (and the names of those theorists associated with them) (Mullins 2002), have been expressed and how they have contributed to our understanding of behaviour at work (Dewe & Cooper 2012). We then shift our focus and take a more detailed look at how, and in what ways, specific organizational theories have been adapted to capture the contemporary experience of work, and more particularly work stress.

TABLE III.1

THE EVOLUTION OF THEORY AND THEORIES OF WORK STRESS: A THEMATIC APPROACH

LOCATING THEORIES IN A CONTEXT THAT CAPTURES WHY THEY EMERGED WHEN THEY DID AND HOW THEY INFORM OUR UNDERSTANDING AND ADVANCE OUR KNOWLEDGE AND PRACTICE

o The transformational nature of change leaves no part of society untouched obligating researchers and practitioners to engage in a continuous process of evaluation that assesses and tests the relevance of our theories.

o It also requires us as researchers to distinguish between developing knowledge and applying that knowledge (Dewe & Cooper 2012, p. 6).

o Understanding the difference between describing a relationship and giving that relationship meaning (Dewe & Cooper 2012, p. 6).

o Questioning whose reality we are measuring by asking where our current methodologies are taking us and what can other creative methodologies do to enhance our understanding (van Maanen 1979).

o Avoiding the temptation of the convenience of established practices frees us to acknowledge the responsibilities we have to those whose working lives we study (Dewe & Cooper 2012).

A thematic approach to theory

Scientific management

Exploring theory through a thematic lens offers us an opportunity to go beyond just bluntly expressing each theme in terms of a set of techniques or methods by locating it within a context that captures why such theories emerged, when they did and how they informed our understanding and advanced our knowledge and practice. You will notice that we don't confine each theme to a set of dates, as we know that theory doesn't progress in an orderly or linear fashion. Ideas run in parallel, often paying little attention to each other, so points of change where new themes emerge become blurred as themes frequently build from the work that has gone on before, often replacing one emphasis with another, leaving structural elements untouched and raising questions about how long theories actually last and how their relevance is maintained. Chronicling Frederick Taylor's ideas and tracing the roots of what became known as scientific management begins in an age that was heralded as 'progressive' (Fry 1976; Zuffo 2011, p. 23), where 'new production factors of emerging enterprises' required new theory (Zuffo 2011, p. 25), where there was a clear need for a more 'systematic management' approach (Wren 2011, p. 12) and where efficiency was not just the key (Zuffo 2011) but represented a means towards organizational and social harmony (Fry 1976).

While Taylor preferred the title of 'task management' rather than 'scientific management' (Wren 2011), and while critics saw his work more in terms of common sense than science, Taylor's intentions 'were to pursue a scientific model' where his work and his methods were in 'systematic equilibrium with the workers' (Zuffo 2011, p. 24). Taylor's theory covered a wide range of practices, some of which, when expressed in more contemporary terms, now illustrate the impact his work has had and explain why his ideas have had 'a continuing grip' on our thinking (Wren 2011, p. 11); terms like job specialization, job analysis, work design motivation, and person-job fit (Giannantonio & Hurley-Hanson 2011, p. 7). It would be wrong not to acknowledge that Taylor's work attracted considerable criticism, and at times hostility, when the metaphor of a machine was used to describe individual behaviour, when establishing 'managerial control' was seen as lying at the heart of all his practices, and where the practices themselves simply lost sight of the fact that they were dealing with people (see Boddewyn 1961, Fry 1976 and Mullins 2002 for summaries of the criticisms). Taylor's ideas 'collided' with a demand for change. Innovation and developments in technical knowledge were needed to meet the growing demands of industrialization, to transform methods of production, to improve efficiency, and to advance progressive management, '[so] above all' Taylor and his ideas were simply 'an expression of his time' (Wren 2011; Zuffo 2011, pp. 24, 25).

Scholars reflecting on Taylor's work accept that he was part of what has been described as the 'progressive age', agreeing that while his work 'can certainly' be discussed, and at times fiercely debated, what cannot be argued is that Taylor 'changed the way people worked in the 20th century' (Giannantonio & Hurley-Hanson 2011, p. 7). He was, argues Zuffo, the first to put the 'human factor' at the heart of his work recognizing that the complexity surrounding work and the person needed to be assessed and understood scientifically; each in balance with the other working in 'a systematic equilibrium', reflecting perhaps 'the first steps between scientific management and applied psychology' (Zuffo 2011, pp. 24, 27). Others capture this theme and see Taylor as something of an organizational behaviourist, recognizing the importance of the social context, the significance of the group, the need for cooperation, the role of incentives, the issue of fatigue, the importance of selection and the morality of management (Boddewyn 1961; Chambers 1973; Fry 1976; Zuffo 2011). Yes, Taylor may have taken a more economic-instrumental approach, and have been somewhat pessimistic but still hopeful in his view on human behaviour (Fry 1976) and rather dogmatic in his views, but his legacy remains because he laid the ground work for 'furthering the search for improving management' by providing 'beginning points' that enabled others 'to extend [their] thinking' and in this way he 'shaped how we live and think today' (Wren 2011, pp. 12, 19). We should not let the debate that continues to swirl around Taylor's methods and techniques, which were a product of the age, distract us from his underlying ideas. It was these that provided the theoretical building blocks that have informed much of our early theory and, indeed, still retain a level of currency for many even today.

TABLE III.2

SCIENTIFIC MANAGEMENT

o   Where 'new production factors of emerging enterprises' required new theories (Zuffo 2011, p. 25).
o   Chronicling Frederick Taylor's ideas and tracing the roots of what became known as scientific management begins in an age heralded as 'progressive' (Fry 1976; Zuffo 2011, p. 23).
o   There was a clear need for a more 'systematic management' approach (Wren 2011, p. 12) where efficiency was not just key (Zuffo 2011) but represented a means towards organizational and social harmony (Fry 1976).
o   Taylor's ideas 'collided' with a demand for change. Innovation and developments in technical knowledge were needed to meet the growing demands of industrialization, the transformation of production, to improve efficiency and to advance progressive management, so 'above all' Taylor's ideas were simply 'an expression of his time' (Wren 2011; Zuffo 2011, pp. 24–25).
o   Taylor's work 'can certainly' be discussed and at times fiercely debated, but 'what cannot be argued' is that Taylor 'changed the way people worked in the 20th Century' (Giannantonio & Hurley-Hanson 2011, p. 7)

Human relations

Reflecting on what was to become known as the 'human relations' era, Moldasch and Weber (1998) point to how alike the approach of Taylor was to that of Mayo, whose Hawthorne studies are regarded as beginning that era. Moldasch and Weber suggest that viewing Taylor's work 'as being purely technocratic' misunderstands his work and more significantly his intention of achieving workplace balance, equilibrium and harmony through scientific study (1998, p. 348). They go on to argue that Taylor's approach is little different from 'even the human relations approach', as Mayo's work also 'involved the promise of improved efficiency *and* social integration (or rather, improved efficiency *due* to social integration)' (Moldasch & Weber 1998, p. 348). Even when the human relations era is described as 'putting the "people factor" into the heart of the subject' (Warner 1994, p. 1153), parallels can be immediately drawn with Taylor's work. Yet trying to understand the human resource era is difficult. Two 'major obstacles to understanding' stand in the way; the Hawthorne experiments and Elton Mayo (Rose 1978, p. 106). Major criticism and controversy surround the Hawthorne experiments as does the 'name stamped upon Hawthorne and its aftermath' (Wallis 1986, p. 158) frequently described as the 'Mayo mystique' (Smith 1998, p. 243).

Human relations shifted thinking from the individual's relationship with the job to one that emphasized work relationships and satisfaction (Cubbon 1969), making the work group and its influence the key to understanding behaviour in organizations (Warner 1994), and capturing Mayo's two assumptions that individuals are driven by the need to establish social networks that offer 'productive cooperation' and that workplace interventions can promote well-being and motivate cooperative behaviour within and between groups, although there is, as some suggest, 'a sense of limitations' that accompanies these assumptions (Sarachek 1968, pp. 189, 197). What was it about the 'work group' that made it so significant, and the key to unlocking organizationally motivated behaviour? Part of the answer may lie in Mayo's recognition of the emerging social problems and alienation that were to accompany the Great Depression, hence the importance of work groups and the social cohesion and meaning they would give, although this may have also reflected Mayo's ability to 'popularize attractive explanations' (Rose 1978, p. 114). Nevertheless despite reservations and concerns, Mayo 'more than anyone else' is generally acknowledged as responsible for replacing the economic emphasis with a social emphasis (Smith 1974, p. 289) with human relations defined as, for example, 'motivating people in organizations to develop teamwork which effectively fulfils their needs and achieves organizational objectives' (Davis 1967, p. 5).

Some of the criticisms surrounding the Hawthorne studies may be partially explained by the fact that they were complex and passed through four distinct phases (Rose 1978), utilizing first an experimental human factor approach exploring output and illumination, followed by and somewhat overlapping with the first phase, a clinical interviewing programme that eventually became more open-ended with respondents talking about 'those concerns that preoccupied them'. This was then followed by more in-depth interviewing exploring what influenced attitudes and behaviour, and finally a more interventional phase involving employee counselling (Rose 1978, p. 110). Add to this the leadership of Mayo, the role of the Harvard Group, the Chicago Group and the 'psychological mayoites' and you have not just 'a surprisingly diverse approach' to human relations (Rose 1978, p. 168), but also a mix of sociology with the growing influence of psychology. Acknowledging the debate around methodology, the failure to give sufficient attention to broader environmental and societal factors, and the role of the organization itself, their managerial perspective, level of scientific rigour, narrowness of approach and simplicity of ideas (Mullins 2002, p. 66); and recognizing the richness, detail and careful analysis that accompanies the arguments of critics and those revisiting, reconsidering, reviewing and looking for or offering explanations to Mayo's work and approach (Bartell 1976; Cubbon 1969; Hassard 2012; Moldasch & Weber 1998;

Rose 1978; Sarachek 1968; Smith 1974; Warner 1994), it is with some trepidation that one asks what can we take from all this?

The question is not without its difficulties, especially when reviewers ponder how, despite all the criticism that has been levelled at the work of Mayo and his colleagues, it is still acknowledged as making 'an important contribution' not just to theory but to management practice as well (Moldasch & Weber 1998, p. 354). Just how crucial the role of the Hawthorne studies was in turning 'hard' scientific management towards 'soft' human relations can be gauged somewhat when words like 'pivotal' or 'crucial' are seen as overstating its significance because economic and social forces were already pushing organizations in that direction. So managers were already 'aware of social and psychological issues in the workplace', and already initiating and developing a human relations style of management before the appearance of Mayo (Hassard 2012, p. 1453). Perhaps the best way to proceed is to follow the dictum suggested by Warner where we simply indicate 'what appears to be novel' from the Hawthorne studies, and acknowledge that what their 'ultimate and wider impact might have been is harder to say' (1994, p. 1152).

So we begin this search for the novel by pointing to the role of work group behaviours (Smith 1974) and 'socio-emotional needs' (Smith 1998, p. 246), the importance of social and cooperative skills, their acquisition, development through training, how they are used and the importance of the use of a 'participatory management' style and its role in conflict resolution (Moldasch & Weber 1998, p. 357). Then, by turning to Mayo and his style of research we can point to his belief in 'knowledge-for-use' (Smith 1998, p. 244), his skill in the use of interviewing, his 'contextualist' approach (Cubbon 1969, p. 111) and his focus on individuals, the work context and the meanings they gave to a situation (Smith 1974, 1998). Nevertheless, because of the 'Mayo mystique' we can also point to just how 'difficult it is to classify Mayo in conventional disciplinary or ideological terms' (Smith 1998, p. 246). The Hawthorne studies are, however, not just about one man, although at times it is difficult to separate the science from the person. The consequences of this confusion nonetheless mean that the significance and importance of broader societal and economic factors, the ideology of the progressive age, the nature of organizations with their prevailing management styles and beliefs all represent issues that were unintentionally sidelined when trying to develop an understanding of the Hawthorne studies (Hassard 2012, p. 1454). None of this may 'make Mayo more credible', but it does suggest that 'he is still worth reading' (Smith 1974, p. 291).

Scientific management and human relations had established two theoretical building blocks – jobs (work) and the person – which shaped how theory was to develop to explain organizational behaviour. With researchers looking beyond human relations, it was systems thinking that captured their imagination (Warner 1994), and so began a journey that was eventually to become known as the 'contingency approach' to organizational behaviour. This was no orderly transition. Organizational psychology and organizational behaviour began to emerge and assume a prominent role (Warner 1994), captured first of all in the work of those who were known as neo-human relationists (Herzberg 1959; Maslow 1943, 1968; McGregor 1960). Enter 'socio-technical systems', rooted in the classical work of the Tavistock Institute of Human Relations (Emery & Trist 1965; Trist & Bamforth 1951), the idea of the organic organization (Burns & Stalker 1961), the signifi- cance of differentiation and integration in organizational structures (Lawrence & Lorsch 1967) and actionable knowledge and action research of Lewin (Coghlan & Brannick 2003; Snyder 2009), and it is clear that the 'contingency theme' embraces a number of approaches. So, to capture this evolution towards what is now more commonly described as the contingency theme, we begin by providing an overview of the important role played by systems thinking. We will use this as a context for understanding how the contingency theme developed and then shift the focus to explore how many of these ideas found their way into stress theory.

TABLE III.3

HUMAN RELATIONS

o   Human relations (Elton Mayo) shifted thinking from the individuals' relation-ship with the job to one that emphasized work relationships and satisfaction (Cubbon 1969), making the work group and its influence the key to under-standing behaviour in organizations (Warner 1994).

o   What made the work group the focus of attention? Part of the answer may lie in Mayo's recognition of the emerging social problems and alienation that was accompanying the Great Depression, so the work group's importance lay in the social cohesion and meaning it would give, 'helping workers to fulfil their social needs and achieve organizational objectives' (Davis 1967, p. 5).

o   Despite the criticism that has been levelled at Mayo's work it is still acknowl-edged as 'making "an important contribution" not just to theory but to man-agement practice as well' (Moldasch & Weber 1998, p. 354).

o   Economic and social forces were already pushing organizations towards a human relations management style before the appearance of Mayo (Hassard 2012).

o   Mayo's contribution was enhanced by his belief in 'knowledge for use' (Smith 1998, p. 244), his skill in the use of interviewing, his 'contextual' approach (Cubbon 1969, p. 111) and his focus on individuals, the work context and the meanings they gave to a situation (Smith 1974, 1998).

General systems theory and the contingency theme

General systems theory, with its roots in biology, encouraged the view that the organization operates as part of a larger environment (Mullins 2002), that the environment influences the performance of the organization (Warner 1994) with which it constantly interacts, and that organizational systems or subsystems could be identified and studied. Few concepts, as Thayer suggests, have 'burst on the intellectual scene with as much promise as General Systems Theory' (1972, p. 481), steering researchers away from earlier approaches which were described as 'closed system thinking' either because they were too mechanistic or paid only passing attention to structure (Kast & Rosenzweig 1972, p. 448; Mullins 2002). General systems theory provided researchers and theorists with a paradigm where they could 'crank into their systems model' much of the earlier knowledge that preceded it (Kast & Rosenweig 1972, p. 448), explore a range of perspectives using open systems thinking, consider the role in this new paradigm of boundaries, and explore the ideas of dynamic equilibrium, steady state and feedback (Kast & Rosenzweig 1972, p. 450).

Yet caution was always present and researchers were reminded from the very beginning that they faced 'new dilemmas' requiring them to recognize that using a biological metaphor that described organizations as 'organic' needs to be tempered, as natural systems are fundamentally different from organizations as systems, since the latter is best described as a 'contrived system' (Kast & Rosenzweig 1972; Katz & Kahn 1966). So simply dichotomizing organizations into either closed or open is not always easy, as invariably most are generally 'partially open or partially closed', recognizing that 'natural systems' emphasize survival, whereas 'organizational systems' emphasis 'effectiveness'; therefore the two may not sit comfortably together, and difficulties are always present when defining precisely the boundaries associated with a system or subsystem (Kast & Rosenzweig 1972, pp. 452–456). All this raises the question of whether general systems theory can, as Thayer suggests, ever fulfil its promise 'or deliver', because the very nature of organizations, their management and purpose means that the effect of 'hierarchy compels us to impersonalize our relationships with each other, thus making it impossible to realize ourselves or beings' (1972, pp. 482–483), thereby limiting what general system theory has to offer. Nevertheless, Kast and Rosenzweig, recognizing the macro nature of general systems theory, argued that stepping down 'a level of abstraction', and turning our attention to a more micro level of analysis provides what they describe as 'a midrange level of analysis', and captures what was already being referred to as a 'contingency view' (1972, p. 459).

The contingency approach refocused attention on the role of structure as significantly influencing organizational performance (Mullins 2002) and explored how different organizational structures 'fit' different organizational environments, or how structure is contingent on environment. The idea of contingency is best expressed in terms of a relationship that is dependent not just on structure or just on the environment but on the transaction between the two, where the better the 'fit' the greater the probability of better performance. The contingency approach does not provide easy answers to organizational performance nor step-by-step solutions, but facilitates, as Kast and Rosenzweig suggest, a greater understanding of what are complex situations where the search increasingly focuses on 'the likelihood of appropriate action' (1972, p. 462).

Two groups of researchers led the way. Burns and Stalker (1961) classified organizational structures ranging from 'mechanistic' to 'organic', depending on whether the environment was stable or dynamic. More 'formal mechanistic' organizational structures, they argue, appropriate when the environment was stable, reduced the ability to adapt or innovate. As environments became more dynamic, a more flexible 'organic structure' was necessary to ensure adaptation and innovation (Burns & Stalker 1961; Sine, Mitsuhashi & Kirsch 2006). At the heart of the Lawrence and Lorsch (1967) approach was the significance of 'environmental uncertainty'. In their work, they recognized that in dealing with environmental uncertainty, organizations needed to balance the increasing demand for differentiation against the need for integration to 'achieve a unified effort'. Organizations that could achieve a state where they are both highly differentiated, yet well integrated, 'cope more effectively with the turbulent environments that science and technology are creating' (1967, p. 47).

This brief overview of these two approaches does not, of course, capture their detailed analysis or their significance in putting to rest the idea that there was one best way to manage or structure an organization. What these two 'mid-range' theories did was to capture the transactional relationship between context and structure, the notion of fit, the dynamics of an 'if-then' relationship (Mullins 2002, p. 565), and best expressed the idea of a structural contingency approach. However, another voice was emerging with growing significance in the discipline of organizational psychology. Rather than the organizational/structure focus, it was the person who became the focal point (Lewin 1952), and following in the Lewinian tradition that 'underpins much of organizational psychology' the concept of person–environment fit became not just a 'dominant conceptual force' but the key either explicitly or implicitly 'to our understanding of behaviour' (Schneider 2001, p. 142).

TABLE III.4

SYSTEMS THINKING (AND THE CONTINGENCY APPROACH)

- Scientific management and human relations had established two building blocks – the job (work) and the person – which shaped how theory was to develop to explain organizational behaviour.
- With researchers looking beyond human relations it was systems thinking that captured their imagination (Warner 1994) and so began a journey towards a theory that was to eventually become known as the contingency approach to organizational behaviour.
- Why contingency? Because behaviour at work was contingent on the transaction between the person and the environment.

o   This transition to a focus on contingency was not to be an orderly transition. The approach itself embraced a number of other approaches influenced by the emergence of, and prominent role of, organizational psychology, the work of those who were known as the neo-human relationists (Herzberg 1959; Maslow 1943,1968; McGregor 1960), the classical work of socio-technical systems in the Tavistock Institute of Human Relations (Emery & Trist 1965), and the idea of general systems theory (Warner 1994).

o   General systems theory steered researchers away from earlier approaches which were described as 'closed systems thinking' either because they were too mechanistic or paid only passing attention to organizational structure (Kast & Rosenzweig 1972, p. 448; Mullins 2002).

o   General systems theory allowed researchers to use the idea of open systems to consider the role of boundaries and explore the ideas of dynamic equilibrium, steady state and feedback (Kast & Rosenzweig 1972, p. 450).

o   The contingency approach refocused attention on the role of organizational structures as significantly influencing organizational performance (Mullins 2002).

o   The idea of contingency is best expressed in terms of a relationship, and is dependent not just on structure or just on the environment but on the transaction between the two, where the better the 'fit' the greater the probability of better performance. This approach facilitates a greater understanding of complex situations where the search increasingly focuses on the likelihood of appropriate action (Kast & Rosenzweig 1972, p. 462).

o   Two groups of researchers led the way – Burns and Stalker (1961) introduced the idea that organizational structures ranged from mechanistic to organic depending on whether the environment was stable or dynamic.

o   Formal mechanistic organizational structures appropriate when the environment was stable reduced the ability to adapt or innovate (Burns & Stalker 1961).

o   As environments became more dynamic, a more flexible organic structure was necessary to ensure adaptation and innovation (Burns & Stalker 1961).

o   The second group of researchers (Lawrence & Lorsch 1967) placed at the heart of their work environmental uncertainty. In dealing with environmental uncertainty organizations had to balance the demands for differentiation against the need for integration to 'achieve a unified effort' (Lawrence & Lorsch 1967).

o   However, another voice was emerging with growing significance – the discipline of organizational psychology. Rather than the organizational structure being the focus it was the person who became the focus and the concept of person–environment fit became not just a 'dominant force' but the key either explicitly or implicitly 'to our understanding of organizational behaviour' (Schneider 2001, p. 142).

From Lewin to person-environment fit

Kurt Lewin has been described 'as one of the most outstanding social scientists of his day' (Burnes & Cooke 2013, p. 420), as 'the practical theorist', and the pioneer of 'actionable-knowledge', and 'action research' (Coghlan & Brannick 2003, pp. 31, 33, 34). His work remains, almost seven decades later, fundamental to our understanding of behaviour at work. It laid the foundations for the study of organizational development and leadership, was central to techniques like 'change management' and consultancy, theory and practice (Burnes & Cooke 2013, pp. 408, 420, 422), and influenced every aspect of management (Coghlan & Brannick 2003). All reflecting his now famous dictum that 'there is nothing so practical as a good theory' (Burnes 2004a, p. 998; Snyder 2009, p. 326). It was his work on 'field theory' that laid the groundwork for much of what was to follow. Central to Lewin's work was the idea of detailing the field (environment), in which behaviour took place to capture its complexities and the forces that shape it (Burnes 2004a), setting the stage for his famous formula where behaviour B 'is a function of the interaction between the person p (or group) and their environment $f(p,e)$' (Burnes & Cooke 2013, p. 412). Lewin's view was that if you were able to identify and map these forces you could better understand why people behave in the way that they do, and what changes would need to be made to bring about changes in behaviour (Burnes 2004a; 2004b; Burnes & Cooke 2013); underlying his view that 'if you want to truly understand something try to change it' (Snyder 2009, p. 226).

Lewin's work still offers a powerful tool for understanding contemporary work behaviour (Burnes 2004a; 2004b), and Lewin's legacy can be 'rightly acknowledged' (Coghlan & Brannick 2003, p. 36). Although the roots of the person–environment fit concept can be traced back to a number of theoretical traditions it is Lewin's work, as Edwards (1996) explains, that is considered 'a pioneer in P-E fit research', has an 'undeniable conceptual and intuitive appeal' and helped to lay the foundations for this approach (1996, 2008a, p. 174). While immediate parallels with Lewin's work can be found when person–environment fit is expressed in terms of needing to think about both the person and the environment when trying to understand behaviour and its causes (Schneider 2001) or that behaviour stems from the relationship between the person and the environment (Edwards 1996) or mapping the sense of fit (Billsberry, Ambrosini, Moss-Jones & Marsh 2005), the concept has clearly developed, as one would expect, in its own direction with its own complexity, dilemmas and challenges. The person–environment fit concept has gripped both scholars and practitioners (Schneider 2001), taking a hold on research, practice and theory. Its two central assumptions – that organizational behaviour rests on the relationship (fit) between the two, and that there is a compatibility between the person and the environment (Kristof 1996; van Vianen 2001, p. 1) – have resulted in 'two traditions' of research: (a) individual differences, where the emphasis is primarily on person variables; and (b) organizational psychology, where the emphasis is on the fit between the person and the environment when predicting individual outcomes

(Edwards 1991; Schneider 2001, p. 142). A third tradition may be emerging describing person–organizational fit where the fit or compatibility is between the person and the organization rather than, for example, the person and the job (Kristof 1996).

The issue that confronts all researchers and practitioners alike is, of course, what we mean by fit. Lewin left the idea of fit somewhat vague, although as Schneider points out, Lewin did go so far as to suggest, without elaborating, that behaviour resulted from some 'constellation' of P and E (2001, p. 145), leaving the idea of what combination constituted compatibility, congruence, togetherness or match to others. Searching for an understanding of fit led Muchinsky and Monahan to outline what they described as 'two types of matches between people and environments': 'supplementary' and 'complementary' (1987, p. 269). The former refers to those who 'gravitate' to an environmental context because they see themselves as similar to others and fitting in, whereas the latter refers to where the needs of the person or environment are 'offset' or compensated by the strengths of the person or environment (1987, p. 271). Muchinsky and Monahan go on to acknowledge how each of their types of fit differs in terms of outcomes variables, what is being measured, the discipline perspective, the stability of the fit, its duration, and interpretational difficulties where in some cases both an 'overmatch' and an 'under-match' may reflect a misfit (p. 269, 276). The 'complementary type' was to be divided further according to 'needs–supplies' and 'demands–abilities'. The former is where individual needs are satisfied by supplies from the environment, whereas the latter is where the demands of the environment are met by the abilities of the person (Edwards 1991, pp. 284-285, 2008a; Kristof 1996, p. 3).

There are now multiple meanings associated with P-E fit, offering multiple conceptualizations and measures, making subtle distinctions as to the structural nature of fit depending on whether the emphasis is on the person or the environment or both, the attribute(s) selected to express the person and the environment, the outcomes being tested, and the distinction between the different theoretical perspectives as to the form the fit is expected to take (Edwards 1991, 1996, 2008a; Edwards & Cooper 1990; Furnham 2001; Kristof 1996; Schneider 1987, 2001). By the time Edwards presented his review of P-E research in 2008, almost a century of research had 'generated hundreds of studies' (2008a, p. 168). Yet from the huge number of studies reviewed, Edwards questions just how much progress has been made, calling on researchers not just to commit to evaluating theory, but to promoting theoretical integration, confronting the meaning of fit, using theory driven approaches to express those dimensions that describe the person and the environment, and testing theories that 'close the empirical loop' reuniting the link between 'theory, to research and back to theory' (Edwards 2008a, pp. 217–222). Others add their voice calling for more work on what it means to have a sense of fit (Billsberry et al. 2005; Edwards & Billsberry 2010), a need to better understand the environmental outcomes of person-environment fit (Schneider 2001), and paying more attention to the methodology for better selecting and operationalizing the fit components (van Vianen 2001).

Our overview is just that; an overview. Most of the work, as Edwards makes clear, has occurred in the last 50 years and represents the work 'by many of the best scholars in P-E fit research' (Edwards 2008a, p. 217). Edwards's work illustrates why P-E fit holds such a central place in organizational behaviour research, captures the intensity of research, the demand for critical analysis, the need for strong theory and the requirement to tackle operational shortcomings, while all the time acknowledging just how important this approach is to understanding behaviour. The two traditions (individual differences and organizational psychology) have generated considerable research (Edwards 1991, 2008a; Furnham 2001; Kristof 1996; Schneider 2001), applied the P-E fit rubric in different ways across a range of areas that emphasize either the person (e.g. vocational choice, recruitment, selection, abilities, interests, values) or the environment (e.g. organizational culture, climate, goals, norms, job stress, job satisfaction, performance). Given, as Schneider notes, the widespread use of the P-E fit concept then, when thinking about its 'many manifestations', it can best be likened to 'a syndrome', helping, when describing the causes of behaviour, to explain the many forms it takes (2001, p. 141). In short, the idea of P-E fit has become fundamental to our understanding of how people in organizations behave. Its significance as a framework for understanding behaviour at work means it has played a crucial role in the way work stress has been researched, and so we now touch briefly on how P-E fit has been used by researchers to understand work stress.

TABLE III.5

FROM LEWIN TO PERSON-ENVIRONMENT FIT

- The work of Lewin stills offers a powerful tool for understanding contemporary work behaviour (Burnes 2004a, 2004b).
- Central to Lewin's work was the idea of detailing the field (environment) in which behaviour took place, to capture the complexities of forces that shaped it (Burnes 2004a).
- Lewin expressed his ideas in the formula that behaviour B 'is a function of the interaction between the person p (or group) and their environment f (p,e)' (Burnes & Cooke 2013, p. 412).
- Lewin's view was that if you were able to identify and map these forces you could better understand why people behave in the way that they do and what changes would need to be made to bring about changes in behaviour (Burnes 2004a; 2004b; Burnes & Cooke 2013).
- Lewin is considered to be 'a pioneer in p-e fit research'. His work has an 'undeniable conceptual and intuitive appeal' and helped to 'lay the foundations for this approach' (Edwards 1996, 2008a, p. 174).

o   P-E fit theory as one would expect has moved in its own direction with its own complexities, dilemmas and challenges.

o   P-E fit theory has gripped both scholars and practitioners (Schneider 2001). Its two assumptions are that organizational behaviour rests on the relationship (fit) between the person and the environment; and there is a compatibility between the person and the environment (Kristof 1996; van Vianen 2001, p. 1).

o   Two traditions of approach have emerged. One that primarily emphasizes person variables and the other approach where the emphasis is on the 'fit' between the person and the environment when predicting individual outcomes (Edwards 1991; Schneider 2001, p. 142).

o   The issue that confronts all researchers and practitioners alike is, of course, what do we mean by fit?

o   Searching for an understanding of fit led to two types of matches between person and environment: supplementary and complementary (Muchinsky & Monahan 1987, p. 269).

o   The former refers to those who 'gravitate' to an environmental context because they see themselves as similar to others and fitting in. The latter is where the needs of the person or the environment are 'offset' or compensated by the strengths of the person or environment (Muchinsky & Monahan 1987, p. 271).

o   A considerable amount of research now offers multiple conceptualizations of the form fit will take, with researchers raising the question of what it means to have a sense of fit (Billsberry et al. 2005; Edwards & Billsberry 2010).

o   More attention needs to be paid to the methodology for better selecting and operationalizing the fit components (van Vianen 2001).

o   Nevertheless the idea of P-E fit has become fundamental to our understanding of how people behave in organizations.

o   P-E fit has been described as 'the most versatile' of theories for understanding work stress, helping to explain its standing as an investigatory tool (Edwards & Rothbard 1999, p. 86; Yang, Che & Spector 2008).

o   Despite the widespread use of P-E fit theory, work stress research has followed its own path.

P-E fit and work stress

Concerns about the 'quality of working life' have been at the heart of organizational psychology research. The contingency theme has come to represent a broad approach to behaviour at work and it too, like the concepts that express it, often reflected movements within movements, and so the quality of working life movement offered a rubric under which researchers could explore the impact of working conditions on well-being. Yet, as we will continue to see, other forces were also at play. The legacy of the socio-technical systems approach had provided researchers with the idea of organizations as open systems interacting with their environments, and the importance of the relationship between the technical with the social in terms of well-being (Ingvaldsen & Rolfsen 2012). This approach, growing out of the Lewin tradition, drew attention to the notion of context and its impact on behaviour, allowing researchers to extend the idea of context beyond organizational boundaries to explore how to best 'design and utilize technology for people and society' (Passmore 1995, pp. 15-16). Society was also changing, with the emergence of large-scale organizations, concerns about productivity, the need for new approaches to management and the accumulating evidence showing the impact of stress and dissatisfaction on well-being (Lawler 1982).

P-E fit has been described as 'the most versatile' of theories for understanding work stress (Edwards & Rothbard 1999, p. 86) helping to explain its standing as an investigatory tool (Yang et al. 2008) and its extensive use by researchers (Edwards & Cooper 1990). Despite the widespread use of P-E fit theory, work stress research has followed its own path, sometimes shaped by the approaches discussed above, sometimes by a sense of urgency to focus on stressful outcomes, sometimes by a need to understand process and always, but not always acknowledged, by the significance of context, the importance of meaning and the ever-present influence of how stress has been defined. So, with hindsight, as we have noted before, work stress research has passed through a number of phases, not necessarily following the orderly way in which we are about to describe them. The 'structural phase' (Cox 1978; Cooper et al. 2001, pp.14–19), essentially a static approach, explored the interaction between a stimulus and a response. This phase allowed researchers to engage in 'structural manipulations', where a third variable was introduced to explore its moderating impact on the stimulus-response interaction, hence the second phase. These two phases, while providing much needed data on the causes and consequences of work stress, failed to capture either the complexity of the relationship or any underlying process (Cooper et al. 2001, pp.14–15). It was the idea that work stress is best viewed as a transaction between the individual and the environment that provided the basis for the third phase, and offered researchers the opportunity to explore the essential nature of the stress process and those psychological mechanisms that link the individual to the environment.

Lazarus and the process-oriented transactional model of stress

The third phase owes much to the work of Lazarus (1966) and his 'process oriented' transactional approach to stress. Lazarus (1999) offered to those wishing to study stress both power and authority by expressing through the idea of transaction that stress did not reside solely in the individual or solely in the environment but in the transaction between the two. What gives Lazarus's view such authority is, as we have described before, how he identifies those psychological processes that link the individual to the environment, and in this way offers a causal pathway for understanding the stress process (Dewe & Cooper 2012, pp. 76, 79). At the heart of Lazarus's theory lies the process of appraisal and the '*relational meaning* that the individual constructs from the person-environment relationship' (2000, p. 665). Lazarus's (2001) theory gives rise to two types of appraisal. The first Lazarus described as 'primary appraisal', noting that what distinguishes this appraisal from secondary appraisal lies less in terms of its timing and more in terms of its content (Lazarus 2001). Primary appraisal refers to 'what is at stake', and it is where the individual gives personal meaning to a stressful encounter; while secondary appraisal is where that meaning is further refined, when the focus shifts to 'what can I do about it', ushering in an appraisal of available coping resources (Lazarus 1999, 2001).

This rather terse overview of Lazarus's transactional view does not capture its elegance of argument or its power of explanation. Its power, as we have described before (Dewe & Cooper 2012, pp. 78-79), lies in the personal meanings individuals create around an encounter and the explanatory potential that resides in those meanings. It also explicitly points to the role of coping and the dynamic nature of the stress process, where individuals are 'constantly evaluating their relationship with the environment' in terms of meaning, coping and the implications for well-being (Lazarus 1999, p. 75). The 'appraisal process' is the link that binds the individual and the environment. It is the process that offers a causal pathway for understanding the stress process, and the reasons why individuals may differ in their reactions to encounters. This process and these links simply reinforce the fact that by ignoring them we are ignoring 'what are the most critical aspects of the stress process' (Dewe & Cooper 2012, p. 77). Nevertheless, while Lazarus's theory has been highly influential in the general stress literature, its impact has been somewhat more muted in relation to work stress (Jones & Bright 2001).

Lazarus's theory has provided 'many valuable insights' (Brief & George 1991, p. 15), and it has been noted that his work 'is well placed' (Harris 1991, p. 21) for developing our understanding of work stress. Where researchers differ in terms of Lazarus's transactional, contextual, process oriented approach is on the emphasis given in his theory to intra-individual (appraisal) processes and the subjective environment (Brief & George 1991; Frese & Zapf 1999; Schaubroeck 1999), building their argument around how it would be 'more useful' for researchers to 'try to discover' as a first priority those work encounters that impact on '*most* workers' rather than focus on 'individual patterns' that make some more vulnerable to stress (Brief & George 1991, p. 16). Reviewers and critics alike are generally in agreement that the theoretical and empirical significance of Lazarus's work rests on the fact that he offers an opportunity to 'frame the questions we need to ask' (Brief & George 1991, p. 18), that our research would be enhanced by 'the thoughtful application' of his work (Harris 1991, p. 28) and that there is a need to investigate all aspects of the stress process (Frese & Zapf 1999; Schaubroeck 1999) if we are to make progress. In this way, the power of concepts like appraisals can be tested empirically and be given the attention they deserve (Dewe & Cooper 2012, p. 79).

TABLE III.6

WORK STRESS THEORY: AN OVERVIEW

- While work stress research and theory has followed its own path it is possible to identify a number of phases it has passed through, not necessarily following the orderly impression we have set out here.
- The structural phase, essentially a static approach, explores the interaction between a stimulus and response (Cox 1978; Cooper et al. 2001).
- The moderator phase introduced a third variable to explore its moderating impact on the stimulus–response interaction.
- These two phases, while providing much needed data on the causes and consequences of work stress, failed to capture the complexity of the stimulus–response relationship or any sense of process. Nevertheless the stimulus–response phases were to provide the building blocks against which theory, definitions and knowledge evolved (Cooper et al. 2001).
- It was when the idea that work stress was viewed as a process – a transaction between the person and the environment – that a third phase was offered, giving researchers the opportunity to explore the essential nature of the stress process and those psychological mechanisms that link the individual to the environment (Lazarus 1999, 2001).
- This third stage owes much to the process-oriented transactional approach to stress (Lazarus 1999, 2001).
- Lazarus (1999) offered to those wishing to study work stress both power and authority by expressing through the idea of a transaction that stress did not reside solely in the individual or solely in the environment but in the transaction between the two (Lazarus 1999, 2001).
- The authority of Lazarus's approach lies in the psychological processes that link the individual to the environment, giving a causal pathway for understanding the stress process (Dewe & Cooper 2012, p. 79).
- The psychological processes are represented by the process of appraisal. Primary appraisal describes 'what is at stake' and is where the individual gives personal meaning to a stressful encounter while secondary appraisal is where the meaning is further refined when the focus shifts to 'what can I do about it', ushering in an appraisal of available coping resources (Lazarus 1999, 2001).

The P-E fit framework and work stress

It was the belief that behaviour at work was best understood in terms of the interrelationship between the person and the environment that led to the wide-spread use of the P-E fit framework for studying work stress (Van Harrison 1978). A number of reasons help explain its generally high level of acceptance. These include the shortcomings of the more traditional stimulus–response approaches, the influence and explanatory potential offered by the writings of Lewin (Edwards & Cooper 1990, p. 293), 'the power' and authority of Lazarus's transactional approach (Dewe & Cooper 2012, p. 76), the instinctive appeal of a framework that provided 'a process of adjustment' (Caplan 1987, p. 249), the description of the interrelationship in terms of fit, matching or congruence (Van Harrison 1978), and that it offers what Edwards and Cooper describe as 'a common sense notion' that what may be a fit for one person is a misfit to another (1990, p. 293). We begin by presenting the basic framework that lies at the core of the P-E fit approach to stress, then the theoretical and measurement issues that stem from the model, explore alternative models and approaches and end by pointing to future directions for research.

We outline the basic P-E fit framework (Caplan 1987; Edwards, Caplan & Van Harrison 2000; French, Rogers & Cobb 1974; French, Caplan & Van Harrison 1982; Van Harrison 1978) by exploring its four constituent elements: the core premise and basic proposition; the different versions of P-E fit; the nature of the form the fit takes; and finally the process of adjustment. At the core of the model is the 'simple yet powerful' premise that stress arises from the fit, match or congruence between the person and environment and not from either acting alone (Edwards et al. 2000, p. 28), establishing the empirical necessity to explore the causal relationship between the person and environment (Van Harrison 1978). At its simplest level stress is defined as the level of mismatch between the person and environment, although as we shall see more exact definitions depend on what components are used to represent the person and environment and which version of the model is being used. The basic proposition that follows from this definition that the greater the misfit the greater the stress (strain) is also subject to the above caveats, and dependent on the nature of the misfit. This means that the often generally assumed assumption that fit is 'good' and misfit is 'bad' needs to be treated cautiously (Edwards et al. 2000; Edwards & Rothbard 1999), helping to explain why analysing the effects of fit requires careful theoretical and methodological consideration (Edwards & Cooper 1990).

The framework proposes two distinct versions of fit (French et al. 1982). The first, S-V fit, concerns the fit between the 'values' (motives, needs and goals) of the person and the environmental 'supplies' to meet those values, whereas the second version, D-A fit, reflects the fit between the 'demands' of the environment and the 'abilities' of the person to meet them (Edwards 1996; Edwards et al. 2000; French et al. 1982). For both versions, P and E can be expressed objectively or subjectively. As each version differs in terms of its underlying process and outcomes Edwards and Cooper caution researchers not 'to minimize these distinctions' or to consider them interchangeable (1990, p. 296). Parallels can be found between these two versions and Lazarus's transactional approach, certainly when expressed subjectively and particularly in respect of the notion where demands are perceived to exceed resources and the appraisal elements of values, goals and motives (1999, 2001; Lazarus & Folkman, 1991); although to realize the full explanatory potential of primary appraisal researchers may wish to investigate further the meanings individuals give to or associate with a misfit or fit.

Nevertheless, whatever version is used, careful attention needs also to be given to the commensurability and consistency of the types of dimensions that are used to best express supplies, values, demands and abilities because to have any sort of meaning the degree of fit between P and E must share the same content (Edwards & Cooper 1990; Van Harrison 1978) so as to express a theoretical correspondence, otherwise 'the proximity of the person and environment to one another' (Edwards et al. 2000, p. 31) loses any sense of relevancy. It is, as Caplan describes, a 'special requirement' of P-E fit theory that 'the conceptual relevance of P and E to each other is [commensurate] and explicit' (1987, p. 252). P-E fit theory also points to the importance of the type of dimension being used and its relevance and priority to the individual (Edwards et al. 2000) capturing the idea that a dimension must be of importance to the individual to warrant the misfit as significant.

It is not just a question of P-E being commensurate in terms of content, there is also, when considering P-E fit theory, the need to understand the importance of the nature of the form fit takes. The importance of this understanding stems from the fact that different forms of fit express significantly different 'functional relationships between fit and strain' (Edwards & Cooper 1990, p. 297). Edwards has identified three types of form that fit may take: (a) the discrepancy between P and E; (b) the interaction between P and E; and (c) the proportion of P fulfilled by E (1990). Because fit 'may follow a variety of functional forms' then, as Edwards cautions, researchers need to recognize the distinctive form that each takes and 'select a form that is consistent with their theoretical assumptions' (Edwards & Cooper 1990, p. 299). Identifying the form that P-E fit takes draws attention to the question of adjustment. At the core of P-E fit theory lies the idea of adjustment defined as the 'amount of improvement over time in P-E fit' (Caplan 1987, p. 251). No assumptions are made about how adjustment takes place, but options/interventions as to how an individual's P-E fit could be improved are offered, with the proviso that there is no one best way to achieve adjustment (Caplan 1987).

Options include: whether one should change P or E or both; that changing P-E fit is not just an individual responsibility; that interventions need to be systematic, evaluated and considered in terms of the costs and benefits to others and more probably initiated at the organizational level (Caplan 1987) although interventions 'must allow for *individualized* treatment' (Van Harrison 1978, pp. 199–200); and that adjustment should be viewed as dynamic with individuals being motivated to resolve misfits (Edwards 2008a). Another of the outcomes of P-E misfit is efforts to resolve it through what French and his colleagues described as introducing the idea of coping more explicitly into the model (French et al. 1982). 'Coping', for these authors, involved efforts to resolve/improve objective P-E misfit, whereas 'defence' refers to efforts to resolve/improve subjective P-E misfit, with the two likely to be interrelated whereby resolving/improving one type of misfit may help resolve/improve the other (Edwards 2008a; Edwards et al. 2000). It is tempting to speculate as to whether the four processes developed by Edwards (1996) to describe 'the effects of excess supplies on well-being' are forms of coping (Edwards & Rothbard 1999, p. 90). The processes of 'conserving', 'carrying-over', 'depleting' and 'inhibiting', as identified by Edwards, certainly all carry a hint of coping. P-E fit theory does not, however, predict how coping strategies are selected or sequenced. Nevertheless, the process of adjustment, and the importance it is given, must send a signal to researchers that the role of coping has been given only limited attention in P-E theory, reinforcing the need for more work to be done to identify those strategies that express the relevance of coping to the issues of fit (Edwards et al. 2000).

While P-E theory is 'strong on many counts', and spans more than six decades of dedicated research, there still remains a need to contemplate what has been achieved and what is needed if theoretical progression is going to continue to be realized (Edwards 2008a, p. 190). Edwards leads the way with reviews that are thorough, comprehensive and detailed (1996, 2008a). He begins by calling for the strength of P-E theories to be constantly evaluated in terms of how well the person-environment relationship expresses the work experience, how well different P-E approaches can be better integrated to capture their combined strengths, the need to confront the meaning of fit, to theoretically anchor the content describing P and E, and to strategically use findings to validate, corroborate or reassess theory (2008a, pp. 217–222).

Three general themes seem to emerge from many of the reviews that signal the direction for future research. They include the need for 'commensurate content' when describing the person and the environment; content where there is not just a theoretical correspondence but a relevance and significance to the person as well. There is also the question of the role of meaning in P-E fit research, and for researchers to refine the notion of subjective perception of values and demands to consider how fit/misfit is appraised capturing the personal meanings and 'individual constructs from the person-environment relationship' (Lazarus 2000, p. 665). This 'theoretically rich' (Park & Folkman 1997, p. 132) role that 'meaning' plays in stress research offers a more precise causal pathway to coping, and offers P-E fit researchers the opportunity to explore what coping strategies are used and to assess their relevance to P-E fit theory.

TABLE III.7

THE P-E FIT FRAMEWORK AND WORK STRESS

○ It is the idea that behaviour is best understood in terms of the relationship between the person and the environment that led to the P-E fit framework for studying work stress (Van Harrison 1978).

○ At the core of the P-E framework is 'the simple but powerful' premise that stress arises from the fit, match or congruence between the person and the environment rather than either working alone (Edwards et al. 2000, p. 28).

○ At its simplest level stress is defined as the level of mismatch between the person and the environment; although more exact definitions depend on the components used to represent the person and the environment. This helps to explain why analysing the effects of a fit requires careful theoretical and methodological consideration (Edwards & Cooper 1990).

○ Two themes at least signal the direction for future research: (a) the need for commensurate content when describing the person and the environment where there is a theoretical correspondence but a relevance and signifi-cance to the person as well (Edwards 1996, 2008a); and (b) to consider how fit/misfit is appraised capturing the personal meanings 'that a person con-structs from the person-environment relationship' (Edwards 1996, 2008a; Lazarus 2000, p. 665).

The notion of balance in stress research

The widely accepted view that stress results from the transaction between the person and the environment introduces the notion of 'balance' and that approaches to work stress may best be described 'as *balance models*' (Meurs & Perrewé 2011, p. 1045). While all the theories we have discussed offer a sense of balance, and while balance may, more often than not, be somewhat narrowly expressed in terms of a sense of disequilibrium at the expense perhaps of emphasizing the more adaptive aspects of the stress experience (Dewe & Cooper 2012; Meurs & Perrewé 2011), it does pro-vide a lens for exploring how theories of work stress have continued to evolve and develop. It is always a hazardous business to categorize theories, and although these so-called balance models share many of the characteristics of the P-E fit approach, what distinguishes them is that they place at the centre of their work demands and more especially resources using these elements and the transaction between them as the context to better understand work stress; see Karasek's demands–control (sup-port) model (Dewe 2017).

We turn first to the work of Karasek (1979) and his job demands–control model that has 'played [such] a dominant role in shaping the [work stress] agenda

(Meurs & Perrewé 2011, p. 1046), and its refinement to include social support (Johnson & Hall 1988). While both control and support can be considered employee resources, we then turn to the more comprehensive job demands–resources model (Demerouti et al. 2001), where the emphasis is on exploring the motivational potential of resources (Schaufeli & Taris 2014) before turning to Hobfoll's (1989) conservation of resources theory and the fundamental role that resource depletion and resource gain play in determining stress.

Karasek's (1979) work certainly captured the attention of researchers (de Jonge, Dollard, Dormann, Le Blanc & Houtman 2000). Karasek's aim was to show that stress results not from a single job demand but from the 'joint effects' between a work place demand and the available resources to individuals 'facing those demands' (1979, p. 287); in this case 'control or job decision latitude'. It is the interactive combination of these two aspects of the job, argued Karasek, that provides the 'instigator' of stress (job demand) with the available decision making latitude the element that provides 'the energy of action', offering an environmentally based stress-management model (1979, p. 287). Generally stated, a combination of high demands and little job decision latitude produced high-strain jobs, whereas low demands and considerable decision latitude produced low-strain jobs. Depending on the demands–decision latitude combination, Karasek (1979) also talked in terms of 'active jobs', where new behaviours were learnt, and 'passive jobs' where the opportunity for learning or problem-focused behaviour declined. Karasek's model has been refined to include another resource: 'social support'. As Johnson and Hall (1988) suggest, this refinement shifted the focus from the individuals' relationship with the job to one that emphasized the importance of relationships between individuals. The refined job demands, control (support) model has attracted considerable empirical attention, and while the model is not without support, findings have been described as mixed (de Lange, Taris, Kompier, Houtman & Bongers 2003). Yet it is clear from the above that Karasek's model expressed the view that resources like decision latitude and support energized the individual to 'cope with the environment' (1979, p. 303), and it is this aspect of his model that requires pursuing.

Two approaches to coping emerge from Karasek's model. The first concerns the active job/learning scenario proposed by Karasek (1979), where jobs high in both demands and control lead to new behaviour patterns, learning and mastery enabling individuals to cope (Taris, Kompier, de Lange, Schaufeli & Schreurs 2003). Karasek (1998) explained that in jobs where control was high individuals had options, could make choices and, if effective, those choices would be learned and integrated into coping patterns. These opportunities would not exist in passive jobs (low in both demands and control) as learning would not only decline but be accompanied by a loss in previously learnt 'problem learning skills' (Karasek 1998, p. 288). While the enhancement of job control properties 'can have positive effects on both learning outcomes and strain' (Holman & Wall 2002, p. 299), and while high control appears to encourage a sense of efficacy in relation to job strain (Taris, Kompier, Geurts, Houtman & van den Heuvel 2010), researchers suggest a more close investigation is needed, of not just the nature of the demands–control interaction but of what they describe as a relationship made more complex because of the way learning and strain may be related (Taris et al. 2003) and the way the process of learning links control to self efficacy (Taris et al. 2010).

The second approach investigates the role that coping plays in Karasek's model, by examining the proposition that resources like control and support enhance well-being through promoting the use of problem-focused coping (Daniels & Guppy 1994; Daniels & Harris 2005). The work by Daniels and his colleagues supported the Karasek idea that control and support provide individuals with choices, and the influence to exercise those choices; that problem-focused coping has differing effects on well-being depending on whether it is being expressed through control or support and that other forms of coping may also be usefully explored (Daniels & Harris 2005). Further work pointed to the fact that 'workers are active in shaping their jobs', and that the way job characteristics are used to express coping will influence the type of coping, again reinforcing the need to differentiate between different forms of coping and their effectiveness (Daniels, Beesley, Cheyne & Wimalasiri 2008, p. 868). Examining how control and support are being used to express coping strategies also raises the issue of when intervening by enhancing job characteristics there is a need to understand whether and in what way this will promote learning and coping (Daniels, Boocock, Glover, Hartly & Holland 2009). Hopefully, the idea that determining what aspects of demands and control are significant for which individuals and what this means to those individuals and which learned new behaviours 'accrue' across working lives (Theorell & Karasek 1996), will draw those researching the job demands, control (support) model closer to the need to explore these questions through the processes and causal pathways suggested by the transactional approach (Daniels & Guppy 1994).

Jobs demands–resources model

Turning to the job demands–resources model, it is clear that this model certainly 'fell on fertile ground' (Schaufeli & Taris 2014, p. 44) by bringing together into one model two research traditions – job design and work stress (Bakker & Demerouti 2007; Demerouti et al. 2001; Schaufeli & Taris 2014). The strength of this model lies in the way it embraces and combines the motivation aspects of job resources from job design research with the stress of job demands from work stress research. In this way the model offers, through its utility, a mechanism for capturing the complexity of the work experience particularly at a time when the workplace is facing major change; the idea that there are other resources beyond just job control and that resources are not just an essential part of stress theory (Lazarus 2001), but offered in their own right an explanatory potential yet to be fully exploited (Hobfoll 1989, 2001). At the heart of the job demands–resources model is the premise that two psychological processes play a role in the development of stress. The first describes the *energetic or health impairment process*, where the cost of job demands exhausts an individual's resources, opening the way for energy depletion and health problems.

The second process is '*motivational in nature*', where resources have an intrinsic role fostering development and growth, and an extrinsic instrumental role leading to goal achievement (Bakker & Demerouti 2007, p. 313; Schaufeli & Taris 2014).

The model in line with other balance approaches proposes at the more general level that 'high demands and low resources lead to strain', whereas 'high demands high resources' lead to greater motivation (Bakker & Demerouti 2007; Schaufeli & Taris 2014). It is the second proposition that captures the 'coping hypothesis' (Demerouti & Bakker 2011). Resources according to this hypothesis become more significant as the situation becomes more demanding, in this way 'gain[ing] their motivational potential', and under these circumstances, this motivational potential is more likely to be used as a coping strategy (Demerouti & Bakker 2011, p. 3). The idea that resources may release high levels of motivation irrespective of the levels of demand (Bakker & Demerouti 2007), the need to distinguish between job resources and personal resources and how they may be interrelated, how individuals shape and craft their jobs and how these perceptions influence the nature of demands and resources and their use (Bakker & Demerouti 2007), all need further research. Similarly whether all demands, and for that matter resources, are equally valued, and whether they are perceived as positive or negative (Cavanaugh et al. 2000; Crawford, LePine & Rich 2010; Schaufeli & Taris 2014; Van den Broeck, Cuyper, De Witte & Vansteenkiste 2010), all illustrate the direction that future research may take. Researchers need to reflect not just on how processes like appraisal (Lazarus 2001) may provide the explanatory context for understanding these issues, but the central role that 'resources' have always played in the transactional model (Lazarus 1999), to understand the coping process.

It was in his 2002 review that Hobfoll correctly concluded that 'in the coming years' resources will remain significant and fundamental to our understanding of well-being (p. 320). The authority of his work and the power of his theory distinguishes his theory of stress from others, particularly the crucial role given to both 'resource loss' and 'resource gain' (1989, 2001, 2002, 2011). To understand stress we must, Hobfoll advocates, understand resources; they are the single most important unit of currency. Resources are defined in terms of four types: 'personal characteristics', 'energies', 'valued conditions', and 'objects' (Hobfoll 1989, p. 517). At the heart of Hobfoll's conservation of resources model lies the idea that individuals endeavour to maintain, protect, defend and build those resources they value, and that stress occurs when those resources are threatened, lost or there is a failure to invest in them (Hobfoll 1989, p. 516; 2001, pp. 341–342). It is crucial, Hobfoll argues, to understand the potency of resource loss, the significance of resource gain and the effort given to 'minimize' resource loss; effort that is the goal of coping (1989, p. 517). Hobfoll's theory offers insights into the importance of 'resource reservoirs', and how they facilitate development, the learning gained from experience, the opportunities resources provide for adaption and growth, the capacity they provide in achieving goals, their fit with coping strategies and the role they play in terms of stress management and interventions (Freund & Riediger 2001; Hobfoll 2002, 2011; Ito & Brotheridge 2003; Quick & Gavin 2001).

TABLE III.8

THE NOTION OF BALANCE IN STRESS RESEARCH

o   The idea that stress results from the transaction between the person and the
    environment also introduces the notion of 'balance models' (Meurs & Perrewé
    2011, p. 1045) although balance is also reflected in much work stress research.
o   What distinguishes these models is that they place at the centre of their
    work demands and more especially resources, using these elements and the
    transaction between them as the context to better understand work stress.
o   Here the work of Karasek is key (1979) – the job demands–control (and
    support) model; as is Demerouti et al.'s demands–resources model (2001)
    and Hobfoll's (1989) conservation of resources theory, and the fundamental
    role that resource depletion and resource gains play in determining stress.
o   From this overview comes a number of themes for future research work
    stress research:

1   The reinforcement of the importance of commensurability, but taking it
    beyond the idea of P-E sharing the same content to the idea that content
    must have a relevancy that expresses the nature of the work experience.
2   Going beyond the structural components that determine fit/misfit to
    exploring the personal meanings it has for the person.
3   To explore the relationship between coping and resources; the role
    resources play in coping options and how they are evaluated (Lazarus
    1999). In 'what way are things resources' and 'resources for what' lead-
    ing to asking 'what do I have' and 'how do I use them' (Freund & Riediger
    2001, pp. 372–378).

Summary

Other theories have of course contributed to our understanding of work stress and
coping. The difficulty with any review rests as much on what is included, as it does
on what has been left out. Our aim here has been to present a broad canvas that captures the way theories have evolved and developed, the themes that have emerged to
drive them forward, the ideas and assumptions that lie behind them, how they have
been buffered by social and economic change, tempered by our growing understanding of the way our knowledge has developed, been applied and disseminated,
how it connects with the issues facing organizations, and the critical contribution
they make. Our aim has also been to acknowledge those forces that shape our discipline, the empirical, theoretical and professional demands placed upon us, the

'creative tensions' necessary to advance our field and the overriding responsibilities we have to those whose working lives we study. From our review we believe it is possible to identify three, not mutually exclusive themes that capture the direction for future research.

Commensurability–relevancy–appraisal and meanings

The first reinforces the importance of commensurability, but extends it beyond the idea that P and E share the same content, crucial as that is, to capture the idea that content must also have a significance to the person in terms of well-being (Lazarus 2001) and, a relevancy that goes beyond the conceptual relevancy of P and E to each other (Caplan 1987) to a relevancy that expresses the nature of the work experience. 'Relevancy' then, involves the idea of significance both in terms of something 'being at stake', and the way the work experience is being expressed in terms of its meaning and its impact on well-being. As we have argued before, researchers need now to give as much attention to the idea of relevancy as they have to concepts like reliability (Dewe & Cooper 2012, p. 162; Dewe, O'Driscoll & Cooper 2010).

The second theme is intended to advance our understanding of the nature of the form fit takes, by going beyond the perceptions of what construes a fit/misfit to how it is appraised, capturing the personal meanings a person constructs around such a state (Lazarus, 1999; 2001). The different approaches reviewed all acknowledge the role played by individual cognitions and appraisal. Drawing a distinction between what a person perceives as a fit/misfit and the meanings associated with it goes beyond the idea of appraising it as threatening well-being, to understanding what 'personal meanings the person attaches to the threat'. It is a distinction between content; the structural components that determine the fit/misfit, albeit subjectively, and its personal meaning. It is these personal meanings which act as a causal pathway and a trigger for coping and emotions (Lazarus 1999, 2001). To ignore them, as we have emphasized and canvassed before, is to ignore one of the most powerful explanatory pathways in stress research, and the possibilities that follow from investigating the different forms of fit/misfit in terms of the meanings associated with them (Dewe & Cooper 2012, pp. 161–162).

Resources

The third theme reinforces the need to continue to explore the relationship between coping and resources. Secondary appraisal is all about 'evaluating coping options' and determining which 'ones to choose and how to set them in motion' (Lazarus 1999, p. 78). It is this 'context' that emphasizes the importance of resources both personal and organizational and the role they play in how coping options are evaluated. It is this link that needs to continue to be pursued. A resource-based focus intimately links personal meanings and coping options, and

acknowledges the need to now place as much emphasis on promoting an understanding of the role of resources and their attributes as has been given to reducing
stress and its consequences (Meurs & Perrewé 2011). Taking a developmental point
of view, as many authors have, offers a way of exploring questions like: how does
learning and development take place?; how are coping strategies and resources
linked?; why, in what way, and what is the nature of that relationship?; what is it
that differentiates one resource from another?; how are they interrelated? (Dewe
& Cooper 2012, pp. 87–88); and 'in what way are things resources?', and 'resources
for what' leading to asking 'what do I have?' and 'how do I use them?' (Freund &
Riediger 2001, pp. 372; 378). Hobfoll himself offers ways forward by discussing,
for example, issues like resource replacement, resource substitution, and the limits
of resources (2001). If, as Hobfoll has suggested, the value of his theory is that it
'provides a broader picture of the coping process', so the opportunity is there for
researchers to continue to refine and develop our understanding of what is a fundamental part of the coping process (2001, p. 363).

Hopes for the twenty-first century

It is clear that change and development has accompanied the fields of management
and organizational behaviour throughout the twentieth century. Yet this change and
these developments – moulded by the times they represent, the values and vision they
express, the goals and aspirations they set out to achieve, the principles they espoused
and the contribution they have made – need constantly to be assessed against changes
in our working lives, our well-being, the nature of society and the world we live in.
Perhaps as we drew closer to a new millennium change and the choices this new
age offered takes on an even greater significance, offering the opportunity for new
beginnings that shed the constraints of the past, challenged the old and encouraged
if not demanded the need for reconstruction and reflection as to where our theories
were taking us and how best they expressed our hopes for the twenty-first century.
So the inevitability of more change was confirmed and it is these changes, new hopes
and new opportunities that heralded the beginning of the new millennium that
introduce the next chapter, and offer with hindsight an ever more turbulent context
for understanding the nature of stress, the challenges we face and the new directions
in which they have led us.

IV

THE NEW MILLENNIUM: DEVELOPMENTS, CHANGE AND TURBULENCE

The inevitability of change accompanied our entry into the new millennium. Some welcomed the new century with a manifesto that championed 'what makes life worth living' (Seligman & Csikszentmihalyi 2000, p. 5), heralding what was to become known as the positive psychology movement. Others having found their voice in the last decades of the twentieth century saw, as the new century progressed, what they described as 'an affective scientific revolution', where the richness of studying discrete emotions came of age – where 'where are we now' was replaced with 'where we are going' (Barsade et al. 2003, pp. 3, 5). Then came the economic crisis that was soon to be discussed in terms of a human crisis, where austerity measures defined the age, determined policy, and left their mark on all of society, causing turbulence, turmoil and anguish that shook the nature of work and drew questions as to where management theories had taken us (Ghoshal 2005; Fotinatos-Ventouratos & Cooper 2015). International coordination and cooperation to combat this crisis led to a call for changes to the way GNP was measured, away from narrow macroeconomic factors to those that measured what expresses the quality of peoples' lives (OECD 2012), ushering in the globalization of well-being (Jané-Llopis, Anderson & Cooper 2012), and even perhaps the explosion of research surrounding the concept of happiness (Rodriguez-Munoz & Sanz-Vergel 2013), the importance of a 'good work' agenda (Bevan 2010, p. 3) and the arrival of the shared economy (*The Economist* 2013a, 2013b).

Organizational psychology and organizational behaviour theories were not immune from these changes, and in response to the turmoil that accompanied them, researchers began to engage in a period of reflection around the theme of 'what was, what is and what may be in OP/OB' (Porter & Schneider 2014, p. 1). If change occurs in waves, then 'three' have helped define the new millennium so far; the positive psychology movement and the affective revolution, the economic crisis and its associated issues as to where management and economic theories had led us, turning well-being into a global issue and prompting the idea of a good work agenda, and finally the need for a period of reconstruction and reflection exploring 'what may be' for theories of OP and OB. This chapter discusses these 'three waves' in more detail and it is against this context together with the change and developments discussed in the earlier two chapters that set the scene for exploring the impact of such change on work stress research.

'The first wave'

The positive psychology movement

In what has now become a defining conceptualization Seligman and Csikszentmihalyi (2000) offered researchers, as the new millennium dawned, if not a new beginning then a new focus; a psychology of positive functioning that was soon to be transformed into the 'positive psychology movement'. Conscious of the past and the need for any discipline to systematically review and revisit the state and focus of its knowledge (Csikszentmihalyi 2003), these authors were aware that by making such an offer researchers would 'not need to start afresh', but more likely just 'redirect their scientific energy' (2000, p. 13). Of course such an offer that suggested that psychology had for too long focused almost entirely on individual vulnerability, at the expense of building a knowledge around individual 'flourishing' and, therefore, needed re-balancing, attracted considerable attention and at times, robust debate (Dewe & Cooper 2014; see Dewe & Cooper 2012, pp. 15–20). But recognizing the value that lay in engaging in such research (Sheldon & King 2001), and the importance of legitimizing 'the study of positive aspects of human experience in its own right' (Csikszentmihalyi 2003, p. 113), an agenda was set that provided 'a remarkable opportunity to do things differently' (Linley, Joseph, Harrington & Wood 2006, p. 9). So the structures were soon in place to confirm that positive psychology was a serious scientific movement (Linley et al. 2006).

In its early years the positive psychology movement was embroiled in a debate at the heart of which was the concern with just how exclusive this emphasis on positivity was going to be (see Dewe & Cooper 2012, pp. 19–20). By narrowing the focus of psychology too much in one direction, the discipline would be in danger of losing that broader perspective necessary to understand individual activity (Lazarus 2003). Researchers were, however, urged to recognize the 'inextricable' nature of the relationship between the positive and the negative (Tennen & Affleck 2003), that one should not be explored at the expense of the other (Folkman & Moskowitz 2003; Lazarus 2003), that you cannot have one without the other (Harvey & Pauwels 2003), that the complexity of the relationship required a more nuanced approach that acknowledges the adaptive qualities of the negative (Held 2004) and that 'strength comes through balance' simply reflecting the way that people live their lives (Bacon 2005, p. 184).

Yet there was always a sense that reconciliation would come through explanation and that the 'even handedness' of positive psychology was represented through its role as an umbrella term, whose strength lay in bringing together under one heading all those different lines of theory that captured individual flourishing (Peterson & Park 2003, p.143; Seligman, Steen, Park & Peterson 2005, p. 410), encouraged reflection on how work may be extended 'to explore or enrich' the positive (Sheldon & King 2001; Simonton & Baumeister 2005, p. 102), and built up, integrated and complemented our existing understanding and knowledge (Gable & Haidt 2005). In this debate as in much of psychology the emphasis was clearly weighted 'towards balance' (Dewe & Cooper 2012, p. 20); understanding how each perspective – negative and positive – contributes to our knowledge, how each contributes to the other and is influenced by the other, and how that focus and balance 'are not mutually exclusive' positions (Bacon 2005, p. 190). As the psychology movement gathered momentum, grew in confidence, and expanded its focus it was this balanced focus of the negative and positive that found expression in what has been described by Wong (2011) as positive psychology version 2.

Three themes run through positive psychology: the 'positive experience', the 'positive personality' and the need to take the 'social context' into account through positive communities and positive institutions (Seligman & Csikszentmihalyi 2000, p. 5). Yet, there is a fourth theme that runs through the positive psychology movement and that is 'the backbone' of the movement 'should be good science' (Snyder & Lopez 2007, p. 11). Recognizing that the value of positive psychology can only be demonstrated through a strategy that unconditionally embraces 'the scientific method' (Dewe & Cooper 2012, p. 21; Peterson & Park 2003, p. 145), then those championing the movement are clear that the highest standards of measurement and methodology have to be adhered to (Lyubomirsky & Abbe 2003; Rand & Snyder 2003). The need is to seek, encourage and support work that reflects these aims (Seligman & Csikszentmihalyi 2001) and, like all movements, research must 'remain at its core' (Simonton & Baumeister 2005, p. 99). It is only the application of rigorous empirical research that will determine how and in what way positive psychology can be supported (Seligman & Csikszentmihalyi 2001). This brief overview of the debate that shadowed the first years of the role of positive psychology and its growth into a movement with aspirations and ambitions we have discussed before (see Dewe & Cooper 2012, pp. 15–20). Here our attention now turns from these 'growing pains' (Wong 2011, p. 69) of those earlier years of the positive psychology movement to explore what progress has been made.

Drawing a distinction between the aims of positive psychology (a different lens and a shared language to understand individual experiences), and what positive psychologists do (understanding the processes and mechanisms that lead to positive experiences), Linley and his colleagues raise the issue, despite 'both laudable and remarkable' achievements made by positive psychology, as to 'which way now' (Linley et al. 2006, pp. 8, 10)? The authors argue that both views have shaped and will continue to shape the direction taken by positive psychology. Identifying what they believe are the major factors that will influence the future direction of positive psychology, Linley and his colleagues point, in addition, to the importance of professional psychological training and the engagement with powerful stakeholders, to the role of research. Here, like other authors, they argue that research must be both rigorous and relevant, avoiding the temptation to engage in popularist science, and integrated across psychology more generally by way of both science and message (Linley et al. 2006, pp. 10–11). So by the middle of its first decade, there is no doubt that the positive psychology movement has made its mark, that 'quite a lot has happened' (Gable & Haidt 2005, p. 103), that 'major advances' have been made as it 'now spans a range of topics' that reflect both the type of science being called for and its progress towards a more balanced discipline (Simonton & Baumeister 2005, p. 99). It can produce a 'progress report' that captures its momentum as a movement (Seligman et al. 2005, p. 410), its growth as a serious 'research corpus' (Linley et al. 2006, p. 8), its character strengths (Bacon 2005), its conceptual utility (Snyder & Lopez 2005) and its remarkable promise (Fredrickson 2005).

Even with the positive psychology movement moving beyond its first decade, commentators continued to use adjectives like explosive (Yen 2010), expansive (Donaldson & Ko 2010), and extraordinary (Hart & Sasso 2011), to describe the breadth, scope and volume of work that fell within its orbit. At the same time the growth of empirical work enabled researchers to 'take stock', and engage in more systematic analysis of the evidence and developmental trends (Hart & Sasso 2011, p. 82; Rusk & Waters 2013; Wong 2011; Yen 2010). Reviewers were able to confirm the continued strong overall growth rate, in addition to identifying the types of publication, the themes covered and emerging trends (Donaldson & Ko 2010; Hart & Sasso 2011; Rusk & Waters 2013; Wong 2011). From the different reviews, it is possible to identify three trends that reflect the changing nature of positive psychology. The first reflects a field that is maturing (Yen 2010), evidenced by the presence of a rigorous scientific base; the second represents a shift in focus from conceptual to empirical studies; and the third an inclusive range of topics researched that have the potential to continue to 'invigorate' the field (Donaldson & Ko 2010, p. 188; Rusk & Waters 2013).

These trends capture the idea of integration and the efforts made to incorporate the values of positive psychology into other fields of study including counselling psychology (Lopez, Magyar-Moe, Petersen, Ryder, Krieshok, O'Byrne, Lichtenberg & Fry 2006), health psychology (Schmidt, Raque-Bogdan, Piontkowski & Schaefer 2011), and positive psychology in the workplace (Mills, Fleck & Kozikowski 2013), the changing way language is used to express through a growing common vocabulary of human behaviour (Rusk & Waters 2013) and the continual broadening of boundaries to reflect the scope and reach of positive psychology (Donaldson & Ko 2010; Fullagar & Kelloway 2012; Hart & Sasso 2011; Rusk & Waters 2013). Perhaps a more contentious trend concerns the idea that 'a more expansive new generation identity' is emerging for positive psychology that calls for bringing further into bal- ance the adaptive processes of both the positive and the negative as they together more fully capture life experiences, emphasizing the 'need to enhance the positives and manage the negatives' (Hart & Sasso 2011, p. 91; Wong 2011, p. 77); what Wong refers to as positive psychology 2.0. Given, as Wong argues, the significant changes that have occurred in the field pushing and expanding boundaries that now embrace topics like resilience, stress related growth and coping, and coupled with the increas- ingly significant role of meaning, then this second generation model of positive psychology focuses both on 'healing the worst AND building the best' (Wong 2011, p. 69) while still holding true to the original mission of positive human functioning (Hart & Sasso 2011; Wong 2011).

Two final points remain. The first concerns the need to acknowledge 'the current and historical importance of humanistic psychology' and its links with positive psy- chology (see Dewe & Cooper 2012, pp.16–17; Rich 2001, p. 9). The second briefly explores the ideas and concepts that represent positive organizational behaviour (Luthans 2002b, 2002c). It is clear that positive psychology 'echo[ed] themes' found in the work of humanistic psychologists (Resnick, Warmoth & Serlin 2001, p. 74), with colleagues asking why only a passing glance appears to have been given to a field rich in history of the positive and where dialogue between the two would be both 'fruitful' and insightful and make a valuable integrative contribution in coming to terms with optimal human functioning (Rathunde 2001; Resnick et al. 2001, p. 93; Rich 2001; Ryff 2003, p. 155; Taylor 2001). Acknowledging what has gone before (Tennen & Affleck 2003), and that 'positive psychology has been strongly influenced by our predecessors' (Seligman & Csikszentmihalyi 2001, p. 89) and 'has many distinguished ancestors' (Seligman 2005, p. 7), still left open questions and debate around the importance of how disciplines, if they are to flourish, need to demonstrate their strong research base supported by established research findings (Csikszentmihalyi 2003; Resnick et al. 2001; Taylor 2001; Seligman 2005; Seligman & Csikszentmihalyi 2001). The debate may not have disappeared but the insights offered by Maslow, as Resnick and her colleagues note, to first use the term positive psychology resonate so clearly with individual growth, human development and positive psychology that they cannot be ignored (Resnick et al. 2001, pp. 74–76).

Why Maslow?

Why only Maslow? Maslow's work had a profound influence on management and organizational thinkers, where his ideas and concepts provided the fields of 'motiva- tion, job design and leadership' with the foundations on which they were able to build (see Dewe & Cooper 2012, p.50; Mullins 2002). Maslow was also, as Rathunde suggests, a persuasive advocate of how science could help to articulate a 'vision of human optimal functioning' (2001, p. 144). Maslow's view that aspects of optimal functioning, including 'peak experiences', had largely been ignored by 'academic psychology' and needed rigorous 'scientific investigation' has, as Rathunde suggests, strong parallels with the ambitions of the positive psychology movement (2001, pp.144–145). It is Maslow's work that we have discussed before (Dewe & Cooper 2012, p. 50) and here we wish to simply reinforce that by going beyond the ideas of self actualization to the next level of motivation, which he called 'self transcendence'. It is that idea that essentially captures the spirit of positive psychology. Maslow had 'compelling doubts' about self actualization as the 'motivational capstone' as, to him, it was not enough, offered a too narrow view of the optimally functioning person and failed to capture 'a sense of the purpose of life' (Koltko-Rivera 2006, pp. 304, 310). 'Self transcendence' is where individuals engage in a higher form of motivation that sets aside their own needs, and it finds expression through 'service to others, an ideal or a cause' (Koltko-Rivera 2006, pp. 303, 306). The idea of 'self transcendence' should now become in practice an essential part of any discussion of Maslow's work.

It was self transcendence that, in Maslow's view, became the highest level of motivation, was clearly separate from self actualization, and provided a route for peak experiences. Its essence, Maslow argued, was reflected in answers to questions like 'what are the moments that give you the greatest satisfaction' or 'what are the moments of reward which make your work and your life worthwhile' (see Koltko-Rivera 2006, p. 305), and its nature clearly mirrored the ideals of the positive personality (Bohart & Greening 2001; McLafferty & Kirylo 2001). Finally, Maslow's (1968) belief in a psychology of being, growth and development appeared to be sorely tested when, in 1969, he commented on what he described as 'a rash' of information about what the world would be like in 2000. He expressed 'alarm' that most of the information dealt with technological changes, leaving him with a sense of 'uneasiness' that the emphasis was 'merely at the material level' – and leaving us to guess (but perhaps knowing) how he would have viewed the first decade or so of the new millennium (Maslow 1969, p. 734).

Positive organizational behaviour

The positive psychology movement was soon to find expression in the workplace through the seminal work of Luthans and his concept of positive organizational behaviour (see Dewe & Cooper 2012, pp. 26–29; Luthans 2002a, 2002b). To Luthans, the opportunity to develop and build new ideas around the theory and research strengths of organizational behaviour offered an exciting opportunity to understand more about 'the good in people' and represented 'a step in the [right] direction' that would advance the field in what are turbulent times (Luthans 2002a, pp. 703–704). Positive organizational behaviour is defined as the 'study and application of positively oriented human resource strengths and psychological capacities that can be measured, developed, and effectively managed for performance improvement in today's workplace' (Luthans 2002a, p. 698). The search began for what Luthans described as positive organizational behaviour capabilities that captured not just the positive but met the criteria of being states and hence 'open to learning, development, change, and management in the workplace' (Luthans 2002a, p. 699).

After much careful theoretical and empirical analysis in search of 'psychological resource capabilities open to development', Luthans and his colleagues identified four which taken together expressed what became known as psychological capital (*see* Dewe & Cooper 2012, pp. 118-120; Luthans & Avolio 2009, p. 293; Luthans, Youssef & Avolio 2007a, p. 19). The four capabilities were 'efficacy', 'hope', 'optimism' and 'resiliency'. This work emphasizes not just the reach of the positive psychology movement but how concepts like positive organizational behaviour and psychological capital have the authority and power to open researchers to a whole new perspective. This is why we have discussed them before (Dewe & Cooper 2012, pp. 26–29, 118–120) and return to them here. Psychological capital is distinguished from human capital (what you know) and social capital (who you know) (Luthans et al. 2007a, p. 20) because its attention is focused on 'who you are' emphasizing development and growth through 'who you are becoming' (Luthans, Youssef & Avolio 2007a, p. 20). This brief overview cannot capture the research activity that has accompanied the development of positive organizational behaviour nor the significance of psychological capital (*see* Bakker & Schaufeli 2008; Dewe & Cooper 2012, pp. 27–29, 118–120; Luthans & Avolio 2009; Luthans & Youssef 2007; Luthans et al. 2007a, 2007b; Nelson & Cooper 2007; Quick, Cooper, Gibbs, Little & Nelson 2010; Turner, Barling & Zacharatos 2005).

Like the positive psychology movement it too has been accompanied by debate and critical analysis (see Dewe & Cooper 2012, pp. 28–29; Fineman 2006; Hackman 2009; Luthans & Avolio 2009; Wright & Quick 2009), but Luthans and his colleagues have been clear as to how psychological capital adds value (Avey, Luthans & Youssef 2010), while academics point to 'how psychological capital is an untapped human resource that can be developed' (Newman, Ucbasaran, Zhu & Hirst 2014, p. S133). In this way, it achieves the goal not just of individual development, but reinforces its role in performance enhancement and management effectiveness. It is clear that when using the umbrella term 'positive psychology at work' to bring together those positive resource capabilities 'of the upmost relevance to organizations' then, when reviewed in terms of their relationship to effective practice, each has 'leverage' to increase performance as well as contributing to individual development (Mills et al. 2013, pp. 154, 160).

An affective revolution

Investigating affect (emotion) at work is 'in the midst of a revolution' (Barsade et al. 2003, p. 33); a revolution that has been slow in coming even though the need for more research to understand this 'missing ingredient' of organizational life (Fineman 2004, p. 720) has long been acknowledged. Described as 'a neglected' part of our understanding (Ashforth & Humphrey 1995; Fox & Spector 2002; Muchinsky 2000, p. 801), recognized as a central and unavoidable part of everyday working lives (Ashforth & Humphrey 1995), expressed in terms of managing emotions being 'implicitly at the core' and lying just below the surface of management's role (Ashkanasy, Hartel & Daus 2002, p. 317) and regarded as an inescapable aspect of managerial life (Rumens 2005), emotion at work has achieved a new status. For some the revolution has spanned the last 30 years, and so comes to the workplace with a long history (Brief & Weiss 2002; Fisher & Ashkanasy 2000; Weiss & Brief 2001). Now galvanized by a dramatic increase in tempo that is taking place (Barsade & Gibson 2007), and buoyed by the fact that emotions matter in organizations (Barsade & Gibson 2007), recent work has shown 'considerable promise' developing a confidence to learn much more about emotions and the questions that need to be posed (Brief & Weiss 2002, p. 300). It is a field of study that is transforming and maturing (Elfenbein 2007). Making emotions at work 'more visible', enhances our understanding of organizational functioning (Fineman 2001, p. 234), meaning that we now need to pay as much attention to feeling as we have to thinking if we are to advance our understanding and capture the reality of work experiences (Muchinsky 2000). Quite simply, 'work is saturated with emotions' (Ashforth & Humphrey 1995, p. 119; Ashforth & Kreiner 2002).

While we are entering an 'exciting time' for researching emotion in organizations (Elfenbein 2007, p. 316), it hasn't always been so; so what has brought about this change? At the risk of ignoring a history of emotion at work describing 'the rich 1930s, the leaner years and the hot 1990s' (Brief & Weiss 2002, pp. 281–282; Weiss & Brief 2001), we begin by acknowledging how expressing emotion in the workplace was viewed as a concern, a disruption that ran counter to the systematic rational processes required to achieve organizational goals and therefore from the organization's point of view such feelings needed regulating (Ashforth & Humphrey 1995; see Dewe & Cooper 2012, pp.106–108). All this helps to explain why emotions, although an integral part of ordinary everyday working life, went 'unacknowledged and neglected in the traditional management literature' (Rumens 2005, p. 117). So it wasn't long before affective research was simply reduced to a focus firmly fixed on job satisfaction as the legitimate measure of emotion in organizations (Barsade et al. 2003; Brief & Weiss 2002); meaning that for decades job satisfaction was 'loosely but not carefully thought' through as a 'surrogate' for affective responses and 'uncritically' assumed to capture feelings at work (Brief & Weiss 2002, p. 286; see Dewe & Cooper 2012, pp.108–110).

But this too was about to change, partly as work itself was changing buffered by the forces of globalization, technology and the arrival of the knowledge economy (Ashkanasy et al. 2002), and coupled with the belief that job satisfaction was no longer able to capture the emotional experience of work. This is a conclusion we and others have drawn before (Barsade et al. 2003; see Dewe & Cooper 2012, pp.108–110), particularly when the explanatory potential in discrete emotions that was crucial to advancing our understanding of work stress and coping

(Lazarus & Cohen-Charash 2001) was somewhat locked out by our reliance on job satisfaction. Work research needs now to better understand and nuance our understanding of those qualities that distinguish one emotion from another (Barsade et al. 2003). But taking our previous conclusions (see Dewe & Cooper 2012, pp. 108–110) a step further it was the growing discontent that surrounded job satisfaction and its assumed affective role that set in motion the opportunity to focus explicitly on workplace emotions.

Job satisfaction – described as a term 'saturated with emotional overtones' – gained a level of scientific credibility as an affective response (Muchinsky 2000, p. 802), but distracted researchers from using it as a stepping stone to explicitly explore emotions at work, and told us more about 'enduring attitudes' associated with a job rather than 'immediate emotions' (Fox & Spector 2002, p. 168). All this, coupled with job satisfaction's long established treatment as measuring affect, and hence its inappropriate use, a primary factor in its inconsistency to predict work behaviours (Weiss 2002), raised questions about its status, definition and measurement (Brief & Weiss 2002; Weiss & Cropanzano 1996). This eventually led to a 'disenchantment' with its usefulness (although its acceptance in practice means that its utility is ensured) that precipitated 'a crisis' that provided researchers with an opportunity to question whether there were other better ways of measuring affect in the workplace (Barsade et al. 2003, p. 10). The opportunity for the revolution had arrived (Barsade et al. 2003), with emotions now taking their place in organizational psychology (Briner & Kiefer 2005); generating a call for a more integrated approach to workplace emotions (Ashkanasy et al. 2002), the need to better understand the nuances that differentiate one emotion from another (Barsade et al. 2003), the role of discrete emotions in the stress process (Lazarus & Cohen-Charash 2001), and the significance of positive emotions (Fredrickson 1998, 2001, 2003, 2005).

Reviewers agree that the study of emotions at work has, in a short space of time, 'taken centre stage' (Gooty, Gavin & Ashkanasy 2009, p. 833). Reviewers of progress now face the unenviable task of considering a large and growing body of knowledge (Briner & Kiefer 2009). We first, in our evaluation of progress, remind ourselves of why we need to understand emotions at work. Four key themes emerge (see Dewe & Cooper 2012, pp.107, 110,117): (a) emotions are central to understanding the work experience (Ashkanasy & Ashton-James 2005; Ashforth & Humphrey 1995; Fox & Spector 2002; Pekrun & Frese 1992); (b) they have the potential to transform the organizational context and individual development and achievements (Pekrun & Frese 1992); (c) they have a critical influence on key organizational outcomes (Ashforth & Humphrey 1995; Barsade & Gibson 2007); and (d) they are crucial to understanding the coping process (Lazarus 1999, 2001; Lazarus & Cohen-Charash 2001). Yet in, or because of, all the hurly-burly of the 'affective revolution', academics in the field expressed concern about the approach to investigating workplace emotions becoming too fragmented (Ashkanasy & Humphrey 2011), and in need of maintaining a sense of systematic and scientific rigour (Ashkanasy & Humphrey 2011; Briner & Kiefer 2009; Gooty et al. 2009).

To inject a greater sense of rigour, Gooty and her colleagues (2009) urged scholars to adopt a more consistent approach to defining emotion, to ensure the nuances that separate discrete emotions are recognized and maintained, to acknowledge the dynamic nature of emotions and to account for the context within which emotions occur. Similarly Briner and Kiefer (2009) call for a more considered approach to the measuring of emotions, to ensure that our methods are congruent with theory, to avoid exaggerated claims concerning emotions and to adopt a more balanced approach to shaping the field that is less managerially driven. Like other critics, Grandey (2008) also reinforces the need to define terms, differentiate between discrete emotions, acknowledge the importance of context, distinguish between different theoretical perspectives and understand the practical and ethical challenges facing workplace investigations. Likewise, the multi-level model of emotion in organizations that spans within person, between persons, interpersonal, groups and teams, and the organization as a whole provides researchers with a framework for understanding the impact of emotions in the workplace (Ashkanasy & Ashton-James 2005; Ashkanasy & Humphrey 2011). All these reflections signal that to achieve a 'richer and broader future' (Dewe & Cooper 2012, p. 117) then it is clear that in addition to appropriate methodological and empirical decisions attention needs to be given to understanding the role of discrete emotions in the workplace, the causal pathways through which these emotions are expressed, their structure, intensity and temporal properties, how exactly they are used, the meanings given to them, their impact on behaviour and the characteristics of the context that triggers them.

TABLE IV.1

THE FIRST WAVE: EXPANDING ORGANIZATIONAL PSYCHOLOGY'S HORIZONS

(If change occurs in waves then three have defined the millennium so far)

The first wave (expanding organizational psychology's horizons)

o   As the new millennium dawned, in what was to become a defining piece, Seligman and Csikszentmihalyi (2000) offered researchers if not a new beginning a new focus: a psychology of positive functioning that was soon transformed into the positive psychology movement.
o   Then came an 'affective revolution' giving voice to investigating emotions at work (Barsade et al. 2003, p. 33). It was a revolution that was slow in coming even though the need for more research to understand the 'missing ingredient' of organizational life was clear (Fineman 2004, p. 720).

'The second wave'

The economic crisis

The positive psychology movement has certainly achieved its goal of drawing researchers' attention to the positive, with its emphasis on individual development and personal flourishing. Seligman and Csikszentmihalyi can rest assured that empirical research has not failed but more the opposite: it has 'confirm[ed] the usefulness of the positions [they] advanced' (Seligman & Csikszentmihalyi 2001, p. 90). The positive psychology movement has influenced every aspect of organizational psychology and contributed to the growth of positive organizational behaviour. However, like any field that is maturing there is still change to come. This change represents not just the need for a balanced model (Wong 2011) but a shift in focus. A shift from what Csikszentmihalyi calls the *direct* or therapeutic approach, where the emphasis has been 'making people *feel* better about their lives' to the *indirect* or enabling approach where the emphasis is on 'helping people *have* better lives' (2009, p. 204). The indirect approach stems from the view that our responsibilities extend beyond our own lives to identifying those conditions that span society and the environment that make individuals more 'optimistic, happy, satisfied' and assisting in making those conditions come about (Csikszentmihalyi 2009, p. 204).

This shift in focus senses and captures a mood that soon was to question the very direction in which theories had taken us, and the need for a time where we engage in a period of reconstruction. It was a mood that quickly was to become engulfed by the profound shock and concern with the way individuals and society had been ravaged by an economic crisis that tore away the facade of much we thought stable and reliable – enter the second wave of change. 'Economic' was soon replaced as preceding the word crisis by 'human', as the costs both emotional and financial 'nigh on impossible' to completely capture carried with them 'a terrible impact on well-being' (Anderson et al. 2011, p. 353) which is still being felt today (Dewe & Cooper 2014). The events of 2008 and the years that have followed have certainly reinforced the fact that we are living in turbulent times (Weinberg & Cooper 2012), even more turbulent than anyone could have predicted, simply because it was, as Clark described, like 'two worlds colliding in mutual incomprehension' (2010, p. 6); the economic, financial systems world with the individuals' world of aspirations and hopes. Forces of economic policy and ideology that at one time celebrated and unconditionally endorsed the ideals of 'market forces' as the flagship for providing prosperity and growth were now wreaking mayhem across all of society, leaving a human crisis that did nothing but offer despair, anxiety, distrust and a struggle to come to terms not just with what was happening but what it meant and how little control there was over anything (Dewe & Cooper 2012, p. 47, 2014; Weinberg & Cooper 2012).

Responses by governments and international agencies to the turbulence of the economic crisis soon had us adding words and phrases like austerity, quantitative easing, downsizing and reconstruction, deficit reduction, spending reviews and economic rebalancing to our vocabulary (Dewe & Cooper 2012, p. 47). Out of this turbulence, and the cold comfort of more financial restraints to come, emerge two sub themes that signal the direction as to where reconstruction and redevelopment should begin so that we can acknowledge where they have taken us and where now they have to go if we are to fulfil our responsibilities to those whose working lives we study. The first questions the assumptions concerning beliefs and practices present in the way corporate capitalism is organized, and explores whether there are alternative ways as to how this economic system could be redesigned and developed to better achieve those values and goals that not only provide individual well-being but a quality of life for all that is inclusive and sustainable (Kasser et al. 2007a).

Associated with this first sub theme is the call for economic metrics like GNP to be recalibrated, so that they better reflect the quality of people's lives, the global interest in happiness and the ideals of the good work agenda. The second sub theme explores how 'management theories' have, influenced by economic ideology, taken a rather narrow reductionist view of managing, making it now time to explore or return to a broader and more integrated approach to management that refocuses on context, leadership, social responsibilities and ethics (Ghoshal 2005). These two sub themes then lead us to our third wave of change that explores 'what may be' for OB/OP theories (Porter 2008; Porter & Schneider 2014, p. 1), what is yet to come and what is needed if our theories are to maintain their significance and relevance. Finally, we touch briefly on what all this means for 'work stress and coping research', before discussing this in more detail in the chapters that follow.

Corporate capitalism and its alternative design

While the psychological consequences of this crisis are well documented, they draw attention to the other side of the coin by asking what psychology can tell us about the 'capitalistic form of economic organization and the strong claims sometimes made about its strengths' (Kasser et al. 2007a, p. 2). Pointing to how reluctant psychologists may be to engage in such an investigation, Kasser and his colleagues in their work point to the values and goals of what they describe as the 'ever increasing influence' of American corporate capitalism, carrying with them 'certain practices and beliefs like self interest, competitiveness, economic growth and high levels of consumption' (2007a, p. 6), and how it is these practices, beliefs and values that must now be questioned; tempering their arguments by acknowledging the complexity of such a form of economic organization and recognizing its successes.

Kasser and colleagues make the case, supported by their research, as to how these goals and values 'conflict with and undermine pursuits long thought by psychologists to be essential to individual and collective well-being' (p. 18), namely, concern for broader society and world issues, the issue of what is important to people, what makes them happy, and the valued individual characteristics of relationships, affiliation, self-worth, generosity and compassion (p. 8). While this overview doesn't capture the richness of the argument outlined by Kasser and colleagues, it does present researchers with two important themes, if not proposals for action, that emerge from their review. The first concerns 'the unique perspective' (p. 18) psychology can bring to understanding the costs and conflicts inherent in the values espoused by such an economic system. The second deals with psychology's role in bringing about change, through the redesign and redevelopment of economic systems, to promote individual characteristics that bring greater well-being through those values that lead to a quality of life that is integrated and sustainable.

Kasser and his colleagues offer a psychological science of economic systems (2007b) that can clearly identify the key assumptions concerning human aspirations and behaviours that are behind such systems, and question whether they foster 'those values, beliefs and behaviours which society wishes its members to move'(p. 68). At the same time, they illustrate how that science can also be used to redesign and develop the way such systems are organized to 'better promote' those individual characteristics that bring 'greater happiness, more social cohesion and greater environmental sustainability' (p. 68). Commentators on the article by Kasser and his colleagues generally find support for and comment on the psychological consequences, showing how by promoting certain goals, values and ideology such economies 'crowd out' the emergence of other more meaningful quality of life values (B. Schwartz 2007, p. 48), or inflate their primacy by showing and endorsing a preference for some values at the expense of others (S. H. Schwartz 2007) or how different goals, values and pressures need to be 'held in balance' (Whybrow 2007, p. 58) or become reflected in and reinforced by public policies (Gowdy 2007).

Other commentators point to the 'steadfast pursuit of economic growth' as the culprit (Easterlin 2007, p. 32) or take the opportunity to answer Kasser et al.'s (2007a, p. 18) question of whether there are alternative forms of capitalism by pointing to 'compassionate capitalism', and how this form of capitalism contributes to individual flourishing through its emphasis on local ownership, engaged human resources and faith and benevolence (Myers 2007, p. 46). Much of this discussion and debate focuses on the contribution psychology can make to our understanding of the psychological costs and consequences of corporate capitalism by 'examining the values and goals that maintain it' (Kasser et al. 2007a, p. 18). This opportunity of a new role and a new focus for psychology would certainly seem to sit nicely alongside the central role that organizational psychology and organizational behaviour play in monitoring and identifying the ever-changing nature of work demands, corporate capitalism and now the economic crisis impose on employees and the affect these demands have on well-being (Fotinatos-Ventouratos & Cooper 2015). Yet it is not just organizational psychology that has a role as a 'sea changer'. Change is also occurring in contemporary economic theory; changes 'that should be encouraged' as they emphasize the active promotion of the 'common good' in economic policies (Ghoshal 2005; Gowdy 2007, p. 35), not forgetting the rekindling of interest by economists in behavioural economics, their adoption of the concept of happiness, and the consequences of these new interests on economic theory and public policy, and the insights they offer economic analysis (Frey & Stutzer 2002). Positive psychology also has a role to play. Its '*indirect* approach' emphasizes the importance of identifying what conditions 'make people more optimistic, happy and satisfied' and then 'helping them come about' (Csikszentmihalyi 2009, p. 204).

Calls for a fuller and broader form of economic analysis, where the focus is on the quality of life, inclusiveness and sustainability return us to the idea of alternative forms of capitalism. Alternative is probably not quite the right word, as it is more the redesigning of capitalism, so that trust can be restored in those institutions and policies that have engaged in activities that led to 'a surge in public antagonism' (Barton 2011, p. 85), where a few prospered at the expense of the wider community. A number of principles emerge that provide a blueprint for what has been described as 're-booting capitalism' (Grayson & McLaren 2012, p. 40). These include reconnecting with stakeholders, re-purposing of goals, resetting time frames to the longer term, and the rebalancing of power (Grayson & McLaren 2012, p. 42). Different approaches capture these principles in different ways. Porter and Kramer, for example, emphasize the 'creation of shared values', where organizational aims must be redefined so that economic value is created in a way 'that also creates value for society by addressing its needs and challenges', acknowledging that the competitiveness of the organization and the 'health of communities around it are closely intertwined' (2011, pp. 64, 66).

Similarly, Barton, calling for 'capitalism for the long term', outlines three ways in which capitalism must be renewed. These include a long term orientation, the acceptance 'that serving all major stakeholders is not at odds with maximizing corporate value' and that 'boards must have the ability to govern like owners' (2011, p. 86). Responsible capitalism (Stears & Parker 2012), for example, has at its core bringing organizations and society close together through developing 'deeper attachments' and commitments with the community so as to infuse a 'strong sense of place', the development of a more 'collaborate mindset' that builds relationships and 'reconnects' with the community and developing alliances beyond the organization that give employees a 'deeper sense of purpose and meaning in their work' and a chance to make an impact beyond the immediate work environment (Stears & Parker 2012, pp. 3–8). Finally 'stakeholder capitalism' builds upon the social nature of value creation, engaging with stakeholders, identifying principles of stakeholder responsibilities, recognizing the connection to the social context, acknowledging that 'cooperation with stakeholders and motivated by values continuously creates new sources of value' and competition is more 'an emerging property than a necessary assumption' (Freeman, Martin & Parmar 2007, pp. 311–312). All of these alternatives have in common a greater sense of social responsibility that requires a reconnecting with the social context, integrating business and social values, the building of a greater sense of purpose that transcends organizational interests and offers a quality of life that is both inclusive and sustainable. Arguing for an alternative type of capitalism brings debate and critique and turbulence. While the debate will grow so too will the need to act not just by governments, organizations and policy makers, but also by individuals placing demands on all to adapt, cope and manage the constant need for change.

GNP, happiness and the good work agenda

At the heart of the economic crisis was the challenge to capitalism itself. Despite the arrival of alternative forms of capitalism and despite the 'exciting and worthwhile opportunity' for psychology to apply its knowledge to redesigning economic systems (Kasser et al. 2007a, p. 18), it is clear from all the debate and discussion that capitalism cannot be transformed by any institution acting independently; change must come via international cooperation working towards agreed solutions (Grayson & McLaren 2012). Yet, it was just this feature – 'the extent of international cooperation' and harmonization of actions – that distinguished this economic crisis from others (Weinberg & Cooper 2012, p. 13). While this may offer some encouragement for those wishing to transform capitalism further hope may be gleaned from the fact that international cooperation and coordination is playing a central role in the policy debate that surrounds whether traditional macroeconomic measures like GNP actually capture 'the most important aspects that shape [the quality of] people's lives and well-being' (OECD 2013; 2012, p. 2) and how much they can be relied upon 'to inform policy debate on all issues' (Commission of the European Communities 2009, p. 2). Parallels can be drawn from the arguments rehearsing the need for the redesign of capitalism but, in this case, the call is for measures of GNP to move beyond traditional economic indicators to those that provide 'a more accurate picture of societal progress' (OECD 2012, p. 2), because 'important conclusions' about well-being are simply 'not apparent from economic indicators alone' (Diener & Seligman 2004, p. 1).

Over the last decade or so the idea that 'well-being' matters has led to a call for social progress to be redefined in such a way so that the focus shifts to measuring a more 'comprehensive picture of well-being' (OECD 2012, p.2) that captures 'the aspects of life that matter to people' (OECD 2013, p. 2). This coupled with a shift in values 'towards metrics that matter' (World Economic Forum 2012a, p. 3) ushered in the OECD's 'Better Life Initiative' that aims to promote 'better policies for better lives' through its 'How's life?' and 'Your Better Life Index' (OECD 2013; 2012, p.1), the workplace wellness alliance (World Economic Forum 2012b) and the reflections around 'GDP and beyond' promoted by the European Union (Commission of the European Communities 2009) and the review by Stiglitz, Sen and Fitoussi (2009). All have well-being at the centre of their calls for refocusing social progress as it 'allows us to come *closer* to what really matters for citizens, their well-being, or more generally the quality of their lives' (Stiglitz et al. 2009, p. 39). All adopt a more person-centred approach, all have had considerable impact, all acknowledge the importance of well-being measures in informing the design, monitoring and appraising of public policy (Dolan, Layard & Metcalfe 2011), and all argue for continued discussion and debate, that considers the 'utility of different kinds of concepts and measures for different purposes' (White, Gaines & Jha 2012, p. 774), continuing research on metrics and the need to ensure 'what we, as a society, care about, and whether we are really striving for what is important' (Stiglitz et al. 2009, p. 63).

It took some time to gather momentum, but the arrival of behavioural economics and its rekindling of an interest in psychology 'challenged traditional economic thinking' (Frey & Stutzer 2005, p. 209), and soon it was the 'psychology of happiness' that tempted economists to acknowledge 'the psychological underpinnings of economic analysis' (Camerer & Loewenstein 2004, p. 3) and engage in new ways and follow new possibilities to tackle old problems (Frey & Stutzer 2005). There are, argue Frey and Stutzer, three reasons why economists should consider happiness research. The first concerns economic policy and how research on happiness can 'usefully inform' policy decisions. The second is the relevance happiness research has to understanding the effects of organizational management, while the third follows from how happiness research helps to better understand the nature and structure of well-being (Frey & Stutzer 2002, pp. 402–403). Perhaps there is a fourth reason that flows from the work of Frey and Stutzer, and that is that happiness research findings add not just 'new knowledge to what have become standard views in economics' but 'challenge those views' as well (Frey & Stutzer 2002, p. 403). What seems to be the growing consensus is that 'through the lens of well-being can lead to concrete changes in direction' offering new approaches to policy analysis and more significantly perhaps the opportunity for new and different policy priorities to take hold (O'Donnell, Deaton, Durand, Halpern & Layard 2014, p. 73).

The economic turmoil and the crisis that swept through society has challenged traditional thinking, required old assumptions to be re-evaluated and seen structures and values that at one time represented the vanguard of contemporary thinking challenged for their narrowness of approach. These challenges have called for a redefinition and transformation of approach that requires more attention to be given to context, more emphasis given to the 'quality of people's lives' and where greater priority is given to understanding the 'nature and meaning of well-being and happiness' so that they too can sit at the heart of strategy, policy and governance. Two further challenges express this desire for change, and reflect this need for more inclusive approaches that comprehensibly capture those factors that shape peoples' lives and the value that lies in them as measures of social progress (World Economic Forum 2012a). These final two challenges are the call for a 'good work agenda' (see Dewe & Cooper 2012, pp. 29–32) and the changes needed to 'management practice' (Ghoshal 2005; Robertson & Cooper 2011). If, as Coats and Lekhi suggest, we are concerned about individuals choosing a life that they value 'then we should care about job quality', helping to explain why the concern about job quality 'is rising up the public policy agenda' (2008, p. 6).

The good work agenda

The 'good work agenda' builds from the proposition that work 'engages all of our skills, talents, capabilities and emotions' (Coats & Lekhi 2008, p. 13), and so it is, 'work that is good work, is the only work, that is good for us' (Coats 2009, p. 10). When asked what good work looks like (Coats & Lekhi 2008), then, good work is good health (Black 2008), positive organizational behaviours, motivated behaviours, opportunities for growth, development and the utilization of talents and skills (Constable, Coats, Bevan & Mahdon 2009), work that is well designed (Grant 2008a, 2008b; Parker & Ohly 2008) and, not forgetting of course competent management (Constable et al. 2009) and trust (Coats & Lekhi 2008). 'Good work' also embraces fulfilling employment (Brown, Charlwood, Forde & Spencer 2006), leading a life of meaning and purpose (Parker & Bevan 2011; Quick & Macik-Frey 2007), and meaningful work that offers self esteem, a sense of fulfilment, environmental mastery and a sense of value (Overall 2008). Turning to the good work agenda is important (see Dewe & Cooper 2012, pp. 29–32) because this is a traditional task that organizational psychology has had a long and rich history in through its work on job design and the role of the quality of working life movement. There are also parallels that can immediately be drawn not just in the language used, but between the ideals of the good work agenda and positive psychology, work stress interventions and the need to understand work in its broadest context. The benefits of 'good work' are clear and, as Constable and her colleagues suggest, the aim of policy makers is not to offer more evidence in support of good work, but to translate this evidence into policy that 'persuades, supports and incentivizes employers' to engage in activities where these ideas and benefits result in 'tangible change in the workplace' (Constable et al. 2009, p. 7).

Management: theory, practice and leadership

Is it the case that management and corporate board practices must take some of the responsibility for the turmoil, the corporate scandals, the managerial excesses and what Fry refers to as 'a chilling pall over the way business is conducted' (2005, p. 48)? While, of course the answer is yes, the more important question is how it came about that 'bad management theories are destroying good management practices' (Ghoshal 2005, p. 75)? The answer lies, it seems, in the way that economics has infiltrated management theory (Ghoshal 2005; Hambrick 2005; Pfeffer 2005), setting in motion an ideology that gives rise to 'a set of pessimistic assumptions' about individuals and organizations and the management practices and behaviours that they engage in (Ghoshal 2005, p. 77). Captured by the language and ideology of economics, and narrow reductionist economic imperatives where behaviour is reduced to its instrumental qualities, self interest and short term maximization of returns (see Dewe & Cooper 2012 pp.38-39; Donaldson 2005; Gapper 2005;

Ghoshal 2005; Pfeffer 2005), those engaged in managerial decision making are isolated from the social context within which they behave, and liberated to engage in such practices free of any 'sense of moral responsibility' (Dewe & Cooper 2012, p. 38; Ghoshal 2005, p. 76). What perhaps is equally telling is that by engaging in such behaviours and practices managers reinforced the idea that these are not only the way to manage but that they are based on credible managerial theory and in this way 'they gain currency' (Ghoshal 2005, p. 77) – and processes are set in motion 'to ensure that they can become self fulfilling' (Pfeffer 2005, p. 96).

Ghoshal's (2005) work was a seminal moment for management theory and reflects in the context of change and crisis the spread of economic theory and its impact on management practice. The Ghoshal paper reflects a key discussion point (see Dewe & Cooper 2012, pp. 38–39) and we return to it again (a) to reinforce the view of the way reductionist economic theories became able to, in a wholesale way, saturate and drive and consume management practice and theory, and (b) to raise the question of 'why has there been such a receptive audience' when there is so much good theory available (Kanter 2005, p. 93)? Kanter explores four reasons. Two of these capture historical trends: first, the push to make organizations more competitive and the search for ways to do this; while the second and not mutually exclusive reason is the growth of corporations, their investors and their power. The third she suggests is that people-centred theories are 'less easy to do' whereas economic theories seem to have 'more reach, resonance and staying power', and from this emerges the fourth reason that economic theories are not all wrong 'they are just too simple and leave out too much' (Kanter 2005, p. 94). Add to this the idea that people theories are less prescriptive, making social scientists more reluctant to engage in policy debate, that ideology 'plays a role' in influencing 'what theories become acceptable' and self-fulfilling and that all must be understood in terms of their time and place within the broader social context (Pfeffer 2005, p. 98), then this leads, of course to what can be done about it?

In his seminal paper, Ghoshal made it clear that in asking what can be done, business schools need to 'own up' to their role and accept that instead of asking what can be done, they should explore what they have been teaching, how they can 'create a new intellectual agenda' and how they need to engage in developing management theories that are 'broader and richer' than those 'reductionist and partial theories' that have dominated contemporary thinking (2005, p. 87). What if, Ghoshal suggests, we think more in terms of context and process, and acknowledge the promising 'good news' (2005, p. 85) that is emerging from the positive psychology movement, and behavioural economics, with its emphasis on well-being and happiness. Other commentators point to the fact that organization success requires all stakeholders to be involved, and that 'value creation means more than shareholder values' (Kanter 2005, p. 95), that we need to be more open and pay more attention to the values 'we are imparting' (Pfeffer 2005, p. 99), that greater emphasis needs to be placed on fulfilling work (Gapper 2005), on the ideals of stewardship (Hambrick 2005), and on the importance of ethics

(Donaldson 2005); all representing a broadness that Ghoshal called for in his 'new intellectual agenda' (2005, p.89) for teaching and for practice. While the various commentators on Ghoshal's article wonder whether the authority and influence of business schools has been somewhat over estimated they all strongly agree that his arguments challenge 'so deeply' the very core of management thinking and practice and therefore 'the status quo in our field' (Nord 2005, p. 92).

If we move from business schools to leadership, then, as we have pointed to before, what responsibilities rest with those who lead and did leadership lose its way (see Dewe & Cooper 2012, pp. 40–43; Podolny, Khurana & Hill-Popper 2005)? Leadership, as Podolny and his colleagues argue, lost its way in a way we are becoming fast familiar with when it became clear that leadership became narrowly focused on economic imperatives, rather than its capacity to 'infuse purpose and meaning into the organizational experience' (2005, p. 5). The search was on for new styles of leadership. A number of themes emerged from this search that included the need to ensure that leadership is seen as extending across all organizational stakeholders, transcending narrowly defined motives and interests, ensuring individual development and in many ways drawing its comfort from the aspirations of the positive psychology movement. While the reality of leadership is complicated, at times full of role conflicts, transforming and changing expectations and the bureaucracy of organizational function and structure (Whittington 2004), the pathway that leadership needs to follow and the current thinking seems to coalesce around the idea of authentic leadership (Avolio & Gardner 2005). Even so the interests around servant leadership (Whittington 2004), spirituality and leadership (Dent, Higgins & Wharff 2005; Fry 2005), prosocial leadership (Lorenzi 2004), ethical leadership (Fulmer 2004), followership leadership (Uhi-Bien, Riggio, Lowe & Carsten 2014) and authentic transformational leadership (Price 2003) cannot be ignored.

An 'authentic style of leadership' builds around ideas about self-awareness; being genuine – 'acting in a way that reflects one's true self' and 'owning one's inner thoughts, beliefs and emotions' (Gardner & Schermerhorn 2004, p. 271). Its definition embraces these ideals and expresses a leadership style where leaders are 'not only true to themselves, but lead others by helping them to likewise achieve authenticity' (Gardner, Avolio, Luthans, May & Walumbwa 2005, p. 344). With its origins in positive psychology and positive organizational behaviour, and capturing the spirit of positive psychological capital, this style of leadership helps create positive ethical cultures (Logsdon & Young 2005), ethical performance (Youssef & Luthans 2005), positive corporate citizenship (Waddock 2005), values that 'enhance personal and institutional development' (Pawelski & Prilleltensky 2005), and positive socially responsible environments (Shorey, Rand & Snyder 2005). Running through these ideas is the need to involve all stakeholders, to transcend beyond narrowly defined interests, to adopt a responsibility to others and to acknowledge the importance of individual development.

Other reviews also point to changes in how leadership is investigated and point to how 'leader-centric' models may 'instill a false sense of certainty', in terms of how leaders influence the performance of individuals and organizations by failing perhaps to recognize the dynamic nature of context (Dinh, Lord, Gardner, Meuser, Liden & Hu 2014, p. 53). Hopefully, leadership research will, 'over the next decade' provide greater insights in how leaders 'can be more effective' in meeting the challenges of the new millennium, and set out 'the relevant leadership processes and dynamics' (Gardner, Lowe, Moss, Mahoney & Cogliser 2010, p. 953) so that the next generation of researchers will wish to move beyond which leadership theory is 'right' to exploring how 'to develop leaders and leadership as effectively and efficiently as possible' (Day, Fleenor, Atwater, Sturm & McKee 2014, p. 79). Other reviewers also capture many of these themes in their reviews and point more specifically to leadership development, a greater need to understand the context of leadership, gender-based differences in leadership, international leadership, the interaction of leadership and technology and a more focused work on the affective aspects of leadership (Lowe & Gardner 2001, pp. 492–504). Finally the three trends that Avolio and his colleagues identify after an exhaustive review of current leadership theories that points to the evolution of leadership research include: the field taking a more holistic view; exploring how 'leadership actually takes place'; and developing alternative approaches and methods for examining leadership (Avolio, Walumbwa & Weber 2009, pp. 441–442). All the reviews point to the need for methodological change and refinement, and all point to a rich history of leadership research and analysis.

TABLE IV.2

THE SECOND WAVE: ECONOMIC (HUMAN) CRISIS AND ITS CONSEQUENCES

o An economic crisis tore away the facade of much that was thought stable and reliable.
o Economics was soon replaced as the word preceding crisis by human as the costs both emotional and financial 'nigh on impossible' to completely capture carried with it 'a terrible impact on well-being' (Anderson et al. 2011, p. 353).
o The consequences included a debate on how corporate capitalism could be redesigned – and asking what psychology could tell us about the 'capitalistic form of economic organization and the strong claims sometimes made about its strengths' (Kasser et al. 2007a, p. 2).
o The 're-booting' of capitalism (Grayson & McLaren 2012, p. 40) and calls for a broader form of economic analysis where the focus is on the quality of life, inclusiveness and sustainability.

o   The calls for measures of GNP to move beyond traditional narrow economic indicators to those that capture the aspects of the 'life that matters to people' (OECD 2013, p. 2).
o   The internationalization of well-being through programmes that shift the focus to well-being by initiatives like 'metrics that matter' (World Economic Forum 2012, p. 3), to promote 'better policies for better lives' (OECD 2012, p. 1).
o   The international interest in happiness (Frey & Stutzer 2002, 2005).
o   The call for a 'good work agenda' (Coats & Lekhi 2008).
o   The rethinking of management practice and leadership (Ghoshal 2005; Hambrick 2005; Kanter 2005; Pfeffer 2005).

A moment to catch up

These early years of the new millennium can at best be described as turbulent, ushering in at times new ideas and developments, whilst at other times offering nothing short of disaster; an economic and human crisis that has required international cooperation on 'a scale never seen before' to ensure that systems and structures once seen as representing our hopes for prosperity and well-being are now being roundly condemned (Weinberg & Cooper 2012, p. 13). From all that the new millennium has offered by way of austerity, uncertainty and anxiety, two themes have emerged from all this turmoil that have remained consistent throughout offering both hope and encouragement: 'development' and 'reconstruction'. 'Development' in terms of new ideas, new approaches and new movements, and 'reconstruction' in terms of refinements to systems and structures, the ideologies that they express and the values that legitimize and foster the pursuit of material goals and single-minded behaviours.

Each offers a way of understanding where we are, what has happened and what may be, but each influences the other as developments soon morph into and become part of the reconstruction or refinement process. Neither calls for an abandonment of what we have. Taken together each represents the two parts of a balanced approach, where the good of what we have is enhanced and reinforced by the careful reconstruction, redefinition and redevelopment of those ideological costs and values that collide with how we want to better express who we are, what we stand for, what we want and what we believe is the best way to achieve that sense of well-being that captures what matters most in life. It only remains now to see what it is that theories of organizational psychology and organizational behaviour have to offer in terms of change, development and reconstruction–refinement.

'The third wave'

'What may be' for theories of organizational psychology and organizational behaviour

'The good news is', as Cooper points out, that 'organizational behaviour [and organizational psychology] move with the times' and reflect 'the issues, concerns and dilemmas of the age and beyond' (2009, p. 7). Staying with, for the moment, our 'development-reconstruction framework' and accepting its somewhat porous boundaries, then it is possible to identify change that is occurring that ushers in both new developments in terms of emerging interdisciplinary subject areas and future challenges that require new pathways and new directions that call for the reconstruction and refining of existing theories, research methods and practice. Before turning to the development and reconstruction themes that map the potential future directions for organizational psychology and organizational behaviour we need to reflect on a debate that routinely engages researchers and practitioners alike. From rather traditional beginnings, where the focus is on the nature of theory, the discussion quickly gathers its voice as attention turns to the issue of an academic–practitioner divide.

Bridging the gap between research and practice

The question of 'what is theory' more often than not generates a more wide ranging discussion that moves from the nature of theory itself to what makes a theory useful, how long do theories last, how do they remain relevant, what is the balance between knowledge generation and knowledge application, how does knowledge transfer, who is responsible for knowledge transfer, what is useful knowledge, and on to 'what constitutes a theoretical contribution' (Corley & Gioia 2011, p. 12; Dewe & Cooper 2012, pp.162-163). Corley and Gioia call for theories to be given more 'scope' requiring researchers to strike a balance between scientific rigour and what they describe as 'pragmatic usefulness', where thinking shifts beyond gaps in the literature to 'engagement with problems in the world' (2011, p.27). This is a challenge they acknowledge, but one which reflects a common theme that we will return to again and have done so before (Dewe & Cooper 2012, pp.162–163), marking the belief that if our work is to become more relevant then linking our theory to practice simply reaffirms the 'applied role' we have and the responsibilities we have to those whose working lives we study (Corley & Gioia 2011, p. 29; Dewe & Cooper 2012, pp.163–164).

Others talk about 'usable knowledge', where the priorities and needs of users are met, but from a standpoint that ensures both 'scientific quality and relevance' (Perry 2012, p. 479). These ideas of 'pragmatic usefulness' and 'usable knowledge' represent ways of bridging this gap or divide between research and practitioners, so what is the gap and what is the nature of the debate that surrounds it? Is it 'a growing and dangerous divergence' between those whose primary concern is for developing knowledge, and those whose primary concern is in applying that knowledge (Hodgkinson 2006, p. 174)? Or is it a feeling that our research is 'abstract and inconsequential' and fails to address more pressing practical issues (Gelade 2006, p. 153)? Or is more to do with highly rigorous, complex and reliable research which does not generalize to a wider audience (Wall 2006)? Or is it because practitioners and researchers often hold 'stereotypical views of each other' (Anderson, Herriot & Hodgkinson 2001, p. 392) or a 'serious disconnect' between those producing the knowledge and those consuming it (Cascio & Aguinis 2008, p. 1062)? Or is it that research should 'be better tuned to practice' (van Dam & van den Berg 2004, p. 482)?

It is, of course, all of those things, as each resonates with the other to produce a divide or gap that builds from the requirement on the one hand for rigorous research the criterion for which cannot be simply jettisoned (Anderson 2007), and the priorities of practitioners that demand a level of practical relevance (Anderson et al. 2011). Paradoxically, there shouldn't be any great research–practitioner divide because 'each have much in common' but 'nonetheless such a divide exists' (Wall 2006, p. 161). So where is the complexity?

Four themes emerge from the debate that help us to understand the underlying complexity. The first concerns the fact that it is not just two audiences with two priorities. Researchers and practitioners are not homogenous groups nor is the research that they do or the priorities that they face (Hodgkinson 2006; Symon 2006). This raises questions about how we distinguish between the two groups and the demands each face, and more importantly how we identify what is the clear cut boundary that separates them (Symon 2006), particularly if there is some level of responsibility for each to share information (Hodgkinson 2006). The second asks how do you achieve a 'pragmatic science' that maintains a sense of relevance and rigour, where knowledge is transferable and meaningful without bordering on the popular yet still meets each other's priorities (Hodgkinson 2006, p. 174; Wall 2006)? The third is the question of 'who are the better custodians of the research agenda' – researchers or practitioners (Symon 2006, p. 170)? Finally, as Symon (2006) concludes, how far are we actually encouraging some sort of researcher–practitioner divide and what are the consequences for each?

Such a debate is important because it is indicative of a need to explore the issues, promotes a level of reflection and at the very least engages the attention of both groups (Gelade 2006; Hodgkinson 2006; Symon 2006). What perhaps emerges out of this debate is that the 'width [of the gap] does matter – but not nearly as much as bridging' it (Anderson 2007, p. 178). So what are the bridging mechanisms? It is difficult to overstate the importance of the case for bridging the divide (Gelade 2006). Two themes emerge both illustrating the idea of 'knowledge intermediaries' (Hodgkinson 2006, p. 177), the importance of promoting two-way communications, mutually beneficial collaborations and partnerships and the 'broadening of horizons' to include engaging in and addressing policy issues (Wall 2006, p. 164).

So the first theme captures the need to be 'more accepting of different perspectives and approaches' (Symon 2006, p. 170), both within and between researchers and practitioners. In so doing, it reinforces the need for greater collaboration that is bi-directionally driven across and between both groups, drawing on the strengths that each group offers in terms of their expertise, and where such collaborations and partnerships build a sense of empathy, mutual understanding and explanation and acceptance of different values and practices (Anderson 2007, pp. 179–181; Cascio & Aguinis 2008; Hodgkinson 2006; Wall 2006).

The second theme simply captures the need for researchers, indeed, for our discipline, to more directly address the issue of policy initiatives and policy development (Anderson 2007; Wall 2006). Organizational psychology is not alone in this matter as management theorists (Rynes 2007a, 2007b), when looking ahead, also draw attention to bridging the divide between research and practice. Perhaps in the spirit of bridging the gap this is why commentators and researchers have begun, as we do again, to re-enforce and reiterate the debate's significance and its complexity and its importance to our discipline, by returning to the question as to how evidence based our discipline is (Briner & Rousseau 2011a, 2011b; see Dewe & Cooper 2012, pp. 155-156), drawing attention again to the challenges that include who determines or arbitrates on what is evidence (Cronin & Klimoski 2011), why we haven't advanced our use of evidence (Thayer, Wildman & Salas 2011), the tools that we need to develop our evidence based expertise (Hodgkinson 2011), and what this means for the diversity of approaches that reflect our discipline (Cassell 2011). It is within this context that we can now return to our development–reconstruction framework, and, accepting its imperfections, explore at the level of developments change that reflects the emergence of interdisciplinary subject areas that have, and are, significantly influencing our approach to and understanding of work stress and coping. In terms of reconstruction we explore future challenges that require new pathways and new directions that call for refining of existing theories, research methods and practice.

Occupational health psychology

Remembering the mutual relationships between each of the dimensions to our framework then in respect of developments, we have in this chapter discussed the growth and maturing of the positive psychology movement, the gathering of speed of the affective revolution and in Chapter II the arrival of cyberpsychology. It only remains now to acknowledge the importance of occupational health psychology, and its significant contribution to our field. The issue of how work influences health and well-being has 'attracted a considerable amount of interest for much of the twentieth century' (Barling & Griffiths 2003, p. 19). Occupational health psychology seeks to identify, understand and develop those psychological processes that help 'to promote and protect' the quality of working life and the health and well-being of workers, illustrating its role as a scientific discipline and an applied field and reflecting both its empirical and societal-policy foci (Barling & Griffiths 2003, p. 30; Schaufeli 2004).

Occupational health psychology is now approaching its twenty-fifth year and represents a multidisciplinary field; and reviewers have begun to consider what lies ahead. Three themes emerge; the first captures the influence of the positive psychology movement and 'a more positive future' that broadens our understanding of health by focusing on positive health as well as ill health, the impact of positive aspects of work on health and well-being including leadership and moods and emotions and, as a more holistic understanding of health growths, then positive interventions. All of this adds much more of 'a balance' to our investigation of health and well-being at work (Barling 2005; Macik-Frey, Quick & Nelson 2007, p. 823; Tetrick 2006). The second theme explores 'new horizons in occupational health' by pointing to the need to investigate the health impact of the changing nature of organizations and working life including developments in technology, virtual work, globalization and the impact of ageing (Macik-Frey et al. 2007, pp. 827–832). Expanding horizons also includes more of a focus on 'organizational health, as well as "workers" and their families' health and well-being' (Tetrick 2006, p. 2) and the need to develop when it comes to societal changes a 'three level hierarchical model' that explores their impact in terms of the external context, the organizational context, and the work context (Schaufeli 2004, p. 504).

The third theme is concerned with the 'methods we use to investigate occupational health', and the need to build on what has become a 'significant body of knowledge' by engaging in, because of the nature of the field experimental and quasi-experimental designs, multi method and mixed method approaches and longitudinal analysis (Barling 2005, p. 308). More descriptive work involves large scale studies, studies that make use of objectively expressed parameters, the continued development of assessment, risk management and intervention tools that build on and enhance their practical focus in terms of evaluation, decision making and knowledge transfer (Schaufeli 2004, p. 510), not forgetting the issues around developing an evidence-based discipline (Briner 2012). We have, across these chapters, identified interdisciplinary areas that have welcomed in the new millennium, found their voice, reflected the changing nature of work and organizations, or continued to establish their presence as an important lens through which to view work, health and well-being. Others may well be in transition, being shaped by an accumulating body of knowledge that has yet to achieve a level of reach, intensity and impact to represent itself as a new approach despite the importance and significance of its focus and relevance; here perhaps is the 'age wave' (Macik-Frey et al. 2007, p. 830) heralding in, if not a psychology of aging, then a psychology of the older person. Others disciplines, while well established, may also be exploring how they may benefit from developing different perspectives or broadening their influence or shifting their boundaries; see, for example, the reshaping of cross cultural psychology (Aycan 2000; Gelfand, Erez & Aycan 2007; Singelis 2000).

New pathways and new directions

Finally, we can turn our attention to the second element of our framework and briefly explore future challenges that identify new pathways and new directions that call for, if not the refining of existing theories, research methods and practice then the momentum for ensuring progress and against which achievements can be judged. Again influenced by the changing nature of work and organizations and by the turbulence and forces discussed earlier then when asked what organizational psychology should do to prosper (Greenberg 2008), commentators suggested adopting a broader social perspective and expanded agenda that eschews reductionist values for values that 'encompass a scientist–practitioner–humanist model' (Lefkowitz 2008, p. 449), bridging the gap between application and scholarship by recognizing that the effective diffusion of knowledge requires greater collaboration and closer consultation notwithstanding the relationship building and academic challenges at stake (Cascio 2008), overcoming methodological barriers to progress (Edwards 2008b), and by adopting a global perspective (Gelfand, Leslie & Fehr 2008). This brief overview cannot capture the richness, depth and cogency of argument that these commentators present when responding to the question outlined above in what was a special issue of the *Journal of Organizational Behavior*.

Concluding this special issue, and drawing on the arguments put forward by the different authors, Porter (pp. 524–526) looks forward by asking four questions: 'has the field made progress over the last 50 years?; has it been sufficiently reflective?; is it better off?; and what will we be saying about the field in 20 years time?' Porter is cautiously optimistic in his answers about future progress, but recognizes that there may not be as much progress in some areas to the extent people think necessary. Nevertheless, while acknowledging that 'there are no experts on the future' Porter (p.525), drawing on his considerable experience and significant contribution to the field, suggests that in the future 'two Cs (context and change) will and should receive more concentrated research and scholarly attention' (Porter 2008, pp. 524–525). Similarly when Porter and Schneider explored 'what may be' for organizational psychology/behaviour, they, after a detailed and comprehensive review that included 'what was and what is', identified what they described as three challenges and four questions. The three challenges included knowing more about the 'O' (organizational context); as without a more direct focus on the setting for behaviour there is a limit to 'the conclusions that can be drawn from research findings'. The second challenge derives from the benefit of knowing more from research that 'cut[s] across' the micro and macro dimensions of behaviour in organizations, i.e. what are the effects on behaviour for example of 'macro changes in terms of structural aspects of the organization.' The final challenge they identify is the need for a greater emphasis to be 'given to international/global aspects of the field' (2014, pp. 15–16).

In terms of whether there will be progress in the future, Porter and Schneider put into question form what they think are 'at least' some of the significant issues that need to be confronted. The first question concerns our ability to build a 'robust evidence-based analysis of behaviour in organizational settings' (p. 15). The second questions whether we can demonstrate an ability to 'achieve a more meaningful integration of findings across the array of topics researched.' The third asks whether through our research findings we can 'achieve a greater impact on managerial practice'; and the final question simply asks about relevance and whether 'our theories [are] up to the task' of expressing and reflecting the impact of change on organizations (2014, pp. 15–18). What we have in these reviews is not just an emerging agenda but a call for reflection that in all respects is a powerful call for constantly reminding ourselves as to where current theories are taking us, how well they express the work experience, how well they translate into practice and how well they allow us to achieve the moral responsibility we have to those whose working lives we study.

TABLE IV.3

THE THIRD WAVE: 'WHAT MAY BE' FOR THEORIES OF ORGANIZATIONAL BEHAVIOUR AND OCCUPATIONAL PSYCHOLOGY?

- o   It is possible to identify change that ushers in new developments in terms of interdisciplinary subject areas (e.g. occupational health psychology), and future challenges that require new pathways and new directions that call for the refining of existing theories, methods and practice.
- o   The 'good news', as Cooper points out, is 'that organizational behaviour [and organizational psychology] moves with the times and reflects the issues, concerns and dilemmas of the age and beyond' (2009, p.7).
- o   However, some issues like the 'gap' between research and practice confront all researchers and the debate remains significant because it signals a need to explore the issues, promotes reflection as to where research is going and at least engages both researchers and practitioners (Anderson 2007; Gelade 2006; Hodgkinson 2006; Symon 2006).
- o   Coupled with the debate surrounding the reach-practice divide is the issue of just how evidence based our discipline is – the potential to be evidence based is present but 'we are not there yet' (Briner & Rousseau 2011a, p. 3; 2011b).
- o   Influenced by the changing of the nature of work and organizations and by the turbulence and the impact of globalization, the spread of technological change and workforce complexities, Porter points to what he suggests are the 'two Cs' (context and change) that in the future should 'receive more concentrated research attention' (Porter 2008, pp. 524–525).

(Continued)

> *(Continued)*
>
> o   In terms of the future progress of our disciplines Porter and Schneider put
>   in question form some of the issues that need to be confronted: what is our
>   ability to build a more meaningful 'robust evidence-based analysis of behav-
>   iour in organizational settings'?; how can a more meaningful integration of
>   findings be achieved across the array of topics researched?; how can we
>   achieve a greater impact on managerial practice?; and are 'our theories… up
>   to the task' of processing and reflecting the impact of change in organiza-
>   tions (Porter & Schneider 2014, pp. 15–18)?

Summary

The first 15 years of the new millennium are best described as turbulent and at worst of crisis proportions. Yet even through the savage difficulties of those middle years of its reign so far, the aftermath that still hangs over us, and the language that continually reminds us, not just of what we have endured, but what is still to come are signs of what must be done, of questions that must be asked, directions that must be followed if progress is going to be made, and responsibilities we must shoulder if we are to maintain a sense of relevance and a strength of purpose that allows our discipline to prosper and enrich the working lives of those we study. Developments both theoretical and empirical have, of course, occurred which have significantly influenced the research process. These developments reflect the continual need to refine and reconstruct our theories and our research so that they capture the nature of the work experience, the costs and the satisfactions that come from that experience and the impact these have on health and well-being. How these different forces of change and the theoretical and empirical refinements that accompany them demand to be, and are reflected in our research, the way they find expression and the meaning this has for analysis, measurement and interpretation, are all explored in the chapters that follow. We first explore the ways in which work stressor research has evolved and developed in the face of change and the call for adaptation and refinement. We then shift our attention to coping research and explore how it too reflects the calls for change, the refinements needed and the meanings these have for future developments before finally exploring the changing nature of intervention strategies and how they reflect change and development.

V

THE EVOLVING NATURE OF WORK STRESSORS: A PROLOGUE TO CHANGE

This chapter first explores how these forces of change, while bringing with them at times turmoil and at other times crisis, also helped usher in new ideas that grew into movements, and new opportunities that gave voice to those calling for the need to reflect, refine and reconstruct established ways of thinking. In doing so, they better express not just the work experience but the consequences of that experience in terms of health, well-being and sustainability. Of course, work stress research was not immune to these calls, and the demand for change. This chapter explores the evolving nature of work stressors, offering a prologue to change. It explores how these forces have helped change, shape and fashion the structure of organizations, the direction of work and the nature of work itself. Within this context, we explore briefly how work stressors have evolved in terms of reflecting both time and context, before turning our attention in the next chapter to those stressors that express aspects of contemporary work, reflect widespread concern, and have received considerable empirical support.

The shaping and refashioning of work

It is somewhat of an understatement to simply point to work as having gone through many changes throughout the last 50 years, although the statement is, in itself, absolutely correct. What lies behind such a statement, as the previous three chapters have pointed out, is the enormity of those changes and their fundamental and sometimes radical impact on work and working lives. Earlier chapters have also, either explicitly or implicitly, made it clear that work and working lives will continue to be transformed, calling for 'fresh approach[es]to work' and how we are 'poised for a revolution in working practices' (Maitland & Thomson 2011, p. 32). Commentators almost universally have, as we have done, pointed to the impact of globalization, the influence and rapacious speed of technological change and the emergence of the 'new workforce' where 'tectonic shifts are taking place' in its composition (Maitland & Thomson 2011, p. 3), not, of course, forgetting how these changes have battered and transformed society more generally. All these changes are, one way or another, with some more than others, 'intimately about us' (Gratton 2014, p. 34) as we experience their effect not just on our working lives but all aspects of our lives. They have infiltrated our feelings, how we relate to others, how we make sense of things and how they continually create the need to manage what we have, what we want and what we value. We also witness the effects that these changes have on others, and how these effects in turn affect us, our capacity to give, our energy levels, the priorities we set and how we manage and cope (Gratton 2014).

It is important when thinking about how these 'forces of change' shape and fashion the nature of work and working lives to take, as Gratton suggests, a 'broad brush' approach that acknowledges both the need for a global perspective that captures the ebb and flow of transactions between nations, whilst also recognizing that 'work takes place in the context of families, expectations and hopes; it takes place within the context of the community and in the context of economic and political structures' (2014, pp. 24–25). Gratton's approach is rich in detail, strong in analysis, cogent and compelling. Gratton's dictum, calling for a broad brush approach, seems to be reflected in those themes commentators point to when describing how work and working lives are being shaped, refashioned and at times transformed. These themes include the restructuring of organizations through acquisitions and mergers as a consequence of global competition, capital and production movements and the demands for rationalization and efficiencies; the shift in emphasis to 'knowledge work' and the impact of these forces of change on the 'everyday realities of work' (Noon et al. 2013, p. 47), in terms of how, when, and where we work, who we work with, the sort of work that we do and the rewards we derive from it.

None of these themes are mutually exclusive; each is part of a complex set of interrelationships, where boundaries merge, are re-established and reshaped and assume more or less potency than before. Each is defined by elements and items that are themselves subject to change, but each separately and all collectively reflect changes to the nature of work and working lives, expressing at the same time the costs such demands for change have on individual well-being. Our aim in this chapter whilst acknowledging the complexity of change, is to explore how, as work and working lives are reshaped and refashioned by change, work stressors also evolve to reflect the changing nature of the work experience and so present researchers with challenges as to the relevance of our measures, their interpretation, meaning and significance to those completing them and their usefulness in capturing the work/well-being relationship. With this aim in mind we return to the first of the three themes outlined above, and consider the restructuring of work and working lives through mergers and acquisitions.

Restructuring organizations through mergers and acquisitions

The research on mergers and acquisitions comes with a long history that reflects its usefulness as a strategy to 'rapidly respond to the demands of a changing global environment' (Cartwright 2008, p. 583), a means of developing and growing global market economies, 'a highly popular form of corporate development' (Cartwright & Schoenberg 2006, p. S1) and an opportunity 'for organizations to enhance profitability or to survive amid ever fierce global competition' (van Dick, Ullrich & Tissington 2006, p. S69). The frequency with which this strategy is used continues to increase, as does the monetary value associated with each acquisition (Cartwright 2008; Cartwright & Cooper 2013; Cartwright & Schoenberg 2006). The complexity that accompanies such a strategy, together with the considerable difficulties in assessing their success and therefore the reporting of positive experiences and returns, the level of financial failures, and their mixed performance in relation to a range of stakeholders (Cartwright & Cooper 2013; Cartwright & Schoenberg 2006; van Dick et al. 2006), 'presents a gloomy picture' and 'an issue of public concern' (Cartwright 2008, p. 583; van Dick et al. 2006, p. S69). While the drive to understand variations in the performance and success of acquisitions has been at the heart of much research (Cartwright 2008; Cartwright & Schoenberg 2006; Cooper & Finkelstein 2016), it has always been accompanied by a growing research interest in the impact of this type of organizational change on those involved and 'their emotional and behavioural response' (Cartwright & Schoenberg 2006, p. S3).

It is clear that mergers and acquisitions are met with 'apprehension and concerns' (van Dick et al. 2006, p. S69), 'uncertainty and fear of the unknown' (Cartwright 2008, p. 586), 'a diminished degree of predictability' (Hellgren, Sverke & Näswall 2008, p. 46) and 'clashes of culture, strategy, operations and personalities' (Allred, Boal & Holstein 2005, p. 23). While individual responses to these fears, apprehensions and concerns have offered researchers a route to explain why mergers and acquisitions underperform (Cartwright 2008), the link between such feelings and stress has been confirmed (Ahammad, Tarba, Liu, Glaister & Cooper 2015). Job insecurity has emerged as the stressor most closely associated with the feelings emanating from mergers and acquisitions, has attracted a considerable empirical following, is regarded as a central construct in understanding 'the dramatic changes' in work and working lives and reflects, on the 'brink of a new millennium', a need to learn more about employment uncertainty and 'the nature of job insecurity' (Sverke & Hellgren 2002, p. 23). Job insecurity falls, like job loss (Karren 2012) under the general rubric of economic stress – those stressors that refer to 'aspects of economic life that are potential stressors for employees and their families' (Probst 2005, p. 268). Job insecurity has, through the notion of job uncertainty, links with the earlier concept of merger stress (Cartwright & Cooper 2013) and has 'detrimental consequences' for employee attitudes and well-being (Sverke & Hellgren 2002, p. 24).

While it is important to focus on well-being, it is equally important, as Cartwright argues, when considering the impact of mergers and acquisitions to focus on how this type of organizational change 'threatens and challenges' social needs, particularly organizational identity (2008, p. 588), not forgetting the growing body of research 'directed at the cultural dynamics of mergers and acquisitions' (Cartwright & Schoenberg 2006, p. S3). Positive benefits also flow from mergers and acquisitions and researchers are catching the mood of positivity by exploring both the role of positive emotions (Cartwright 2008) and their cultivation (Kusstatscher 2006) throughout this type of organizational change. How individuals respond to the merger or acquisition depends on how the integration process is managed. Appelbaum and his colleagues offer a behavioural approach to guide managers through all stages of the merger and acquisition process, drawing attention to the importance of communication, the role of culture, the complexities surrounding the change process and the role of managers, as such a process 'assumes significant effort and dedication' (Appelbaum, Gandell, Yortis, Proper & Jobin 2000a, p. 658; Appelbaum, Gandell, Shapiro, Belisle & Hoeven 2000b). These authors (Appelbaum et al. 2000a, p. 649), point to what they describe as the 'merger syndrome', characterized by the centralization of the integration process, a corresponding decrease in communications and stress so the 'level and quality of planning' (Nguyen & Kleiner 2003, p. 447) becomes crucial for success both in regard to those involved in the process and more significantly those who lead it.

While the 'influence of OB research continues to be overshadowed by that of financial scholars' (Cartwright 2008, p. 995), and while mergers and acquisitions are 'complex settings for research', three issues emerge from this brief overview: (a) that our knowledge of the emotional and behavioural responses to mergers and acquisitions continues to develop; (b) that leadership is key to the integration process; and (c) that researchers need to better understand and learn more about the properties, nature and consequences of job insecurity.

As work and working lives are reshaped and refashioned by change, work stressors also evolve to reflect the changing work experience presenting researchers with the challenge as to the relevance of our work stressors measures, their interpretation, meaning and significance to those confronted with completing such measures and their usefulness in capturing the work/well-being relationship. Three themes reflect the reshaping and refashioning of work stressors.

TABLE V.1

ORGANIZATIONAL RESTRUCTURING THROUGH MERGERS AND ACQUISITIONS

o   Mergers and acquisitions are a useful strategy 'to rapidly respond to the demands of a changing global environment' (Cartwright 2008, p. 583).

o   While the drive to understand the performance and success of mergers and acquisitions has been at the heart of much research it has always been accompanied by a growing research interest in the impact of this type of organizational change on those involved and 'their emotional and behavioural response' (Cartwright & Schoenberg 2006, p. 53).

o   It is clear mergers and acquisitions are met with 'apprehension' and 'concerns' (van Dick et al. 2006, p. 569), 'a diminished degree of predictability' (Hellgren et al. 2008, p. 46) and 'clashes of culture, strategy, operations and personalities' (Allred et al. 2005, p. 23).

o   While 'the influence of organizational behaviour research in mergers and acquisitions continues to be overshadowed by that of financial scholars' (Cartwright 2008, p. 995) work stress researchers need to understand and learn more about the properties, nature and consequences of job insecurity.

The shift to knowledge work and the reshaping of work

Turning to the remaining two themes of this chapter, we first explore the growth of the service sector, where we saw the transition towards what became known as the 'new economy' quickly transformed into the 'knowledge economy' and where we are living and working in an age of information and knowledge. The story of the knowledge economy is, as Brinkley explains, a tale of how 'general purpose technology' combined with 'intellectual and knowledge assets – the intangibles' fuelled 'a profound shift' in demand 'towards high valued added, knowledge intensive goods and services' (2008, p. 9). The transformation of the economy, and in its wake, work and working lives rested on three changes: (a) the rise of knowledge intensive industries and high-tech manufacturing; (b) a shift away from investments in traditional physical assets to intangible assets such as 'software, human and organizational capital, research and development, brand equity, design and copyright'; and (c) the demand for a highly skilled workforce (Brinkley, Fauth, Mahdon & Theodoropoulou 2010, pp. 5, 9–10).

Knowledge is now an economic good, and its 'most important property' is that it is 'the ultimate economic renewable' because 'the stock of knowledge is not depleted' and its value increases as it is shared with others (Brinkley 2006, p. 5). What's more, knowledge 'has become central to the production of organizational value' (Brinkley et al. 2010, p. 17). Nevertheless, because, as a commodity, 'knowledge' is everywhere, this immediately presented the need for improved measures of what is 'knowledge work', who are the 'knowledge workers', is 'knowledge work' good work (Brinkley et al. 2010), and how does the term knowledge economy help us understand the changing nature of work and working lives? Because we live in a world where the speed of innovation is so great, defining the economy or the age is fraught with difficulties. Whether we have ever left the information age or the knowledge economy remains a moot point for, as each generation of technological change brings with it new opportunities, so knowledge itself changes in the way it is created, how it is marketed, the demand for it, the way it is accessed, evaluated and assessed, the way we think about it and the way it is consumed and used.

Describing the economy as a 'knowledge economy' shouldn't be interpreted as implying that there is a 'non-knowledge economy' as this descriptor is used to describe 'a change in economic structures, and the way firms and people operate across all sectors affecting a very wide range of occupations' (Brinkley 2008, p. 13). So when we think of the many ways in which the economy has been described there is one common theme running through them, that is, that 'the economy is becoming increasingly weightless' (Coyle & Quah 2002, p. 8). The descriptor of weightlessness captures the idea that 'creating value depends less and less on physical mass, and more and more on intangibles, such as human intelligence, creativity, and even personal warmth' (Coyle & Quah 2002, p. 8). Using weightlessness as a descriptor leaves behind the undertones associated with the idea of knowledge, freeing us and helping us better understand the impact of ubiquitous technology, the notion of seamless interconnectivity, the significance of context, the nature of 'network individualism' and its role as a 'social lubricant' (Rainie & Wellman 2014, p. 107), and the potential of a technologically driven transformation of work, working lives and lives in general.

So what does this mean for 'work'? We begin by acknowledging as we have done before (Dewe & Cooper 2012, pp. 34–35), the growth of the service sector, the job-generating ability of knowledge-based industries, the importance of innovation and entrepreneurialism, research and development, value-added design, product differentiation, fashion and marketing, the intensity of competition and the ever presence of globalization (Brinkley 2008). At the same time, management development and skill enrichment will become 'even more crucial' (Confederation of Business Industry 2007, p. 10), requiring a constant need for a greater emphasis on human resource management (Saridakis & Cooper 2013), a shift to resource-based strategies (competing through people), the expression of human resources through forms of employee engagement, value-driven rather than control-driven organizational cultures, more socially responsible management styles, an emphasis on sustainability that extends beyond the green agenda to sustainable working lives, the importance of facilitation, collaboration and lifelong learning (see Dewe & Cooper 2012, pp. 36–37), and the ideas of partnership being something more than 'a well meaning slogan' (Taylor 2005, p. 22). Work for many will become more intense, more goal and deadline directed, more project and team organized, assume an 'emotional quality', require the ability to boundary span, have the potential to be more flexible, will require a greater maintenance of work–life balance, and emphasize the importance of context, meaning and well-being (Dewe & Cooper 2012, p. 37).

Three themes emerge from this change: (a) the reshaping of organizations to reflect more organic and network structures; (b) the emphasis on resource-based strategies, and human resource management's pivotal role in bringing about sustainable success both operationally and strategically; and (c) the intensity of work itself, as the patterns of work change (Dewe & Cooper 2012, p. 37). As we have noted before (Dewe & Cooper 2012, pp. 33–34, 37), the third theme encompasses how work is arranged in relation to both time and place, the way work goals are organized, set, achieved and evaluated, how it assumes a more emotional quality, how uncertainty is more likely to accompany the work experience, how the demands for a sense of work–life balance are achieved, how the social aspects of work become more complex in terms of establishing and maintaining working relationships, communicating and collaborating, how facilitation and cooperation become skills required at all levels of management, how changing work values reflect changes in the meaning of work, and the constant need to reconcile the conflicting demands between 'what we want from work and what work provides' (see Dewe & Cooper 2012, pp. 34, 37).

Many of the changes mentioned above 'will be experienced [by workers] in different strengths across different sectors, industries and workplace' (Donkin 2010, p. 248). Yet embedded in all the rough and tumble of this change, the turbulence it creates and the economic chaos that at times accompanies it, there has remained a constant theme to focus on 'what makes good work', to understand 'why job quality in a changing economy matters' (Coats & Lekhi 2008, p. 11), to recognize that 'if we care about the capabilities of individuals to choose a life that they value then we should care about job quality' (Coats & Lekhi 2008, p. 6), that 'finding meaning in work matters to people' (Parker & Bevan 2011, p. 5) and that while it is 'a trickier task' policy makers should be concerned with measuring progress towards 'fulfilling employment' (Brown et al. 2006, p. 1). The 'good work' agenda has also attracted the attention of those monitoring the scale, growth and importance of knowledge work. While acknowledging that job quality is a pathway to health and well-being, and accepting that job quality is important across the workforce 'regardless of the degree of knowledge content in their jobs', the question 'is knowledge work better for us' is one that demands attention (Brinkley et al. 2010, p. 6). Accepting the difficulties associated with terms like 'knowledge worker' and 'knowledge economy' Brinkley nevertheless, in trying to get to grips with whether knowledge work is good work, raises the all-important question of whether the knowledge economy has 'a dark side' (2008, p. 9).

While Brinkley's research to date is reassuring, in the sense that 'this new working elite' has not made worse those existing 'divides' in the labour market, it has not, he goes on to add, done anything to improve them, concluding that 'there is no room for complacency' (2008, pp. 9–10). It wasn't long before other researchers also began to point to the 'dual nature' or 'double-edged' side to technology (Day et al. 2010; Tarafdar et al. 2007), and 'these dual and sometimes dark, effects of the implementation and use of Information and Communication Technologies' (Tarafdar et al. 2007, p. 302). The 'explosive growth of [these] end-use computing and networking technologies' (Ragu-Nathan et al. 2008, p. 417), their implementation and application, was soon to be associated with stress and a phenomenon called technostress. Technostress described 'the state of mental and physiological arousal observed in certain employees who are heavily dependent on computers in their work' (Arnetz & Wiholm 1997, p. 36). Two avenues for research accompanied the concept of technostress. The first concerned the need to understand exactly what it is about these technologies that 'ultimately leads to stress' (Ayyagari et al. 2011, p. 832). The second explored the impact of technostress, the issue of computer anxiety (Shu, Tu & Wang 2011), its pathway towards technophobia (Thorpe & Brosnan 2007) and, not forgetting of course, techno-enthusiasts (Coget 2011).

The ubiquitous nature of technology, its networking and interconnectivity capabilities soon led researchers to look beyond the concept of technostress to other types of behaviours and attitudes when considering the role of technology and its impact on the nature of work and our working lives. A body of research was soon to grow around topics that ranged from problematic internet use (Hetzel-Riggin & Pritchard 2011), to internet abuse and internet addiction (Griffiths 2010), the quality, quantity and management of emails (Whittaker, Bellotti & Moody 2005), cyberbullying (Sabella, Patchin & Hinduja 2013), sensitivity to mobile phones (Rubin, Cleare & Wessely 2008), the benefits and dangers of social networking (Turel & Serenko 2012), cyberloafing (Lim & Chen 2012) and teleworking (Bailey & Kurland 2002). Researchers have not just limited their attention to the impact of technology on behaviours, attitudes and well-being. Technology's reach extends beyond organizational boundaries, and so researchers have continued to track and explore issues like work–family (life) balance (Brough & Kalliath 2009), extending that research from the more traditional focus on spillover to issues of crossover (Bakker, Westman & van Emmerik 2009), segmentation and integration (Ashforth, Kreiner & Fugate 2000; Kreiner 2006) along with the issue of flexible working (Pardey 2013). Since the boundaries of time and place of work have been blurred and at times lost in terms of how, when and where work is performed, it's not surprising to find that researchers have also been building a corpus of research around topics like workaholism (Snir, Harpaz & Burke 2006), counterproductive work behaviours (Sackett 2002), dysfunctional behaviour (Robinson 2008), corruption in organizations (Burke, Tomlinson & Cooper 2011) and employee morale (Bowles & Cooper 2009).

A transformed weightless economy with its emphasis on value creation through intangibles that embrace knowledge, skills and creativity, its reshaping of the nature and character of work where the emphasis is on resource-based strategies, the growing significance of human resource management, and management styles that emphasize value driven leadership, collaboration, facilitation and team work, provided the context (see Dewe & Cooper 2012, p. 37) for the emergence of a new generation of work stressors. Before we turn to examine some of these new generational stressors in more detail we briefly turn our attention to the evolution of work stressors more generally, exploring how measures of more traditional stressors need to adapt and more importantly maintain their relevance in a world where work is constantly changing in terms of how, when and where work is performed and experienced.

TABLE V.2

THE SHIFT TO KNOWLEDGE WORK

o   The transformation of the economy and in its wake work and working lives rested on three changes: '[t]he rise of knowledge intensive industries and high tech manufacturing, a shift from investments in traditional physical assets to intangible assets such as 'software, human and organizational capital, research and development, brand equity, design and copyright' and the demand for a highly skilled workforce' (Brinkley et al. 2010, pp. 5, 9–10).

o   So when thinking of the many ways in which the economy can be described, a key concept is that 'the economy is becoming increasingly weightless' (Coyle & Quah 2002, p. 8).

o   Using 'weightless' as a descriptor helps us to better understand the impact of ubiquitous technology, the notion of seamless interconnectivity, the significance of context and technology's role as 'a social lubricant' (Raine & Wellman 2014, p. 107).

o   It wasn't long before researchers began to point to the 'dual nature' or 'double-edged' side to technology (Day et al. 2010; Tarafdar et al. 2007) with its implementation and application soon to be associated with stress and a phenomenon called technostress, questioning what it is about these technologies that 'ultimately leads to stress' (Ayyagari et al. 2011, p. 832).

o   Technology's reach extends beyond organizational boundaries and so researchers have continued to track and explore issues like family–life balance (Brough & Kalliath 2009).

The evolving nature of work stressors

'In one way or another', argues Barling and his co-authors, work stressors 'have attracted considerable empirical attention and public fascination' (Barling, Kelloway & Frone 2005, p. 3), not least because each of us has a strong personal interest in understanding what the causes of work stress are, and what it means to experience them. This helps to explain why, despite significant advances in our understanding of job stressors, it still remains, according to one of the seminal writers in the field 'an unfinished enterprise' (Beehr 1998, p. 843). You can understand why there is such an interest as stressors are, by nature, products of environmental circumstances, and as these circumstances change, then so must stressors change both in form and struc-ture if they are to maintain a relevance despite the fact that some appear to take on 'a timeless quality' (Jex & Yankelevich 2008, p. 498). It is these changing circumstances that also provide the context from which, as we have discussed (see Dewe & Cooper 2012, p. 94), new generations of stressors emerge. So, to provide a sense of how work stressors, products of a changing environment, adapt we briefly explore what is a rich history of change before turning to describe in more detail a new generation of stressors. Finally we explore how the constancy of change challenges established measurement practices, questioning not only their capacity to capture the work con-text, but also their utility and relevance to express the work experience, its intensity, its meaning and its ability to convey affect.

TABLE V.3

THE RESHAPING OF WORK

o   You can understand why there is such an interest in stressors as they are, by nature, products of environmental circumstances and as these circum-stances change, then so must stressors change both in form and structure, if they are to maintain a relevance despite the fact that some appear to take on 'a timeless quality' (Jex & Yankelevich 2008, p. 498).

o   So it is against a backdrop of social, economic and political upheaval demand-ing jobs, a greater urgency to restructure, a more complex human resource management environment, and the ever presence of technological change and innovation that these changes simply reinforce feelings of job insecurity, the intensity of work, the demands of technology and a deterioration in working relationships and work behaviours (Dewe et al. 2010).

o   Work stress researchers have been 'confront[ed] with a something of a dif-ferent challenge' (Barling et al. 2005, p. 3), that is, that there are a considerable number of issues – potential stressors (e.g. terrorism, organizational politics

> and justice) – that organizations and employees face that have been explored in the general psychology literature but have not been addressed 'from a work stress perspective' and so haven't yet received the empirical attention that this perspective offers (Barling et al. 2005, p. 3).
>
> o   A further challenge for work stress researchers is to 'be alert' to questions of whether 'the standard ways of working' still prevail and the need in terms of stressor relevance give adequate attention to the variety of 'non standard ways' of working that are rapidly increasing. So it is no longer the case that non-standard work can be assumed 'to look like' standard work – making 'non-standard working' a topic 'in its own right' (Ashford et al. 2007, p. 67), and raising implications for stressor identification.
>
> o   Also the reshaping of work means challenges for measurement – how the consistency of change challenges established measurement practices, questions their capacity to capture the contemporary work context, their usefulness and relevance to express that work experience, its intensity, its meaning and its ability to convey affect (Dewe & Cooper 2012).

Stressors: A brief history of change

Challenges and difficulties confront anyone exploring the history of stressors, for it is a history of the concept of stress itself, a history within a history, a history of change and a history that needs to confront, like the discipline itself, the old assumptions about the 'images we carry of work', and the new work that is emerging (Ashford et al. 2007, p. 67), and what it is that makes a form of organizing new (Puranam, Alexy & Reitzig 2014). The idea that the history of stressors is, in many ways, nothing more and no different from the history of stress itself arises because the role and significance of stressors has been simply enshrined in that history when stress, as an independent variable, was defined as a stimulus and identifying potential sources of stress became the principal theme of stimulus-based models of stress (Cooper et al. 2001, p. 15). Definitions offer a sense of time and place, and present researchers with an understanding of why particular approaches prevailed, and so this definition (stimulus) and this time gave researchers the licence to begin to identify and categorize the nature of stressors themselves (see Dewe & Cooper 2012, pp. 90–92; Dewe et al. 2010).

Identifying sources of work stress can be traced, as we have noted before (see Dewe & Cooper 2012, p. 94), to the work of Kahn and his colleagues when they noted that 'conflict and ambiguity are among the major characteristics of our society and we are marked by them' (Kahn, Wolfe, Quinn, Snoek & Rosenthal 1964, p. 3). Pointing to two 'dominant societal trends' (Kahn et al. 1964, p. 5) – the growth of large corporations with their rules, regulations and levels of bureaucracy and the

increasing significance of technology – Kahn and his colleagues laid the foundations, and the first category of stressors were expressed through the concepts of role
conflict, role ambiguity and later role overload. Stressors that, even today, still have
a remarkable presence and continue to attract considerable attention (Dewe et al.
2010), with researchers exploring how changing work roles and demands 'continue
to enrich and develop' our understanding (Hellgren et al. 2008, p. 61) and where
and why more research is needed before our work can be said to be complete
(Beehr & Glazer 2005). Others were soon to contribute with frameworks for cate-
gorizing stressors laying the groundwork and setting the benchmarks against which
change and evolution could be measured (Beehr 1985, 1998; Beehr & Newman
1978; Cooper & Marshall 1976, 1980; Ivancevich & Matteson 1980; McGrath 1970;
Quick & Quick 1984; Sutherland & Cooper 1988). As noted in earlier chapters,
as our understanding of the concept of stress developed and focused more on its
'transactional' properties, the definition of stress as a stimulus has taken on 'more of a
historical value' (Dewe et al. 2010, p. 3), but the idea of continuing to understand the
nature of stressors through their evolving properties remains crucial if the authority
of the term is to be maintained and assume a level of relevance.

Before moving to the evolving nature of stressors, it is interesting to touch on
the idea of a history within a history. As mentioned, the history of stressors is part
of the broader history of the stress concept as it moved through various iterations
from a focus on its interactional properties (stimulus-response) to the sequencing
and unfolding of a stressful encounter, where definitions required researchers to
explore the nature of the 'transaction', and those processes that linked the individual and the environment (Lazarus 1999). But the development of stressors has
had its own history within a history as for a time research attention turned to the
idea of the role and importance of critical life events (Holmes & Masuda 1974;
Holmes & Rahe 1967; Dohrenwend & Dohrenwend 1974). The debate that followed this work ranged (Cooper & Dewe 2004, pp. 41–51) across a number of
issues but settled on two: whether life events were best measured objectively or
subjectively (see Dohrenwend & Shrout 1985; Jones & Kinman 2001; Lazarus,
DeLongis, Folkman & Gruen 1985), or whether 'daily hassles and uplifts' (Kanner,
Coyne, Schaefer & Lazarus 1981, p. 1) had more utility as a measure because
they more closely reflected individual experiences (Jones & Kinman 2001). The
debate ebbed and flowed for almost a decade before the interest in critical 'life
event research' began to wane (Cooper & Dewe 2004, pp. 47–51). Two reasons
are offered for this. Both touch a nerve when considering the measurement of
stressors. The first offered by Lazarus (1999) concerned the failure to give enough
attention to the meanings individuals give to such events, and the second stems
from the view that the 'list of events did not keep up-to-date or [remain] comprehensive enough' (Cooper & Dewe 2004, p. 51).

We now turn to how stressor research has been nurtured and shaped by the forces
discussed, not just in this chapter, but in those chapters that have preceded it. Looking

back over the 1980s, Burke points to what he describes as 'increasingly important contemporary sources' of stressors tempered by 'the effects of the economic recession' (1988, p. 93; Dewe & Cooper 2012, p. 94) including mergers and acquisitions, job future ambiguity and insecurity and organizational locking-in where employees felt 'boxed-in'. 'It would not be an exaggeration', Burke concluded from his review, to say that 'occupational stress has become a central topic in the field of organizational behavior' (1988, p. 106). The 1980s also witnessed the spread of computers through the workplace, with mounting concerns about how this innovation may 'present more difficulties' in terms of adaptation and coping 'than many work situations' (Briner & Hockey 1988, p. 135). By the 1990s Dewe and his colleagues noted that against a backdrop of social, economic and political change, more cognitively demanding jobs, a greater urgency to restructure, a more complex human resource environment, and the ever presence of technological change and innovation, these forces simply reinforced feelings of job insecurity, the intensity of work, the demands of technology and a deterioration in working relationships and work behaviours (Dewe et al. 2010, pp. 233–239; Dewe & Cooper 2012, p. 94). So by the time the new millennium was to mark its first five years the term 'contemporary stressors' had grown to cover, because of their salience and reach, those stressors that captured the impact of technology, the issue of job insecurity, the continually evolving nature of work–life demands, and the challenging behaviours they provoked (Barling et al. 2005; Sulsky & Smith 2005; Cooper & Robertson 2013).

Yet it was not to end there, as researchers were to be confronted by 'something of a different challenge' (Barling et al. 2005, p. 3). This challenge required researchers to recognize that there are a considerable number of issues – indeed potential stressors – that organizations and employees faced that have been explored in the general organizational behaviour/psychology literature, but have not been addressed 'from a work stress perspective' and so have not yet received the empirical attention that this perspective offers (Barling et al. 2005, p. 3). Examples of these issues and their potency as stressors include: terrorism (Inness & Barling 2005); poor leadership (Kelloway, Sivanathan, Francis & Barling 2005); organizational politics (Harris & Kacmar 2005); and organizational justice (Cropanzano, Goldman & Benson 2005); not forgetting the growing body of work on workplace violence (Budd, Arvey & Lawless 1996; Kelloway, Barling & Hurrell 2006; LeBlanc & Kelloway 2002). While our attention is on contemporary work stressors, their evolution and how they are expressed in work, we need also to acknowledge the research that continues on more established stressors and how they are refined and need to be continuity assessed to ensure that they maintain a sense of relevance and express the nature of the work experience. Examples here would include the work on refining our understanding of the nature of role stressors (Beehr & Glazer 2005; Hellgren et al. 2008), issues of crossover (Bakker et al. 2009) and segmentation and integration in relation to work–life balance (Ashforth et al. 2000; Kreiner 2006).

Finally, work stress researchers, like all in the discipline, need to be alert to the 'change that is clearly afoot' and how the assumption that the 'standard ways of working' still prevail, fails to give adequate attention to the variety of 'non-standard ways' of working that are rapidly increasing. It is no longer the case that non-standard working can be assumed to 'look like' standard working, making 'nonstandard work a topic worthy of study' in its own right (Ashford et al. 2007, p. 67). Researchers need now to ensure that meeting the challenges of capturing the nature and experiences of what is best described as a 'blended workforce', where standard and nonstandard workers work together, needs at the very least new theories and new measures that 'are central to filling in a portrait of this new future' (Ashford et al. 2007, p. 106). In a similar way, when the question of 'what makes a form of organizing new?' is posed, then, as Puranam and his colleagues suggest, this requires an exploration of what it is that is 'novel and unique' about solutions to the universal processes of organizations (Puranam et al. 2014, p. 177). The detailed analysis by Puranam and his colleagues, and their approach to the issue of novelty and newness, represents another challenge for researchers wishing to better understand the changing nature of how work is organized and how measures need to be attuned to those work features that make a difference. From here and from this context of change, history and evolution we turn in the next chapter to exploring a new generation of stressors and the measurement challenges that face researchers when attempting to capture the contemporary work experience.

Summary

Our aim in this chapter, whilst acknowledging the complexity of the forces of change, is to explore how, as work and working lives are reshaped and refashioned by change, work stressors also evolve to reflect the changing nature of the work experience and so present researchers with challenges as to the relevance of our measures, their interpretation, meaning and significance to those completing them and their usefulness in capturing the work/well-being relationship. By thinking in terms of three themes that express the forces of change we signal the importance of the context and the descriptive knowledge it provides to understanding why different stressors emerge when they do; the importance of refining our measures so they reflect the changing nature of the work experience endorsing the significance of the concept of relevance and reflecting its importance as a methodological tool. We suggest that three themes reflect the reshaping and refashioning of work stressors: organizational restructuring through mergers and acquisitions; the shift to knowledge work; and the reshaping of work. These three themes represent the 'global focus' (Gratton 2014, p. 24) but, as Gratton reminds us, 'work takes place in the context of families, expectations and hopes; it takes place within the context of the community and in the context of economic and political structures' (2014, p. 25).

So the identifying and measuring of stressors is all about us, because we have a strong personal interest in understanding what the causes of work stress are, and what it means to experience them; suggesting and endorsing the importance of refining stressor measures and the significance of the concept of relevance. But as we intimated in the beginning of this summary this prologue sets a context and offers through that context the prescriptive knowledge that gives us the opportunity to understand why stressor measurement is important, how stressors are anchored by a time and place and why tools like refining our measurement practices and establishing their relevance are so critical to meeting the obligations we have to those whose working lives we research.

VI

A NEW GENERATION OF STRESSORS AND THE CHALLENGES OF MEASUREMENT

This chapter begins by exploring a new generation of work stressors that capture and express the change that has occurred. It illustrates how work stressors of all kinds are shaped and fashioned by such change and how this imposes on researchers an obligation to ensure that stressors reflect the work experience, its meaning and its impact. We turn briefly in this chapter to the idea of 'economic stress', and from there begin our discussion of stressors that reflect this new generation. These stressors include job insecurity and its allied concept of flexibility, technostress, and work–life balance crossover and segmentation. We also explore what are the new generation of work behaviours that are provoked by this change, stressors which include counter-productive behaviours, addictive behaviours, bullying, and violence and aggression. Finally, we focus, as we have done before, on the challenges measuring work stressors presents for researchers, exploring the difference between describing a stressor and defining it, and giving it meaning, and whether and in what way workplace stressor measures are actually measuring what we think they are (see Dewe & Cooper 2012, pp. 95–97). We also rehearse, as we have before, the fact that the multi-dimensional nature of stressor measures means that there is a need to explore the idea of 'within' stressor relationships, investigating the relationships between items in a scale and the consequences this has for interpretation. We then turn our attention to the relationship between stressors, their potential cumulative relationship, their combined influence and whether stressors have specific or more general affects (see Dewe & Cooper 2012, pp. 95–97; Trenberth & Dewe 2006).

Concepts like 'economic distress', and later 'economic stress', took root following the difficult recessionary economic times of the 1980s and the need to better integrate and understand the impact of the economy and economic circumstances and their consequences on the 'structure and quality of family life' (Voydanoff 1990, p. 1099). The two indicators that were soon to capture the nature of economic stress were job insecurity and job loss (Klehe, Van Vianen & Zikic 2012; Voydanoff 1990), coupled with economic strain and economic deprivation. While acknowledging the devastating and tragic consequences of job loss (Karren 2012), our attention here is directed towards what has been described as one of the challenges facing organizational psychology in the new millennium: understanding those 'threatening characteristics' and what are now fast becoming 'universal features' that accompany employment – 'uncertainty and job insecurity' (Fernandez-Ballesteros 2002, p. 2). Our review of job insecurity follows the pattern of other researchers (De Witte 2005; Greenhalgh & Rosenblatt 1984, 2010; Klandermans & van Vuuren 1999; Probst 2005; Reisel & Probst 2010), and explores job insecurity the concept, its measurement and consequences, its management and future directions for research.

Job insecurity

To understand the concept of job insecurity, we need to acknowledge the powerful way in which the concept of job security shaped early theories of needs and motivation, where continuity of employment was fundamental to the meaning of work, motivation and job satisfaction (Greenhalgh & Rosenblatt 1984, 2010; Herzberg 1959; Maslow 1943). So, it is not surprising, when economic and organizational factors threatened such a central individual need, that the primary concern of researchers turned to the issue of job insecurity and its consequences. It was the seminal work of Greenhalgh and Rosenblatt (1984) that laid the foundations for understanding the meaning of job insecurity, and their model offered a 'primary theoretical' framework for exploring its nature, causes and consequences (Greenhalgh & Rosenblatt 2010, p. 7). At the risk of understating the detail and richness of their work, these authors conceived of job insecurity in terms of a perceived threat derived from organizational cues and messages to the probability of a loss of job continuity or the loss of valued job features, and the sense of powerlessness that accompanied such a threat (1984, pp. 440–442; 2010, p. 9). Job insecurity was defined by these authors as the 'perceived powerlessness to maintain desired continuity in a threatened job situation' (1984, p. 438), and embraced four 'essential features' that included 'desired continuity', 'threat', 'job features at risk' and 'powerlessness' (2010, pp. 9–10).

Other definitions were soon to follow, as reflects a concept in transition (see De Witte 1999; Sverke, Hellgren & Näswall 2002), with job insecurity definitions generally capturing the notion of a 'subjective experience reflecting uncertainty about future employment' (Sverke, De Witte, Näswall & Hellgren 2010, p. 175). Job insecurity was soon classified as a work stressor (Barling & Kelloway 1996; Probst 2005; Strazdins, D'Souza, Lim, Broom & Rodgers 2004; Sverke et al. 2010), with the seriousness of its consequences not standing 'that far behind' those of other economic stressors including job loss (Klehe et al. 2012,

p. 747). Measures too were soon to follow a more systematic approach, with
instruments capturing the essential features of Greenhalgh and Rosenblatt's
framework (Ashford, Lee & Bobko 1989), or through considering its utility by
developing a more simplified version of the Ashford model (Lee, Bobko & Chen
2006) or cross-nationally validating the Job Insecurity Scale first developed by De
Witte (see Elst, De Witte & De Cuyper 2014).

Others have operationalized job insecurity by: identifying different levels of job
insecurity (Mohr 2000); or distinguishing between how secure employees think
they are versus the perception of how likely they are to keep their job (Sverke,
Hellgren & Näswall 2006); or by considering the discrepancy between the level of
security they believe they have and the level they would prefer (Jacobson & Hartley
1991); or by considering the merits of single item versus multi-dimensional measures (see Sverke & Hellgren 2002; Sverke et al. 2002, 2006). While researchers
acknowledged that different research objectives will demand the need for different
measures, many point to conceptual and operational issues that still need to be
discussed and debated when job insecurity is the focus. These include global versus
multi-dimensional, objective versus subjective, qualitative versus quantitative, and
cognitive versus affective approaches to measurement (Hellgren, Sverke & Isaksson
1999; Sverke & Hellgren 2002; Sverke et al. 2002, 2006). Exploring these issues
will give a sense of how the notion of job insecurity was shaped, its boundaries set
and its nature expressed. So, we turn first to the objective–subjective debate, one
that confronts all work stressor researchers when investigating the realities of the
work experience.

The refining and reshaping of job insecurity – its multi-faceted characteristics; its subjective and objective characteristics

If job insecurity is, as most definitions assume, individual and subjective (Sverke
et al. 2006), and if this subjectivity is the 'cornerstone' from which our understanding builds (Sverke et al. 2002, p. 243), then where does the distinction between
the objective and the subjective lie? It lies, it seems, in that job insecurity implies
uncertainty about the future (De Witte 1999), and whilst the quality and nature
of this uncertainty is itself in need of further exploration (Bussing 1999), it is the
forces that give rise to this uncertainty, these 'objective threat[s]' (Greenhalgh &
Rosenblatt 1984, p. 440) or antecedent conditions, that would seem to separate the
objective from the subjective, suggesting that in this way job insecurity may 'occur
as a contextual phenomenon' (Sverke et al. 2006, p. 5). However, as it is these forces
that help shape the individuals' perceptions of the threat (Greenhalgh & Rosenblatt
2010), it is this interaction, as we shall see, that is generally viewed as best expressing
the experience of job insecurity (Sverke et al. 2006). Some researchers also suggest
that feelings of job insecurity can occur irrespective of whether an objective threat
is present (Kinnunen, Mauno, Natti & Happonen 1999).

Nevertheless, if these forces or antecedent conditions are reflective of objective insecurity, then they could include macro-environmental factors (De Witte 2005), the nature of the employment contract (Bussing 1999; Strazdins et al. 2004), various formal or informal organizational communications and announcements, organizational prompts and clues intended or unintended and rumours (Greenhalgh & Rosenblatt 1984, p.441; 2010), and perhaps personality characteristics (Sverke et al. 2006). More 'research is warranted' to better understand the role individual characteristics play in relation to job insecurity (Sverke & Hellgren 2002, p. 37), just as it is clear more attention needs to be given to advancing our understanding of objective insecurity (Bussing 1999). It is also important to recognize that job insecurity involves an interaction between its objective and subjective components, that definitions reflect the mismatch between the two, and that both are part of this wider complexity that when taken together as a process offers considerable explanatory power (Klandermans & van Vuuren 1999). So, if 'the starting point' for understanding job insecurity depends on individual perceptions (Kinnunen et al. 1999, p. 244), and if 'most authors agree' that job insecurity is subjective (De Witte 2005, p. 1), then how is subjective insecurity experienced?

Understanding 'subjective job insecurity' involves three steps: (a) understanding the process; (b) understanding how perceptions of the experience are derived; and (c) understanding what they are being built on. The process was first outlined by Greenhalgh and Rosenblatt, where they described the perceived 'subjective threat' as emerging from a cognitively transformed objective threat (1984, p. 440). This focus, and this process, imply that it is these perceptions that inform the 'subjective reality', as distinct from the 'objective reality', and help to explain how two individuals faced with the same situation experience it differently (Sverke et al. 2002, p. 243). Others use the language of Lazarus's (1999) transactional stress theory to reinforce the idea that stressors generally achieve their meaning and significance through such cognitive processes, that meaning is dependent on such a process and that it is this meaning that exerts its power and authority (Kinnunen et al. 1999), suggesting that job insecurity stems from the individual's appraisal of the work environment (Hellgren et al. 1999). It is possible to quibble and point to the need to better understand the meanings individuals actually give to job insecurity, as distinct from how they feel or the probability of events occurring, or some mismatch or discrepancy or the level of uncertainty. However, the fact that researchers are attempting to distinguish between 'describing the event' and 'giving it meaning', suggests that the ideas embodied in the concepts of appraisal (Lazarus 1999) are attracting the attention they deserve (Dewe & Cooper 2012).

Job insecurity – its quantitative and qualitative characteristics

This still leaves the question of what is being appraised or evaluated. Researchers have for some time distinguished 'loss of continuity of employment', often seen as more global and unitary in its approach, from the loss of important job features

(Hellgren et al. 1999, p. 180), seen more in terms of job insecurity's multi-faceted character and the need to capture as broad a view as possible of its nature (Rosenblatt, Talmud & Ruvio 1999). In terms of a multi-faceted approach, and the dictum that enough facets of the wider employment relationship are included to ensure that the nature of the uncertainty being faced is captured (Sverke & Hellgren 2002), then this wider view would certainly include the sense of 'powerlessness' that accompanies uncertainty, loss and threat (Greenhalgh & Rosenblatt 1984, 2010). The discussion around the global versus the multi-faceted nature of job insecurity drew researchers towards labelling the focus on perceived loss of job continuity as 'quantitative job security', with the loss of features of the employment relationship being labelled 'qualitative job security' (Hellgren et al. 1999). The use of the quantitative–qualitative descriptors drew attention to the need to explore the differential consequences of these two aspects of job insecurity (Hellgren et al. 1999), although meta-analysis does point to quantitative job insecurity having a stronger relationship with outcome variables, perhaps because of the way in which it expresses more of the job insecurity experience (Sverke et al. 2006). Nevertheless both, as research suggests, are important work-related stressors (De Witte, De Cuyper, Handaja, Sverke, Naswall & Hellgren 2010; Roskies & Louis-Guerin 1990; Sverke et al. 2010).

Job insecurity – its cognitive and affective characteristics

Researchers were to offer one further refinement to better our understanding of the nature of job insecurity. This refinement came when the distinction was made between the relative emphasis on 'cognitive versus affective' elements of job insecurity and their measurement (Borg & Dov 1992; Huang, Lee, Ashford, Chen & Ren 2010; Huang, Niu, Lee & Ashford 2012; Ito & Brotheridge 2007; Pienaar, De Witte, Hellgren & Sverke 2013). The former refers to the perception of the possibility of a loss of job continuity, or of the loss of particularly satisfying features of the job (i.e. negative job changes), whilst the latter focuses on the affective elements of the experience – the emotional reaction or as Pienaar and his colleagues succinctly put it 'thinking about it' and 'feeling about it' (2013, p. 4). This distinction, it was argued, is necessary, although both are expected to relate to one another, not just because 'it made intuitive sense' (Pienaar et al. 2013, p. 4), but because the perceived judgment of a loss of continuity or job features is simply different from one's worry, anxiety or concern about this change (Huang et al. 2010, 2012). The distinction was also necessary to ensure that the same emphasis and empirical examination be given to the affective nature of job insecurity as had been given to its cognitive nature, and to this end there is a need to continue to work towards achieving agreement on how this distinction should be operationalized (Huang et al. 2010).

From its early beginnings the distinction between cognitive and affective job insecurity continued to garner support with researchers agreeing that these two dimensions can be clearly separated (Huang et al. 2010, 2012; Mauno & Kinnunen 2002;

Pienaar et al. 2013; Staufenbiel & Konig 2011) although discussion still continues to swirl around the elements that capture the nature of each dimension. This distinction, and this research, draws researchers closer to the work of Lazarus (1999) and his concept of appraisal, particularly 'primary appraisal', where individuals construct personal meanings from the events themselves. In this way researchers point to the 'appraisal of threat' defined by Lazarus as consisting 'of the possibility of some damage in the future' (1999, p. 76), and generally the attempt to capture this appraisal by assessing the amount of perceived uncertainty or likelihood of future job or job facet discontinuity (Huang et al., 2012; Mauno & Kinnunen 2002; Pienaar et al. 2013; Staufenbiel & Konig 2011). This work is important because of the potential explanatory power that resides in concepts like appraisal.

Perhaps having made this distinction, the field is now ready when exploring cognitive job insecurity to move to the next level of analysis, where the focus is on capturing the personal meanings that accompany uncertainty and likelihood; meanings that are subjectively distinct from the components that create them. Evidence may already be present in the literature when concepts like powerlessness (Greenhalgh & Rosenblatt 1984) are thought of more in terms of giving meaning to experiences like uncertainty or likelihood, or whether notions like survival or having someone to blame need now to be revisited and examined through the lens of appraisal and meaning (Jacobson 1987). All the while taking encouragement from the work of Roskies and Louis-Guerin in terms of the importance of the 'mediating role' played by '*subjective appraisal of risk*', emphasizing the need for more work on better understanding these processes and their meaning (1990, p. 356). Whatever direction future research takes, examining item content remains important (Staufenbiel & Konig 2011), as does how items best characterize the experience being investigated to ensure both relevance and fit (Sverke et al. 2006). It is clear that cognitive and affective job insecurity are independent but related. Each offers a mechanism for understanding their differential effects in terms of antecedent conditions and outcomes (Huang et al. 2012; Pienaar et al. 2013; Staufenbiel & Konig 2011), and how, when and in what way each are related (Huang et al. 2010, 2012).

Consequences of job insecurity

Considerable work has been done on refining and shaping the concept of job insecurity, giving researchers a more robust framework within which to examine its consequences, although agreement has yet to be reached on the 'exact definition' of job insecurity (Selenko & Batinic 2013, p. 725) and the need for 'a *commonly* used scale' (Elst et al. 2014, p. 365). Nevertheless 'an extensive research tradition' has confirmed the negative consequences of job insecurity on individuals and organizations (De Witte 2005, p. 2), points to job insecurity as 'one of the more important stressors' (De Witte 1999, p. 173), reinforces the view that job security can no longer be taken for granted (Roskies, Louis-Guerin & Fournier 1993), confirms that job insecurity has all the characteristics of a chronic stressor (De Witte 2005) as 'an ambiguous,

chronic menace' (Roskies & Louis-Guerin 1990, p. 346), and that in line with the
Lazarus tradition that the anticipation of harm (i.e. job insecurity) can have 'effects
as potent as experiencing the harm itself' (De Witte 1999, 2005; Roskies et al. 1993,
p. 619; Sverke & Hellgren 2002). Job insecurity has far-reaching short and long term
consequences, which impact on the organization and its effectiveness, on employee
attitudes, performance and other work related behaviours, emotions, health and
well-being (Cheng & Chan 2008; De Witte 1999, 2005; Sverke & Hellgren 2002;
Sverke et al. 2002, 2006), with moderator analysis pointing to the consequences of
job insecurity for different types of employees and occupational groups (Cheng &
Chan 2008; Roskies & Louis-Guerin 1990; Sverke et al. 2002).

When questioning where job insecurity research is heading (Klandermans &
van Vuuren 1999), then, it is clear that the call for more longitudinal work to
explore issues of causality, its long term effects – including its duration and how
the process develops – and at what point in that process do different consequences
of job insecurity emerge (Cheng & Chan 2008; De Witte 2005; Elst et al. 2014;
Klandermans & van Vuuren 1999; Sverke et al. 2002) is very important. It is also
important that the long term consequences of 'choosing to emphasize or ignore
the danger of job loss or deterioration' (Roskies & Louis-Guerin 1990, p. 357)
are being heeded or receiving the attention they deserve. Reviewers continue to
emphasize the need for more research on how the different aspects of job insecurity relate to different consequences to better understand its differential effects
(Klandermans & van Vuuren 1999; Sverke & Hellgren 2002; Sverke et al. 2006),
the need for more work on its spillover effects on relationships outside of work
as well as on other relationships at work (Greenhalgh & Rosenblatt 2010; Sverke
et al. 2006), the need for work that continues to explore how job insecurity is
related to factors like work intensity, burnout, compliance behaviours and depression (Sverke et al. 2006), not forgetting its organizational consequences (De Witte
2005; Greenhalgh & Rosenblatt 2010), to continue to explore the role of moderators and their buffering of the negative impact of job insecurity (Cheng & Chan
2008; De Witte 2005; Sverke et al. 2002) and the need to continue to develop and
test theoretical frameworks (De Witte 2005).

All these demands simply reflect a field that is, at one level, not just required to
broaden our knowledge and, at another to provide a more in-depth understanding
(De Witte 2005, p. 5), but is also required to keep up with the accelerated rate of
organizational change. It is a topic that will continue to 'characterize working life',
testing the resources of those who work in organizations and those who research
such experiences (Sverke et al. 2002, p. 259).

Job insecurity interventions

When the question is raised as to how the negative consequences of job insecurity
can be reduced (Sverke et al. 2006), two approaches emerge from the literature.
The first is process focused and emphasizes the necessity for intervention strategies

(De Witte 2005), offering what may be strategies that represent best practice. These practices have, as their aim, the need to 'reduce the unpredictability and uncontrollability' associated with job insecurity and in this way 'avoid or at least mitigate' some of its negative consequences (De Witte 2005, p. 4). Such strategies include providing accurate information, by making communications 'open and honest' particularly about future events, by encouraging participation in the change process, by designing a process that is perceived as fair and equitable, and by recognizing the importance of individual differences, personality, the need for social support and where possible a greater sense of balance in terms of efforts and rewards (De Witte 2005, pp. 4–5; Sverke et al. 2006, pp. 17–20). Nevertheless, as De Witte suggests, reducing the consequences of job insecurity 'is not wholly possible' as a 'certain degree of insecurity…is perhaps unavoidable in economically troubled times' (2005, p. 4) requiring organizational strategies to also broaden their focus to contextual issues like social support, employability and the balance between effort and rewards. While researching these practices and evaluating their impact has been described as a 'fruitful direction for future research' (Sverke et al. 2006, p. 20), there is no doubt about the difficulties faced as ambiguity, uncertainty and concern are all hallmarks accompanying job insecurity which are inescapable during times of economic upheaval but also since job insecurity is now simply likely to remain central to the work experience (De Witte 2005; Sverke et al. 2006).

Job insecurity – the concept versus the concept of employability

The second approach also reflects organizations in a state of 'perpetual motion', where the need to question and challenge established concepts, theories and practices to test their relevance, their utility and their ability to reflect contemporary work experiences seems to be the only constant (Baruch & Hind 1999, p. 295). At the nub of this second approach is the notion that job security is 'no longer a valid concept' (Baruch & Hind 1999, p. 295), and is 'increasingly becoming a thing of the past' (Kluytmans & Ott 1999, p. 261). This means that intervention strategies need now to explore a different basis for establishing job security, one that moves beyond the notion of 'lifetime employment' to one where the emphasis is on 'lifetime employability' (Forrier & Sels 2003, p. 103). Here the emphasis is on employability, where continuous individual self development (Baruch & Hind 1999) offers an opportunity to build one's capacity for being continuously employed (Forrier & Sels 2003), to hone one's abilities to 'make employment transitions' (De Cuyper, Bernhard-Oettel, Berntson, De Witte & Alarco 2008, p. 490), to retain and improve one's 'attractiveness' in the labour market (Rothwell & Arnold 2007, p. 24), to successfully adapt to the demands of today's economy (Fugate, Kinicki & Ashforth 2004), ushering in a new type of employment relationship (Baruch & Hind 1999) and illustrating the nature of boundaryless (Arthur 1994) and protean (Hall 2004) careers.

The term 'employability' has, over its history, served a number of purposes with it now being seen more in terms of an 'alternative to job security', functioning as a mechanism for developing transferable career opportunities both within (internal employability) and beyond (external employability) current employment (Forrier & Sels 2003, p. 104). In this way it serves as a vehicle for career development and advancement (De Cuyper & De Witte 2010), a personal resource that should be fostered (De Cuyper, Makikangas, Kinnunen, Mauno & De Witte 2012), a channel for being responsive to one's value (Direnzo & Greenhaus 2011), whilst at the same time illustrating both its benefits for individuals and its relevance for combatting the menacing prevalence of job insecurity (De Cuyper et al. 2008). In addition to distinguishing between 'internal and external employability' researchers also point to the difference between quantitative and qualitative employability, where the former refers to all job opportunities, whereas the latter takes more of a quality focus taking into account whether the job opportunity is 'somewhat better' than the current job (De Cuyper & De Witte 2010, p. 637).

While employability is largely person centred (Fugate et al. 2004), those components that describe it cover a range of personal issues including, for example, how people see themselves (career identity), how prepared and capable they are to change (personal adaptability) and their capacity to recognize and realize career opportunities (social and human capital), helping to make employability a 'synergistic collection' of personal attributes that are 'energized and directed' by a person's career identity (Fugate et al. 2004, pp. 18, 19–25). Nevertheless, as befits a concept in development, the list of dimensions and the items that represent them has been expanded and broadened (De Cuyper et al. 2012; Forrier & Sels 2003; Fugate & Kinicki 2008; Rothwell & Arnold 2007; Langan-Fox & Cooper 2014), making it difficult on the one hand to reach agreement on the items that make up each dimension and, indeed, the dimensions themselves (Forrier & Sels 2003), yet necessary on the other hand to provide insights that allow a sense of conceptual clarity, consistency and relevance to emerge – notwithstanding employability's 'time and place related' nature (Forrier & Sels 2003, p. 107) and the potential pattern and complexity of relationships that give it its synergistic qualities.

Nevertheless, despite these complexities, the notion of employability and perceived external employability (De Cuyper et al. 2012) has achieved a resonance among researchers, where it is now regarded 'as the upcoming critical resource for workers in times of high job insecurity' (De Cuyper & De Witte 2010, p. 636). So employability, however it is conceptualized, heralds the beginning of a new era, a fundamental shift in employment relations, where the organization 'is simply another stakeholder' albeit a significant one in individual career development (Baruch & Hind 1999, p. 300), and where organizations along with policy makers need now to consider how employability is managed (Kluytmans & Ott 1999), what processes are involved (Forrier & Sels 2003), what constitutes best practice, and whether personal employability planning will soon become the new human resource language of the future. As the concept of employability becomes comfortably embedded in the ebb and flow of management practice, it offers researchers the opportunity to further our understanding of whether, and in what way, employability may reflect a form of 'work specific proactive adaptability' (Fugate et al. 2004, p.14), a mechanism for 'securing one's labour market position' (De Cuyper et al. 2008, p.488), a personal coping resource (De Cuyper et al. 2012), the role it plays in relation to well-being (De Cuyper et al. 2008; Chen & Cooper 2014) and how its different dimensions relate to one another, their patterning and their differential effects.

Flexibility and flexicurity – a postscript

As the notion of employability continues to gain currency, it too needs to be sensitive to other changes in working life, and so is often linked to the increasingly 'flexible nature' of the labour market and, like job insecurity, as we head into the new millennium, another 'threatening characteristic' of the changing nature of work (Klandermans & van Vuuren 1999; Fernandez-Ballesteros 2002, p. 2; Sverke & Hellgren 2002). Of course 'flexibility' has long been a part of working life, with scholars when thinking about the transformation of work including flexibility under the heading of 'new ways of working'; a term that covers not just the changes transforming work but how they facilitate flexibility 'in the time and location of work' (Blok, Groenesteijn, Schelvis & Vink 2012, p. 5075). Like employability, flexibility is first described in terms of work (internal) or job (external) flexibility; with internal (work) flexibility reflecting time, function and permanent contract, whereas external (job) flexibility reflects function but no contract (Hesselink & van Vuuren 1999, p. 276). There is also a growing interest in the concept of flexicurity, where in some form and in some combination general or precise elements of each are brought together, although there are issues that surround how flexicurity is defined (Chung 2012). Nevertheless the objective of promoting both flexibility and security combined in some form or another offers new opportunities to establish different approaches to employment policies (Ackers & Oliver 2007; Sparrow, Hird & Cooper 2015), practices and conditions.

A substantial body of research has grown around the nature, type, scope, prevalence and uptake of flexibility, spanning a wide range of contexts, which include type of work, work characteristics, work-employment arrangements, management and organizational processes, policies and procedures. This research also explores a wide range of issues including its consequences and outcomes, its impact on well-being, its antecedents, its costs and benefits, its challenges and obstacles, its trends, its issues for gender, its role as a stressor, its impact on work–life balance and work–family conflicts and its contributions to the changing rhythm of life, values, hopes, aspirations and expectations. This postscript is simply to acknowledge the importance of flexibility in shaping the structure and management of contemporary organizations, its significance in transforming working lives, its impact on all aspects of society, its negative and positive role in redesigning the employment relationship and psychological contract.

TABLE VI.1

A NEW GENERATION OF STRESSORS

JOB INSECURITY

- ○ 'A perceived threat derived from organizational cues and messages to the probability of a loss of job continuity or the loss of valued job features and the sense of powerless that accompanies such a threat' (Greenhalgh & Rosenblatt 1984, pp. 440–442; 2010, p. 90).
- ○ Job insecurity has been refined and reshaped and explored in terms of its subjective–objective characteristics (Sverke et al. 2006), its quantitative–qualitative characteristics (Hellgren et al. 1999) and its cognitive–affective characteristics (Borg & Dov 1992; Huang et al. 2010; Huang et al. 2012; Ito & Brotheridge 2007; Pienaar et al. 2013).

JOB INSECURITY AND THE CONCEPT OF EMPLOYABILITY

- ○ The distinction between 'lifetime employment' and 'lifetime-employability' (Forrier & Sels 2003, p.103) reshapes the meaning of employability.
- ○ In the case of the latter the nature of employability changes to reflect an emphasis on continuous individual self-development (Baruch & Hind 1999) that offers an opportunity to build one's capacity for continuous employment (Forrier & Sels 2003), to hone one's ability to make employment transitions (De Cuyper et al. 2008) and to retain and improve one's 'attractiveness' in the labour market (Rothwell & Arnold 2007, p. 24).
- ○ Employability is now seen as an 'alternative to job insecurity' functioning as a mechanism for developing transferable career opportunities both within and beyond current employment (Forrier & Sels 2003, p. 104). Employability is now regarded 'as the upcoming critical resource for workers in times of high insecurity' (De Cuyper & De Witte 2010, p. 836).

FLEXIBILITY AND FLEXICURITY

- ○ *Flexibility*: The transformation of work including 'new ways of working' that facilitates flexibility in terms of 'the time and location of work' (Blok et al. 2012, p. 5075).
- ○ *Flexicurity*: The objective of promoting both flexibility and security combined in some form or other offers new opportunities to establish different approaches to employment policies, practices and condition (Ackers & Oliver 2007).

Technostress

Why technostress and why now? Although the term technostress was first introduced by Brod in 1982, the word and its meaning have really found a voice and a place in work stress research, as we have moved further into the new millennium. The reasons for this are partly due to the tempo of technological change, creativity and innovation, partly due to its reach and inclusiveness, partly due to new generations of applications tumbling over themselves to be the first in the market, partly due to generations of people wanting instant information, gratification and inter-connectiveness; and partly due to the need to better understand technology's 'dark side' in addition to recognizing its benefits and common good. When the focus shifts to 'work', then the reasons for understanding technostress include the increasing dependence of organizations on information and communication technologies (ICTs), the constant need to meet the gap between 'existing' knowledge and 'needed' knowledge, the need to understand how these technologies change work arrangements and organizational cultures resulting in 'a fundamental shift' in working relationships and the need to come to terms with the paradox between technology's 'liberating effects' on the one hand and its demands and pressures on the other (Ragu-Nathan et al. 2008, p. 418).

So this section begins by first exploring the nature and definitions of technostress, and allied concepts like computer anxiety, technophobia and Information Communications Technologies (ICTs) stress. We then outline what are described as 'techno creators/stressors' (Tarafdar, Tu & Ragu-Nathan 2010) and 'techno inhibitors' (Fuglseth & Sorebo 2014), and explore their consequences. Lastly, we move on to a discussion on internet abuse and internet addiction (Griffiths 2010), problematic internet use (Kim & Davis 2009), email use (Whittaker et al. 2005), cyberbullying (Sabella et al. 2013), the benefits and dangers of social media (Turel & Serenko 2012), and cyberloafing (Lim & Chen 2012).

Technostress, computer anxiety and technophobia

A decade and a half into the new millennium, technostress still had the qualities and feel of a 'new concept', but by then it was coupled with an expanding literature on why we 'feel technostressed' (Shu et al. 2011, p. 924). The contextual factors that helped shape definitions of technostress are all too familiar, and capture not just individuals having to deal with, manage and cope with the constantly changing and evolving nature of technology, but the profusion and variety of demands and responses that accompanies their use (Ragu-Nathan et al. 2008; Tarafdar, Tu, Ragu-Nathan & Ragu-Nathan 2011). So it is not surprising to find that the two themes of adaptation and negative impact are part and parcel of most definitions. Both of these themes are captured by Brod when he defines technostress as 'resulting from the inability of an individual or organization to adapt to the introduction and operation of new technology' (1982, p. 754) later adding 'in a healthy manner' (see Ayyagari et al. 2011, p. 832). Most definitions, while emphasizing the negative impact on individuals, capture its adaptational side with commonly agreed definitions expressing these themes in ways that view technostress as 'one of the fallouts of an individual's attempts and struggles to deal with constantly evolving ICTs and the changing cognitive and social requirements related to their use' (Tarafdar et al. 2007, p. 303).

So how does computer anxiety differ from technostress? The difference, it seems, stems from the fact that technostress is more of a general construct that is concerned with the 'fallout' that follows from the individual's ability to deal, manage or cope with technology that is continually evolving and developing (Shu et al. 2011). Computer anxiety, on the other hand, stems from a 'fear of technology in general, and of computers in particular' (Thorpe & Brosnan 2007, p. 1258). The nature of computer anxiety is expressed through beliefs that include, for example, one's understanding of, confidence in and ability to use a computer, one's emotional feelings towards the computer, the physical arousal that accompanies using or thinking about using a computer, and more general beliefs about the role of computers in society (see Beckers & Schmidt 2001, p. 36). So, computer anxiety is generally defined in a way that reflects a 'fear for computers when using the computer or when considering the possibility of computer use' (Chua, Chen & Wong 1999, p. 610), and while appearing to 'harbour components of trait anxiety' (Beckers, Wicherts & Schmidt 2007, p. 2860), its complexity and multi-dimensional structure challenges the need to develop suitable intervention strategies. Nevertheless, it is clear that computer anxiety poses a significant threat to individuals' health and well-being (O'Driscoll et al. 2010).

From her comprehensive and detailed review, Powell suggests that future research into computer anxiety may wish to 'revisit' the role of managerial support, the role privacy and security play in computer anxiety today, the role and utility of alternative research methods and the need to ensure that measures continue to reflect the complex and evolving nature of technology, its multi-dimensional nature and its general versus specific qualities (2013, pp. 2378-2379). The issue of whether computer anxiety reaches levels that reflect a form of phobia needs to be treated with some caution, and where conclusions are tentatively expressed to simply capture that for some, computer anxiety 'may enter into the framework of problematic fears' (Thorpe & Brosnan 2007, p. 1258). Finally, the term ICT stress describes 'the condition brought on by interruptions at work, time pressures and technical problems in connection with ICT use' (Thomée, Eklöf, Gustafsson, Nilsson & Hagberg 2007, p. 1301). It differs from technostress in that its focus is on those 'situational factors that impede a person's ability to use ICT' (O'Driscoll et al. 2010, p. 274). When thinking about ICT stress, Thomée and his colleagues conclude that it is important to take the quantity and the quality of ICT exposure into account since each may lead to different effects (Thomée et al. 2007).

Techno creators/stressors and their consequences

While not entirely sequential, but once having identified that technology has its 'dark side' with negative effects, the next step was to explore the different ways in which ICT technologies 'create stress for people using them' (Tarafdar et al. 2007, p. 304; Stich, Farley, Cooper & Tarafdar 2015). Researchers point first to how the stress-creating effects of ICT include its ubiquitous nature, its capability for continuous connectivity, its competitive pressures to keep up to date, its demands on technical capabilities, its increasing complexity and sophistication, its ability to provide through multiple sources large amounts of information and its requirement for multi-tasking (Ragu-Nathan et al. 2008, pp. 421–422; Tarafdar et al. 2007, pp. 304–306). Emerging from this context, and driven by the idea that technostress 'is a problem of adaptation', five techno creators/stressors have been identified that 'provide theoretical and empirical shape' to technostress (Tarafdar et al. 2007, p. 322). They include: (a) 'techno-overload' (the requirement to work faster and longer); (b) 'techno-invasion' (being constantly connected and the consequent spill-over into all aspects of life); (c) 'techno-complexity' (more time spent learning and understanding coupled with feelings of inadequacy); (d) 'techno-insecurity' (the constant threat of job insecurity, of being replaced by computers or by others with better skills); and (e) 'techno-uncertainty' (the impact of constant change, new developments and upgrades) (Ragu-Nathan et al. 2008; Tarafdar et al. 2007, p. 315; Tarafdar et al. 2010, 2011).

Two other potential stressors could be added to this list. Both reflect the organization's culture with technostress being greater in organizations where there is both a more centralized power structure and a highly innovative culture (Wang, Shu & Tu 2008). Coovert and his colleagues also add to the list of potential stressors by pointing to 'electronic performance monitoring', showing how such activities extend beyond just monitoring task performance to service observations and work behaviour monitoring that can take place through what they describe as 'unobtrusive inspections' involving eavesdropping and surveillance (Coovert, Thompson & Craiger 2005, p. 308). Research also shows how certain technology characteristics (e.g. usability, intrusiveness, privacy invasion and dynamism) are related to more commonly measured stressors like work-role overload, role ambiguity, work–home conflict and job insecurity (Ayyagari et al. 2011). Others, taking a demands–resources perspective, point to how different ICT characteristics have this dual role functioning at times as either a demand or a support and, in this way, point to the need to better understand how and in what way such characteristics operate to 'minimize harm and maximize individual and organizational benefits' (Day et al. 2010, p. 340). This theme is also present in research that explores those factors that facilitate or enhance individual engagement with technology, focusing on issues that include, from the individual's perspective, computer self-efficacy (Shu et al. 2011) and perceptions of mastery or perceived control, and from an organizational point of view the importance of factors like training, organizational culture, technical and social support not, of course, forgetting how the absence of these may create barriers to engagement (O'Driscoll et al. 2010, pp. 283–296; Tarafdar et al. 2010). These approaches also reflect the idea of 'technostress inhibitors', where strategies that involve technical support, building employee ICT literacy and facilitating involvement all have the potential to reduce the effects of technostress creators/stressors (Fuglseth & Sorebo 2014).

The 'negative' or 'unconstructive' consequences of technostress (Tarafdar et al. 2010, p. 305) are often explored through frameworks that group consequences according to whether they are 'adverse psychological' or 'adverse IS user-related' outcomes (Tarafdar et al. 2011), or end-user satisfaction (psychological strain) or end-user performance (behavioural strain) (Tarafdar et al. 2010). These frameworks are generally part of more complex models developed to explore the causal pathways that account for the roles played by antecedent conditions, individual and organizational moderating variables and inhibiting mechanisms. Research captures the range and variety of consequences including, for example, health issues (Coovert & Foster Thompson 2003), anxiety and frustration (O'Driscoll et al. 2010), depression and sleep disturbances (Thomée et al. 2007), role overload, role conflict, commitment (Tarafdar et al. 2011), hassles (Day et al. 2010), dissatisfaction (Ragu-Nathan et al. 2008; Tarafdar et al. 2010) and productivity issues (Tarafdar et al. 2007, 2010, 2011). It is the impact of technostress on productivity that has drawn attention to what has become known as the 'productivity paradox' (Tarafdar et al. 2007, p. 322). Technostress 'creators/stressors' have been found to have a negative impact on 'productivity' (Tarafdar et al. 2010; Tarafdar, Ragu-Nathan, Ragu-Nathan & Tu 2005), particularly for those individuals with a high dependency on technology (Karr-Wisniewski & Lu 2010). These results, as Tarafdar and colleagues suggest, simply 'reinforce the belief' that unless technostress is managed then the expected increases in productivity will fail to follow (2007, p. 322).

New concerns for health and well-being: technology's new behaviours

It is not just the relationships between technostress creators/stressors and their psychological and behavioural consequences that have captured the attention of researchers. The power, attraction, magnetism and fascination for the internet, the desire for its social and connectivity applications, the opportunities they provide to express and shape one's life, identity and relationships, and its constant availability and presence fosters new behaviours and new concerns for health and well-being. We begin this section by first exploring 'problematic internet behaviours'. While acknowledging the enormously positive contribution that the internet has made to our lives, terms like problematic, excessive, over-use[ers], addiction–addictive–addicts, and obsession–obsessive have more often than not crept into our language and are now frequently and commonly used when describing behaviours associated with the internet (Beard & Wolf 2001; Caplan 2002, 2003; Davis 2001; Young 2004;

Whang, Lee & Chang 2003). At the same time we are also conscious of the debate that accompanies and swirls around the different terms, particularly when addiction is being used to describe such internet behaviours (e.g. Beard & Wolf 2001; Caplan 2002; Griffiths 2010;Young 2004; Stich et al. 2015).

Each term offers different perspectives and understandings on the nature and meaning of this type of internet behaviour. So while there may be different types of dependency (Beard & Wolf 2001), with different types of users having different reasons for using different internet functions (Griffiths 2010), it may be important and there may be a need to distinguish between specific versus general internet use (Davis 2001), recognizing the difference between internet use and the activity being assessed through the internet that becomes the core focus of behaviour (Kim & Davis 2009; Griffiths 2010). Nevertheless, the debate continues to raise questions about the subtleties and 'conceptual undertones' that separate the different terms and their long term effects (Beard & Wolf 2001, p. 378; Griffiths 2010), the similarities and differences between internet addiction and other addictions (Young 2004) and 'what it actually is that people are addicted to' (Beard & Wolf 2001, p. 381). The debate will continue to lie in the shadows and in wait for those wishing to explore the area, and regardless of how often the term addiction is used, or used interchangeably with problematic behaviour, it is clear 'that there are people developing a harmful dependence on the internet' (Beard & Wolf 2001, p. 382). The research literature has developed around both the term internet addiction (Douglas, Mills, Niang, Stepchenkova, Byun, Ruffini, Lee, Loutfi, Lee, Atallah & Blanton 2008;Young 2004) and problematic internet behaviour (Beard 2002; Caplan 2002, 2003).

Problematic internet use

Because the term problematic involves 'fewer theoretical overtones' (Beard 2002, p. 4), we will limit our focus to 'problematic internet behaviour'. Why does this sort of behaviour occur? A range of reasons provide a context for understanding why such behaviour emerges and include, for example, opportunity for access, affordability, anonymity, convenience, escape, disinhibition, social acceptability and the hours spent working and so using the computer for such activities (Griffiths 2010, pp. 467–468). Davis's (2001) model emphasized and saw individual cognitions as the 'main source of abnormal behaviour', and specific PIU (Pathological Internet Use) as involving 'overuse and abuse of specific Internet functions' (2001, pp. 188, 192). Davis (2001) also drew attention to generalized internet use across a range of functions including simply wasting time as distinct from specific internet use that involved a dependence on a specific function of the internet. Arguing that his model provided the framework for exploring PIU's multi-dimensional relationships, the task as he saw it 'becomes empirically testing this model' (2001, p. 194) and so it was the groundbreaking work of Caplan (2002, 2003) that laid the foundations as the exploratory 'initial work' to identify the dimensions of a construct 'that lends itself to empirical operationalization' (Caplan 2002, pp. 573, 556).

Caplan's work (2002, 2003) identified a number of cognitive and behaviour dimensions or symptoms of PIU. These included (Caplan 2003, p. 634) 'compulsive use' (the inability to control, reduce or stop online behaviour accompanied by feelings of guilt at the time spent online), 'mood alterations' (the extent internet use is used to change negative states), 'preference for online social interaction' (the perception of greater social control and greater social benefits that flow from the internet than from face to face interactions), 'excessive internet use' (the degree to which an individual feels that their time on the internet is excessive), and 'withdrawal' (the degree of difficulty of staying away from the internet). With perhaps a preference for online social interaction being 'a key indicator' reflecting the belief that this may lead over time to more 'compulsive and excessive use' of the internet (2003, p. 638), Caplan (2003) identified that future work on PIU may wish to consider exploring areas like 'communication apprehension', 'unwillingness to communicate' and 'social skills', suggesting that by exploring across disciplines we can only continue to develop our understanding of PIU and our obligation to offer intervention strategies that help those dealing with PIU (Caplan & Turner 2007).

As our understanding of PIU and its measurement developed, it was only natural that researchers should turn their attention to identifying those characteristics that may make some individuals more likely to engage in PIU than others. Our aim here is to just give a sense of what has been, and what continues to be a rapidly expanding field of enquiry. Loneliness, shyness, depression and self esteem were soon found to predict PIU (Caplan 2002; Ceyhan & Ceyhan 2008; Kim & Davis 2009; Saunders & Chester 2008; Whang et al. 2003), with researchers at times distinguishing between emotional loneliness (emptiness and restlessness due to the absence of a relationship) and social loneliness (feelings of boredom and marginality due to no significant friendships or sense of belonging), with PIU associated with low levels of social loneliness and high levels of emotional loneliness (Moody 2001, p. 394). It is interesting to note 'an implicit contradiction' (Kim & Davis 2009, p. 491), when it comes to social activities including loneliness, as the internet may for some fulfil their social needs for friends, associates and relationships that are not satisfied elsewhere, suggesting that more work is needed on what exact function the internet is being used for and what it may be fulfilling (Kim & Davis 2009). Researchers have explored the issue of PIU and gender (Hetzel-Riggin & Pritchard 2011), whilst reviews provide a good understanding of the range and variety of characteristics explored (Huang 2010; Kelly & Gruber 2010). 'Giving a sense' of this research is just that, and while it cannot do justice to the rich, comprehensive and complex literature that has grown around those individual characteristics that help predict PIU, the importance of this work can be gauged by the call that this work needs to continue to advance so that by distinguishing these 'defining characteristics' (Kelly & Gruber 2010, p. 1845), we are seeking ways to provide avenues for help as much as we are seeking to better understand the condition and its meaning and structure.

Cyberloafing, cyber incivility and cyberbullying

Other behaviours also reflect the growing use and availability of the internet and allied technologies. While 'idling on the job' has always been a concern for organizations, the arrival of the internet has certainly 'revolutionized' idling, with cyberloafing being the IT way of whiling away time (Lim 2002, p. 678). Cyberloafing concerns the use of the internet while at work to voluntarily engage in surfing 'non-job related web sites' for personal purposes (Lim 2002, p. 677). When viewed through the lens of exchange theory and organizational justice, cyberloafing has been described as a form of deviant work behaviour and as falling under the rubric of 'production deviance' (Lim 2002, p. 677). In this way when employees sense some imbalance or injustice stemming from the employment relationship then to redress this state the internet provides an attractive, constant and safe opportunity to take back 'what they feel their employer owes them' in a way that offers few personal misgivings for them when 'balancing', so to speak, 'the ledger' (Lim 2002, p. 680). With the internet employees now have 'an easier way to redress their perceived grievances' that is almost undetectable and instantly gratifying (Lim, Teo & Loo 2002, p. 69).

But perhaps 'cyberloafing' has another more positive side to it, because it may serve as an emotion-focused coping strategy. The work by Lim and Chen (2012) certainly points in this direction – browsing activities were found to have a positive effect on emotions, reinforcing the view that browsing offers a momentary re-energising escape from job demands (Oravec 2002), a 'necessary break' that is fast becoming the new IT 'office toy', equivalent to and replacing earlier forms of stress reducing gadgets. In this way it represents a 'middle ground' by describing this sort of behaviour more in terms of its 'cyber-stimulating' properties (Anandarajan & Simmers 2005, pp. 777, 787). The work by Henle and Blanchard (2008) also points to the coping properties of cyberloafing, suggesting that cyberloafing is perhaps more likely to be used when confronted with role ambiguity or role conflict and less likely to be used when confronted with role overload, influenced by how likely it is that sanctions would be imposed for using such a technique. Whether the term cyberloafing or cyber-stimulating is used, it is important, as Lim and Chen (2012) conclude, to develop our understanding of employee attitudes towards cyberloafing – why they engage in it, what motivates them, what properties best express the idea of 'zoning out', how much is acceptable and when do these properties take on a more negative role – if we are to better appreciate cyberloafing's positive and negative qualities (Lim & Chen 2012).

Cyber-incivility has its origins in what has become known as email stress, email overload and email-related stress (Hair, Renaud & Ramsey 2007; Reinke & Chamorro-Premuzic 2014), and follows the seminal paper on work incivility by Andersson and Pearson (1999). The level of cyber-incivility in the workplace and its 'growing threat' to well-being (Giumetti, et al. 2013, p. 297) 'underscores the need for further study' (Francis, Holmvail & O'Brien 2015, p. 191), helping to explain what is a rapidly growing field of research exploring the incidence, nature and experience of incivility committed through email communications (Francis et al. 2015; Giumetti et al. 2013). It is clear that email has fundamentally changed how we communicate, and while supposedly offering flexibility and control brings with it a 'continuous and tangible reminder' of the feelings of overload it creates (Barley, Meyerson & Grodal 2015, p. 901), its potential to convey emotion (Byron 2008) through misunderstandings of meaning, tone and injudicious use of language (Brown, Duck & Jimmieson 2014) and the everyday way in which this creates conflict and leads to feelings of anger, recriminations, disputes and severe hurt (Friedman & Currall 2003).

All this because emails make it easier to respond, to react immediately, to make demands and requests that take time away from the task at hand, to interrupt concentration (Barley et al. 2015, p. 888), to provide fewer, if any cues to interpretation and meaning (Byron 2008), offering none of the features for understanding meaning that accompany face-to-face communication (Baruch 2005; Friedman & Currall 2003; Sproull & Kiesler 1986). They trigger little need to give attention to or even adhere to acceptable forms of social behaviour – the 'online disinhibition effect' (Suler 2004, p. 321) – perhaps because emails are more of a 'series of intermittent, one directional comments' than a conversation (Friedman & Currall 2003, p. 1327). Emails are also lacking in 'grounding', in that achieving a sense of understanding and a shared sense of participation in the process is missing, making it 'more profoundly asocial' (Friedman & Currall 2003, pp. 1327, 1329) – and simply adding to and supporting the likelihood of 'emotional inaccuracy' (Byron 2008, p. 320). There is no doubt that these features that accompany the flow of emails bring their own consequences both to the sender and the receiver (Barley et al. 2015; Brown et al. 2014; Day et al. 2010; O'Driscoll et al. 2011; Reinke & Chamorro-Premuzic 2014).

The consequences of 'cyber-incivility' need to be considered within the spectrum of workplace behaviours. Although incivility is described in terms of 'low-intensity deviant behaviour' (Andersson & Pearson 1999, p. 457), it is surrounded by ambiguity as to the intention to harm (Andersson & Pearson 1999; Francis et al. 2015), influenced by 'email miscalibration' – questioning whether we are as good at communicating effectively as we think we are (Kruger, Epley, Parker & Ng 2005, p. 925) – and accompanied by our fallibility as email users (Byron 2008). All of these comments offer opportunities for future research, and it should not be overlooked that unwittingly offending causes as much emotional hurt as calculated rudeness, deliberate ambiguity and antagonistic or derogatory use of language. It is also interesting to note that the spectrum of workplace behaviours that express cyber-incivility now extends to a separate area of study and concern called cyberaggression (Weatherbee 2010), where emails are deliberately used to convey aggression or where the email is used in a way where the receiver perceives it as being aggressive. This type of behaviour, as Weatherbee goes on to indicate, 'is a more serious problem' and represents a form of 'interpersonal deviance' (Weatherbee 2010, p. 37). It is important, when thinking about cyber-incivility, to remind ourselves that the behaviours engaged in and the nature of the technology itself suggests why its consequences can be so damaging, helping to explain why this type of communication is so different from face-to-face communication.

Email messages can, for example, be repeatedly read and alternatively interpreted, in addition to being carefully crafted and redrafted to ensure the message has its impact and indeed the response has its added effect (Friedman & Currall 2003). Behaviours and feelings can be displayed by sending and resending the email, carbon-copying it to a range of others (Giumetti et al. 2013), deliberately avoiding follow-up requests or sending condescending replies, or by showing little or no interest in others or regard for others (Cortina, Magley, Williams & Langhout 2001). Symbols or 'so called emoticons' can be used to get a point across (Kruger et al. 2005, p. 926) or to masquerade behind, all helping to aggravate, increase confusion, conflict and ambiguity of message; not forgetting that the incivility of a message can lead to a string of 'tit-for-tat' exchanges (Andersson & Pearson 1999).

Email management, and particularly email overload, has been discussed in terms of the use of techniques like filtering or batch processing (Barley et al. 2015) and the benefits that flow from reducing the frequency of checking emails (Kushlev & Dunn 2015). It is also important to recognize that all emails communicate emotions, and are particularly open to misinterpretation, so increasing awareness of this through training helps in establishing norms of behaviour and protocols for how emails are used (Byron 2008). Yet, as Barley and his colleagues point out email management is a more complicated matter, extending beyond issues of volume alone and needs to be seen in terms of the ebb and flow of daily communication patterns and procedures, and the anxieties and behaviours that accompany such activities; so that for any intervention strategy to be successful it needs to address this 'sociomaterial entangle-ment' (Barley et al. 2015, p. 903).

As befits a rapidly growing field of research a number of avenues for future research are offered by researchers. These include, for example: comparing cyber-incivility with face-to-face incivility (Giumetti et al. 2013); understanding more about how receivers make attributions about the intentions of the sender (Francis et al. 2015); the culture of email communications in organizations; the use of qualitative methods to better understand how worry and email stress are experienced (Jerejian, Reid & Rees 2013); making greater use of the transactional model and its concepts of primary and secondary appraisal to better understand email stress in addition to gathering more information on the type of email related tasks and the source of email traffic (Brown et al. 2014); and more generally in terms of work incivility exploring those organiza-tional conditions that make possible or restrain incivility, the role played by individual differences, and how people cope with incivility (Cortina et al. 2001).

We now turn to another form of personal deviance – cyberbullying (Baruch 2005; D'Cruz & Noronha 2013; Privitera & Campbell 2009). The study of bully-ing has a long history (Rayner, Hoel & Cooper 2001), and is now well established as a significant area of research (Samnani & Singh 2012), with researchers now beginning to explore its changing face as we enter the cyber age (Law, Shapka, Hymel, Olson & Waterhouse 2012) and the myths and realities that accompany the concept of cyberbullying (Sabella et al. 2013). It is clear that emails and other forms of social media now provide a different type of bullying and 'a different route for abusive behaviour' (Baruch 2005, p. 368). While a considerable amount of research has investigated the impact of cyberbullying on young people, research on cyberbullying at work has been described as 'sparse' (D'Cruz & Noronha 2013, p. 325), as a work in progress (Privitera & Campbell 2009); making it, when compared to our understanding of more traditional face-to-face forms of workplace bullying, 'much less understood' (D'Cruz & Noronha 2013, p. 325).

Nevertheless workplace research has begun by identifying the role that emails play as a mechanism for bullying, and the importance of email as 'an enabler' for what might become 'vicious behaviour' (Baruch 2005, p. 368). Researchers have also found that cyberbullying co-existed alongside more traditional forms of face-to-face bullying, that those cyberbullied also experienced face-to-face bullying, that it does operate in the workplace and that it has the ability to 'change the face of bullying' (Privitera & Campbell 2009, p. 399). Research identifying the distinguishing features of workplace cyberbullying paints a vivid portrait of its potential impact (D'Cruz & Noronha 2013, p. 329). Three core features capture the nature of workplace cyberbullying: (a) its boundaryless spread; (b) 'its concreteness and permanence'; and (c) 'its invisibility and anonymous' shape. The first expresses its scope – whether person or work-related and directed, its anytime, anywhere, anyplace, anybody qualities with accompanying work–life balance issues. The second refers to the fact that it is there in front of you, on your screen, immediately readable, downloadable and always there for repeated viewing. The third core feature adds to its impact and complexity as initially at least it is only the receiver who knows about it, and may find it difficult to determine or not know who it came from, why it came, whether it is real and what intentions come with it or flow from it. And if these features are not enough then the qualities and nature of this behaviour, like many of the behaviours we have discussed, will change and develop as fast as the technology itself and those generations of new applications that shape it taunting and challenging researchers to keep pace (D'Cruz & Noronha 2013, pp. 339-342).

To these behaviours we could add what has been described as the 'dark side' of smart phone usage – compulsive behaviour and how the features of smart phones and the characteristics of users influence stress levels (Lee, Chang, Lin & Cheng 2014). Then there is social media, with its 'all-encompassing nature' (van Osch & Coursaris 2013, p. 702) and the benefits and dangers of social networking websites (Turel & Serenko 2012) including online deception; how 'the unknown and invisible' engage in exploitation and the challenges this presents (Tsikerdekis & Zeadally 2014, p. 72). One way to think of the different behaviours we have discussed is to collect them all under the heading of 'counterproductive behaviours', 'actions that workers engage in that harm their organization or organizational members' (Bowling & Gruys 2010, p. 54), and then further divide them into two dimensions that are 'interpersonal-organizational' or 'task relevance directed' (Gruys & Sackett 2003, p. 39). Considerable work has gone into developing frameworks for understanding the nature, structure and categories of counterproductive behaviours (Griffin & Lopez 2005; Gruys & Sackett 2003; Martinko, Gundlach & Douglas 2002; Sackett 2002), and in furthering our understanding of their dimensions and measurement (Bowling & Gruys 2010).

Reviews point to the growing body of work around individual and contextual factors that may help explain why 'counterproductive behaviour' is engaged in

(Robinson 2008), and special editions point to the range of perspectives taken to understand such behaviours (Popovich 2010). Other researchers, noting the unique features of technology, point to the need to distinguish this form of behaviour from other forms of counterproductive behaviours, suggesting that these techno-driven behaviours be now collected under the title of cyberdeviancy as 'a step towards achieving conceptual clarity' (Weatherbee 2010, p. 40). It is clear that as the pace of technological change brings with it greater connectivity, facilitated by more innovative and creative ways of communicating, not just with each other but applications communicating with other applications, this will predictably bring with it similar creative and inventive ways of engaging in counterproductive behaviours or cyberdeviancy (Weatherbee 2010).

Researchers argue that more work is needed to look into how these behaviours can be predicted and managed (Griffin & Lopez 2005), the role selection processes play in helping to reduce these behaviours (MacLane & Walmsley 2010) and the contribution researchers can make by bringing more clarity and understanding to what is a complex set of behaviours (Bowling & Gruys 2010; Popovich 2010; Weatherbee 2010). We have of course focused on the dark side of technology, since our interest has been in its role as a stressor and the behaviours it facilitates. But it is just as important, from time to time, to remind ourselves of its 'positive side' and of the benefits it brings, the educational, training and learning opportunities it offers, its role as a resource, a coping mechanism, a social support, a mechanism for monitoring our health, feelings and well-being, the way it can simply stir our imagination, broaden our outlook, awaken our ambitions, energize, refresh and replenish our spirit, and how it grants us the authority and the freedom to follow our dreams and what may yet be seen.

TABLE VI.2

TECHNOSTRESS

o   The paradox between technology's 'liberating effects' on the one hand and its demands and pressures on the other; enter technostress (Ragu-Nathan et al. 2008, p. 418).
o   The contextual factors that helped shape definitions of technostress are all too familiar and capture not just individuals having to deal with, manage and cope with the consistently changing and evolving nature of technology, but the profusion of the demands and responses that accompanies their use (Ragu-Nathan et al. 2008; Tarafdar et al. 2011). So it is not surprising to find that the two themes of adaption and negative impact are part and parcel of most definitions of technostress.

(Continued)

(Continued)

o   Technostress is generally defined in ways that reflect 'one of the fallouts of an individual's attempts and struggles to deal with constantly evolving ICTs and the changing cognitive and social requirements related to their use' (Tarafdar et al. 2007, p. 303).

o   So how does computer anxiety differ from technostress? The difference it seems stems from the fact that technostress is concerned with the 'fallout' that follows from the individual's attempts to deal with, manage and cope with technology that is evolving and developing, whereas computer anxiety stems from a 'fear of technology in general and of computers in particular' (Thorpe & Brosnan 2007, p. 1258).

o   The way ICT 'creates stress' for those using it includes its ubiquitous nature, its capability for continuous connectivity, its competitive pressures to keep up to date, its demands on technical capabilities, its increasing complexity and sophistication, its ability to provide multiple sources of large amounts of information and requirements for multitasking (Tarafdar et al. 2007, p. 304; Ragu-Nathan et al. 2008, pp. 421–422).

o   Five techno creators/stressors have been identified that 'provide theoretical and empirical shape' to technostress. They include 'techno-overload, techno-invasion, techno-complexity, techno-insecurity and techno-uncertainty' (Ragu-Nathan et al. 2008; Tarafdar et al. 2007, p.315; Tarafdar et al. 2010; Tarafdar et al. 2011).

o   Added to the above list of techno creators/stressors are potentially organizational culture (Wang et al. 2008) and electronic performance monitoring (Coovert et al. 2005, p. 308).

o   Research also shows how certain technology characteristics (e.g. usability, intrusiveness, privacy invasion) are related to more commonly measured stressors like work role overload, role ambiguity and work–home conflict and job insecurity (Ayyagari et al. 2011).

o   New concerns for health and well-being stem from technology's new behaviours. These include problematic internet use (PIU) (Davis 2001), cyberloafing, cyber incivility, email stress and cyberbullying (Lim 2002; Lim & Chen 2012; Oravec 2002; Hair et al. 2007; Reinke & Chamorro-Premuzic 2014; Andersson & Pearson 1999; Barley et al. 2015; Baruch 2005; D'Cruz & Noronha 2013; Privitera & Campbell 2009).

Work–life balance: From spillover to crossover

The third stressor is often described in terms of work–home conflict, reflecting the influence of the forces of change outlined in earlier chapters. Here we begin by outlining how these forces have forced researchers to refine the concept of work–life balance, so as to give a context for understanding not just the challenges researchers face, but also reflect on not only the blurring of the boundaries of work and home but the changing nature of work itself. These challenges are cogently outlined by a number of researchers (Brough & Kalliath 2009; Guest 2002; Kalliath & Brough 2008), even to the extent of commenting on the elusive meaning that accompanies the concept of balance itself. It is clear that organizational behaviour cannot be understood or explained by 'variables within the organization alone' (Brough & Kalliath 2009, p. 581), reinforcing the importance not just of the concept of work–life boundaries itself, but also the changing boundaries of organizational behaviour.

Guest (2002, p. 256) refers to 'three broad sets of overlapping influences' that have heightened the interest in work–life balance. These he describes as developments at work (the intensifying of the nature of work, spurred on by advances in technological advances), community concerns that centre on the deteriorating quality of life, and the generational and gender composition of a changing workforce with changing values. Brough and Kalliath note that the advances of technology have created an 'almost seamless interface' between home and work (Brough and Kalliath 2009, p. 581), supporting their earlier comments that these developments create 'a need to examine existing organizational behaviour theories and corporate influences at the interfaces of work and family' (pp. 581–582).

All researchers on this topic (Guest 2002; Kalliath & Brough 2008) draw attention to what appears to be a continuing challenge as to what is meant by 'balance', despite what Brough and Kalliath refer to as work–life balance reflecting a 'virtual explosion in research in recent years' (2009, p. 581). Researchers have expanded the debate swirling around the word balance, to argue that we should think now less in terms of balance and, through a framework of personal resources allocation, more in terms of 'resource allocation' (Grawitch, Barber & Justice 2010) or the matter of choice, leading to terms like 'work–life articulation' or 'work–life harmonization' (Gregory & Milner 2009, pp. 1–2). As Gregory and Milner suggest, these alternatives 'reflect a mutual reinforcement of the two spheres' (2009, p. 2), although they also suggest these alternatives bring their own problems; the debate continues.

The refining of future research

Despite the debate about just what balance means, or whether alternatives better express the work–life balance research, 'work–family balance has become a driving force in itself' (Brough & Kalliath 2009, p. 581), with research making theoretical and empirical advances. Perhaps the best example of these advances is the transmission of work on life being thought more in terms of 'crossover' than 'spillover', where previously demands 'of work [were] transferred to and interfere with the nonwork domain for the same person' (i.e. spillover); whereas in the case of crossover work 'demands and their consequent strain crossover between closely related persons' (Bakker et al. 2009, p. 207). As Bakker and his colleagues suggest job demands 'first spillovers from work to home and then crosses to the partner'

(Bakker et al. 2009, p. 207). As Westman, whose work has been at the centre of the spillover–crossover movement, says: 'it follows that work–life balance may crossover from one spouse to another. I do suggest that spillover is a necessary but not sufficient condition for crossover' (Westman, Brough & Kalliath 2009, p. 588). What intrigued Westman was the idea of crossover implying 'a process that involves contagion of demands and their consequent arousal across closely related or otherwise linked persons' (Westman et al. 2009, p. 589). So what are the mechanisms underlying crossover (Westman et al. 2009, p. 591)?

'One of the main crossover mechanisms' identified by Westman and Vinokur (1998), Westman suggests, is 'empathy'. Westman (Westman et al. 2009, p. 591) continues, in her conversation with Brough and Kalliath, 'that based on findings the crossover effects appear between closely related partners who share the greater parts of their lives together' (Westman et al. 2009, p. 591). This conversation concludes when it comes to future research pointing to the need to explore the possibility of crossover of positive emotion, and the role of individual differences and gender in explaining how empathy as a process may operate. What the crossover idea does is shift the direction of focus, and through the lens of empathy, shows how such a process may work in organizations, particularly in team working. Do the emotions of a team member have, for example, this contagious crossover effect making this a new focus to explore and advance our understanding of team effectiveness (Bakker et al. 2009; Westman et al. 2009)? This also raises the issue of borders within organizations, through how work is organized. Thinking in terms of borders, and the contagiousness of positive emotions, offers a new way to view work–life balance that questions the traditional use of a conflict framework, and perhaps points to the wider issue of where and what borders are being crossed and the implications of this on what is meant by balance (Guest, 2002).

The ideas of individual differences: segmentation and integration

The idea of 'borders' is the focus of theories when exploring the concept of work–life balance, but the concept of borders offers another focus, introducing the idea of individual differences by exploring how individuals express how segmented or integrated they prefer these two domains to be. 'Segmenters' (Kreiner 2006, p. 485) are those who 'prefer to keep the two domains as separate as possible', in contrast to those 'integrators' whose preference is 'essentially removing boundaries between the two and blending facets of each' (Kreiner 2006, p. 486). This segmentation approach expands research on work–life balance by focusing on an individual difference perspective. As Kreiner (2006) argues, these preferences have not been given the attention they deserve when understanding work–life balance (Kreiner 2006). This focus on individual difference also offers researchers an opportunity to explore how individuals cope with or negotiate 'daily role transitions' (Ashforth et al. 2000, p. 472;

Kreiner, Hollensbe & Sheep 2009). This understanding of negotiation or coping processes will become even more important, particularly since technology has blurred the work–life boundaries, helping researchers to explore the changing roles individuals play both at work and at home (Kreiner et al. 2009) and the policies organizations develop to integrate non-working lives into work, with phrases like 'having to wear different hats' (Ashforth et al. 2000, p. 472) becoming part of our common parlance and expressing the changing transition between roles and the changing nature of work (Ashforth et al. 2000; Rothbard, Dumas & Philips 2001).

As mentioned earlier, researchers are well aware, when pointing to how technology has blurred the boundaries between work and life, of the need to know how these changes are coped with and to suggest that future research will need to focus on 'how do individuals engage in daily role transitions as part of their organizational life' (Ashforth et al. 2000, p. 472). More work will inevitably be needed to focus on the changing natures of boundaries, not forgetting whether technology has simply erased the work–life boundary and created the 'almost seamless interface between work and family' (Brough & Kalliath 2009, p. 581).

As the work on individual differences advances, then this may mean organizational policies created to give a sense of integration 'may not be beneficial to all and may have drawbacks for some' (Rothbard, Phillips & Dumas 2005, p. 253). This also introduces the notion that organizational policies should be sensitive to the ideas that express 'congruence of boundary management' (Rothbard et al. 2005, p. 253), and the idea of how crossover works in how teams are managed (Bakker et al. 2009) – and, indeed, how crossover may influence how other parts of the organization are managed. Not forgetting that the crossover of positive emotions needs now to be broadened (Bakker et al. 2009; Westman et al. 2009) to include a more positive emphasis in work–life balance models and, indeed, how the crossover process works and what other ways than empathy may be driving the crossover process (Bakker et al. 2009). All of which leads us back to the elusive concept of what is meant by balance.

Of course individual differences research points to the complexity of these work–life relationships, and demands that future research needs to explore the role these differences play. It is argued that this research should be broadened to include gender differences (Westman et al. 2009), and to explore how these complexities can be investigated using alternative methodologies (Bakker et al. 2009; Westman et al. 2009), including being more aware of 'cross cultural sensitivity' and the gains that can be derived from it (Brough & Kalliath 2009, p. 582; Powell, Francesco & Ling 2009), and building a broader understanding of work–life balance (Fisher 2001). Work–life balance research also raises the question of 'how much of our self is defined by work' (Ramarajan & Reid 2013, p. 621). These authors suggest this is a difficult question to answer, since changes like job security, workforce diversity and 'the spread of technology' are all masking the division between work and non-work, requiring workers, their organizations, and occupations to 'renegotiat[e] these relationships' (Ramarajan & Reid 2013, p. 621), and requiring research to focus on the other side of the coin, and explore how these changes are influencing their non-work identities (Ramarajan & Reid 2013). The reality is that these types of questions have possibly contributed to the interest in and the growing literature on workaholism.

TABLE VI.3

WORK-LIFE BALANCE: SPILLOVER OR CROSSOVER

- The blurring of the boundaries of work and home.
- The three 'broad sets of overlapping influences' that have heightened the interest in work–life balance. These influences are the intensification of work spurred on by technological advances, community concerns that centre on the deteriorated quality of life and the generational and gender composition of a changing workforce with changing values and expectations (Guest 2002, p. 256).
- An 'almost seamless interface' between home and work (Brough & Kalliath 2009, p. 581).
- The refining of work–life balances theories had led to the transmission of work on life thought more in terms of 'crossover' than spillover – where work demands 'crosses over to the partner' (Bakker et al. 2009, p. 207). As Bakker and his colleagues suggest job demands 'first spillover from work to home and then crosses to the partner' (Bakker et al. 2009, p. 207).
- As Westman, whose work has been at the centre of the spillover–crossover debate, says: 'it follows that work–life balance may crossover from one spouse to another' – 'it involves a contagion of demands and their consequent arousal across clearly closely related or otherwise linked individuals' (Westman et al. 2009, p. 589).
- Work–life balance research has also explored the issue of individual differences in terms of segmentation and integration of work. 'Segmenters' (Kreiner 2006, p. 485) are those who 'prefer to keep the two domains separate as possible', in contrast to those 'integrators' whose preference is to 'remove boundaries between the two and essentially blending facets of each' (Kreiner 2006, p. 486).
- This individual difference focus is on how individuals negotiate 'daily role transitions' (Ashforth et al. 2000, p. 472) and organizational policies that are created to give a sense of integration may not be beneficial to all (Rothbard et al. 2005, p. 253). Not forgetting that the crossover of positive emotions raises the question of whether the focus on a work–life conflict model needs now to be broadened (Bakker et al. 2009; Westman et al. 2009).

The growing interest in workaholism

The topic of workaholism has attracted considerable interest and therefore 'it should come as no surprise then that opinions, observations and conclusions about workaholism are both varied and conflicting' (Burke 2000, p. 1). While reviews are quick to point to the fact that there is little agreement 'about its meaning' (Snir et al. 2006, p. 369), a consensus seems to be building around the idea that our understanding would be advanced if the term was better considered in terms of a syndrome (Aziz & Zickar 2006). The work that has, it seems, attracted most researchers' attention when describing workaholism as a proposed syndrome is the tripartic model proposed by Spence and Robbins (1992), where workaholism was described as 'involving an excessive involvement in work, a drive to work and a lack of work enjoyment' (Aziz & Zickar 2006, p. 52). This led to a workaholic being described if two dimensions were high ('work involvement' and 'drive to work'), and the third ('lack of work enjoyment') was low (Aziz & Zickar 2006, p. 53). It also allowed the opportunity to refine workaholism into further categories including, for example, the 'enthusiastic workaholic' (high on all three dimensions) and the 'work enthusiast' (high on work involvement and its enjoyment and low on work drive) (see Aziz & Zickar 2006, p. 53).

Using the Spence and Robbins model to cluster employees into profiles provided 'considerable support for conceptualizing of workaholism as a syndrome' (Aziz & Zickar 2006, p. 60). This study also pointed to workaholics experiencing less work–life balance than non workaholics, and pointed to the need to think of workaholism as a syndrome when developing interventions, because focusing on and examining 'the specific symptoms instead of the global construct' is a more effective approach in design (Aziz & Zickar 2006, p. 61), as is exploring why work cultures allow such behaviours to be accepted and permitted to 'flourish' (Burke 2000, p. 14). Indeed 'while workaholic behaviors relate closely to levels of well-being' the findings are mixed, although research draws attention to the 'critical role' that each dimension plays in the health and well-being of workaholics, helping it seems to explain the inconsistency in findings about the impact of workaholism. The key factor is how the three dimensions combine, and it is this that appears to determine the pivotal role they play in leading to problematic health and well-being (McMillan & O'Driscoll 2004, p. 517).

The future direction for research, despite all this creative work, is to find 'a consistent definition and operationalization of workaholism [as this] is explicitly needed before further progress can be made' (Patel, Bowler, Bowler & Methe 2012, p. 2) leading to a more 'thorough understanding of what constitutes the workaholic' (Aziz & Zickar 2006, p. 61) and its measurement. Despite issues surrounding the definition and measurement of workaholism the model offered by Spence and Robbins opens the way forward to continue to explore the three dimensions that combine to define a workaholic whilst researchers also explore the value organizations place on workaholism, and 'those strategies that maximize its benefits and tactics to minimize its costs is imperative' (McMillan & O'Driscoll 2004, p. 518); 'hopefully' as Burke suggests, to research in this area may be enhanced by bringing the literatures of clinical and organizational psychology closer together to 'encourage more research in this area' (2000, p. 14). Future research also points to the development of a more refined perspective to emerge when distinguishing between workaholics and, for example, the 'work enthusiast', not ignoring the other profiles that can be generated from the work of Spence and Robbins (1992). The idea of the work enthusiast and the enthusiastic workaholic offers now a more positive perspective to emerge that could be explored using the context of the positive psychology movement.

All these demand that the direction of future stressor research should continue to reflect on a number of measurement practices; themes that we have discussed elsewhere (Dewe & Cooper 2012, p. 95), but we believe as we have redeveloped these themes they are important enough to be rehearsed again. These themes for future research represent refining, relevance and reliability. This chapter reflects all three – researchers have explored how stressors have constantly been *refined* to reflect the influence of societal, technological and economic forces; in this way *reflecting* how measures remain relevant to reflect the work experience; and then finally their *reliability* where the argument now goes beyond its traditional statistical value to question whether our reliance on it may mask the relevance of what is being measured, introducing the idea of whether measures have 'a use-by' dimension. It is these and other measure issues we want to discuss in the concluding section of this chapter.

Measurement: The themes of refinement, relevance and reliability

We have identified three contemporary stressors that reflect current work experi- ences, and that reflect social, economic and political forces that create the context that allows these new work stressors to evolve. It is also this context and these forces that point to the need for researchers to consider whether existing measurement practices of more classical stressors are mindful of how well these measures reflect contem- porary work experiences. As this chapter illustrates, concepts such as refining and relevance (see Dewe & Cooper 2012, p. 95) will give a new meaning to robustness – where measures are only robust if they are relevant and express the contemporary work experience – expanding its meaning beyond its more narrow traditional meth- odological definition. Robustness, along with the concepts of refining and relevance, will assume an importance alongside the place reliability is traditionally given in stressor measurement. This is why, as Beehr (1998) suggests, work stressor measure- ment is a never ending business. Refining stressors requires constantly asking the question whether work stressor measures are actually measuring 'what we think they are' (Dewe & Cooper 2012, p. 93). How well do they capture the current work experience? Researchers have of course, as this chapter illustrates, engaged with, and acknowledged, the significance of how the context shapes stressors, and therefore concepts like refining and relevance and the associated concept of robustness all need to become an important part of evaluating measurement practices.

The idea of refinement is graphically illustrated by Hellgren and his colleagues (Hellgren et al. 2008), when they explore the future challenges facing 'work role measurement'. These researchers conclude when considering contemporary or 'classical stressor' measurement, it is 'important to consider them in terms of how [they express] today's employees' experience [of] work' (Dewe & Cooper 2012, p. 93). Refinement has at its core the concept that stressors are 'seen more in terms of their ability to describe an experience than to actually define it' (Dewe & Cooper 2012, p. 95). If stressors reflect a context, then stressor measurement must evolve to describe that context so their meaning is continually changing and, as we have pointed out before, 'persisting with a stressor measure because it exhibits strong psychometric properties may not, in fact be advancing our understanding of what is being measured' or the work being experienced (Dewe & Cooper 2012, p. 95).

The concept of refinement is not mutually exclusive from the concept of relevance, as each is part of a process where relevance reflects the outcome of the process of refinement. Perhaps 'relevance' is a broader view, as it represents those forces that require the need for refinement. Perhaps it reflects, as Ashford and colleagues (Ashford et al. 2007, p. 67) point out, the need to better understand what our model of what 'standard work' reflects, as we cannot assume that standard work models look like contemporary work and reflect the changing work experience, as 'at the very least new theories and new measures are central to filling in a portrait of this new future' (Ashford et al. 2007, p. 106). But refinement and relevance also depend on how our measurement practices change and adjust. So, just as we have illustrated the creativity of researchers to refine the nature of stressors, so that they express contemporary work experiences, this creativity needs also to be reflected in the way measures are used in analysis to express these stressors to ensure this creativity is not lost (Dewe & Cooper 2012). In our view the creativity of researchers does not stop at refining stressors or identifying new ones. It extends, if relevance is going to be maintained, to consider how such measures are going to be used in analysis and how that allows 'a portrait of this new future' to emerge (Ashford et al. 2007, p. 106). So 'measurement practice' is the other half of the relevance equation. We explore, as we have before (Dewe & Cooper 2012, pp. 95–97), how measurement practices may begin this process of change under two general broad headings: 'within-relationship' (the relationship between items in a measure that pattern to create the nature and context of the experience) and 'between-stressors relationships' (what role does each stressor play in terms of its relationship with other stressors, (see Dewe & Cooper 2012, pp. 95–97). Not forgetting distinguishing between the items being measured and the issue of the way they are appraised and given personal meanings (primary appraisal) (Lazarus 2001), the positive side of stressors – those aspects of the experience that may be valued (Beehr & Grebner 2009), and whether stressors have specific or more general effects (Dewe & Cooper 2012, p. 97).

As we have explored before (see Dewe & Cooper 2012, pp. 93–97), the 'within-relationship' focuses on the pattern of scores derived from the items in a stressors scale. The idea here is that respondents may have identical mean scores but through their pattern of items they have checked in the scales they may have a quite different experience. So here we argue for more attention to be given to the 'pattern of items', in this way being more sensitive not just to the multi-dimensional nature of stressors, but to what mean scores may actually express and the explanatory potential that resides in them (Dewe & Cooper 2012, p. 96; Dewe & Brook 2000). We are not, of course, suggesting mean scores be abandoned, as their utility secures their continued use. But patterns or clusters of stressor items provide an explanatory context which the blunt use of mean scores masks. The idea of between-stressors covers issues like the relationship between different stressors, and the nature of that experience of one stressor on another (see Dewe & Cooper 2012, p. 97). What role does each play in terms of its relationship with other stressors? What is the nature of their cumulative effect and 'the consequences of experiencing one on the experiencing of another' (Dewe & Cooper 2012, p. 97)? It is the accumulative effect of stressors which has yet to receive the attention it deserves.

The meanings given to stressors

The way in which work stressors are appraised or given personal meanings, as distinct from the nature of the events themselves, has been touched on in this chapter. The appraisal process is, as Lazarus (2001) describes, fundamental to his transactional theory of stress, as appraisals represent the psychological processes that link the individual to the environment and the emotional pathway that flows from them. As we have expressed before (see Dewe & Cooper 2012, p. 96), an event at work triggers the appraisal process, where individuals give personal meaning to the event (Lazarus 2001). Ignoring this 'primary appraisal' process in work stress research is to overlook perhaps the most powerful explanatory pathway that resides in the transactional model and 'what can be achieved through a view of stress centred on relational-meaning' (see Dewe & Cooper 2012, p. 79). This 'primary appraisal stage is important in determining how individuals will respond to perceived demands' (Mackey & Perrewé 2014, p. 262).

It is this context and idea that has drawn researchers to explore the 'challenge-hindrance model' of stressor research (Cavanaugh et al. 2000), although as Webster and her colleagues point out, this model of stress while implying the primary appraisal process does assume 'a priori that certain stressors would be experienced as either challenges or hindrance' (Webster, Beehr & Love 2011, p. 506). Nevertheless, this work is important because it illustrates to work stress researchers how introducing the challenge-hindrance of assumed meanings, associated with particular stressors, brings this important distinction to the general attention of work stress research and offers, as originally attended, a fruitful way of understanding why some stressors may not lead to negative emotions (Cavanaugh et al. 2000). This work is also important because it not only captures the positive–negative qualities of stressors, but also draws attention to the complexity associated with the meanings associated with stressors. Meanings can be both positive and negative, raising questions about the stress process, its various phases and stages, the way meanings may change through the process and of course coping. In their results, challenge-related stressors are positively associated with job satisfaction, whereas negatively (hindrance) related stressors are associated with behaviours like job-search and turnover (Cavanaugh et al. 2000).

'The major propositions in the [Cavanaugh et al. 2000] model have been supported' (Webster et al. 2011, p. 505), as is the idea that stressors can have positive and negative consequences (Edwards, Franco-Watkins, Cullen, Howell & Acuff 2014), and the model 'is growing in prominence in the research literature' (Webster et al. 2011, p. 505). It achieves its power from the transactional model of stress, as primary appraisal (personal meanings) are believed to be the link, the causal pathway, between the stressor and outcomes (Lazarus 2001; Webster et al. 2011, p. 506). This helps to explain the differential effects of stressors, and perhaps why some stressors trigger their own unique outcomes, suggesting 'that the stressor-outcomes relationship may be more specific than generally assumed' (Dewe & Cooper 2012, p. 97). However, the challenge-hindrance model points researchers to the authority of personal meanings; to ignore personal meanings is to overlook the explanatory power they have (Dewe & Cooper 2012).

Summary

This chapter set out to capture the creativity of researchers when working towards the refinement and relevance of the measurement of stressors so that they reflect the contemporary work experience. Whilst not wishing to ignore the emphasis given to reliability in research our point is, as we have said before, 'that uncritically accepting the *a priori* labelling of a stressor as always reflecting the same events or of having the same meanings' (Dewe & Cooper 2012, p. 95) fails to capture the evolving nature of stressors and the ability of measures to adequately reflect the work experience. 'Persisting with a stressor measure simply because they exhibit sound psychometric properties may not, in fact, be advancing our understanding of what it is being experienced or the nature of the stressor itself' (Dewe & Cooper 2012, p. 95). Reliability is important but this chapter illustrates the importance of the concepts of refinement and relevance and, indeed, of creativity, and these should not be lost at the expense of the convenience of reliability. This chapter also points to the explanatory power of personal meanings, as distinct from the events themselves, and how it is these meanings initiate the causal pathway that links to the emotion experienced. Again it is these personal meanings which represent such a powerful explanatory force that should not be overlooked by researchers; and perhaps now, as the research illustrates, they should be emphasized as a core feature of future research (Dewe & Cooper 2012).

VII

COPING WITH STRESS, FUTURE DIRECTIONS AND CHALLENGES

There is no doubt that stress coping research has captured the creativity and imagination of researchers, resulting in what has been described as a 'boundless enthusiasm for' such research (Aldwin 2000, p. 73) and 'a dramatic proliferation' (Somerfield & McCrae 2000, p. 620) of this type of research over the last three decades (Dewe & Cooper 2012). One reason for this 'enthusiasm' is not just that coping is critical to our understanding of stress, but that it is clothed in a sense of 'immediate personal relevance' to all of us (Aldwin 2000, p. 73). This 'proliferation' of research has of course not been free of controversies and debate, as writers question how coping should be defined (Dewe & Cooper 2012, p. 136; Folkman & Lazarus 1991; Folkman 1982), how it should be measured (Coyne & Racioppo 2000), its complexity (Aldwin 2000) and whether as Burke (2002, p. 83) suggests as 'researchers perhaps our expectations were too high'.

The coping research context and the growing variety of coping strategies

Our intention in this chapter is to build on the creative research and reviews that reflect the current field of stress coping research (see Folkman & Moskowitz 2004), and to use these to set out and acknowledge the challenges facing this field of research. So, in this chapter, our aim is first to explore the growing variety of coping strategies that may reflect the way social and economic turmoil characterizes the first years of this century. At the very least, it illustrates an evolving field of research. From our exploring the growing varieties and complexity of coping strategies we point to two issues. The first signals that researchers need now, because of the growing varieties of coping strategies, to be more sensitive to the complexities of measuring coping and how measures are constructed to ensure participants can express the range of strategies they may use.

This is advice that has long been offered to coping researchers in ways that illustrate its importance and helps to explain the direct way that advice has been given (Coyne & Gottlieb 1996; Coyne & Racioppo 2000; Dewe & Cooper 2012, pp.144–145; Folkman & Moskowitz 2004). This advice is usually accompanied by a more general debate around the use of coping checklists, and while it may be viewed as just one part of that wider debate, the growing varieties of coping strategies makes it more difficult to ignore, gives it a greater sense of urgency and makes it more pertinent, particularly when we are reminded how coping strategies are so sensitive to the context and to the way the encounter has been appraised (Lazarus 1999, 2001). This is not to ignore all the other advice given when designing coping measures, but just to counter a 'convenience factor creeping in' (Coyne & Gottlieb 1996; Dewe & Cooper 2012, p.144), stifling our knowledge of coping, the relevance of our measures and our understanding of the range of strategies used. Of course it also challenges researchers to consider the issue of 'length' when designing coping measures. We are not arguing that coping checklists should be abandoned, their utility is clear, but that we do need to recognize their limitations in understanding a complex process like coping, but be mindful of how sensitive checklists need to be to describing participants 'thoughts and actions in detail' (Coyne 1997; Lazarus 1993, p. 236; Oakland & Ostell 1996).

The second issue the growing variety of coping strategies signals is not just that their growth emphasizes the importance of being sensitive to the complexities of measuring coping strategies, but also points to the evolving nature of 'classifying' them; accepting that classifying coping strategies does 'provide a useful way of talking about many kinds of coping in broad' terms (Folkman & Moskowitz 2004, p. 751). Classifying coping strategies is often the first challenge coping researchers confront, and so measures that restrict the range of coping strategies must necessarily change the nature and scope of the classification framework derived. In the context of a growing variety of coping strategies, the complexities that shape their classification become immediately apparent, particularly since the consequences of classifying them from restricted measures has a fundamental impact on our understanding of how coping strategies are being used. So 'classifying coping strategies' may need to be seen more in terms of a movable feast, as our knowledge of the variety of coping strategies continues to grow. The work on classifying coping strategies tends to illustrate the point that a classification framework of coping strategies develops in conjunction with our knowledge of the varieties of coping strategies individuals use and the complexities associated with their measurement.

The classification of coping strategies builds on the classic work by Folkman and Lazarus (1984), who introduced what they later described as a 'broad brushstrokes' approach (Folkman and Moskowitz 2004, pp. 751–752), built around the focus of the strategies as either being 'problem-focused' or 'emotion-focused', and setting the benchmark for researchers to follow. As discussed previously (Dewe & Cooper 2012, pp. 138–140) as research on coping advanced, it led Folkman to extend the 'problem-focused', 'emotion-focused' framework to include 'meaning-focused' and 'relation-focused' coping, as these two categories reflected 'major gaps in the original formulation' (Folkman 2011, p. 454). It was these four strategies that marked the beginnings of what Folkman and her colleague described as helping 'the synthesis of findings across studies' although adding to how it 'runs the risk of masking important differences within categories' (Folkman & Moskowitz 2004, p. 752). Illustrating the evolving nature of classifying coping Folkman pointed to the need in 2011 to include future orientation coping, religious and spiritual coping and interpersonal coping (Folkman 2011, p. 454) to any synthesis of findings. This brief summary of the history of classifying coping strategies cannot claim to capture the richness of the work or the reviews it is based on, nor the controversy surrounding the measurement of coping strategies, and is intended to do nothing other than to reinforce the complexity of classifying the varieties of ways of coping that have emerged making this task an evolving one.

More particularly it points to how these new varieties of coping may reflect strategies that are sensitive to the changing work context, and the personal meanings given to the experiences of contemporary work. Acknowledging the complexities of the measurement of coping strategies, and the challenges it presents, means researchers need to be as sensitive to the limits of the measures they use as they are to the growth in our knowledge of the variety of ways of coping, the complexities this creates for measurement and the importance of understanding the context within which coping occurs. Other challenges also face coping researchers, and this chapter turns to them after exploring and commenting on the growing varieties of coping. These include understanding (a) what it means to cope effectively, (b) the idea of coping flexibility (Kato 2012) and other perspectives like (c) coping and ageing, (d) coping and gender, and (e) coping and personality. Finally, the chapter ends by exploring the future, by questioning 'where to from here'. As Folkman and Moskowitz suggest, when it comes to coping measurement it 'is probably as much an art as a science'. 'The art' they argue, lies in 'selecting an approach that is most appropriate and useful to the researcher's question' adding the rider 'sometimes the best solution may involve several approaches' (2004, p. 751).

The varieties of coping

The growing variety of coping strategies tracks an ever complex and ongoing process. Folkman and Moskowitz (2004) provide a framework that we have built around and used and adapted to structure our discussion to signal this growth in coping varieties. We begin our discussion of the growing varieties of coping strategies by turning to what Folkman and Moskowitz described as these 'dynamic and new directions' in coping research (2004, p. 756) by first exploring religious coping as it carries the idea of a resource, a sense of control and neatly raises the issues of appraisals.

Religious coping

Why religious coping? While religion has been 'well documented' in terms of its beneficial health effects, the way those beneficial health effects come about has not been given the attention it deserves as a coping resource (Krägeloh, Chai, Shepard & Billington 2012, p. 1147). Religious coping has all the hallmarks that reflect the forces of change spilling across the face of society. It involves, for example, the search for meaning (Park 2005), its 'relevance for personality functioning' (Emmons 1999, p. 875), its expected relationship with personality factors like 'conscientiousness' and 'openness to experience' (McCrae 1999), and its relationship to 'forgiveness' (McCullough & Worthington 1999). It is often described as an emotion-focused coping strategy (Worthington & Scherer 2004), but for the most part its psychological function 'is still being debated' (Krägeloh et al. 2012, p. 1138). 'Religious coping' does reflect the ideals of the positive psychology movement through that movement's focus on flourishing or personal growth (Seligman & Csikszentmihalyi 2000), its utility aided by the publication of a religious coping scale (Pargament, Koenig & Perez 2000) and especially because of its usefulness for exploring 'to help find the strength to endure and to find purpose and meaning in circumstances that can challenge the most fundamental beliefs' (Folkman & Moskowitz 2004, p. 759).

It is clear that religious coping is more complex, when the notion of religious coping is discussed in terms of 'religiousness' and 'spirituality,' but nevertheless each captures the 'psychospiritual of people's lives' and in this way enhances our understanding of coping (Emmons 1999, p. 876). Pargament and his colleagues (Pargament et al. 2000) when developing their religious coping scale were concerned less with religiousness, and more with specifically 'how the individual is making use of religion to understand and deal with stressors' (Pargament et al. 2000, p. 521). Their functional view was built around the 'variety of purposes religion plays in day to day living and in crisis'. These included: (a) the search for meaning; (b) the search for control; (c) comfort/spirituality, intimacy/spirituality – 'as a mechanism for facilitating social cohesion'; and (d) life transformation (Pargament et al. 2000, p. 521). The power of this scale rests in the different ways each of these dimensions of religious coping can be used.

Using religious coping as an illustration of a variant of coping 'provides a richer understanding of the many expressions of religion in coping' (Pargament et al. 2000, p. 540). It challenges researchers to be more sensitive when constructing a coping scale and shows the care that is needed to best capture the nature and the variety of coping strategies and their use, whilst being mindful to meeting the constraints of scale length. While we are not suggesting that expressing religious coping strategies must be included in workplace coping scales, we are drawing attention to this type of coping and its place in understanding coping with work stress. As reminded by Krägeloh and his colleagues, work stress coping scales do not generally include items that 'ask about a very broad range of coping responses that involve the use of religious concepts' (Krägeloh et al. 2012, p. 1138) because as these researchers acknowledge 'questionnaire length remains a major consideration' (p. 1138).

However, what we are suggesting is that capturing the variety of coping strategies is complex, and researchers need to understand this complexity when construct-ing coping scales. This complexity is also determined by the context, shaped by the forces of economic, political and social change, and the changing nature of work within which coping takes place, requiring researchers to be sensitive to the coping strategies relationship with the context and the meanings (appraisals) individuals give to the stressors. These forces have, of course, over the years also resulted in 'changes in religious and spiritual expression' (Zinnbauer, Pargament & Scott 1999, p. 890), leading to a debate exploring the contemporary meanings in society of religion and spirituality (Zinnbauer et al. 1999).

'When asked about how they cope with their most stressful situations, many people make mention of religion' (Pargament et al. 2000, p. 520). The positive ben-efits of this type of coping are described as 'very well documented' (Krägeloh et al. 2012, p. 1137). But it is clear that finding out what it is about religion that provides these benefits 'is an intriguing empirical question' and a field that 'can be an enor-mously fertile source of insights' (Baumeister 2002, p. 166). So it is not surprising that exploring religion as a coping resource has emerged as a growing interest, although this research comes with its own challenges like, for example, the 'importance to examine the dynamic ways in which people use their religion in specific situations' (Ano & Vasconcelles 2005, p. 462).

Interestingly, research has investigated not just what religious coping means, and how it is used and measured, but has also explored why it has a beneficial effect (Pargament et al. 2000), ultimately leading to the theme of how do individuals 'make use of religion to understand and deal with stressors' (Ano & Vasconcelles 2005, p. 462). This has broadened out to include themes of 'what do people *expect* of religious coping' (Loewenthal, Cinnirella, Evdoka & Murphy 2001, p. 293), how religious coping is used relative to other coping strategies (Krägeloh et al. 2012), the functions of Christian prayer in the coping process (Bade & Cook 2008), religion as a meaning-making framework in coping with life stress (Park 2005), and why there should be such 'inattentiveness to the relevance of religion' (Emmons 1999, p. 875; McCrae 1999). All, as Pargament suggests, offering the opportunity to 'gain a more complete understanding of religion and human nature more generally' (2002, p. 239).

This research generally explores the use of religious coping in the context of men-tal illness and trauma, although not entirely ignoring work stress. Religious coping research reflects a number of themes that may illustrate the change in emphasis that coping researchers have been developing. It explores, for example, the context within which religious coping is being used, and the tempestuous social and economic turmoil that that context represents, perhaps helping to illustrate why religious coping strategies reflect a search for meaning; highlighting the ideas of searching for meaning, 'a sense of coherence which includes the ability to make stressors comprehensible and meaningful' (Park, Cohen & Murch 1996, p. 72). Religious coping also embraces in its wake themes like 'stress-related growth' (Park et al. 1996), and the themes of 'benefit finding', 'flourishing' and 'forgiveness,' embracing the ideas of the positive psychology movement.

Meaning-focused coping

The significance of the context, and its role in changing the nature of coping, has found expression in the growing literature on 'strategies that involve a great deal of intrapsychic cognitive processes of "meaning making"' coping (Park 2005, p. 709). The idea of meaning-making coping is 'particularly relevant in situations [contexts] that are not solvable' (Park 2005, p. 710), making this coping reflective of the social, economic and political turmoil that is characteristic of this century. The idea also captures perhaps Park's idea of 'global meanings' that represent the individual's 'internal cognitive structures that individuals construct about the nature of the world' (2005, p.709) and in such turmoil are discrepant with appraisal meanings that are concerned with 'what can be done to cope with the situation' (Park 2005, p. 709). It is where individuals 'search for [some] meaning once a context has been appraised as stressful' (Park and Folkman 1997, p. 122); and it is where some level of sense is sought to give the context 'meaning', leading to the idea of sense-making coping (Davis, Nolen-Hoeksema & Larson 1998).

It is this search for meaning that leads to the ideas of 'benefit finding' and 'benefit reminding' coping (Tennen & Affleck 2005). Benefit finding 'has been linked to psychological and physical health and it plays a prominent role in theories of cognitive adaptation to threatening circumstances' and has been understood as a coping strategy 'by many investigators and theorists' (Tennen & Affleck 2005, pp. 584, 589). Taking one's time to remind oneself of the perceived benefits and using this to 'comfort themselves [throughout] difficult times' represents its sense as a process of 'working through' or 'rebuilding', as individuals 'over time' come to see the situation as having beneficial qualities (Tennen & Affleck 2005, p. 590).

However, as Tennen and Affleck (2005) question, when in the coping process individuals actually make these 'selective evaluations' a coping strategy, and how it should be measured as such needs further empirical investigation. In the context of the complexities of determining when and whether 'benefit finding' is being used as a coping strategy, Tennen and Affleck (2005, p. 591) list alternative ways as to 'how might we understand this phenomenon'. In these alternative ways, Tennen and Affleck (2005, p. 591) draw attention to the idea that benefit finding may reflect 'growth or change' and so lead us to the ideas of 'stress related growth' or 'personal growth derived from negative events' (Tennen & Affleck 2005, p. 591).

Stress related growth

A considerable literature has continued to grow over the last two decades on 'stress related growth', particularly in relation to traumatic life events, but growth 'following from negative events on a daily level has been largely unexplored' (Losavio, Cohen, Laurenceau, Dasch, Parrish & Park 2011, p. 761) although the term stress related growth aims to provide a broader view to avoid the impression that growth only arises from trauma (Aldwin & Levenson 2004). There is still much to learn about the nature of growth and 'how growth is achieved' particularly in 'terms of individual adjustment' (Park 2004, p. 69). This learning begins by exploring what we mean by growth, and as alluded to above one of the more complex issues in understanding growth is in separating the notion of coping from 'self-enhancement tendencies' (Park 2004, p. 71); separating 'attempts people make [to] feel better' from growth being actually enacted as a deliberate coping effort (Park 2004, p. 71). This leads to growth being assessed as 'positive change'; then how, when and why does this positive change take place and what does this mean 'in the lives of those who experience it' (Park 2004, p. 73)? It is the quality of this transformation that is needed to be understood and 'the good that has come out of having to face them [stressors]' (Tedeschi & Calhoun 2004, p. 7). Researchers are urged to do 'more descriptive work in this area before foreclosing on the operationalization of growth' (Park 2004, p. 70).

Faced with these challenges in defining 'growth' and separating deliberate ways of coping from ways 'individual make them[selves] feel better' (Park 2004, p. 71), researchers have explored the role of different coping strategies and their association with the concept of 'growth' in terms of investigating what types of coping strategies are supportive of 'growth' (Folkman 1997). This focus has profound implications for coping research, since this focus challenges researchers to consider 'positive states', and the implication that in stressful negative events individuals can also experience positive psychological states (Folkman 1997). For future coping research Folkman argues the emphasis should be towards exploring those coping strategies that help 'sustain positive psychological states in the context of lasting stress, the conditions that trigger the search for positive psychological states and the intensity and duration of positive psychological states necessary to help sustain individuals in coping with the negative parts of the stressful event' (Folkman 1997, p. 1218).

Other researchers have also investigated the role of coping and 'growth', as difficult it may be, acknowledging the difficulties as to what is meant by the nature of 'growth' (Nolen-Hoeksema & Davis 2004; Park 2004) and its operationalization. Researchers suggest that one of the dimensions of 'growth' is learning new coping skills. This is seen as part of the 'growth' process, and 'growth' may be represented when individuals are placed in a situation where that situation requires them to do things they have not done before (Wortman 2004). Nevertheless Wortman adds the rider that we still need to 'be tough minded' about the concept of growth and 'what the data actually shows' (Wortman 2004, p. 89). The consequences of this meaning to growth may mean perhaps that the research focus needs to be more directed to changes in coping strategies rather than the approach that simply explores the association of coping with 'growth' *per se*. This raises the issue of whether the 'growth' process can be clearly separated from the coping process, or is a coping process in itself (Tedeschi & Calhoun 2004), requiring researchers to distinguish between 'growth' as a process or an outcome (Park & Helgeson 2006) both involving coping. Interestingly, the work by Bjorck and Byron showed that 'in general' growth (positive change) 'was unrelated to intended changes in coping' (2014, p. 97), although as the authors point out their work was built on coping intentions but did address this important issue.

What does all this mean for coping research? First it points to the fundamental importance of 'meaning' in the stress process. Not just in the meanings offered by appraising an event, but 'meaning making' as a coping strategy, although separating the two is not always easy. But what is clear is the powerful presence of 'meaning' and how its explanatory potential pervades coping research. Then it points to how in a negative stressful event individuals can experience positive states, raising the question of whether those coping strategies that give rise to these positive states differ from those coping strategies grappling with the negative states (Folkman 1997). The question of what type of stressful events promote 'growth' and what are the other factors that promote 'growth' other than coping (Wortman 2004) is another empirical issue as is deciding on what is meant by the nature of growth. As coping is a transaction between the individual and the environment, then does the same coping strategy used in that process differ in its function as the process evolves? If we are looking at a process, then, it is clear in the future, the call for longitudinal research is never far from the conclusions of researchers.

Proactive coping

This theme of positivity has found its voice in 'proactive coping', and expresses many of the goals of the positive psychology movement. Proactive coping is, as Folkman and Moskowitz describe, 'helping the field move forward' (2004, p. 756), and represents what Folkman describes as 'touching on the protective aspects of the stress process' (Folkman 2009, p. 73). Proactive coping differs from traditional definitions of coping, broadening the idea of coping because of its 'future orientation' (Folkman & Moskowitz 2004, p. 757). While there has been some debate as to whether other coping styles (anticipatory, preventative) have this future orientation the debate has essentially moved to focus more on whether proactive coping raises the issue of where the boundaries of defining coping should lie (see Dewe & Cooper 2012, p.142; Schwarzer & Taubert 2002).

Proactive coping is all about 'act [ing] in advance to prevent' stressors or 'to mute their impact' (Folkman 2009, p. 73). It is described by others as 'an effort to build up general resources that facilitates promotion toward challenging goals and personal growth' (Schwarzer & Taubert 2002, p. 28). In this way it reflects a positive-challenging-appraisal perspective (Aspinwall & Taylor 1997). So proactive coping emphasizes 'goal management rather than risk management' (Schwarzer & Taubert 2002, p. 28). This type of coping develops themes that capture aspects of the conservation of resources theory (Hobfoll 2001), expressing the language of the positive psychology movement through its notions of 'challenge', 'flourishing' and 'personal development' (see Dewe & Cooper 2012, pp. 15–17). It comes with a long history (Aspinwall & Taylor 1997) and raises and emphasizes the focus of timing when developing our understanding of how coping works in the stress process (see Dewe & Cooper 2012, pp.141–142).

'Proactive coping' reflects the broadening of our understanding of coping (Schwarzer & Taubert 2002), and embraces many of the changes in perspective offered by the positive psychology movement. It is also associated with the idea of the proactive personality and the proactive leader, and neatly captures the notion of positive appraisals and the significance of the transactional view of stress. It points to the way our measures and methods need to change if the complexities of the coping process are going to be understood, perhaps shifting the focus from the quantitative to perhaps a more qualitative approach to capture the subtleties of coping (see Dewe & Cooper 2012, pp.144–145; Schwarzer & Taubert 2002). As Folkman suggests, proactive coping must be considered as 'an important addition to the stress and coping model' (2011, p. 455).

Culture and collective coping

Globalization, with its long tentacles that inevitably lead to 'culturally diverse populations', is making its presence felt in coping research, as researchers begin to challenge 'the prevailing Western, individualistic…values and orientation' that accompanies coping research (Bhagat et al. 2012; Kuo 2013, p. 374). This work has found expression in 'collective coping', argued to be a central component of the coping repertoire of diverse populations. These 'emerging findings on culture-specific collective coping are critical' (Kuo 2013 p. 375), when 'existing stress and coping research has been increasingly criticized for perpetuating a Western, European, individualistic worldview in its theories' (Kuo 2013, p. 376).

Other departure points with traditional coping research also illustrate the significance of culture-specific coping (Bhagat et al. 2012). These are summarized by Bhagat and his co-authors (2012, p. 208) as 'from dualistic to dichotomous thinking – … where one can be simultaneously optimistic and pessimistic.' 'Eastern cultures … socialize their members in dualistic thinking'. They also include 'existential-coping' ('acceptance of what cannot be changed and discovering meaning and purpose of individual existence'). Both these latter culture-specific coping strategies tend to chime with and would benefit the development of our understanding of meaning-making coping and our ideas about stress related growth. But the primary focus has been on 'collective coping', as it is this strategy that underpins 'cultural differences and specificities in coping patterns across culture' (Kuo 2013, p. 376). It is the collective that provides the coping resource (Bhagat et al. 2012).

Collective coping is conceptualized as a 'constellation of behaviours of multi-faceted stress responses shaped and enhanced by collectivistic norms, values and tendencies' (Kuo 2013, p. 377). It is this 'implicit' seeking out for help from the collective that provides the individual with the support without it meaning the loss of face or shame, and marks it out from social support which is explicit in its nature and its behaviour (Bhagat et al. 2012; Kuo 2013). It is individuals who are culturally mutually dependent on the collective and place its importance above their own goals (Kuo 2013).

Why is this important? Because when workforces, as a consequence of globalization, are becoming more internationalized and culturally diverse, this must alter the way we think about coping and its nature. Assessing its effectiveness in the light of the dominance in coping research that the role of individualism has played in comparison to collectivism (Kuo 2013) gives us another context to explore meaning-focused coping, stress related growth and indeed work–life balance. Not forgetting the opportunity it provides to explore the role that culture plays as an explanatory tool (Kuo 2013). In the end, it empowers us 'with a better insight into human experience in coping with stress' (Bhagat et al. 2012, p. 210).

Collaborative coping and communal coping

There is, however, another side to collective coping, distinct from its cultural roots, and one that may reflect the way 'contemporary work' is organized. Team working, where individuals work more collaboratively, suggests that the collective (the team) may become the focus of coping, taking on a new meaning where workers are more likely, when work is organized like this, to use team coping or collaborative coping in the way they cope. Here it is the 'team' or the network that becomes the coping resource. Indeed, the downside of collaborating in teams suggests a new type of stressor – 'collaborative overload' - expressing the nature of contemporary work and the changing nature of role overload (Cross, Rebele & Grant 2016). There is also the growth of interest in 'communal coping' (Folkman & Moskowitz 2004, p. 759), where prosocial behaviours reflect this coping style that is conscious of, and reacts to, the social context by ensuring that coping actions 'are delayed if they would be distress[ing] to another member of the social environment' (Folkman & Moskowitz 2004, p. 759).

However, there is a dark side to communal coping – anti-social coping (Folkman & Moskowitz 2004, p. 759) More research on collaborative or team coping and communal coping may reflect why Folkman describes 'the social aspects of the stress process' as being 'very promising and deserving of further study' (2009, p. 75). There is one aspect of collaborative and communal coping that has received relatively little attention and that has been the sharing of good news or 'what do you do when things go right' (Gable, Reis, Impett & Asher 2004, p. 228). Both these types of coping have the potential of sharing good news and the positive benefits that can follow from doing so (Gable et al. 2004).

Leisure coping

The significance of 'leisure coping' reminds us that all coping with stress does not just occur or confine itself to a work context. Leisure coping research may help individuals 'find new meanings and directions in life' (Iwasaki, MacKay & Mactavish 2005a, p. 6), as well as reflecting themes increasingly common to mainstream coping; research like, for example, 'transforming oneself to grow through finding new opportunities and perspectives' (Iwasaki et al. 2005a, p. 5–6) as well as an opportunity for constructing the meanings of leisure as a coping strategy (Iwasaki et al. 2005a), and as a 'positive diversion or time out' (Iwasaki, Mactavish & MacKay 2005b, p. 81), or its role in stress related growth (Chun, Lee, Kim & Heo 2012) – not forgetting the role of leisure in influencing spiritual well-being (Heintzman & Mannell 2003).

'Running somewhat parallel to work stress and coping is the work of leisure and coping' (Dewe et al. 2010, p. 58), with a growing belief that 'examining the ways in which individuals engage in leisure to cope with stress appears to have important implications both conceptually and practically' (Iwasaki, MacKay, Mactavish, Ristock & Bartlett 2006, p. 164), because it enhances our understanding and broadens our understanding of coping and informs and provides a useful framework when designing interventions (Iwasaki 2003). Not overlooking the fact that leisure provides a range of opportunities 'for people to exercise higher levels of freedom of choice and sense of control, in comparison to activities in more constrained domains of life such as work' (Iwasaki 2003, p. 184).

Although there has been 'considerable discussion' around the term 'leisure', since it was first defined as 'free time' (Dewe et al. 2010, p. 58), its meaning, as we have noted before, has for some time broadened and moved away from that 'objective' view built around describing types of leisure activities to a more contextual view where it is investigated more in terms 'of its function, relevance and meaning in people's lives' (Dewe et al. 2010, p. 59). In this way, it seems, there is the opportunity to capture the contemporary view of the experience of work, and what leisure means in this context. Organizations have in many ways captured leisure, or at least the exercise dimension of leisure, as a way of defining their well-being interventions. Yet its original meaning of 'free time' has also a resonance and chimes with contemporary work experiences now though, raising the question as to where leisure 'fits in' to peoples' already overloaded working lives, and what leisure means to them and its role in their life.

The question of whether and where leisure can be 'fitted in' to what are already busy contemporary working schedules remains a moot point. Nevertheless the growing research on leisure coping and its richness and vitality means that its role in the coping process should not be ignored, because it has the ability to enrich and offer a new perspective to our understanding of coping. Yet there would seem to be a certain irony in its importance and its role in coping, when leisure is continuously promoted as having an increasingly significant part in what is characterized as a modern lifestyle. On the other hand, contemporary working lives are so busy, individuals haven't the opportunity to participate in such a touted lifestyle. Perhaps leisure has now a ritualistic quality, in that people feel they 'have to' become involved in some leisure activity, and this perhaps leads to reducing the benefits and freedoms that flow from participating in it.

Nevertheless the view that leisure plays a significant role as a coping function 'is well supported in the literature' (Coleman & Iso-Ahola 1993; Dewe et al. 2010, p. 59). Perhaps the most thorough, inclusive and wide-ranging framework of leisure coping (Iwasaki 2003) is the two dimensional approach by Iwasaki and Mannell (2000). These authors describe their model as distinguishing between people's relatively enduring *leisure coping beliefs* 'about the ways in which their leisure involvements help them cope with stress', as compared with how 'their leisure provides for coping with the stress they encounter' (Iwasaki & Mannell 2000, p. 177); that is, their situation-specific behavioural and cognitive *leisure coping strategies* (Iwasaki & Mannell 2000). In this latter view, coping acts as a resource as well as a coping strategy (Schneider & Iwasaki 2003; Iwasaki 2003), making the point that individuals will use different leisure coping strategies depending on the characteristics of the stressor. Their model offers three ways leisure may act as a coping strategy: in a 'palliative way' (time out, or refreshing, psychologically regrouping, gaining a new perspective, renewing energy); through 'companionship'; and through 'mood enhancing' (Iwasaki 2003; Iwasaki & Mannell 2000, pp.164–165).

However, thinking in terms of the social and economic disruption that seems to be part and parcel of this century, it would be interesting to determine whether such disruption has *shaken leisure coping beliefs* and how these beliefs, in this new millennium, have changed about the perceived role and involvement in leisure now plays in helping people cope, since its role may now be a different sort of resource than it may have been in the past. The role of leisure may now take on a more formal character, with a growing industry that surrounds the different activities that can be participated in. This is accompanied with the more formal notions of what now constitutes healthy lifestyles. Yet despite the health and well-being benefits of leisure, we need to remind ourselves that its primary characteristic is its 'autogenic' qualities that suggest its participation should represent something that is part of one's lifestyle that is enjoyed, suits the individual and offers the capacity building that helps to cope with stress.

Nevertheless leisure research as a *coping strategy* now seems to reflect many of the features of mainstream coping research through the language used to describe leisure coping strategies as a vehicle for 'transforming oneself to grow', capturing the goals and ideals of the positive psychology movement, or types of leisure 'help[ing] them find meanings and directions in life' (Iwasaki & Schneider 2003, p. 110). This suggests a meaning-focused coping aspect. Leisure coping also reflects how it 'may equip people to possess positive attitudes to life', bridging the work on discrete positive emotions (Iwasaki & Schneider 2003, p. 110). Leisure has also been described as offering 'breathers' from stress, 'sustainers' of coping effort, and 'restorers' (Iwasaki & Schneider 2003, p.110; Iwasaki et al. 2005b), reflecting the revived interest in the attributes of resilience. Not forgetting the implications that leisure holds for work–life balance and its dimension for offering support, friendship and companionship (Iwasaki & Mannell 2000, p. 168). Noting also the ongoing work, where researchers have investigated leisure and its influence on spiritual well-being (Heintzman & Mannell 2003).

The implications for general coping research lie in the existence of this corpus of research that has not just 'managerial and theoretical implications' (Iwasaki & Schneider 2003, p. 108), but reminds us that coping occurs in settings other than those where the stressors are located, that work boundaries do not necessary define our loci of research. At the very least it certainly raises issues of work–life balance; and also reminds us that ignoring this form of coping is to fail to understand the richness of the coping process.

Changing the face of coping: Positive emotions

When discussing the role of positive emotions in coping, Folkman and Moskowitz (2004, p. 764) introduce it in their review as 'an exciting development in the field of coping'. Others capture this sense of excitement by describing the fact that 'discrete emotions' are 'the coin of the realm' when understanding the coping process (Lazarus & Cohen-Charash 2001, p. 45). Indeed, the general field of studying emotions at work has been described as 'an exciting time' (Elfenbein 2007, p. 316). The work on positive emotions (Fredrickson 2001) and the growing influence of the positive psychology movement partly explain this 'excitement' and have 'opened a new avenue for coping research' (Folkman & Moskowitz 2004, p. 764).

It is the emphasis on positive emotions that has captured the attention of coping researchers. This attention has been stimulated by the ideas of growth and flourishing (Seligman & Csikszentmihalyi 2000), and the recognition that job satisfaction, as a surrogate measure of emotions, had broadly assumed 'the mantle' for investigating emotions at work (Dewe & Cooper 2012, p. 109). Perhaps now it is a time for change with researchers tackling the issue of discrete emotions at work, building on and taking their cue from the work by Lazarus and Cohen-Charash (2001) where they reiterate the significant role discrete emotions play in the transactional stress process, illustrating their causal pathway from the appraisal to coping that facilitates the emotional response; illustrating at the same time how positive appraisals lead to positive emotions. It is, as O'Driscoll (2013, p. 90) argues, 'crucial that more attention in coping research [be given] to emotional states since these appear to be at the heart of psychological well-being'.

While of course investigating positive emotions or any emotion for that matter at work comes with its difficulties, due somewhat to the rather restricted view, concerns and consequences that managers have of such a focus, it is clear that 'emotions give a broader focus of organizational life' (Dewe & Cooper 2012, p. 110). As with any emerging area of investigation researchers must face issues around definition and measurement of emotions that point to the need to 'fine tune' both, needing, for example, to capture the nuances that separate one emotion from another in terms of their focus, 'intensity, duration, meaning and significance' (Dewe & Cooper 2012, p. 112), helping to 'liberate' them from negative emotions. Nevertheless, there is a growing and active research base emerging that illustrates the power and role of positive emotions which opens 'a new avenue for coping research' (Folkman & Moskowitz 2004, p. 764).

The scope of this work is broad, as Folkman and Moskowitz illustrate in their review, by beginning with 'the growing awareness of the presence of positive emotions in the stress process' and how positive emotions can occur even in the most dreadful stressful situations (Folkman & Moskowitz 2004, p. 764) raising issues for those interested in coping research. The first issue questions how independent are those coping strategies associated with negative effect from those associated with positive effect (Folkman & Moskowitz 2004, p. 765)? This question illustrates the complexity of coping and of stressful encounters, and the role in that encounter of the positive, its meaning and the significance it plays.

So what are these positive emotions? Simply noting the growth of positive emotions, and producing a list of them, runs counter to what scholars suggest is the best way forward. The idea is to avoid lists and rather to develop our substantive knowledge by recognizing those qualities which make positive emotions significant, and move towards distinguishing between them on the basis of their qualities and how their nature and discreteness flows from the context within which they are expressed (Lazarus & Cohen-Charash 2001, p. 49). In this we must acknowledging the fundamental work of Fredrickson and her theory that positive emotions 'broaden and build', they are 'open and expansive', unlike negative emotions that 'narrow people's ideas about possible actions' (2010, p. 21). Her work 'charts a new course' in our understanding and significance of positive emotions (Fredrickson 2001, 2003, 2005, 2010, p. 21). Not forgetting the role the positive psychology movement has played in drawing researchers' attention to the issue of positivity (Fredrickson 2010), and the importance of people being able to 'flourish' and maximize their talents (Seligman & Csikszentmihalyi 2000). Nor forgetting the relationship between positive and negative emotions in a stressful encounter, when they occur, the role each plays in relation to the other, their intensity, duration and significance, the coping that initiates them, and the context within which they occur (Folkman & Moskowitz 2004).

So our aim here is to note the range and the creativity researchers have shown in identifying positive emotions. These include zest (Peterson, Park, Hall & Seligman 2009), 'hope' (Reichard, Avey, Lopez & Dollwet 2013), 'forgiveness' (Fehr, Gelfand & Nag 2010); in addition to the more common 'joy, love, happiness pride, gratitude and compassion' (Dewe & Cooper 2012, p. 113). For coping research this means recognizing a face of coping that has been hidden by the traditional focus of stress coping research, and coping's traditional role, of diminishing distress and fragility.

Emotion approach coping

Another development that may have been prompted by the interest in positive emotions is the work being done by exploring coping through 'emotional approach coping' (Austenfeld & Stanton 2004, p. 1335; Stanton, Kirk, Cameron & Danoff-Burg 2000). This work primarily stems from the way emotion focused coping has generally been measured, and because the 'generally accepted conclusion' (wrongly) is that emotions are associated with 'dysfunctional outcomes' comes generally from measures that take an avoidance emotion behaviours focus that contaminates and inflates that view (Austenfeld & Stanton 2004, pp. 1335, 1339).

The 'adaptive potential' of emotion approach coping, where emotions are 'acknowledged, understood, and expressed', and where through this approach, emotions are 'actively processed and expressed in the context of coping' (Austenfeld & Stanton 2004, pp.1340, 1341; Folkman & Moskowitz 2004, p. 761) has supported the belief in their adaptive potential. The meticulous work by Austenfeld and Stanton and colleagues has led to the development of the 'emotion approach coping' scale, with two dimensions: 'emotion processing' (e.g. 'I take time to figure out what I am really feeling') and 'emotion expressing' (e.g. 'I feel free to express my emotions'), each dimension demonstrating 'differential relations with other variables' (Austenfeld & Stanton 2004, pp. 1342–1343; Folkman & Moskowitz 2004, p. 761). In this way, these authors (Austenfeld & Stanton 2004) have shown the adaptive potential of coping through emotion approach coping in different stressful contexts, and indicate those factors that moderate the relationship between this type of coping and outcomes.

Working through the development of coping through emotion approach scales reminds us of the need to refine scales, making them relevant to the context, the time and the work experience and our advances in knowledge. While it may not be possible to relate this refinement of emotional-focused coping using an emotional-approach perspective to the forces of change, it does emphasize the importance of relevance in this case as a consequence of our developing knowledge. We need to remember that when giving coping strategies labels it is the context that determines that descriptor's relevance and meaning. This also reminds us that descriptors have a time dimension, requiring researchers to think in terms of how long it is before a label has reached its 'use by' date, and is at odds with the context it supposedly represents, or when the measure does not reflect the state of our knowledge. As we have discussed before it is one thing to give labels to describe coping data, but another to ensure that label's relevance when that coping strategy is assessed within the context of a stressful encounter (Dewe & Cooper 2007, 2012; Dewe et al. 2010).

TABLE VII.1

THE GROWING VARIETY OF COPING STRATEGIES

The growing variety of coping strategies may well reflect the social and economic turmoil that characterizes the first years of this century. The coping process is intensely built around individual appraisals that build a powerful personal context that is sensitive to the changing work context, the personal meanings given to the work experience and the coping process; helping to explain the changing nature of coping varieties and the refining of traditional coping strategies.

RELIGIOUS COPING

- o   Has all the hallmarks that reflect the forces of change spilling across the face of society.
- o   It involves for example the search for meaning (Park 2005).
- o   Its 'relevance for personality functioning' (Emmons 1999, p. 875).
- o   Its expected relationship with personality factors like conscientiousness and being open to experience (McCrae 1999).
- o   Its relationship to forgiveness (McCullough & Worthington 1999).
- o   It reflects the ideals of the positive psychology movement (Seligman & Csikszentmihalyi 2000).

MEANING-FOCUSED COPING AND STRESS-RELATED GROWTH

- o   The significance of the context and its role in changing the nature of coping has found expression in the growing literature on 'strategies that involve a great deal of intrapsychic cognitive processes of "meaning making" coping' (Park 2005, p. 709).
- o   Meaning-making coping is 'particularly relevant in situations [contexts] that are not solvable' (Park 2005, p. 709).
- o   It is the search for meaning that leads to the ideas of benefit-finding and benefit-reminding coping (Tennen & Affleck 2005).
- o   Drawing attention to the idea of benefit-finding may reflect 'growth or change' and so leads us to the idea of stress-related growth, or 'personal growth derived from negative events' (Tennen & Affleck 2005, p. 591).

(Continued)

(Continued)

PROACTIVE COPING

- The theme of positivity has found its voice in proactive coping and this expresses many of the goals of the positive psychology movement.
- Proactive coping differs from traditional definitions of coping, broadening the idea of coping because of its 'future orientation' (Folkman & Moskowitz 2004, p. 757).
- While there has been some debate as to whether other coping styles (anticipatory, preventive) have this future orientation the debate has essentially moved to focus more on whether proactive coping raises the issue of where the boundaries of defining coping should lie (Dewe & Cooper 2012; Schwarzer & Taubert 2002).
- Proactive coping is all about 'acting in advance to prevent' stressors or 'to mute their impact' (Folkman 2009, p. 73).

CULTURE AND COLLECTIVE, COLLABORATE AND COMMUNAL COPING

- Globalization inevitably leads to 'culturally diverse populations' and is making its presence felt in coping research, moving the focus in coping from 'individualistic coping' to 'collective' coping (Bhagat et al. 2012; Kuo 2013).
- Collective coping is conceptualized as 'a constellation of behaviours of multifaceted stress responses shaped and enhanced by collectivistic norms, values and tendencies' (Kuo 2013, p. 377).
- Culture offers a lens to alter the way we think about coping; providing another context within which coping can now be located and researched.
- There is, however, another side of collective coping, distinct from its cultural roots and one that may reflect the way contemporary work is organized.
- Team working, where individuals work more collaboratively, suggests that the collective (the team) may be the focus of coping, offering new avenues for coping research.
- This may also reflect a growing interest in 'communal coping' (Folkman & Moskowitz 2004) where prosocial behaviours reflect this coping style (Folkman & Moskowitz 2004).

LEISURE COPING

- The significance of leisure coping reminds us that coping with work stress does not just occur in or confines itself to a work context.
- Researching leisure as a coping strategy provides an opportunity for constructing the meanings of leisure coping (Iwasaki et al. 2005a, p. 1).
- Leisure coping research helps individuals 'find new meanings and directions in life' (Iwasaki et al. 2005a, p. 6).

o   In addition it reflects themes increasingly the concern of mainstream coping research, like for example 'transforming oneself to grow through finding new opportunities and perspectives' (Iwasaki et al. 2005a, p. 12).

o   Not overlooking the fact leisure provides a range of opportunities 'for people to exercise higher levels of freedom of choice and sense of control in comparison to activities in more constrained demands of life such as work' (Iwasaki 2003, p. 184).

o   Indeed the role of leisure and the beliefs that surround it as to its role in contemporary society may have changed since it is accompanied by its own industry, so that as its role changes we should not forget its autogenic qualities that gives leisure its potential – something that is part of one's lifestyle, that is enjoyed, and offers the capacity building that helps to cope with stress.

o   While leisure research come with a rich history, its changing role in society, the blurring of boundaries between work and life and the way lifestyles are also being reshaped offer opportunities to research how leisure coping is changing ensuring its potential as a coping strategy is recognized.

EMOTION APPROACH COPING RATHER THAN EMOTION AVOIDANCE COPING: 'A NEW AVENUE FOR RESEARCH'

o   The significance of the 'affective revolution' and the positive psychology movement opens 'a new avenue for coping research' (Folkman & Moskowitz 2004, p. 764).

o   The above may have provided the context that prompted the research interest in emotion approach coping (Austenfeld & Stanton 2004).

o   Emotion approach coping signals a shift in focus from the more traditional view that takes an avoidance emotion approach (Austenfeld & Stanton 2004, pp. 1335–1336).

o   Emotion approach coping involves emotion processing (e.g. I take time to figure out what I am really feeling) and emotion expressing (e.g. I feel free to express my emotions) (Austenfeld & Stanton 2004, pp. 1342–1343).

The meaning of coping effectively

In their review of the idea of coping effectiveness, Folkman and Moskowitz point to it remaining 'one of the most perplexing in coping research' (2004, p. 753; see Dewe & Cooper 2012, pp. 147–150). Two theories guide our understanding of effectiveness, (see Dewe & Cooper 2012, pp. 147–150) and as we have discussed before our review of these theories is simply to set the context and to understand that what is now needed is to supplement these theories by developing an understanding of what is actually meant by coping effectiveness – to arrive at what does effectiveness mean to those coping with work stress. These theories fall under two general headings: 'outcomes', and the 'quality of fit between coping and the demands of the event' (see Dewe & Cooper 2012, pp. 147–148; Folkman & Moskowitz 2004, p. 754). However, these two approaches to understanding effectiveness have been described as modest (Lazarus 2000), as 'the most vexing of problems is what we mean by effectiveness and how do we measure it' (Lazarus 2000, p. 672); illustrating the importance of the context in determining the evaluation of effectiveness and who it is that is making that evaluation (Folkman & Moskowitz 2004). The outcomes approach views effectiveness in the sense of goals that are valued and significant to the individual and relevant to the context (Folkman & Moskowitz 2004, p. 754).

However, this approach to effectiveness tends to 'mask important complexities' (see Dewe & Cooper 2012, pp. 147–150; Folkman & Moskowitz 2004, p. 754). Folkman & Moskowitz (2004) point to the need to take into account the nature of the outcome in terms of it being short-term or long-term, each requiring different evaluations of effectiveness, the impact of one outcome on another, the issue of the nature of resolution and who makes the evaluation of how effective an outcome is (2004, pp. 754–755). Then there is the 'cost' of the outcome, as outcomes may be achieved but carry costs, and what this means in terms of it being evaluated as effective (see Dewe & Cooper 2012, pp. 148–149). Perhaps this means that more work needs to focus on the qualities of outcomes in terms of their meaning, exploring what has actually been resolved, how resolution is evaluated, and their impact on the individual and how that colours the quality of the meaning and determines what is actually achieved (Folkman 1997, 2011; Folkman & Moskowitz 2004). Determining these qualities of outcomes may not be an easy task (Folkman & Moskowitz 2004).

The second approach explores effectiveness in terms of the 'goodness of fit' between the nature of the encounter and the coping strategies used. Here the focus moves from the outcome to the 'process', although by the very way fit is expressed outcomes cannot be ignored (Dewe & Cooper 2012, p. 148; Folkman 1982; Folkman & Moskowitz 2004). At the heart of this approach is the suitability of the coping strategy in relation to the characteristics of the context. Evaluating the 'goodness of fit' is explored through the individual's appraisal of the encounter (Folkman 1982; Folkman & Moskowitz 2004). This approach needs agreement, first on the idea of 'fit' making theoretical sense and, second, that researchers accept the importance of the role of appraisals which is critical to this approach. This means what constitutes a 'good fit' must be accompanied by a more refined understanding of the meanings that accompany that 'fit', and the contextual and individual differences that surround it (see Dewe & Cooper 2012, pp. 149–150; Folkman & Moskowitz 2004). Indeed, this is a powerful argument that reinforces the need to give more attention to the way stressors are appraised, as they provide the personal context that in this case advances our understanding and assessment of the goodness of fit and coping effectiveness.

Yet despite the research that accompanies both these approaches, the question of what is actually meant by 'effectiveness' (Dewe & Cooper 2007) is left open. This is a question that reflects a sense of frustration over progress so far when reviewers (Somerfield & McCrae 2000, p.622) comment 'what is meant by effective coping' and indeed 'what is ineffective coping' and 'by what criteria' should it be judged (Dewe & Cooper 2012, p.147; Somerfield & McCrae 2000).Yet both for outcomes and 'fit' there is the need to understand the nuances that reflect their qualities, how they give meaning and the context within which they are made as it is only in this way can we achieve a sense of what it means to cope effectively (see Dewe & Cooper 2012, pp. 148–149). Exploring the meaning of outcomes and 'fit' cannot be understood without descriptive knowledge of the context and the role played by individual differences (see Dewe & Cooper 2012; Folkman & Moskowitz 2004), adding to the complexity of arriving at what it means to cope effectively.The context gives the interpretive meanings to outcomes and offers a way of understanding why coping strategies are used, and their effectiveness (Dewe & Cooper 2012, pp. 148–149). Without this descriptive knowledge we are only getting 'half the story' (Dewe & Cooper 2012; Zeidner & Saklofske 1996, p. 506) suggesting the need for a qualitative approach to capturing what it means to cope effectively.

The relationship between 'personality and coping' has had a fractious history in relation to stress research, but it adds another layer of complexity to understanding and assessing effectiveness of coping (Dewe & Cooper 2012, pp. 149–150). Nevertheless research points to the role that personality has in influencing coping and its effectiveness. In fact, Watson, David and Suls (1999) in their review clearly conclude that general traits like extraversion and conscientiousness 'should be routinely assessed in research on stress, coping and adaptational outcome' emphasizing this view by concluding that these 'basic traits of personality would encourage the development of more complex conceptual models' (p. 135). As we have mentioned before (Dewe & Cooper 2012, p. 150), personality may also dispose individuals towards using a particular coping strategy, influencing how flexible they are in coping (Folkman & Moskowitz 2004). It may also determine how they may prefer to use a coping strategy, when and in what order coping strategies are used, how coordinated they are, how determined they are to use a particular coping strategy, and how personality will influence appraisals, aims and expectations (O'Brien & DeLongis 1996, p. 808).

Coping flexibility

Coping effectiveness draws attention to the idea of 'coping flexibility' (Folkman & Moskowitz 2004). Coping flexibility has been defined as 'the ability to discontinue an ineffective coping strategy and produce and implement an alternative coping strategy' (Kato 2012, p. 263). This idea of flexibility acknowledges the ideas of 'fit', but extends it through the definition above by pointing to a reciprocal process involving two types of coping: evaluative coping and adaptive coping. Evaluative coping refers to the recognition evaluation - that the coping is not producing the ideal outcomes. But it is not a question of 'abandoning' the strategy, as flexibility requires adaptive coping: 'considering an alternative strategy' and 'creating alternatives and implementing them' (Kato 2012, p. 263). This process 'includes aspects of repertoire coping' (Kato 2012, p. 263). Testing the flexible coping hypothesis has led to the development of the coping flexibility scale (Kato 2012) and findings that point to flexible coping producing adaptive outcomes (Kato 2012).

Coping flexibility refers not just to how individuals vary their strategies across events, but whether such flexibility is appropriate (Cheng 2001), pointing to the role that individual differences play in coping flexibility (Cheng 2001; Cheng, Kogan & Chio 2012), with findings supporting the fact that more flexible individuals experience higher levels of well-being (Cheng et al. 2012). Cheng and her authors are 'advocates' for the idea of whether interventions focused on coping flexibility can equip employees to cope with the changing work context more effectively. Their work showed that employees in such a flexibility focused intervention 'reported [not just] the largest increase in levels of coping flexibility [but also] a corresponding decrease in depression' supporting this type of intervention (Cheng et al. 2012, p. 272). Interestingly those higher in coping flexibility 'are more likely' to better detect 'subtle' changes in the environment and tend to use a variety of coping strategies to cope with stressful encounters (Cheng et al. 2012, p. 274).

This view of coping flexibility points to its 'role as a relevant resource that fosters adjustment to the changing work environment' (Cheng et al. 2012, p. 273). It also emphasizes the transactional view of stress as 'a dynamic process that is receptive to situational changes', offering a concept of 'active adjustment to the changing environment' (Cheng et al. 2012, p. 273). Coping flexibility points to the patterning of coping, and therefore creative measures are required in order to understand the way coping strategies pattern and are derived, and the role they play in that pattern in relation to one another. This is fundamental knowledge if we are to enhance our understanding of coping and how as a process it works. It also raises the role of individual differences bearing in mind how personality influences coping particularly in the way it may prioritize coping strategies (O'Brien & DeLongis 1996, p. 808). It also points to the significance of the role that appraisals, goals and aspirations play.

Coping: A postscript

Coping and ageing

Exploring the varieties of coping shouldn't be regarded as reflecting the full gamut of coping research. Researchers have, for example, explored coping using a 'life cycle approach' (Kirkwood & Cooper 2014; Frydenberg 2002), with its emphasis on the vitality of coping, but pointing to how coping goes beyond a 'means to help people deal effectively with stress' to 'motivate[ing] them to engage in self-actualizing behaviours that contribute to life's challenges' (Frydenberg 2002, p. v). Other reviewers of lifespan research (Aldwin 2011), while noting the measurement complexity that accompanies ageing research, argue for a developmental framework to be more embedded in stress research, and again emphasize the need for 'a positive perspective' pointing to the need to understand in the ageing process 'what is gained in late life as well as what is lost' (p. 29).

Coping and gender

Reviews (Helgeson 2011; Tamres, Janicki & Helgeson 2002) on coping and gender point to an expanding literature. These reviews are rich and wide ranging, but when the future directions for coping and gender research are discussed, they reveal the need to better articulate gender differences in coping and the complexities that accompany this research. Helgeson begins her review by suggesting that researchers need to begin by 'moving beyond the examination of sex differences in stress and coping and focus on explicating the reasons for those differences' (p. 80). Acknowledging the work on the influences of status and gender roles, Helgeson's general conclusion is that 'little research has explicitly examined whether sex differences in stress and coping are due to these variables' (p. 80). Her second point is that where the research goal is to understand whether one sex uses a coping strategy more than the other, this requires a shift from an absolute (mean scores) to a relative position, and needs consideration as a 'simple comparison of men and women on a certain coping strategy is not necessarily informative with respect to gender' (p. 80) since 'relative coping reveals a different pattern of sex differences than analysis of absolute coping' (Tamres et al. 2002, p. 25). Although Tamres and colleagues did find that whether 'the analysis was absolute or relative women clearly engaged in more support seeking than men' (Tamres et al. 2002, p. 25).

Helgeson also advises caution when thinking in terms of whether certain coping strategies are more adaptive for men or women, since findings have 'not been conclusive' (p 81). So, as Helgeson argues, these inconsistencies in findings suggest there may be other variables that 'are more important than gender – or other variables that need to be considered in the context of gender – that predict coping' (p. 81), suggesting that the nature of the stressor 'could be a good candidate' (p. 81) but pointing out that this too is likely to be influenced by gender.

Nevertheless, the question of whether certain coping strategies are more adaptive for men and women should be decided 'when they are faced with similar stressors that have similar demands' (Helgeson 2011, p. 81). All the same, these reviews urge researchers to be more sensitive to the nature of the stressor (Helgeson 2011; Tamres et al. 2002). Just as important a finding is where researchers 'need to be aware' (Helgeson 2011, p. 80) that in the majority of studies reviewed women are appraising the stressor as 'more severe than men' (Tamres et al. 2002, p. 26), suggesting that working from the appraisal rather than the 'objective' stressor may enhance our understanding of the role of sex differences in coping. Finally, as Helgeson suggests, research points to the concept that at times 'men and woman are physiologically reactive to stressors that are relevant to their gender roles' (p. 81). This research, like others in the field of stress and coping, is confronted with the difficulties that surround how coping is measured. So researchers are urged to be more sensitive to, and give 'greater care' to, how coping is 'delineated' to benefit the interpretation of findings (Tamres et al. 2002, p. 27). But also researchers should focus on what has been described as 'gender schematicity' (Bem 1981), where not only do 'people differ in the extent to which they adhere to gender roles, people also differ in the extent to which they encode the world in terms of gender' (Helgeson 2011, p. 81).

Coping and personality

Researchers have also shown an interest in coping and personality, with this work moving through three generations of research (Suls, David & Harvey 1996), with the latest being described as a growing revival of interest in the role that personality plays in stress research (Ben Porath & Tellegen 1990; Cartwright & Cooper 2009a). As noted in the section on determining coping effectiveness, researchers suggest that general traits like extraversion and conscientiousness 'should be routinely assessed in coping research' (Watson et al. 1999, p. 135). The view that emerges from the coping-personality research is that researchers should now be as sensitive to what a person is like, and that this view should assume as much attention as is traditionally given to what a person does (Costa & McCrae 1990). As mentioned earlier the relationship between coping and personality has been fractious, and this is best explained by Lazarus when looking back at the role of personality research in stress research. Its role in stress research Lazarus suggests was not lost on researchers, but it was more the case that 'other research agenda[s] were more important to us at the time' (1990, p. 42). Indeed it was Lazarus's works that helped to guide and provide a context for this third generation of personality of research.

   The challenge for those interested in personality and coping is the problem that faces all those interested in coping research, perhaps more apparent in this type of research, because here you have the stability of the Big 5 measure of personality set against all the debates and challenges that face the search for what could possibly resemble a stable solution that measures coping strategies. It is this dilemma that seems more visible for those exploring the personality-coping relationship, with this frustration best captured by Carver & Connor-Smith (2010, p. 685) when they suggest what is a 'bewildering number of distinctions made' between the broad categories of coping. Researchers are acutely aware of this difficulty, and reviews point to the future directions research should take when investigating a relationship where one part of the relationship offers stable measurement (Big 5) and the other where the boundaries that express coping's qualities are not yet reflecting a similar stability (Carver & Connor-Smith 2010; Connor-Smith & Flachsbart 2007). Despite these challenges researchers need to note the consistent role in the coping and personality relationship that extraversion, conscientiousness and openness play.

TABLE VII.2

A POSTSCRIPT TO COPING RESEARCH

Exploring the varieties of coping strategies should not be regarded as reflecting the full gamut of coping research. Coping research covers a wide range of topics, all illustrating the complexities of the field. Some examples of these perspectives that enrich the field are listed below.

COPING FLEXIBILITY

o   'The ability to discontinue an ineffective coping strategy and produce and implement an alternative coping strategy' (Kato 2012, p. 263; Cheng 2002; Cheng et al. 2012).

COPING AND GENDER

o   The need to better articulate gender differences in coping and the complexities that accompany this research (Helgeson 2011; Tamres et al. 2002).

COPING AND AGEING

o   Introducing a lifecycle and lifespan approach and a development framework (Aldwin 2011; Frydenberg 2002).

COPING AND PERSONALITY

o   An emphasis on the role that personality plays in coping research (BenPorath & Tellegen 1990; Costa & McCrae 1990; Suls et al. 1996; Watson et al. 1999).

COPING AND CULTURE

o   A shift from the prevailing Western individualistic values and orientation – because of culturally diverse populations – to the idea of collective coping (Bhagat et al. 2012; Kuo 2013).

Where to from here?

Concluding their review, Folkman and Moskowitz point to how 'despite the complexities inherent in the study of coping research', it 'continues to hold great promise for explaining who thrives under stress and who does not', arguing that coping research as a field of study is maturing, with this maturity reflected through its ability to accommodate 'healthy debate and thoughtful criticism' (2004, p. 768). Debate and criticism will continue as researchers, through their creativity, understand the need to refine concepts, and offer new ways of applying their findings if we are to better consider the fundamental importance coping plays in our understanding of the stress process. This places an obligation on researchers to lead; to avoid the convenience factor – the accepting of the status quo – and build on the continued pursuit of innovative practices that have made this maturity possible (Dewe & Cooper 2012).

It is not our aim to make coping research seem impossibly difficult, but there is no doubt it is complex, although with many avenues for fruitful research. Researchers have also shown their creativity by using and pointing to the benefits that follow from the use of 'within-person, process-oriented' approaches which include emotional narratives (Lazarus 1999) and daily process designs (Tennen, Affleck, Armeli & Carney 2000; Dewe & Cooper 2012, p. 145). In this way, researchers need to take on the dictum of Coyne and Racioppo (2000, p. 659) that 'coping research can be only be solved by "radically refashioning coping research"' (see Dewe & Cooper 2012, p. 144), emphasizing 'the continual need to search for alternative eco-logically sensitive approaches' (Dewe & Cooper 2012, p. 144). If we were to identify the three themes that have expressed the way the concept of coping has matured they would be 'meaning', 'context' and 'measurement'. These three themes are not mutually exclusive and it is their interdependence that explains the explanatory potential that resides in them, and illustrates the crucial role they play in advancing our understanding of the complexities of the stress process, and how people adjust to the challenging experience of work in challenging times (indeed in tumultuous times). We will comment on each of the three.

Meaning

Two points follow: how the importance of 'meaning' is fundamental to our understanding of the stress process; and the potential benefits that a meta-view of coping offers in enhancing our understanding as to how coping strategies are used to give meaning to their type and nature. We turn first to 'meaning making' and the critical role it plays in understanding coping and stress research (Park 2011; Park & Folkman 1997). The importance of its role is illustrated by Park (2011) by the way she distinguishes the different points in her meaning-making model of coping and the different roles played by meaning; the role of global meanings, situational/appraisals and meaning-making coping. Meaning-making coping has a strong following in the coping literature.

However, in the work stress literature, where meaning-making coping may be flourishing, the significance associated with the explanatory power of appraisal (personal meanings) languishes in comparison, and has not been given the attention it deserves (Dewe & Cooper 2012, p. 77; Dewe et al. 2010). Although Park (2011), in her review, indicates there is still work to be done on 'meaning making' coping in terms of it being measured and the ways measures capture the different types of meaning-related constructs. Yet the work stress literature seems to still debate the role of appraisal, even though it is these personal meanings that individuals give to stressors that set the very context for coping and the causal pathway for emotions (see Dewe et al. 2010; Dewe & Cooper 2012, p. 77; Frese & Zapf 1999; Schaubroeck 1999). As we have argued before (Dewe & Cooper 2012) the explanatory author-ity that 'personal meanings' offer is not in doubt, and ignoring them is to ignore one of the most crucial steps in the stress process – and in this case the opportunity to enhance our understanding of that process (Dewe et al. 2010; Dewe & Cooper 2012, p. 77). We should also bear in mind the work of the growing research pro-gramme that explores the personal meanings of stressors appraised as challenges and hindrances and its explanatory potential (LePine, Podsakoff & LePine 2005; LePine, LePine & Jackson 2004; Webster, Beehr & Christiansen 2010; Webster et al. 2011).

The coping literature – particularly that exploring coping flexibility – brings to our attention a meta-view of coping (Cheng et al. 2012). The significance of this view is that it focuses on how coping strategies are used; how different coping strategies relate to each other and the roles they play in that relationship, emphasiz-ing as we have done before the importance of investigating the patterns of coping and profiling those patterns providing the opportunity for researchers to investi-gate the 'variability of patterns' and at the same time illustrating the dynamics of the coping process (Cheng 2001, p. 815; Dewe & Cooper 2012, pp. 146–147). It is this meta-view of coping that moves researchers to think in terms of coping pat-terns or clusters (Dewe 2003), and extending that thinking to the dynamics of the pattern and the roles coping strategies play in the pattern. It allows researchers to ask the questions 'why that pattern and what does it mean?' It provides a context for exploring coping and shifts our focus to what may be a more fruitful level (Dewe & Cooper 2012).

Context

Thinking of 'context' is important because it gives meaning to our understanding of coping. It is clear contexts operate at different levels. There is the social, economic and political context, and how this shapes our goals, values and expectations ('global meanings') (Park 2011; Park and Folkman 1997). Then there is personal meaning (appraisals) that set the context for coping and work stress research (local meanings) (Park 2011; Park & Folkman 1997). Then there is what can describe as the 'method context' – the patterning and clustering of coping strategies provided by a meta-view of coping (Cheng 2001). All of these help to explain why coping has been described as a contextual process, and help to explain how difficult it is to derive a stable solution for coping strategies. Stress research can focus at any of these levels, but recognizing that each level is co-dependent in some way for, as Rousseau and Fried explain, 'context comes from Latin root meaning "to knit together"' (2001, p. 1).

So when introducing the concept of meaning, researchers need to be more sensitive to the different nature of the contexts in which meanings reside and what that means for measurement and interpretation (Dewe & Cooper 2012). It at least requires work stress researchers to acknowledge that meanings create contexts and they are a powerful explanatory tool.

Measurement

Meaning and context point to the ever-present issue of measurement. Two points are clear, and they are not mutually exclusive. The first covers issues we have rehearsed before. When researchers look to answer the question 'whose reality are they measuring' (Cooper & Dewe 2004; Dewe & Cooper 2012, p.161; Dewe et al. 2010), this requires a knowledge base that includes meaning and context, and measures that 'are ecologically sensitive that express how individuals think and feel' (Dewe & Cooper 2012, p. 161). This directs researchers towards considering the subtleties in measurement, which requires (as we have discussed before) distinguishing between measures that 'describe a relationship and [those] giving that relationship meaning' (Dewe & Cooper 2012, p. 161). Because of the turmoil of recent times researchers need, and are acutely aware of, and have, when considering 'whether our measures are measuring what we think they are' (Cooper & Dewe 2004; see Dewe & Cooper 2012, p. 161; Dewe et al. 2010) and where our measures are taking us (Dewe & Cooper 2012), developed creative measurement techniques and so seemingly accepted the need of continually refining measures. 'Refining' is a measurement issue that needs to become a regular practice, reflecting our need to continually build, renew and develop our measurement practices (Dewe & Cooper 2012). Creative methods that are ecologically sensitive to context and meanings and reflect 'in-depth, idiographic techniques that attempt to map the psychological terrain' (Snyder 1999, p. 327) 'need now to become a more significant part of our measurement repertoire' (see Dewe & Cooper 2012, pp. 144–145).

Interestingly, measurement builds its own context, with its own rules and procedures for how data should be organized and analyzed, with its own themes of 'fit' about how measures relate to the experience of work but also reminding researchers how, because measurement is contextual, it is subject to change. We should also emphasize that measurement is not independent of the advances made in our knowledge, so measures must express these changes ensuring that relevance is given the same emphasis as traditionally has been given to reliability (Dewe & Cooper 2012).

The second point in terms of measurement is its focus, the idea of a meta-view of coping (Cheng et al. 2012), and the potential explanatory power that this view gives to understanding 'coping in use'. The importance of this phrase 'meta-view', building on, and expanding the view of Cheng (2012) and her colleagues, is that its focus lies in, and draws attention to, the patterns or clustering of coping strategies, giving voice to Folkman and Moskowitz's (2004, p. 753) point that coping strategies 'seem to travel together'. The strength of taking a meta-view offers a perspective that lies in the patterns or clusters of coping strategies, providing a context that allows our understanding of the coping process to develop by offering a closer examination of the nature of coping patterns and clusters; how strategies pattern or cluster allowing perhaps the meaning of that pattern or cluster to be explored, how coping strategies work together and the variety of roles coping plays – support, compensatory or inhibiting – in that pattern or cluster (Dewe 2003). Viewed coping strategies in a pattern or cluster (a coping context) allows researchers (Dewe & Cooper 2012, p.147) to question why that combination, and how it expresses how the coping strategies are being used. This meta-view may also help to explain how a particular coping strategy may, depending on the pattern or cluster, play different roles (Dewe 2003; see Dewe & Cooper 2012, p. 147). If we are to enhance our descriptive knowledge of the nature of coping, researchers would be advised to consider the idea of a meta-view as an approach to doing that.

Summary

Research into coping with work stress brings with it 'a boundless enthusiasm', perhaps because this research has an 'immediate personal relevance' to all of us (Aldwin 2000, p. 73). This does not mean that coping research is free of controversies, critical debate and discussion – far from it, as researchers question how it should be measured (Coyne & Racioppo 2000) and its complexity (Aldwin 2000) as an area of study. Our intention in this chapter has been to explore the challenges facing coping researchers by exploring the coping research context focusing on the growing variety of coping (Folkman & Moskowitz 2004) strategies that may reflect the social and economic turmoil that captures the first years of this century. From the growing of varieties of coping we point to two measurement issues: the design of coping checklists, and the classification of coping strategies. The first issue is that now because of the growing varieties of coping strategies researchers need to be more sensitive to the context and to the way the encounter has been appraised (Lazarus 1999, 2001) when designing coping measures, to ensure participants can express the range of strategies they may use. If coping checklists offer a utility to researchers then researchers need to be mindful of their limitations and their design, particularly their contextual sensitivity to describing participants 'thoughts and actions in detail' (Lazarus 1993, p. 236). The second issue flows from the first and concerns the classification of coping strategies; often the first challenge facing researchers and so dependent on how sensitively coping strategies have been measured. Work on classifying coping strategies develops in conjunction with our knowledge of the growing varieties of coping strategies individuals use and the complexities associated with their measurement. So, as the coping research literature illustrates, the classifying of coping strategies is dependent on the sensitivity of our measures to the growth in the variety of coping strategies, making this issue of classification an evolving one; but empirically strategic if our knowledge is going to continue to develop in a consistent way. Irrespective of the research objectives poor measurement practices will fundamentally limit our progress and our ability to answer the important question of how coping strategies are actually being used; placing any attempt to classify them in doubt. This chapter turns to other challenges facing coping researchers, all in their way reflecting the need for consistent measurement. It reviews issues as to what we mean by coping effectiveness and coping flexibility before turning to the almost parallel fields of coping and gender, coping and ageing, coping and personality, and coping and culture. The chapter ends by returning to three themes that capture the essence of future coping research: meaning, context and measurement. It is these three themes that we argue will set the future agenda for coping research, allowing this field to signal its maturity and acknowledge its creativity when exploring how individuals cope with challenging if not tumultuous times.

VIII

INTERVENTIONS AND CHALLENGES

Stress interventions are a central interest to those engaged in researching work stress. Despite its long history, intervention research 'remains a thorny and complex issue' (Biron & Karanika-Murray 2014, p. 85). A number of reasons help to explain this complexity. These reasons are partly economic and social, representing the forces we have discussed earlier including the long arm of globalization, and the rapacious speed of technology reshaping work and the type of work, and the way we work. They also reflect the way the economy and society is changing, crafted, described, refined and expressed through the restructuring of organizations, a diverse work-force and the meanings attached to health and well-being.

These forces have at the same time reshaped the face of organizational psychology. With a change in focus from interactional models to transactional models where studying the process becomes the goal when explaining work behaviours, the importance of meaning and its explanatory potential, the influence of the positive psychology movement where its influence extends beyond the importance of how individuals flourish, to the renewal and enriching of the idea of psychological wellness (Lyubomirsky & Abbe 2003), and how in understanding the realities of work you now need to balance the negative and the positive to get the full picture of the work experience. Change also comes from recognizing that to understand the nature of work, research needs to explore the explanatory power that resides in the context and how it shapes behaviours, the power in qualitative analysis and what it offers as a methodology for capturing the meaning of the work experience, not forgetting that describing a relationship is different to giving that relationship meaning (Dewe & Cooper 2012, p. 6) – all this helping to explain why terms like health promotion, wellness and 'workplace health friendliness' (Drach-Zahavy 2008, p. 197) all make intervention research and its strategies and practices 'thorny and complex' (Biron & Karanika-Murray 2014, p. 85).

The changing face of organizational psychology adds a further level to the complexity of intervention practice. Ironically interventions remain complex because of the creativity of researchers themselves recognizing for example, the requirement to rethink old concepts, their fit and relevance for describing the contemporary work experience. The need to infuse concepts like employability with new meanings and life, to reflect the realities of contemporary work experiences is one example, as is our 'mental maps' of the new patterns of working and whether our theories and models of work reflect these new ways of contemporary working (Ashford et al. 2007). But research also points to emerging new areas to integrate into intervention practice, adding to its complexity. These include, for example, building into intervention practice personal meanings and appraisals of stressors, new behaviours that include for example cyber addiction, problematic computer behaviour, cyber-deviance, workaholism, the changing meaning of health, the boundaries of work and its impact on work–life balance, not forgetting the meaning of balance in the context of the contemporary nature of work, to just mention a few (Brough, O'Driscoll, Kalliath, Cooper & Poelmans 2009).

All of these changes raise the question of how to tackle the intervention literature. This chapter takes a creative approach but begins traditionally, by turning first to a brief history of intervention research by exploring the seminal work on the theory of preventive stress management that forms a context for understanding stress interventions and how they have developed (Hargrove, Quick, Nelson & Quick 2011). Then to illustrate the complexity of intervention practice this chapter explores the debate surrounding the practitioner–academic divide (Briner & Rousseau 2011a), the role of the good work agenda and the importance of the quality of work to health, its meaning and a life of purpose (Coats & Lekhi 2008). Then the chapter changes its focus and 'since most studies focus on the effectiveness of organizational interventions' (Biron & Karanika-Murray 2014, p. 85) explores the issue of their evaluation, examining the argument that intervention research should now move beyond narrowly confining the evaluation of interventions to outcomes and focus more on 'how and why' an intervention works (Nielsen 2013, p. 1042) by exploring process and implementation issues that set the context for understanding the intervention's success. Then from this emphasis on evaluation the chapter moves to ask where in this work on interventions and their evaluation is the guidance that could come from the training and development literature in terms of the transfer of learning and the different levels of evaluation practice? (Baldwin & Ford 1988; Kirkpatrick 1994). Then in a change in tempo the chapter finally examines how accounting for people may offer a way of expressing the 'wellness' of the organization through the concept of intellectual capital (Caicedo & Martensson 2010; Kahn, Stevenson & Roslender 2010; Roslender et al. 2006), and explores what this literature offers those researchers interested in well-being and occupational health interventions.

TABLE VIII.1

THE CHALLENGES FACING INTERVENTION RESEARCH

THE CONTEXT

o Despite its long history, intervention research 'remains a thorny and complex issue' (Biron & Karanika-Murray 2014, p. 85).

o A number of reasons help to explain this complexity: globalization, the rapacious speed of technology and its reshaping of work, the type of work and the way we work. All of these reflect the way the economy and society is changing, crafted, described, refined and expressed through the restructuring of organizations, a diverse workforce and the meanings attached to health and well-being.

o These changes have at the same time reshaped the face of organizational psychology. With a change in focus from interactional models to transactional models where the emphasis is on process as the goal when explaining work behaviours, the importance of the explanatory power of meaning in stress research, the influence of the positive psychology movement where its influence extends beyond its importance of how individuals flourish to the renewal and enriching of concepts like psychological wellness (Lyubomirsky & Abbe 2003, pp. 292–293).

o All these changes, and the realities of the context of work, help to explain why terms like health promotion, wellness and 'workplace health friendliness' confront those interested in stress management interventions (Drach-Zahavy 2008, p. 197) and make it a 'thorny and complex issue' (Biron & Karanika-Murray 2014, p. 85).

The theory of preventive stress management

The theory of preventive stress management (Quick & Quick 1979) 'with its origins in public health and preventive management' (Hargrove et al. 2011, p. 182) has served as the seminal work presenting researchers with a context and benchmark by offering a preventive stress management framework for developing a theoretical and empirical understanding of organizational practices with the aim of 'look[ing] at [the] ways managers can take a healthy, preventative approach to stress' (Quick & Quick 1979, p. 15). The framework is structured in terms of a 'platform and a translated overlay' (Hargrove et al. 2011, p. 182). The platform describes the stress process including both positive (eustress) and negative responses (stress) and outcomes (individual and organizational). The 'translated overlay' identifies the different interventions and their intervention points in the stress process. Three levels of intervention are identified: *primary, secondary and tertiary*. *Primary* intervention aims at reducing stressors, 'managing the level of stress so it is not overwhelming for the employee rather than to eliminate it'; *secondary* interventions offer the resources and techniques for individuals to manage organizational stressors, and these can be 'stressor-directed, symptom-directed or generalized' (Quick & Quick 1979, pp. 18, 21); while *tertiary* interventions include the rehabilitation phase, aimed at the recovery of individuals having experienced stressful outcomes.

The subtext of the theory of stress management helps to illustrate the richness and potency of the model. Quick and Quick (1979) noted that sufficient levels of stress are needed so managing the stress is important, and that primary levels of intervention may not be 'effective for all individuals nor will be possible in all settings' (p. 21). They also note that in any level of intervention the role of management is crucial; it requires 'committed leadership – not only should leaders strive to produce healthy organizations but should also strive for happy organizations' (Hargrove et al. 2011, p. 187), and recognizing that not all stressors have their origins or impact in the workplace, that stress can be positive and beneficial to both individuals and organization. Their framework (Quick & Quick 1979) was to promote health both individual and organizational, and the focus was not just on the objective stressors but their perception of them. They note that any intervention should be culturally sensitive, not just in terms of the organization but 'the cultural demands of the societies in which they [the organization] operate[s]' (Hargrove et al. 2011, pp. 184, 187; Quick & Quick 1979). Much of the language of this framework (Quick & Quick 1979) can be found in the literature and indeed in contemporary research that has followed it, illustrating its seminal value and significance.

Interestingly, reviewing their work (Hargrove et al. 2011, p. 190) 33 years after its conception, Hargrove and his fellow authors including Jonathon and Jim Quick and Debra Nelson provided insights from the research that had accompanied their framework and discuss a number of ways it can be taken forward. The first is to emphasize that their theory 'serves more as a backdrop or framing theory', making it systemic in nature (p. 190). Their theory had not really exploited the positive aspects of the model (p. 190), and it 'explicitly sidestepped "coping" at the outset and came slowly to its incorporation into the theory' (p. 190). The language these authors acknowledged was more towards 'managing rather than coping' (p. 190) but later as these approaches were seen more in terms of meaning and tone, coping was integrated into the theory. The role and the importance of the appraisal process in determining the nature of the stressor reinforced its role in the stress process. The understanding it provides when developing intervention strategies provided intervention researchers with a transactional model (Lazarus 1999) to express their endeavours, where the stress resides not solely in the individual or the environment but in the transaction between the two. Finally 'a deep dive into emotions and emotion regulation' may also provide a potent explanatory opportunity in 'understanding preventive stress management practices' (Hargrove et al. 2011, pp. 190–191).

Since the work of Quick and Quick (1979) and their collaborating authors a rich and expanding literature on interventions has grown that seems now to be at a crossroads, although reviews may be reaching a consensus as to where future empirical efforts should be directed. Reviewers (Burke 2014; Brough, Dollard & Tuckey 2014; Cox et al. 2010; Nielsen, Taris & Cox 2010) point to the innovations that have moulded contemporary intervention research – globalization, technology, developments in coping research like the emphasis on proactive coping, and the positive psychology movement to name a few (Dewe & Cooper 2014). Nevertheless each review seems, in its own way, to get to the point relatively quickly where reviewers acknowledge that intervention research 'has not yet been translated into interventions that are guaranteed to effectively, systematically and substantively improve the health and well-being of employees' (Nielsen et al. 2010, p. 220), or that 'interventions that effectively manage occupational stress continue to have mixed impact' (Brough et al. 2014, p. 1) or 'the evidence is mixed' (Burke 2014, p. 1). But Nielsen and her colleagues question how 'being an applied discipline' (p. 219) and having built a considerable knowledge of the antecedents of health and well-being, where should our priorities lie? The answer it seems is to better our understanding of 'how the effectiveness of interventions can be improved' by moving our research focus towards understanding the process where research 'addresses the design, implementation, [and evaluation] of interventions' (Nielsen et al. 2010, p. 220) or as Nielson and Randall put it 'opening the black box' (Nielsen & Randall 2013, p. 603).

Underlying these arguments lies the issue of what are the responsibilities of an applied field. Reviewers point to the 'lack of attention paid to process and contextual factors influencing the intervention' (Burke 2014, p. 9), the need to arrive at the appropriate principles of evaluation and asking why intervention researchers have not called on the training and development literature as there are marked parallels and much that can be learnt. There is also the moral responsibility we have to those whose working lives we research (Dewe & Cooper 2012). So to get to the question of how best can research benefit from exploring the explanatory potential that resides in an evaluative focus and how does exploring the context and process aid our understanding of what makes an effective intervention, we need first to explore the role of an applied discipline.

The role of an applied discipline – the academic–practitioner divide debate

Most of organizational psychology, because of its traditional applied focus, is beset by an under-current that there is a widening 'gap' or divide between those who research it (academics) and those who apply it (the practitioner), and perhaps more significantly those who are listening to the debate, or are concerned that this 'gap' exists.

So, we begin by exploring the answers – if there are answers – to three questions. Is there a widening gap between what is researched and those who attempt to apply it (Anderson et al. 2001)? How evidence-based is organizational psychology (Briner & Rousseau 2011a)? What is meant by good work (Coats & Lekhi 2008)? In answering these three questions, or at least the first two, the solution seems to lie in the issue of relevance. Turning to the first question the proposition seems to be that unless steps are taken to bridge the gap we are, as a discipline, losing our pragmatism as a science and drifting towards becoming 'a pedantic and popular science' and through them to a 'puerile science' (Anderson et al. 2001, p. 394); or that our work has lost its edge in the sense of being practically useful – its utility is questioned (Corley & Gioia 2011). But the argument is more complex and involves on the one hand balancing rather than choosing between the two dimensions of originality and utility (Corley & Gioia 2011), or on the other hand balancing between rather than choosing between the two dimensions of rigorous research and relevant practice (Anderson et al. 2001, p. 392) – dimensions that express the nature of our discipline and the nature of the divide. Both sets of authors see ways for bridging the rigour-relevance gap.

Corley and Gioia (2011) question how our theoretical contributions can 'most influence practice?' or 'what constitutes a theoretical contribution?' (p. 12), coming down to 'the long standing theme' of 'relevance to practice' (p. 21). The solution is by working towards 'an orientation to' what they describe as 'prescience' – 'it involves anticipating and influencing the type of managerial knowledge needed to deal with coming societal and organizational concerns – what we need to know to enlighten both academic and reflective practitioners' (2011, p. 23). To Corley and Gioia a prescience view 'anticipates the conversations both scholars and societal leaders should be having and influences the framing of those conversations in conceptual terms' (2011, p. 23). It draws attention to what we need to know and 'understand from a theoretical point of view that have relevance for significant organizational and societal issues and problems' (2011, p. 24). Prescience directs researchers towards organizationally relevant future issues, giving managers a focus that is 'sensegiving' and 'sense-making' (p. 28). This requires that as a discipline we need to be able to change our practices that 'better account for the issues and problems central to the organizations we study' (2011, p. 28). The significance of relevance we have emphasized before (see Dewe & Cooper 2012, p. 7) and our motivation here is to raise the consciousness of researchers to its significance and the pivotal role it plays in our discipline.

Anderson and his colleagues through a rich and detailed argument point to the importance of recognizing the significant role stakeholders have in focusing the research emphasis in a direction that allows pedantic or popular research to express our discipline and so we need to engage in 'political activity in order to reduce or redirect the influence of key stakeholders' (2001, p. 391). By widening the range of stakeholders 'in our research endeavours' from the beginning we 'will then pursue research that addresses problems of pressing concerns' (2001, p. 408) allowing 'researchers *and* practitioners'… 'to [fully] appreciate what are the most appropriate questions that need to be addressed, let alone what form the answers might take' (2001, p. 408), ensuring that 'pragmatic science dominates our field, to the benefit of individuals, teams, and organizations alike, in this period of major organizational and social change' (2001, p. 409). These two paragraphs cannot capture the richness of the arguments made, including exploring the nature of different stakeholders and their influence and the importance of relevance to the nature of our discipline. The messages are clear and offer ways of bridging the divide, illustrating in their argument 'islands of excellence' (Anderson et al. 2001, p. 409). Although we may be risking the temptation to turn complex arguments into simple ones, relevance – a powerful tool for researchers – has, it seems, to have two sides to it. One is to ensure that our work expresses the contemporary work experience (prescience) and the robustness of our research is defined in terms of its relevance; giving new meaning to the concept of robustness. Its other side ensures relevance applies not just to the researcher's perception but also in the view of those other stakeholders who play a role in setting the research context and agenda broadening the research context. The importance of a concept like relevancy is that it plays a fundamental role in establishing methodological rigour. Relevance as we have argued before (see Dewe & Cooper 2012, pp. 7–8) should now be as common a concept when thinking about best practice as has been traditional with reliability.

When it comes to the second question that asks whether organizational psychology is an evidence-based discipline then the review by Briner and Rousseau (2011a) suggests not yet, although they do point out that 'given that new information replaces or refines existing information, the evidence base we use is inevitably a work in progress' (2011a, p. 4). As these authors go on to emphasize, it 'is an active process' (2011a, p. 6). Just how close we are to being evidence-based has implications for the researcher–practitioner divide, particularly when such a case is contingent on 'the judicious use of information, practitioner expertise and judgment, evidence from the local context, a critical evaluation of the best available research evidence, and the perspectives of those people who might be affected by the decision' (2011a, pp. 6–7). Briner and Rousseau's review of the key characteristics of evidence-based practice, and their estimation of how evident they are in organizational psychology concludes that as a profession, and being mindful of the barriers faced and those factors we have control over to reach that status, we are not there yet but 'as a profession well positioned, should we wish to do so' (2011a, p. 11).

So against this context Briner and Rousseau offer two 'important means' for bridging the gap between the researcher and practitioner: 'practice-orientated evidence and systematic reviews' (2011a, p. 11). Turning to the first, practice-oriented evidence, this offers a way, when appropriately designed, 'of communicating and sharing ideas that serve the interests of both' researcher and practitioner (p. 12). These offer a way of integrating the knowledge of practitioners and researchers 'at all stages of the research process' and in this way 'overcome the knowledge production problem' 'by producing practice-oriented scientific knowledge' (2011a, p. 13).

The second approach, systematic reviews, are 'fundamental to evidence-based practice' and equally to contributing to closing the gap between researcher and practitioner (2011a, p. 14). These reviews are designed to systematically 'identify and critically' appraise evidence relevant to both 'the causes and possible solutions of organizational problems' (Briner & Rousseau 2011a, p. 14). Underlying these two techniques are opportunities for the collaboration of practitioner and researcher, where shared information allows researchers to understand, acknowledge and learn from the practitioner perspective, as they (the practitioner) learn from the role of the researcher, all built around an organizationally relevant issue. Recognizing the issues practitioners face and the organizational pressures on them, Briner and Rousseau suggest that the role of our discipline as 'knowledge brokers' (p. 20) should be emphasized and the skills of a facilitator be reinforced. It is in the collaborative effort between researcher and practitioner where the strength of these techniques lies. Each technique should now be seen as an 'essential part' of 'the organizational psychologist toolkit' (Briner & Rousseau 2011a, p. 18).

The review by Briner and Rousseau (2011a) is the opening paper debating the role of evidence-based practice in organizational psychology in *Industrial and Organizational Psychology*. The contributors to the debate 'don't dispute the significance of evidence-based practice nor the need to bridge the researcher–practitioner divide but rather consider the best way to get there' (Dewe & Cooper 2012, p. 156) raising issues that point to the complexities and hurdles faced when getting there. The arguments are diverse and, as we have rehearsed before (Dewe & Cooper 2012, p. 156), include for example the question of who decides what we mean by evidence (Boatman & Sinar 2011), what we can learn from other branches of psychology (Catano 2011) and indeed other disciplines, and the question of whether we already have the evidence but need to now better understand why we don't use it or even care to use it (Thayer et al. 2011). Others take a more methodological perspective and bring to the debate the notion that any technique for instilling evidence-based practice in our work needs to be conscious of the diversity of methods in our field and we should not lose sight of those creative alternative methods 'that don't quite fit', cautioning against a proposal that relies on and offers the technique of systematic reviews as the best way ahead (Cassell 2011, p. 25). Or perhaps, as Hodgkinson (2011) suggests, the way forward is to broaden, combine and adapt the techniques that we have already built up rather than emphasizing one particular technique. What is central, argues Briner, is that evidence-based practice is about '*integrating research evidence with the expertise of the practitioner*' (2012, p. 40).

So we have a context into which intervention research may be well placed to add to the debate where researchers are grappling with the issues swirling round the researcher–practitioner divide and the ways this gap can be bridged. But the context of intervention research heralds other changes too that face intervention researchers, including, for example: the influence of the positive psychology movement and its impact on the content of interventions (Fullagar & Kelloway 2012); the impact of globalization and technology on the nature of the work experience and the structure of employment and the diversity of the workforce, raising at the very least the question of the nature of contemporary working and working patterns of people and whether our models of work that interventions are built on reflect them (Ashford et al. 2007); the theoretical changes that explore the ideas of a transactional view where the emphasis is on understanding the process (Lazarus 2001); and the changing nature of health and well-being (Drach-Zahavy 2008). Still leaving the question of what do we actually mean by good work and the role of the good work agenda (Coats & Lekhi 2008)?

The positive messages about individuals flourishing and growth that flows from the positive psychology movement has energized researchers to once again explore the question of 'what makes good work' and what is meant by 'a good work agenda' (Coats & Lekhi 2008) – a theme that runs throughout this book. Why, question Coats and Lekhi, 'does good work matter?' (2008, p.11). They point to how good work has been 'rising up the political agenda' because good work 'or not can affect health, life expectancy and life chances' (2008, p. 11). More importantly perhaps, they capture the contemporary idea that what is needed is a broader view that scopes the idea of good work as going beyond the conventional boundaries of health and safety issues 'to embrace a much wider range of complex issues' (Coats & Lekhi 2008, p. 11). Like the internationalization of well-being, political policy has taken up this concern at a national level as well as an international level with the International Labour Organization (ILO) developing the notion of 'decent work' (Coats & Lekhi 2008, p. 11).

While pointing to the issue of the prevalence of work stress and its affect on health and the costs of this on individuals, families, organizations and society generally, Coats and Lekhi (2008) argue as we noted earlier, that work has to be 'seen as a fully human activity that engages all our talents, skills, capabilities and emotions' (p. 13). What separates the labour market from other markets is that it is a market in people and not a market in things, and when viewed like this it cannot be viewed as anything other than as 'a social act', and so individuals need to be able to choose 'a life that they value' (Coats & Lekhi 2008, p. 13). So if we care 'about a life that they value' then we should care about job quality (Coats and Lekhi 2008, p. 6). What 'trumps all the arguments is the robust epidemiological evidence that the quality of employment has on health, life expectancy and opportunity' (Coats & Lekhi 2008, p. 14).

When detailing 'good work' many of the phrases used to describe it are familiar to organizational behaviour readers as they include control, resources and decision latitude, but what distinguishes this approach is that 'good work goes to the heart of what it means to be human' for without good work 'we are deprived of many of the capabilities we require to choose a life we value' (Coats & Lekhi 2008, p. 16). So good work has underlying it the ideas of social capital, of partnership between employer and employee, mutual trust that does engage, as Coats and Lekhi (2008) argue, the opportunity to use our skills, maximizing our potential, talents and abilities bound together to provide a life of value, meaning and purpose expressing a social act and a fully human activity (Coats and Lekhi 2008). None of this can be achieved without strong leadership and good management. This view of good work chimes with the quality of working-life movement and job redesign and job enrichment. But in good work there is a sense of a broader canvas, which recognizes the broader social context that expresses the nature of work and the forces which shape work and give the individual the opportunities that express a life of value. Perhaps as well it inspires those interested in stress management inventions to understand how important their work is and reinforces the significance of evaluating interventions when set against how important the quality of work is to health, meaning, and a life of value.

TABLE VIII.2

THE CHALLENGES OF AN APPLIED DISCIPLINE

o The stress management literature, it seems, becomes 'a meeting place' – the ground where the issues that surround the nature, obligations and expectations of how an applied discipline meets the challenges of using its knowledge, and more significantly translating that knowledge in a way that it is beneficial to all those whose responsibilities concern the quality of working life (Nielsen et al. 2010).

o Here in this one topic you can find the language that shadows the arguments of the researcher–practitioner divide – 'applied psychology is defined not by the methodology that it uses but by the problems that it seeks to address' (Cox, Karanika, Griffiths & Houdmont 2007, p. 349).

o The issues that capture the challenges of a discipline aspiring to become evidence based – 'how do we determine what is acceptable evidence?' (Cox et al. 2007, p. 350).

o And the good work agenda – 'is it reflective of the reality of organizational life'? (Cox et al. 2007, p. 358).

o The topic of interventions seems to have reached a crossroads. Gone is the need for more work on what factors reduce the quality of working life; 'no more of the same' (Cox et al. 2010, p. 217).

o The focus of intervention research should be now through their evaluation and the process that it entails; evaluating how stress management interventions are using that knowledge to enhance working life (Cox et al. 2010).

o Reviews on intervention research illustrate a rapidly growing literature (Biron, Karanika-Murray & Cooper 2013; Biron et al. 2014b; Burke 2014; Cox et al. 2007; Nielsen et al. 2010) clearly identifying the challenges and issues faced by researchers.

Stress interventions and the emphasis on evaluation

When you begin to examine the stress management intervention literature it immediately becomes apparent that it is a 'meeting place' – the ground where the issues that surround the nature and obligations and expectations of how an applied discipline meets the challenges of using their knowledge and more significantly translating that knowledge in a way that is beneficial to *all* those whose responsibilities concern the quality of working life (Nielsen et al. 2010). Here, in this one topic you can find the language that shadows the arguments of the researcher–practitioner divide ('applied psychology is defined not by the methodology that it uses but by the problems that it seeks to address'– Cox et al. 2007, p. 349), the issues that capture the challenges of a discipline aspiring to become evidence-based ('how do we determine what is acceptable evidence?' – Cox et al. 2007, p. 350), and of course the good work agenda ('it is reflective of the reality of organizational life' - Cox et al. 2007, p. 358).

The topic of interventions seems to have reached a crossroads. Gone has the need for more work on what reduces the quality of working life – 'no more of the same' (Cox et al. 2010, p. 217). The focus now should be on an examination of the process of evaluation, evaluating how effective stress management interventions are and using that knowledge to enhance working life (Cox et al. 2010). This, argues Cox and his colleagues, will be *'challenging* – the starting point' for further research that offers innovation and creativity in its scope and *'promising'* where interventions will point to new research directions that 'bring us closer to our goal of improving working life, health and well-being' (Cox et al. 2010, p. 218).

So what does a model of process evaluation look like? The reason why a process evaluation is somewhat absent in organizational-level stress management research is, argues Nielsen and Randall (2013, p. 602), that researchers are still unsure what elements should be taken into account despite the work being done on identifying such elements. However, there is still a requirement for an integrational framework that 'describes the elements that need to be included in process evaluations of organizational-level stress management interventions' (Nielsen & Randall 2013, p. 602). The model developed by Nielsen and Randall (2013) proposes that the process elements can be organized into three themes: the context; the intervention design and implementation; and participants' mental models (Burke 2014; Nielsen & Randall 2013, pp. 602, 603). The context theme reflects 'the fit' between the intervention and those organizational contextual factors that 'facilitate and hinder successful implementation' (Nielsen & Randall 2013, p. 606). Because the context is complex this theme is discussed in terms of its *omnibus* and *discrete* nature. The omnibus view asks questions in relation to 'where and when' did the intervention take place and 'how did it fit with the culture and conditions of the intervention group' (Nielsen & Randall 2013, p. 607). Omnibus contextual issues also question the capacity of the organization to conduct interventions exploring the organization's experience in developing and utilizing intervention strategies. The discrete view of context explores the specific events that the organization may have been facing and dealing with and 'may influence the effects of the intervention' (Nielsen & Randall 2013, p. 607).

The second theme outlines 'the design and implementation of the intervention' (Nielsen & Randall 2013, p. 603). It involves three elements: *initiation* (who initiated the intervention and for what purpose did it target the problem, and did it reach the target group); *intervention activities* ('risk assessments and action plans'); and *implementation strategy* (who were the drivers of change, who participated in the process, was there a significant sense of participation from employees in the decision making process, what role did senior managers play and how did they support the intervention, and similarly what was the role and support of middle managers and consultants, how was the information on the intervention communicated, and what information was given to participants) (Nielsen & Randall 2013, pp. 603, 604–607). The final theme concerns participant's *mental models*. This theme is divided into two categories and broadly concerns the participants' reactions and behaviours. The two categories include *mental maps* ('readiness for change and perceptions and appraisals of the intervention activities') and *changes in mental maps* (did learning take place and as a result did changes occur in behaviours and attitudes) (Nielsen & Randall 2013, pp. 603, 607–608).

Reviews of intervention research illustrate a rapidly growing literature (Biron et al. 2012; Biron et al. 2014a; Burke 2014; Cox et al. 2007; Nielsen et al. 2010) clearly identifying the challenges and issues faced by researchers. It is these challenges and issues that we focus on to explore what is needed to release the explanatory potential of interventions and how this knowledge can be used to work towards the goal of enhancing the work experience. It is clear from reviews (Cox et al. 2007; Nielsen 2013; Nielsen et al. 2010) that intervention research needs to move beyond narrowly confining the evaluation of interventions to outcomes and focus more on '*how and why*' an intervention works (Nielsen 2013, p. 1042) so as to provide 'sustainable improvements' (Nielsen 2013, p. 1042) and to not limit 'the opportunities of transferring evidence to practice' (Nielsen et al. 2010, p. 221). When turning to the '*why*' this focus broadens intervention research by pointing to the need when evaluating interventions to explore the process or 'implementation issues' (Nielsen 2013) and their impact on an intervention's effectiveness, moving the evaluation phase away from trying to evaluate effectiveness in terms of its content alone; although both are necessary to give a thorough understanding of effectiveness (Cox et al. 2007). It is the focus on the 'why' and on process issues that provides a context within which the content of the evaluation is placed and assessed (Cox et al. 2007; Nielsen 2013; Nielsen et al. 2010). Not forgetting, as Burke reminds us, interventions need monitoring and 'invigorating' to prevent what he describes as 'fade out' (2014, p. 3). 'Focusing on the content of the intervention without considering the attitudes and behaviours of those targeted by the intervention is unlikely to bring about real understanding of why and how a specific intervention has worked' (Nielsen et al. 2010, p. 228). However, this is not without its complexities.

These complexities that accompany stress management evaluations we have touched on above. They include for example exploring what we mean by an applied discipline (Cox et al. 2007, p. 349) and settling perhaps for bringing together empirical robustness with practical relevance that reflects the reality of the work experience. Following the logic of Cox and his colleagues (Cox et al. 2007) this brings with it responsibilities that include determining what is acceptable evidence. Should for example practical evidence be sacrificed by the methods used making it 'not fit for purpose' (Cox et al. 2007, p. 350)? That is of course if attention is given to the question of what is the purpose of the evaluation; and also bearing in mind that describing a relationship does not necessarily give it meaning (Dewe & Cooper 2012, p. 7) or indeed the knowledge to take forward what the result means in terms of the reality of the workplace. Cox et al. (2007) address the question of 'why' (what the results mean) by pointing to whether this meaning comes from evaluating content alone or by broadening the canvas and exploring these results against the context of the evaluation process – implementing factors that may influence the quality of the evaluation. Here Cox and his colleagues (2007) point to how this broader process focus on evaluations has already struck a chord with researchers. As the content and the context 'are unlikely to be separate from the systems within which they operate', Nielsen & Randall (2013, p. 602) point to the importance of this broader canvas approach to interventions giving meaning to their effectiveness.

There is still work to be done in relation to process evaluations. These include for example the implementation factors that should be included or at least identifying the critical ones although the literature now offers proposed frameworks (Cox et al. 2007; Nielsen & Randall 2013). The process focused evaluation will generate different data that suggests different methods that go beyond traditionally used methods simply because the distinction is being made between implementation failures versus content (programme) failures (Nielsen & Randall 2013, p. 602). Nevertheless these challenges also offer promise as they 'hold considerable potential' to advancing well-being and the quality of working life (Cox et al. 2010, p. 218).

The promise of this broader focus on process evaluations offers: (a) a requirement to determine the purpose of the evaluation; (b) methods that are 'fit for purpose,' emphasizing a mixed-methods approach (Cox et al. 2007); (c) the need to distinguish between content and implementation factors and their impact on effectiveness/success (Nielsen & Randall 2013; Nielsen et al. 2010); (d) that this broad canvas gives meaning and answers the 'why' question more effectively; (e) the impact this focus is already having on our knowledge of implementing interventions by identifying the role and significance of line managers to the success of an intervention (Nielsen 2013), and the role and behaviours of those employees as being more than 'passive recipients' to an interventions success (Nielsen 2013, p. 1029); (f) the potential of this broader focus offers the opportunity to explore the transferability of implementing strategies across organizations; (g) how the management of the implementation process is crucial to the success of an intervention (Cox et al. 2007); and, (h) how this broader focus releases researchers' creativity offering them the opportunity to move beyond the traditional approach to content (Biron et al. 2014b; Cox et al. 2010; Nielsen et al. 2010) and explore for example linking leadership style training to well-being (Kelloway & Barling 2010) and balancing work–home demands (Brough & O'Driscoll 2010) and with content moving towards accommodating the ideas of the positive psychology movement – promoting health with individual flourishing, the ideas of psychological capital and gains derived from positive psychological scholarship (Biron 2014; Burke 2014; Cameron & Caza 2004; Luthans et al. 2007a; Meyers, van Woerkom & Bakker 2013). All of these points offer a way forward with many already leaving their mark on the direction of future research.

Intervention theory is like other theories in organizational psychology, being refined to reflect the realities of working life (Cox et al. 2007). The introduction of a process view of interventions points to the importance of the context and its role in shaping and influencing outcomes. It is not, as reviewers make clear (Cox et al. 2007) a one or the other choice as this would not express the realities of working life – 'outcomes are not separate from process' and process provides the context that gives the outcomes meaning (Cox et al. 2007, p. 357). It also means that a process view liberates researchers to think of methods that express the context and the meanings that can be derived from it; freeing researchers to think of those methods that express this meaning and 'fit' the experience of contemporary work. Underlying these arguments is the crucial role that 'research design' plays when offered this broader view of stress management interventions and how it is 'fit for purpose' in providing the meanings that emerge and are crucial in developing our understanding (Cox et al. 2007, p. 358). We too have adopted a broad brush approach to reviewing the literature on stress management interventions to capture the changes and challenges confronting researchers. In this way we have sacrificed for the sake of brevity and hopefully for getting the arguments across, the richness of the work cited, its attention to detail and the depth of argument to give a rather terse overview of a literature that is challenging and encouraging and reflective of the creativity of those guiding the field.

TABLE VIII.3

INTERVENTION RESEARCH: TOWARDS A PROCESS EVALUATION FOCUS

o   It is clear from reviews that intervention research needs to move beyond narrowly confining evaluations to outcomes and focus more on 'how and why' an intervention works so as to provide 'sustainable improvements' (Neilsen 2013, p. 1042) and to not limit 'the opportunities of transferring evidence to practice' (Nielsen et al. 2010, p. 221).

o   The 'how and why' focus broadens intervention research by pointing to the need when evaluating interventions to explore the process or 'implementation issues' (Neilsen 2013).

o   It is the focus on the 'how and why' and on the process issues of evaluations that provides a context within which the intervention is placed and assessed (Cox et al. 2007; Nielsen 2013; Nielsen et al. 2010).

o   There is still work to be done in relation to process evaluation research. This includes what implementation factors should be included or at least identifying those that are the critical ones, although the literature now offers proposed frameworks (Cox et al. 2007; Nielsen & Randall 2013).

o   Process focused intervention will generate different data that suggests different methods that go beyond traditionally used methods simply because the distinction is being made between implementation factors versus content (programme) factors (Nielsen & Randall 2013, p 602).

o   Nevertheless these challenges offer promise as they 'hold considerable potential' to advancing well-being and the quality of working life (Cox et al. 2010, p. 218).

The guidance from the field of training and development

When you explore the reviews of stress management and occupational health, particularly those that focus on evaluation, you get an immediate sense of the work and guidance that could come from the discipline of training and development. Two areas from this discipline come to mind. The first is the issue of the transfer of training (Baldwin & Ford 1988) and the other more obvious one is evaluation (Kirkpatrick 1994). It is clear from the training and development literature that understanding whether training has transferred from an intervention into the workplace depends on the level of evaluation and so each transfer of training and evaluation is needed to understand the success of an intervention. Exploring the training and development field and its work on these two topics of transfer and evaluation may offer stress management researchers 'innovation in design' through 'understanding the science of other disciplines' (Cox et al. 2007, p. 357).

The framework for examining training transfer (Baldwin & Ford 1988) identifies three antecedents for transfer. These are trainee characteristics, training design and the work environment. These three antecedents have direct or indirect conditions of transfer. The conditions of transfer include both 'the generalization of material learned in training to the job context and maintenance of the learning over a period of time on the job' (Baldwin & Ford 1988, p. 64). These conditions of transfer are also influenced by the training materials being learned and retained (1998, p. 65). The conditions of transfer that direct attention to generalization and maintenance of learning and the requirements of learning and retention resonate with the ideas of 'fit' and indeed to the relevance of the content to allow learning to transfer and the purpose of the evaluation to determine whether and in what way learning has been achieved.

But it is the antecedents for transfer that have a powerful presence for the stress literature. These three (trainee characteristics, training design and the work environment) certainly have parallels with Nielsen and Randall's (2013) model through their themes of context, intervention and its design and mental models. A closer examination illustrates the power of these antecedents and their importance to transfer. Trainee characteristics include 'skills, motivation and personality' (Baldwin & Ford 1988, p. 64). Certainly the motivation to learn is acknowledged in the stress literature. The second, training design, incorporates 'learning principles; the sequencing of training material and the job relevance of the training content' (Baldwin & Ford 1988, p. 64) and the language of the importance of design is also reflected in the stress literature. The third is the work environment and in many ways this asks the question what makes a good transfer climate, exploring those factors like support, constrains and opportunities and their role in hindering or advancing transfer. Again process models have recognized the work environment as a central part of their focus. However, whether the stress management literature by using the language of transfer recognizes that this language reflects a coherent framework that is designed to model the transfer of learning, and whether that is their intention remains a moot point. The language of transfer 'is more than a function of original learning in a training programme. For transfer to have occurred learned behavior must be generalized to the job context and maintained over a period of time on the job' (Baldwin & Ford 1988, p. 63). It is these ideas of retention and learning and their generalization and maintenance that signal a future direction that stress intervention research may wish to follow.

When the training and development discipline turns its attention to evaluation then the seminal work of Kirkpatrick (1994) comes immediately to mind (Abernathy 1999). Kirkpatrick's theory describes four levels of training evaluations: reaction, learning, behaviour (transfer) and organizational results-performance (Kirkpatrick 1994). Despite its simplicity, or because of it, the four levels of evaluation theory are the benchmark for those thinking of the training criteria to guide evaluation. There are two things that the training and development literature agree on: the importance of evaluating training and 'the difficulty of doing so' (Alliger, Tannenbaum, Bennett, Traver & Shotland 1997, p. 341). Kirkpatrick's four levels of training evaluation represent a taxonomy, simply classifying the four levels of evaluation. To be of value evaluations must be robust, 'meaningful to decision makers and must be able to be collected within typical organizational constraints' (Alliger et al. 1997, p. 342). This suggestion would seem to resonate with the stress intervention literature.

Kirkpatrick's scheme is not without its critics (Abernathy 1999; Holton 1996), with calls for the four levels to be expanded to include two new levels: 'human good and societal value' and 'return on investment' (Holton 1996, p. 5). Then there are the measurement issues that accompany the four level approach, particularly going beyond financial data towards a learning and growth perspective, the ideas of continuous learning and human capital (Abernathy 1999) all reflecting changes in the nature of working life and the goals of evaluation that make the question 'am I measuring the right thing' extremely important (Abernathy 1999, p. 23). It should also be noted that for most organizations evaluations are carried out at level 1 (trainee reactions) because data 'is easy to collect' but 'not related to other, more meaningful indicators for training evaluation' (Alliger et al. 1997, p. 342) – for example, did changes in behaviour or learning take place, and what has transferred to the workplace? Evaluation has four general purposes: proving, planning, learning and controlling, all of which influence the nature of the evaluation, its style and approach (Easterby-Smith 1994).

The evaluation literature is being shaped and refined by changes to the work experience, reflecting that evaluation despite its complexity must be responsive and relevant. The training and development literature on evaluation provides a corpus of knowledge and a context for those stress and occupational health researchers interested in evaluation. If stress and occupational health researchers are being urged to 'be aware of the limitations of standard designs and paradigms but should also attempt to address them' (Nielsen et al. 2010, p. 228), then the training and development literature may be the first place they turn to as it too is looking for a new generation of evaluation models by reminding itself that methods and paradigms are continuously engaged in a process of refinement (Pawson & Tilley 1997).

Accounting for people as a means of expressing the 'wellness' of an organization

The discipline of accounting is accompanied with now a rich history, grappling with the idea of accounting for people. The debate, sometimes controversial, spans how important and in what way such 'intangibles' as the people side of organizations are to organizations, how they should be measured, what it is that measurement is trying to make tangible and what are the social, moral issues surrounding such measurement attempts (Caicedo & Martensson 2010; Roslender 2009a, 2009b). What perhaps strikes at the heart of this debate, and this argument is one familiar to the experiences of organizational psychology, is that societal changes, global competition and aggressive technological advances have produced what is a 'weightless society', where 'creating value depends less on physical mass and more and more on intangibles such as human intelligence, creativity and even personal warmth' (Coyle & Quah 2002, p. 8). So if these intangibles are now the drivers of organizational growth then the challenge of how to measure them becomes even more important.

The importance of this to those interested in the health and well-being of individuals is that accounting for people now goes beyond its earlier manifestations e.g. human asset accounting and human resource accounting, by being drawn to the idea of intellectual capital as an organizing concept around which accounting for people should coalesce (Caicedo, Martensson & Roslender 2010). Why intellectual capital? As explained by Roslender and colleagues (2006), in a 'weightless economy', 'information economy or knowledge society a new type of asset was increasingly becoming the basis for sustained wealth creation. Organizations were therefore required to acquire, enhance and retain this asset if they wished to be successful in the wealth creation stakes. As the term intellectual capital indicates, this asset has its origins in employees' (2006, p. 53), using 'a simple dichotomy to better understand the process of growing intellectual capital via the relationship between' what they describe as, *primary intellectual capital* ('people and their attributes') and *secondary intellectual capital* ('what they create') (Roslender 2009b, p. 343; Roslender and Fincham 2001; Fincham & Roslender 2004). It is secondary intellectual capital that provides the context within which employees 'can flourish' and develop (Roslender 2009b, p.343).

This idea of building accounting for people around the idea of intellectual capital has significance for those interested in stress and occupation health interventions. The first reason for this is the concept intellectual capital focuses attention on employees 'as the critical source of value creation' (Roslender 2009a, p. 151) and perhaps more significantly encourages researchers when considering measurement issues to think what such a concept offers, since it captures and demonstrates the realities of contemporary work by demonstrating the 'enduring potential that people have to deliver, advance [and] progress organization' (Roslender 2009a, p. 151). The second reason why this work is important to intervention studies is that intellectual capital also opens the way to develop innovative approaches for measuring individual growth and development and more importantly offers the way to explore 'wellness as intellectual capital' (Roslender et al. 2006, p. 48), 'workforce health as intellectual capital' (Kahn et al. 2010, p. 227) and employee health and well-being (Caicedo et al. 2010, p. 436). Such an approach to accounting for people 'merits significant applause' (Caicedo et al. 2010, p. 437).

The experiences of those interested in accounting for people through the lens of intellectual capital have uncanny parallels with organizational psychology. Under the framework of intellectual capital there is the opportunity to explore individual growth and development reflecting shades of the positive psychology movement, not forgetting the work on psychological capital (Luthans et al. 2007a), and of course the work on health, wellness and well-being. In terms of the latter what is important to those interested in well-being and occupational health interventions is the way the concept of intellectual capital has given accounting for people researchers the impetus to expand the concept to include health, wellness and well-being and see them as being at the core of expressing the concept of intellectual capital (Caicedo & Martensson 2010). This view is justified by the fact that 'employee health is not only associated with quality of life for the individual and with wealth in society' but that 'it is a critical resource that supports productivity in organizations and should thus be accounted for' (Arneson & Ekberg 2005; Caicedo & Martensson 2010, p. 286). The talents individuals possess are best seen when there are the opportunities to use them, 'consequently primary and secondary intellectual capital is to be seen as forming two sides of the same coin of human creativity, and potential' (Roslender et al. 2006, p. 58).

Taking the view that 'a fit and healthy workforce is a very valuable organizational asset' then employee wellness becomes a further dimension when intellectual capital is debated (Roslender et al. 2006, pp. 58–59). This does not mean that because there is agreement that organizing under the umbrella of intellectual capital is the way forward for accounting for people, there is a consensus about measurement, but more a recognition of the complexities surrounding measuring it and those components that express it. The concept of intellectual capital, its nature and meaning has also been intensely debated (Dumay 2009; O'Donnell, Henriksen & Voelpel 2006). But two things stand out when thinking about the work done on measuring health and wellness under the banner of intellectual capital: the crucial role of practitioners in developing measures; and a more qualitative approach to better express the nature of such intangibles and their meaning. Both of these resonate with the intervention literature and the experiences of those who research it.

'Accounting for employee health and well-being would be facilitated by embracing a self-accounting approach' (Caicedo et al. 2010, p. 453; Roslender et al. 2006; Roslender 2009b) when exploring the measurement of health and wellness in organizations. This narrative approach follows an emerging practice in measuring intellectual capital more generally where, in this case, it is employees articulating 'their experiences of improved health and well-being within the workforce' (Caicedo et al. 2010, p. 453). Similarly the idea of health statements, a Swedish development, builds on the endeavours of practitioners, researchers and policy makers to counter the growth in sick leave levels with the aim of them 'being accounted for to regain relevance and accordingly managed'(Caicedo & Martensson 2010, p. 291). While this narrative self-statement approach is at an initial stage with no agreed format, Swedish organizations have taken to such an approach simply because 'of the expectation' behind them to 'influence employers to improve employee health' (Caicedo & Martensson 2010, p. 292). The idea of the self accounts is the value of getting 'commentaries provided by the participants themselves… conveying the reality of initiatives [interventions] and encouraging others to be involved' (Roslender et al. 2006, p. 61).

Here perhaps is the point where those interested in the evaluation of well-being and occupational heath interventions could consider whether self-accounts could represent a more sophisticated form of level 1 (employee reactions) evaluation, as discussed by Kirkpatrick (1994). They could represent a touch point where these creative accounting for people approaches, under the banner of intellectual capital measurement, meet the stress management researchers, offering each group the opportunity to explore their approaches to evaluation of health and well-being evaluations, and to explore what could flow from such a meeting in terms of knowledge building and future research. Interestingly Roslender (2009b) draws attention to the idea of 'Intellectual Capital Statements' (2009b, p. 347), building on a Danish development providing another narrative approach that offers insights for those interested in knowledge management (2009b, p. 347).

We began this section on accounting for people by mentioning its rich history. Our aim here was to point to the parallels that touch accounting for people researchers and those researchers interested in stress management interventions and so by drawing attention to what may be interdisciplinary touch points we have not commented on the rich history of those interested in accounting for people. The phases that accounting for people has moved through as a discipline, and the ideas it embraces, have not always be seen as generally or readily accepted, or even convincing by all as having a 'special affinity' with established accounting practice and procedures (Fincham & Roslender 2003; 2004, p.333). What each phase illustrates is a body of creative, innovative and insightful knowledge which can be drawn on by those wishing to progress accounting for people initiatives (Roslender et al. 2006), in a way that now simply best expresses the nature of temporary organizations, the society they reflect and the values they hold. What now is being witnessed via intellectual capital, is the emergence of a new discourse, a greater awareness and a need, perhaps more compelling than before, to better represent those invisible resources – intangibles – that capture the 'dynamics of value creation' in organizations (Fincham & Roslender 2003, p. 782; 2004). If, as Fincham and Roslender suggest, 'the case of intellectual capital accounting' is presented as a concept reflecting 'clusters of ideas to be selected and interpreted in a variety ways' then those interested in work stress interventions may wish to pay attention to these ideas and to interpret the ways they can be placed in their work (Fincham & Roslender 2004, p. 332).

TABLE VIII.4

STRESS MANAGEMENT INTERVENTIONS: WHAT ABOUT THE GUIDANCE FROM TRAINING AND DEVELOPMENT AND ACCOUNTING FOR PEOPLE?

TRAINING AND DEVELOPMENT

o   The guidance that comes from the work on transfer of training (learning) (Baldwin & Ford 1988) and the more obvious work on levels of evaluation (Kirkpatrick 1994).

o   It is clear from the training and development literature that understanding whether learning from training has transferred depends on the level of evaluation of its goals and objectives. The antecedents of transfer depend on the characteristics of participants in the training, the design of the training and the work context – what makes a good transfer climate? These three transfer conditions would resonate with those interested in the evaluation process of stress management interventions.

o The seminal work on levels of evaluation developed by Kirkpatrick (1994) points to moving beyond when evaluating an intervention level 1 (employee reactions) to higher levels that focus on learning (its maintenance and retention), behaviour (transfer) and organizational results and performance. To be of value evaluations must be robust and 'meaningful to decision makers and must be able to be collected within typical organizational constraints' (Alliger et al. 1997, p. 342). Another suggestion that would seem to resonate with the stress intervention literature.

o Exploring the training and development literature may offer stress management researchers 'innovation in design through understanding the science of other disciplines' (Cox et al. 2007, p. 357).

ACCOUNTING FOR PEOPLE AND THE WAY WELLNESS IS EXPRESSED THROUGH THE CONCEPT OF INTELLECTUAL CAPITAL

o Accounting for people comes with a rich history, particularly in terms of 'intangibles' – the people side of organizations, how they should be measured, what measurement is trying to make tangible, and what are the social and moral issues surrounding such measurement attempts (Caicedo & Martensson 2010; Roslender 2009a, 2009b).

o What is at the heart of intangible measurement is that societal changes, global competition and aggressive technological advances produce what is a 'weightless society' where creating value depends less on physical mass and more on intangibles such as 'human intelligence, creativity and even personal warmth' (Coyle & Quah 2002, p. 8).

o So if these intangibles are now the value drivers of organizational growth then the challenge of how to measure them becomes even more important.

o Accounting for people is drawn to the organizing concept of intellectual capital to express the idea that in this changing context it is the people who are important for value creation.

o Using a simple dichotomy to better understand the process of growing intellectual capital, it is described in terms of primary intellectual capital ('people and their attributes') and secondary intellectual capital ('what they create') (Roslender 2009a, p. 343; Roslender & Fincham 2001; Fincham & Roslender 2004).

o It is the idea of secondary intellectual capital that provides the context within which employees can flourish and develop (Roslender 2009b).

(Continued)

(Continued)

o   The concept of intellectual capital focuses attention on employees as 'the critical source of value creation' (Roslender 2009a, p. 151).

o   Then intellectual capital opens the way to develop innovative approaches for measuring individual growth and development, and more importantly offers the way to explore wellness and well-being as intellectual capital (Roslender et al. 2006, p. 48), workplace health as intellectual capital (Kahn et al. 2010, p. 227) and employee health and well-being (Caicedo et al. 2010, p. 436).

o   'A fit and healthy workforce is a very valuable organizational asset' (Roslender et al. 2006, pp. 58–59).

o   Two things stand out when thinking about the work done on measuring health and wellness under the banner of intellectual capital. The first is the crucial role played by practitioners in developing measures (accounting for employee health and well-being would be facilitated by embracing a 'self-accounting approach' – Caicedo et al. 2010, p. 453; Roslender et al. 2006; Roslender 2009b); and 'health statements' (Caicedo & Martensson 2010, p. 291). The second thing that stands out is the narrative approach. The idea of the self accounts is the value of getting 'commentaries provided by the participants themselves... conveying the realities of initiatives [interventions] and encouraging others to be involved'(Roslender et al. 2006, p. 61).

Summary

This chapter on interventions reflects how one area of research and study can seem to be a melting pot for many of the issues facing those working in an applied field. As interventions are the 'doing' side of the discipline it is no wonder that it is a meeting point for those issues facing an applied approach. Much of what we have discussed throughout this book reflects parts of the transactional approach to work stress, and each topic has their own 'doing points', requiring researchers to continually be aware of the issues of process, context and relevance and always being conscious of how those concepts mould our work and 'fit' it to reflect the contemporary work experience. In this chapter we have seen intervention researchers introduce a process view of interventions, pointing to the importance of the context and its role in shaping and influencing outcomes, and simply refining their work to better reflect the realities of working life. This has reinforced the principles of refining and relevance as significant driving forces to make our research robust in terms of its meaning to those whose working lives we study. The term robustness has also been refined not just to refer to its traditional methodological meaning but now its relevance to express the nature of contemporary working lives. In terms of the context that guides intervention work we have also pointed to two other disciplines – training and development, and accounting for people – that may from their perspectives offer intervention researchers opportunities to think in terms of a broader context to better understand interventions and their evaluation by exploring the 'meeting points' where each discipline may add to our understanding. As Biron and colleagues suggest, 'integrating occupational health with daily business remains a serious issue and one of the most challenging parts of occupational health interventions' (2014b, p. 277). A challenge that those cited in this chapter aspire to meet.

IX

CONCLUSIONS

This book has been about the forces of change, and the challenges they present to those interested in work stress and coping research. Researchers have of course been confronted with contextual changes before. But what distinguishes this period is the speed of change, its international consequences and its reach, touching all and ranging across all aspects of society. Leaving all 'with a sense of loss and no little drop in faith in the systems which have underpinned modern, economically developed societies' (Weinberg & Cooper 2012, p. 1). While turbulence inevitably brings uncertainty and stress, these times also brought with them profound, almost unimaginable consequences to well-being and the quality of lives 'nigh on impossible' to capture completely (Anderson et al. 2011, p. 353). These consequences were accompanied by feelings that 'so deeply' challenged the very core of management thinking and practice and, therefore, 'the status quo in our field' (Nord 2005, p. 92), that the creation of 'a new intellectual agenda' for teaching and practice (Ghoshal 2005, p.89) was required. So, accompanying the turbulence, there was a sense that 'bad management theories are destroying good management practice' (Ghoshal 2005, p. 75) leading to people suffering unimaginable insecurity and stress.

So issues like refining measures and theories to express the new realities of work, the significance of the explanatory potency of the concept of relevance to our methods, and its key role in bringing together researcher and practitioner, are issues we believe will strengthen our discipline, allowing it to meet the responsibilities we have to those whose working lives we research. In this concluding chapter we want to explore these issues not in terms of establishing a 'new intellectual agenda' (Ghoshal 2005) because issues like 'refining and relevance' are already embedded in and express the nature of our discipline, but to point once more to their potency, acknowledging the need for descriptive knowledge and the new pathway it offers. Rather than letting these issues remain undercurrents of concern, we herald them as important tools for reshaping our research toolkit, and in this way acknowledge the somewhat 'unobtrusive way' they have contributed to our creativity.

There are, of course, other issues we want to draw attention to now, not exactly mutually exclusive, including concepts like 'refinement and relevance'. But also there are some that we have emphasized before – the importance, for example, of the concept of 'meaning' and its many roles in work stress research (Dewe & Cooper 2012, p. 6), the importance of 'context' and its explanatory potential, and how these issues collectively remind us that we have a moral responsibility to those whose working lives we research. We have explored the forces of change through the concepts of globalization, technology and the reshaping of the workforce, work and society. But each of those forces is changing as well and forging new perspectives on issues. So in setting a context to our discussion of the challenges ahead for our discipline, it is important to note the changing character of those forces and the world within which we do our research.

The changing nature and character of the forces of change

It seems in the discourse surrounding globalization and the turmoil of the economic (human) crises, there is now, through the World Social Forum, the need to look 'for a *different kind* of globalization' (Teivainen 2002, p. 628). This alternative form of globalization is still being debated, in terms of how structurally it can be organized, and how sustainable, social and economic processes, can be developed and integrated (Ayres 2004; Buttel & Gould 2004; Teivainen 2002). The idea is that globalization is multifaceted, and there are likely to be different futures for different facets (Ritzer 2011). 'Green shoots'– in the changing nature of globalization – can be found in the globalization of the concept of well-being (OECD 2013), the internationalization of happiness research (Frey & Stutzer 2005) and the search via the 'good work' agenda (Coats & Lekhi 2008) for the ideal of meaningful work.

These 'shoots' reflect the belief that the narrowness of traditional economic indicators like GDP cannot capture 'the aspects of life that matter to people' (OECD 2013, p. 2), and that by refocusing measuring 'social progress' through concepts like well-being, we can get *'closer* to what really matters for citizens' (Stiglitz et al. 2009, p. 39). This new look to globalization sets the stage for not just thinking about how an applied discipline like organizational psychology can make a difference to 'refining' corporate capitalism (Kasser et al. 2007a), but offers an opportunity and freedom in this broader context, to consider its role and contribution; releasing the power of psychological concepts, and the properties they express, to alter the way globalization is defined. So by lifting the limitations imposed by the more traditional narrow economic definitions, a new facet of globalization is emerging that expresses a more inclusive approach that is concerned with the quality of social progress, offering a new approach to measuring what matters (World Economic Forum 2012a) and signalling the need to give globalization a more 'human face' (Huq & Tribe 2004, p. 921).

Looking for change in the nature and character of technology is simply like exploring its history; identifying its transformational qualities and witnessing how it too has in this transformational process been transformed. So although the boundaries are difficult to capture, because of the speed of innovation and creativity, technology's changing character can be broadly summed up as the computer, the internet, the internet of people and the internet of things. We are entering the 'age of anytime, anyplace, anywhere' (Kleinrock 2008); 'from computer to computer, human to human, human to thing and thing to thing' (Tan & Wang 2010, p. V5–376). Technology's character is now frequently described in words to reflect the age we live in, inevitably defined in terms of the latest generation of creative products on the market, rather than simply describing the age in terms of an information age. Although whether we have ever moved from an 'information age' remains a moot point since we are more likely to describe the age in terms of the flow and availability of information, and how it has changed our behaviours, using words that sum up the age, such as connectivity or interconnectivity, mobile, wired, ubiquitous, contextual, systems, networked, connected, a social lubricant, access, applications or apps and online (Rainie & Wellman 2014; Scoble & Israel 2014). No wonder the descriptor of 'weightless' to describe the nature of the age has stood 'the test of time' (Coyle & Quah 2002, p. 8). The nature and character of technology has changed, but perhaps it is this dynamic transformational property of technology that is its defining quality, and it is this that represents the spirit of the age. Because of this defining transformational quality, rather than attempting to understand it by focusing on the speed at which technology transforms, a more productive route to understanding its quality lies in exploring how 'behaviours have changed' by being part of this technological transformational process. In this way technology's qualities are defined by the way it has changed our behaviour; how we now talk in terms of our cyberbehaviour and have added a new addition called cyberpsychology to our field.

It is interesting to note that in Colbert and colleagues' editorial on the digital workforce (Colbert, Yee & George 2016) the emphasis is on behaviours in an 'exciting transformation of work, work practices and workplaces' and the 'wealth of possibilities' (Colbert et al. 2016, p. 737) for managers to lead and increase performance. In terms of behaviours, they point to the work by Prensky (2001), who describes 'digital natives', usually young people 'completely at home in the world of digital devices' and 'digital immigrants', 'adults who have readily adopted technology as it has become available' (Colbert et al. 2016, p. 731). They point to how 'digital natives entering the workforce differ in their expectations of work and work practices, as well as how these differences might influence the future workplace' (Colbert et al. 2016, p. 731). Interestingly they draw attention to how the increased use of technology may reflect 'declining levels of empathy,' whereas digital competences 'and fluency' could lead to 'gamers' (digital game players) developing 'leadership skills' (Colbert et al. 2016, p. 732). Immediately, it is possible to see changes to the design of jobs, how work is organized, and 'the prevalence of technology in employees' lives may also impact [on] identity development and expression [and] interpersonal relating' (Colbert et al. 2016, p. 733). It also offers a new way of thinking about intergenerational issues in the workforce, and if generations are 'never fully "unplug[ed]"'(Colbert et al 2016, p. 731) and the consequences for work–life balance. All of this endorses the idea of how behaviour is the defining perspective to understanding this technological transformation of the age we live and work in.

The third of the forces of change – work, society and sustainability (Gratton 2014) – have also gone through a transformational process, with the hand of globalization and technology helping to write the script of their transformational change. Words express this change and express if not the world we have then, at least the world that is wanted: 'inclusiveness', 'sharing', 'balance', 'trust', 'transparency', 'connectiveness' and 'sustainability'. The way that work, and society, has been transformed and reshaped by the forces of globalization and technology reflects their power and reach. Looking at the reshaping of work three themes emerge. *Structurally it has changed* in terms of time and place – a blurring of boundaries that reflect the idea of anytime, anyplace and always ready (Kleinrock 2008). *The nature of jobs has changed* reflecting an emotional intensity that attracts new styles of working and new types of work, all reflecting the complexities of a diverse workforce. The third theme requires *different management and leadership styles* that express authenticity coupled with a collaborate style.

This reshaping of work goes beyond just illustrating the power of globalization and technology, because it represents the new context within which we research, and it is the work context that is one of the defining changes of the age. From this reshaping and transforming of work comes at least two consequences that reframe our responsibilities as researchers. The first focuses on and requires the need to confront the old assumptions about 'the images we carry of work', and the new ways of working that are emerging (Ashford et al. 2007, p. 67). This requires giving attention to the variety of 'non standard ways' of working which are rapidly increasing. So it is no longer the case that non–standard work can be assumed to 'look like' standard work, making 'non standard working' a topic 'worthy of study' in its own right 'and also is an ideal context for testing and developing theory about organizations, work, and workers' (Ashford et al. 2007, p. 67). The second theme that stems from the transformational nature of work is what has been described as 'social sustainability'. It concerns the costs imposed on people through organizational and management processes, practices and procedures 'that have serious harmful effects on employees' physical and psychological wellbeing' (Pfeffer 2009, p. 5), or what would make working lives more sustainable where individuals have a quality of working life that is more productive, meaningful and satisfying (Pfeffer 2009, 2010). These forces of change have set for researchers what could be called a 'development' context (Viney 1993) of change, transforming working lives, society and life generally, and in that process transforming themselves. Why 'development'? Because it provides the fertile ground from which new ideas can be developed, old perspectives compared with the new reality emerging, and a context against which we can assess the relevance of our research and those practices that stem from it. A background against which we can evaluate the progress we are making in understanding behaviour at work.

The role of meaning in work stress research

It is the theme of meaning that seems to permeate work stress research, with the potential to provide the descriptive knowledge needed to release a richer understanding of the stress process. While acknowledging the complex roles played by meaning in the stress process, there has been for some time 'a sense that we only have scratched the surface in our understanding of the contribution that appraisal plays in the coping process' (Snyder 1999, p. 331). This is true in work stress research, where the personal meanings (appraisals) given to stressors have not attracted the attention they deserve (Dewe & Cooper 2012, p. 97). 'Appraisals' point to the distinction between simply describing a relationship, and exploring what gives that relationship meaning (Dewe & Cooper 2012, p. 6). Not knowing how a stressor is appraised would seem to diminish our understanding of the role of positive and negative meanings, their causal pathways and their explanatory potential. Not forgetting our ability to fully contribute to the growing body of knowledge that flows from the positive psychology movement, offering a balance between meanings expressing 'a demand and meaning [that acts] as a resource' (Dewe & Cooper 2012, p. 161). 'Appraisals' mean that we are keeping 'an eye on the societal context in which our models live', and by reinforcing this message, Snyder adds 'if our societal values shift as we move into the next century then coping researchers should keep their hands on the pulse of this changing society' (1999, p. 331).

Measuring the role of meaning in the stress process requires researchers to 'be faithful to the dynamic unfolding nature of the phenomena under investigation' (Thoits 1995, p. 63), with calls for 'utilizing the in-depth ideographic approach that attempts to thoroughly map the psychological terrain' (Snyder 1999, p. 327). Both researchers cited point to what has become a more persistent call for measures that represent a more 'ecologically sensitive' approach to capturing the meanings that permeate the stress process, if we are to exploit their explanatory power (Dewe & Cooper 2012, p. 161). To emphasize how close these techniques are to our field and being used to good effect, researchers point to the parallels that can be found in different branches of our own discipline, by pointing to methods like 'the diagnostic approach of a therapist building a model of a client's problem situation' (Oakland & Ostell 1996, p. 142). The warning is that if we are going to advance our understanding of 'appraisals and coping', which are complex processes rich in meaning, 'the status quo mentality about our measures, however, will not suffice' (Snyder 1999, p. 327). Understanding meanings in work stress research is fundamental to our progress, and so the status quo offers no excuse or solution, nor does the convenience that accompanies established measures. What is going to be needed is for researchers to harness their creativity that permits the explanatory potential of 'meaning' to be the centre of attention, so as to release and show the benefits that flow from using measures that focus on providing descriptive knowledge.

The importance and explanatory power of context

Meaning points to the importance of context. 'Contextualization can occur in many stages of the research process, from question formulation, site selection and measurement to data analysis, interpretation, and reporting' (Rousseau & Fried 2001, p. 1). The context 'enhances our understanding of organizational behaviour and the validity of our work' (Rousseau & Fried 2001, p. 1). Thinking contextually is 'a way of approaching research', where that descriptive knowledge or 'a thicker description of the setting' helps 'in understand[ing] the factors that give rise to the researcher's observation' (Rousseau & Fried 2001, p. 6). Meanings build 'contexts', as do methods, and so at this level, without this descriptive knowledge, you are losing not just explanatory power but only getting half the picture. To illustrate this point we have called for personal meanings (appraisals) in work stress research to be given the attention they deserve (Dewe & Cooper 2012, p. 97). It is clear that these 'meanings' initiate the causal pathway to affect helping to explain why, for example, respondents react differently to the same stressor (Dewe & Cooper 2012).

'Methods' also produce boundaries in their quest for rigour, and also set a context and a paradox, whereby by promoting rigour they may lose on the way the sense of creativity by limiting the boundaries or using the traditions that rigour sets. We are not, of course, suggesting the abandoning of the need for rigour, far from it, but only the idea that it necessarily sets boundaries and traditions that researchers need to be alert to in their search for creativity. In this case, we have also called for what has been described as a 'meta-view of coping' (Cheng 2001), where the emphasis is on the way coping strategies pattern or cluster, providing a context for understanding the role each strategy is playing in the pattern (Dewe 2003). This provides a new opportunity and a new context to understand how coping strategies are used, and the different roles they play, adding meaning to the complexities of classifying coping strategies.

The transactional approach offered by Lazarus (1999, 2001) contextualizes the stress process using appraisals (personal meanings) as the mechanism that links the person to the environment, illustrating the 'theoretically rich' role that meanings play in the stress encounter (Park & Folkman 1997, p. 132). In work stress, the call for creativity in methods has long been present (Dewe & Cooper 2007; Folkman 2011; Lazarus 1997, 2000; Somerfield & McCrae 2000) – 'researchers pointing to the benefits that follow from the use of "within-person, process oriented" approaches, which include emotional narratives (Lazarus 1999) and daily process designs' (Dewe & Cooper 2012, p. 145). It was Lazarus (2000) who pointed to how the debate that surrounds the over-dependence on coping checklists may well have masked the creativity that researchers are already using in coping research. Rousseau and Fried also point to context's role becoming more important, as an explanatory tool, as 'the domain of organizational behaviour is becoming more international giving rise to the challenges in transporting social science models from one society to another' (2001, p. 1).

Refinement and the rigour–relevance debate

Here we want to explore the significance of refining our measures, the rigour–relevance debate and the moral and ethical consequences that flow from it. 'Refinement' is about ensuring that measures reflect the realities of the work experience. It is the process that is intimately linked to 'relevance', and gives a new meaning to robustness, where measures are only robust if they are relevant and express the contemporary work experience; and in our view relevance should rank alongside the emphasis given in research to reliability. 'Refinement' requires researchers to ask 'are our measures measuring what we think they are' (Dewe & Cooper 2012, p. 93), and how well do they express the work experience? Refinement means that more frequently than not measures are 'seen more in terms of their ability to describe an experience rather than to actually define it' (Dewe & Cooper 2012, p. 95). Relevance is also described in terms of 'generating insight practitioners find useful for understanding their own organizations and situations better than before' (Vermeulen 2007, p. 755). This suggests that relevance comes with a requirement to better understand the realities of work; working towards presenting 'research that matters… requires multiple commitments: commitment to ongoing interaction with the subjects of study (e.g. managers and employees) and unremitting commitment to rigorous scientific standards' (Vermeulen 2007, pp. 757–758). Hence the rigour-relevance debate.

The 'rigour–relevance' debate comes with a long history (Gulati 2007), and 'the either/or debate is moot' (Gulati 2007, p. 775). A number of themes flow that express this position. The first is that rigour and relevance are not opposites (Gulati 2007) and it is necessary to strike a balance between the two (Gulati 2007; Tushman & O'Reilly 2007; Vermeulen 2007). Each does not assume significance without the other (Gulati 2007), and 'a quest for understanding (*rigor*) with little thought of use (*relevance*)' does not represent balance (Tushman & O'Reilly 2007, p. 769). It is to misunderstand the implications this has for practice, and engaging in research that matters and our commitment to those whose working lives we research (Vermeulen 2007). It also means 'that discovery [is] interactive'(Gulati 2007, p. 780) requiring scholarship that should be 'engaged' with practitioners (Tushman & O'Reilly 2007, p. 771), requiring 'boundary spanning research focused squarely on phenomena of interest to managers' (Gulati 2007, p. 775) and synergistic in its dialogue between practitioner-researcher (Gulati 2007) and how this rigour–relevance balance can enrich the research process (Vermeulen 2007) providing 'actionable knowledge' (Hughes, Bence, Grisoni, O'Regan & Wornham 2011, p. 43). The 'rigour–relevance' debate is complex, with the themes above reflecting the need to slip the shackles of the debate, recognize the significance to a field that is applied and see practitioners 'as informants as well as consumers of one's academic research' (Vermeulen 2007, p. 755); that is, active partners in the relationship.

Perhaps 'relevance' has an inner side and an outer side. The inner side is ensuring that our measures reflect the realities of the work experience, as we have emphasized throughout the book, whereas the outer side is 'researchers discovering through interactions with managers what is important to them' (Gulati 2007, p. 780). Neither the inner nor the outer perspective is mutually exclusive. Each shows a reality that can be achieved (Hodgkinson & Rousseau 2009), that places relevance at the forefront, offering 'a depth to existing scientific constructs and theory as well as an enhanced appreciation of their potential applications' (Hodgkinson & Rousseau 2009, p. 543). Pointing in its wake to the significance of, and the power and authority of the explanatory potential that resides in the context and meanings, giving descriptive knowledge the mechanism for achieving the balance between rigour and relevance. It is also important to remember that there is an ethical and moral argument that binds relevance to rigour. Is it ethical to have measures that fail to capture the reality of the work experience (inner relevance)? And are we meeting our moral responsibilities if we are not asking the right questions (outer relevance) that matter most to those whose working lives we study?

This book has attempted to highlight the central research and practice issue regarding stress in the workplace. We have provided an historical account of the key concepts on stress and coping, and showed the movement toward creating well-being cultures in the workplace of the future. Well-being has become the most topical HR issue of our times, as organizations attempt to reduce sickness absence and presenteeism, and increase productivity. There is a global move toward redefining the objectives in the workplace and society more generally, away from GDP and towards the concept of Gross National Well-being. This current movement has its history as far back as Bobby Kennedy, who in 1968, when he was seeking the Democratic Party nomination for President, said in a speech at the University of Kansas:

> Too much and for too long, we seemed to have surrendered personal excellence and community values in the mere accumulation of material things. Our Gross National Product, now, is over $800 billion dollars a year, but that Gross National Product – if we judge the United States of America by that – that Gross National Product counts air pollution and cigarette advertising, and ambulances to clear our highways of carnage. It counts special locks for our doors and the jails for the people who break them. It counts the destruction

of the redwood and the loss of our natural wonder in chaotic sprawl. It counts napalm and counts nuclear warheads and armored cars for the police to fight the riots in our cities. Yet the gross national product does not allow for the health of our children, the quality of their education or the joy of their play. It does not include the beauty of our poetry or the strength of our marriages, the intelligence of our public debate or the integrity of our public officials. It measures neither our wit nor our courage, neither our wisdom nor our learning, neither our compassion nor our devotion to our country, it measures everything in short, except that which makes life worthwhile.

That is the challenge for our children's future and of the workplace of the future, a culture that values the well-being of all our employees.

REFERENCES

Abernathy, D. J. (1999). Thinking outside the evaluation box. *Training & Development*, 53, February 19–23.

ACAS (2012). Cyber bullying in the workplace is on the rise. Workplace snippet: November.

Ackers, L., & Oliver, L. (2007). From flexicurity to flexsecquality: The impact of the fixed-term contract provisions on employment in science research. *International Studies of Management & Organizations* 37, 53–79.

Ahammad, M., Tarba, S., Liu, Y., Glaister, K., & Cooper C.L. (2015). Exploring the factors influencing cross-border mergers and acquisitions. *International Business Review* 25, 445–457.

Aldwin, C. M. (2000). *Stress, coping and development: An integrative perspective.* New York: The Guilford Press.

Aldwin, C. (2011). Stress and coping across the lifespan. In S. Folkman (Ed.). *The Oxford handbook of stress, health and coping.* (pp. 15–34). Oxford: Oxford University Press.

Aldwin, C. M., & Levenson, M. R. (2004). Posttraumatic growth: A developmental perspective. *Psychological Inquiry* 15, 19–22.

Alliger, G. A., Tannenbaum, S. I., Bennett, W., Traver, H., & Shotland, A. (1997). A meta-analysis of the relations among training criteria. *Personnel Psychology* 50, 341–358.

Allred, B., Boal, K. B., & Holstein, W. K. (2005). Corporations as stepfamilies: A new metaphor for explaining the fate of merged and acquired companies. *Academy of Management Executive* 19, 23–37.

Anandarajan, M., & Simmers, C.A. (2005). Developing human capital through personnel web use in the workplace: Mapping employee perceptions. *Communications of the AIS* 15, 776–791.

Anderson, N. (2007). The practitioner-researcher divide revisited: Strategic-level bridges and the roles of IWO psychologists. *Journal of Occupational and Organizational Psychology* 80, 175–183.

Anderson, N., Herriot, P., & Hodgkinson, G. P. (2001). The practitioner-researcher divide in industrial, work and organizational (IWO) psychology: Where are we now and where do we go from here? *Journal of Occupational and Organizational Psychology* 74, 391–411.

Anderson, P., Jané-Llopis, E., & Cooper, C. (2011). The imperative of well-being. *Stress and Health* 27, 353–355.

Andersson, L. M., & Pearson, C. M. (1999). Tit for tat? The spiralling effect of incivility in the workforce. *Academy of Management Review* 24, 452–471.

Andersson, L., Jackson, S. E., & Russell, S.V. (2013). Greening organizational behavior:
An introduction to the special issue. *Journal of Organizational Behavior* 34, 151–155.

Ano, G. G., & Vasconcelles, E. B. (2005). Religious coping and psychological adjustment to stress: A meta-analysis. *Journal of Clinical Psychology* 61, 461–480.

Appelbaum, S. H., Gandell, J., Yortis, H., Proper, S., & Jobin, F. (2000a). Anatomy of
a merger: Behavior of organizational factors and processes throughout the pre-
during-post-stages (part 1). *Management Decision* 38, 649–661.

Appelbaum, S. H., Gandell, J., Shapiro, B. T., Belisle, P., & Hoeven, E. (2000b).
Anatomy of a merger: Behavior of organizational factors and processes throughout the pre- during- post stages (part 2). *Management Decision* 38, 674–684.

Arneson, H., & Ekberg, K. (2005). Evaluation of empowerment processes in a workplace health promotion intervention based on learning in Sweden. *Health
Promotion International* 20, 351–359.

Arnetz, B. B., & Wiholm, C. (1997). Technological stress: Psychophysiological symptoms in modern offices. *Journal of Psychosomatic Research* 43, 35–42.

Arthur, M. B. (1994). The boundaryless career: A new perspective for organizational
inquiry. *Journal of Organizational Behavior* 15, 295–306.

Ashford, S. J., Lee, C., & Bobko, P. (1989). Content, causes, and consequences of job
insecurity: A theory-based measure and substantive test. *Academy of Management
Journal* 32, 803–829.

Ashford, S. J., George, E., & Blatt, E. R. (2007). Old assumptions, new work. *The
Academy of Management Annals* 1, 65–117.

Ashforth, B. A., & Humphrey, R. H. (1995). Emotion in the workplace: A reap-
praisal. *Human Relations* 48, 97–125.

Ashforth, B. A., & Kreiner, G. L. (2002). Normalizing emotions in organizations:
Making the extraordinary seem ordinary. *Human Resource Management Review* 12,
215–235.

Ashforth, B. E., Kreiner, G. E., & Fugate, M. (2000). All in a day's work: Boundaries
and micro role transitions. *Academy of Management Review* 25, 473–491.

Ashkanasy, N. M., & Ashton-James, C. E. (2005). Emotion in organizations:
A neglected topic in I/O psychology but with a bright future. In G. P. Hodgkinson
& J. K. Ford (Eds.). *International Review of Industrial and Organizational Psychology*
20. (pp. 221–268). Chichester: John Wiley & Sons.

Ashkanasy, N. M., & Humphrey, R.H. (2011). Current emotion research in organizational behavior. *Emotion Review* 3, 214–224.

Ashkanasy, N. M., Hartel, C. E. J., & Daus, C. S. (2002). Diversity and emotion: The
new frontiers in organizational behavior research. *Journal of Management* 28,
307–338.

Aspinwall, L. G., & Taylor, S. (1997) A stitch in time: Self-regulation and pro-active
coping. *Psychological Bulletin* 121, 417–436.

Austenfeld, J. L., & Stanton, A. L. (2004). Coping through emotional approach: A new look at emotion, coping, and health-related outcomes. *Journal of Personality* 72, 1335–1363.

Avey, J. B., Luthans, F., & Youssef, C. M. (2010). The additive value of positive psychological capital in predicting work attitudes and behaviors. *Journal of Management* 36, 430-452.

Avolio, B. J., & Gardner, W. L. (2005). Authentic leadership development: Getting to the root of positive forms of leadership. *The Leadership Quarterly* 16, 315–338.

Avolio, B.J., Wallumbwa, F., & Weber, T. J. (2009). Leadership current theories, research and future directions. *Annual Review of Psychology* 60, 421–449.

Aycan, Z. (2000). Cross-cultural industrial and organizational psychology. *Journal of Cross-Cultural Psychology* 31, 110–128.

Ayres, J. M. (2004). Framing collective action against neoliberalism: The case of the 'Anti-Globalization' Movement. *Journal of World-Systems Research* 10, 11–34.

Ayyagari, R., Grover, V., & Purvis, R. (2011). Technostress: technological antecedents and implications. *MIS Quarterly* 35, 831–858.

Aziz, S., & Zickar, M. J. (2006). A cluster analysis investigation of workaholism as a syndrome. *Journal of Occupational Health Psychology* 11, 52–62.

Bacon, S. F. (2005). Positive psychology's two cultures. *Review of General Psychology* 9, 181–192.

Bade, M. K., & Cook, S. W. (2008). Functions of Christian prayer in the coping process. *Journal for the Scientific Study of Religion* 47, 123–133.

Bailey, D. E., & Kurland, N. B. (2002). A review of telework research: Findings, new directions, and lessons for the study of modern work. *Journal of Organizational Behavior* 23, 383–400.

Bakker, A. B., & Demerouti, E. (2007). The job demands-resources model: State of the art. *Journal of Managerial Psychology* 22, 309–328.

Bakker, A. B., & Schaufeli, W. B. (2008). Positive organizational behaviour: Engaged employees in flourishing organizations. *Journal of Organizational Behavior* 29, 147–154.

Bakker, A. B., Westman, M., & van Emmerik, I. J. H. (2009). Advances in crossover theory. *Journal of Managerial Psychology* 24, 206–219.

Balch, O. (2014). The 'new wave' in sustainable business. *The Guardian* G2, Thursday 15 May, 3.

Baldwin, T. T., & Ford, J. K. (1988). Transfer of training: A review and directions for future research. *Personnel Psychology* 41, 63–105.

Barjis, J., Gupta, A., & Sharda, R. (2011). Knowledge work and communication challenges in networked enterprises. *Information Systems Frontier* 13, 615–619.

Barley, S. R., Meyerson, D. E., & Grodal, S. (2015). E-mail as a source and symbol of stress. *Organizational Science* 22, 887–906.

Barling, J. (2005). 'And now the time has come…'. *Journal of Occupational Health Psychology* 10, 307–309.

Barling, J., & Griffiths, A. (2003). A history of occupational health psychology. In J. C. Quick & L. E. Tetrick (Eds.). *Handbook of occupational health psychology.* (pp. 19–33). Washington, DC: American Psychological Association.

Barling, J., & Kelloway, E. K. (1996). Job insecurity and health: The moderating role of workplace control. *Stress Medicine* 12, 253–259.

Barling, J., Kelloway, E. K., & Frone, M. R. (2005). Editors' overview: Sources of work stress. In J. Barling, E. K. Kelloway & M. R. Frone (Eds.). *Handbook of work stress.* (pp. 3–5). Thousand Oaks, CA: Sage.

Barsade, S. G., & Gibson, D. E. (2007). Why does affect matter in organizations? *Academy of Management Perspectives* 21, 36–59.

Barsade, S. G., Brief, A. P., & Spataro, S. E. (2003). The affective revolution in organizational behavior: The emergence of a paradigm. In J. Greenberg (Ed.). *Organizational behavior: The state of the science.* (pp. 3–52). Mahwah, NJ: Lawrence Erlbaum Associates.

Bartell, T. (1976). The human relations ideology: An analysis of the social origins of a belief system. *Human Relations* 29, 737–749.

Bartelson, J. (2000). Three concepts of globalization. *International Sociology* 15, 180-196.

Barton, D. (2011). Capitalism for the long term. *Harvard Business Review* 89, 85–91.

Baruch, Y. (2005). Bullying on the net: Adverse behavior on e-mail and its impact. *Information & Management* 42, 361–371.

Baruch, Y., & Hind, P. (1999). Perceptual motion in organizations: Effective management and the impact of the new psychological contracts on 'survivor syndrome.' *European Journal of Work and Organizational Psychology* 8, 295–306.

Baumeister, R. F. (2002). Religion and psychology: Introduction to the special issue. *Psychological Inquiry* 13, 165–167.

Beard, K. W. (2002). Internet addiction: Current status and implications for employees. *Journal of Employment Counseling* 39, 2–11.

Beard, K. W., & Wolf, E. M. (2001). Modification in the proposed diagnostic criteria for internet addiction. *CyberPsychology & Behavior* 4, 377–383.

Beckers, J. J., & Schmidt, H. G. (2001). The structure of computer anxiety: A six-factor model. *Computers in Human Behavior* 17, 35–49.

Beckers, J. J., Wicherts, J. M., & Schmidt, H. G. (2007). Computer anxiety: 'Trait' or 'state'? *Computers in Human Behavior* 23, 2851–2862.

Beehr, T. A. (1985). Organizational stress and employee effectiveness: A job characteristics approach. In T. A. Beehr & R. S. Bhagat (Eds.). *Human stress and cognition in organizations: An integrated perspective.* (pp. 57–82). New York: John Wiley & Sons.

Beehr, T. A. (1998). Research on occupational stress: An unfinished enterprise. *Personnel Psychology* 51, 835–844.

Beehr, T. A., & Glazer, S. (2005). Organizational role stress. In J. Barling, E. K. Kelloway & M. R. Frone (Eds.). *Handbook of work stress.* (pp. 7–33). Thousand Oaks, CA: Sage.

Beehr, T. A., & Grebner, S. L. (2009). When stress is less (harmful). In A. S. G. Antoniou, C. L. Cooper, G. P. Chrousos, C. D. Spielberger & M.W. Eysenck (Eds.). *Handbook of managerial behavior and occupational stress.* (pp. 20–34). Cheltenham: Edward Elgar.

Beehr, T. A., & Newman, J. E. (1978). Job stress, employee health, and organizational effectiveness: A facet analysis, model, and literature review. *Personnel Psychology* 31, 665–669.

Bem, S. L. (1981). Gender schema theory: A cognitive account of sex typing. *Psychological Review* 88, 354–364.

Ben Porath, Y. S., & Tellegen, A. (1990) A place for traits in stress research. *Psychological Inquiry* 1, 14–17.

Benson, J., & Brown, M. (2011). Generations at work: Are there differences and do they matter. *The International Journal of Human Resource Management* 22, 1843–1865.

Bevan, S. (2010). *The business case for employee wellbeing.* A report prepared for Investors in People. London: The Work Foundation.

Bhagat, R. S., Segovis, J. C., & Nelson, T. A. (2012). *Work stress and coping in the era of globalization.* New York: Routledge Taylor & Francis Group.

Billsberry, J., Ambrosini, V., Moss-Jones, J., & March, P. (2005). Some suggestions for mapping organizational members' sense of fit. *Journal of Business and Psychology* 19, 555–570.

Biron, C. (2014). Conclusion: Positive versus stress interventions – Does it really matter? In C. Biron, R. J. Burke & C. L. Cooper (Eds.). *Creating healthy workplaces: Stress reduction, improved well-being, and organizational effectiveness.* (pp. 321–325). Farnham: Gower Publishing Ltd.

Biron, C., & Karanika-Murray, M. (2014). Process evaluation for organizational stress and well-being interventions: Implications for theory, method, and practice. *International Journal of Stress Management* 21, 85–111.

Biron, C., Karanika-Murray, M., & Cooper, C. L. (Eds.) (2012). *Improving organization interventions for stress and well-being: Addressing process and context.* Abingdon: Routledge.

Biron, C., Burke, R. J., & Cooper, C. L. (Eds.) (2014a). *Creating healthy workplaces: Stress reduction, improved well-being, and organizational effectiveness.* Farnham: Gower Publishing Ltd.

Biron, C., St-Hilaire, F., & Brun, J. -P. (2014b). Implementation of an organization intervention on quality of life: Key elements and reflections. In C. Biron, R. J. Burke & C. L. Cooper (Eds.). *Creating healthy workplaces: Stress reduction, improved well-being, and organizational effectiveness.* (pp. 261–280). Farnham: Gower Publishing Ltd.

Bissing-Olson, M. J., Iyer, A., Fielding, K. S., & Zacher, H. (2013). Relationships between daily effect and pro-environmental behavior at work: The moderating role of pro-environmental attitude. *Journal of Organizational Behavior* 34, 156–175.

Bjorck, J. P., & Byron, K. J. (2014). Does stress-related growth involve constructive changes in coping intentions? *The Journal of Positive Psychology* 9, 97–107.

Black, C. (2008). *Working for a healthier tomorrow: Review of the health of Britain's working age population*. Presented to the Secretary of State for Health and the Secretary of State for Work and Pensions. London: TSO, 17 March.

Blok, M. M., Groenesteijn, L., Schelvis, R., & Vink, P. (2012). New ways of working: Does flexibility in time and location of work change work behavior and affect business outcomes? *Work* 41, 5075–5080.

Boatman, J. E., & Sinar, E. F. (2011). The path to meaningful evidence. *Industrial and Organizational Psychology* 4, 66–71.

Boddewyn, J. (1961). Frederick Winslow Taylor revisited. *Academy of Management Journal* 4, 100-107.

Bohart, A. C., & Greening, T. (2001). Humanistic psychology and positive psychology. *American Psychologist* 56, 81–82.

Borg, I., & Dov, E. (1992). Job insecurity: Correlates, moderators and measurements. *International Journal of Manpower* 13, 13–17.

Bowles, D., & Cooper, C. L. (2009). *Employee morale: Driving performance in challenging times*. London: Palgrave Macmillan.

Bowles, D., & Cooper, C. L. (2012). *The high engagement work culture: Balancing me and we*. London: Palgrave Macmillan.

Bowling, N. A., & Gruys, M. L. (2010). Overlooked issues in the conceptualization and measurement of counterproductive work behavior. *Human Resource Management Review* 20, 54–61.

Boyd, D. M., & Ellison, N. B. (2008). Social network sites: Definition, history and scholarship. *Journal of Computer-Mediated Communication* 13, 210–230.

Bramble, T. (2006). 'Another world is possible': A study of participants at Australian alter-globalization social forums. *Journal of Sociology* 42, 287–309.

Brief, A. P., & George, J. M. (1991) Psychological stress and the workplace: A brief comment on Lazarus' outlook. In P. L. Perrewé (Ed.). *Handbook on job stress* [Special Issue]. *Journal of Social Behaviour and Personality* 6, 15–20.

Brief, A. P., & Weiss, H. M. (2002). Organizational behavior: Affect in the workplace. *Annual Review of Psychology* 53, 279–307.

Briner, R. B. (2012). Developing evidence based occupational health psychology. In J. Houdmont, S. Leka & R. Sinclair (Eds.). *Contemporary occupational health psychology: Global perspectives on research and practice*. (pp. 36–56). Chichester: Wiley-Blackwell.

Briner, R. B., & Hockey, G. R. (1988). Operator stress and computer-based work. In C. L. Cooper & R. Payne (Eds.). *Causes, coping and consequences of stress at work*. (pp. 115–140). Chichester: John Wiley & Sons.

Briner, R. B., & Kiefer, T. (2005). Psychological research into the experience of emotion at work: Definitely older, but are we any wiser. *Research on Emotions in Organizational Settings* 1, 289–315.

Briner, R. B., & Kiefer, T. (2009). Whither psychological research into emotion at work? Feeling for the future. *International Journal of Work Organization and Emotion* 3, 161–173.

Briner, R. B., & Rousseau, D. M. (2011a). Evidence-based I-O psychology: Not there yet. *Industrial and Organizational Psychology* 4, 3–22.

Briner, R. B., & Rousseau, D. M. (2011b). Evidence-based I-O psychology: Not there yet but now a little closer. *Industrial and Organizational Psychology* 4, 76–82.

Brinkley, I. (2006). *Defining the knowledge economy*. London: The Work Foundation.

Brinkley, I. (2008). *The knowledge economy: How knowledge is reshaping the economic life of nations*. London: The Work Foundation.

Brinkley, I., Fauth, R., Mahdon, M., & Theodoropoulou, S. (2010). *Is knowledge work better for us? Knowledge workers, good work and wellbeing*. London: The Work Foundation.

Brinkley, I., Jones, K., & Lee, N. (2013). *The gender job split: How young men and women experience the labour market*. London: Touchstone Extras TUC.

Brod, C. (1982). Managing technostress: Optimizing the use of computer technology. *Personnel Journal* 61, 753–757.

Brough, P., & Kalliath, T. (2009). Work-family balance: Theoretical and empirical advancements. *Journal of Organizational Behavior* 30, 581–585.

Brough, P., & O'Driscoll, M. (2010). Organizational interventions for balancing work and home demands: An overview. *Work & Stress* 24, 280-297.

Brough, P., O'Driscoll, M., Kalliath, T., Cooper, C., & Poelmans, S. A. Y. (2009). *Workplace psychological health: Current research and practice*. Cheltenham: Edward Elgar.

Brough, P., Dollard, M. F., & Tuckey, M. R. (2014). Theory and methods to prevent and manage occupational stress: Innovations from around the globe. *International Journal of Stress Management* 21, 1–6.

Brown, A., Charlwood, C., Forde, C., & Spencer, D. (2006). *Changing job quality in Great Britain 1998–2004*. Employment Relations Research Series No 70. London: DTI.

Brown, R., Duck, J., & Jimmieson, N. (2014). E-mail in the workplace: The role of stress appraisals and normative response pressure in the relationship between E-mail stressors and employee strain. *International Journal of Stress Management* 21, 325–347.

Brynjofsson, E., & McAfee, A. (2014). *The second machine age: Work, progress and prosperity in a time of brilliant technology*. New York: W.W. Norton & Company Inc.

Budd, J. W., Arvey, R. D., & Lawless, P. (1996). Correlates and consequences of workplace violence. *Journal of Occupational Health Psychology* 1, 197–210.

Burke, R. J. (1988). Sources of managerial and professional stress in large organizations. In C. L. Cooper & R. Payne (Eds.). *Causes, coping and consequences of stress at work*. (pp. 77–114). Chichester: John Wiley & Sons.

Burke, R. J. (2000). Workaholism in organizations: Concepts, results and future research directions. *International Journal of Management Reviews* 2, 1–16.

Burke, R. J. (2002). Work stress and coping in organizations: Progress and prospects. In E. Frydenberg (Ed.). *Beyond coping: Meeting goals, visions and challenges.* (pp. 83–106). Oxford: Oxford University Press.

Burke, R. J. (2014). Improving individual and organizational health: Implementing and learning from interventions. In C. Biron, R. J. Burke & C. L. Cooper (Eds.). *Creating healthy workplaces: Stress reduction, improved well-being and organizational effectiveness.* (pp. 1–22). Dorchester: Dorset Press.

Burke, R. J., Tomlinson, P., & Cooper, C. L. (2011). *Crime and corruption in organizations.* Aldershot: Gower Press.

Burnes, B. (2004a). Kurt Lewin and the planned approach to change: A re-appraisal. *Journal of Management Studies* 41, 976–1002.

Burnes, B. (2004b). Kurt Lewin and complexity theories: Back to the future. *Journal of Change Management* 4, 309–325.

Burnes, B., & Cooke, B. (2013). Kurt Lewin's field theory: A review and re-evaluation. *International Journal of Management Reviews* 15, 408–425.

Burns, T., & Stalker, G. M. (1961). *The management of innovation.* London: Tavistock.

Bussing, A. (1999). Can control at work and social support moderate psychological consequences of job insecurity? Results from a quasi-experimental study in the steel industry. *European Journal of Work and Organizational Psychology* 8, 219–242.

Buttel, F., & Gould, K. (2004). Global social movement(s) at the crossroads: Some observations on the trajectory of the anti-corporate globalization movement. *Journal of World-Systems Research* 10, 37–60.

Byron, K. (2008). Carrying too heavy a load? The communication and miscommunication of emotion by email. *Academy of Management Review* 33, 309–327.

Caicedo, M. H., & Martensson, M. (2010). The makings of a statement: Accounting for employee health. *Journal of Human Resource Costing & Accounting* 14, 286–306.

Caicedo, M. H., Martensson, M., & Roslender, R. (2010). Managing and measuring employee health and wellbeing: A review and critique. *Journal of Accounting and Organizational Change* 6, 436–459.

Camerer, C. F., & Loewenstein, G. (2004). Behavioral economics: Past, present, future. In C. F. Camerer, G. Loewenstein & M. Rabin (Eds.). *Advances in behavioral economics.* (pp. 1–51). New York: Princeton University Press.

Cameron, K. S., & Caza, A. (2004). Contributions to the discipline of positive organizational scholarship. *American Behavioral Scientist* 47, 731–739.

Campbell-Kelly, M. (2007). The history of the history of software. *IEEE Annuals of the History of Computing* 29, 40-51.

Caplan, R. D. (1987). Person-environment fit theory and organizations: Commensurate dimensions, time perspectives and mechanisms. *Journal of Vocational Behavior* 31, 248–267.

Caplan, S. E. (2002). Problematic internet use and psychosocial well-being: Development of a theory-based cognitive-behavioral measurement instrument. *Computers in Human Behavior* 18, 553–575.

Caplan, S. E. (2003). Preference for online social interaction: A theory of problematic internet use and psychosocial well-being. *Communication Research* 30, 625–648.

Caplan, S. E., & Turner, J. S. (2007). Bringing theory to research on computer-mediated comforting communication. *Computers in Human Behavior* 23, 985–998.

Cartwright, S. (2008). Mergers and acquisitions: Why 2+2 does not make 5. In J. Barling & C. Cooper (Eds.). *The Sage book of organizational behavior.* (pp. 583–601). London: Sage.

Cartwright, S., & Cooper, C.L. (2009a) (Eds.). *The Oxford handbook of personnel psychology.* Oxford: Oxford University Press.

Cartwright, S., & Cooper, C. L. (2009b). Counting cost of presenteeism. *Professional Manager* 2.

Cartwright, S., & Cooper, C. (2013). The impact of mergers and acquisitions on people at work: Existing research and issues. In C. L. Cooper (Ed.). *From stress to well-being: Stress management and enhancing well-being.* V2 (pp. 131–149). Basingstoke: Palgrave Macmillan.

Cartwright, S., & Schoenberg, R. (2006). Thirty years of mergers and acquisitions research: Recent advances and future opportunities. *British Journal of Management* 17, S1–S5.

Carver, C. S., & Connor-Smith, J. (2010) Personality and coping. *Annual Review of Psychology* 61, 679–704.

Cascio, W. F. (2008). To prosper organizational psychology should … bridge application and scholarship. *Journal of Organizational Behavior* 29, 455–468.

Cascio, W. F., & Aguinis, H. (2008). Research in industrial and organizational psychology from 1965 to 2007: Changes, choices and trends. *Journal of Applied Psychology* 93, 1062–1081.

Cassell, C. (2011). Evidenced based I-O psychology: What do we lose on the way? *Industrial and Organizational Psychology* 4, 23–26.

Catano, V. M. (2011). Evidence-based I-O psychology: Lessons from clinical psychology. *Industrial and Organizational Psychology* 4, 45–48.

Cavanaugh, M. A., Boswell, W. R., Roehling, M. V., & Boudreau, J. W. (2000). An empirical examination of self-report work stress among US managers. *Journal of Applied Psychology* 85, 65–74.

Ceyhan, A. A., & Ceyhan, E. (2008). Loneliness, depression, and computer self-efficacy as predictors of problematic internet use. *CyberPsychology & Behavior* 11, 699–701.

Chambers, P. (1973). Frederick Winslow Taylor: A much-maligned management pioneer. *Management Review* 62, 62–64.

Chartered Institute of Personnel & Development (2012). *Diversity and inclusion: Fringe or fundamental?* With Bernard Hodes Group. November. London: CIPD.

Chartered Institute of Personnel & Development (2013a). *Megatrends: The trends shaping work and working lives.* London: CIPD.

Chartered Institute of Personnel & Development (2013b). *The state of migration: Employing migrant workers.* March. London. CIPD.

Chen, T. M. (2011). *How networks changed the world.* IEEE Network: November/December 2–3.

Chen, P., & Cooper, C. L. (2014). *Work and well-being.* Oxford: Wiley Blackwell.

Cheng, C. (2001). Assessing coping flexibility in real-life and laboratory settings: A multimethod approach. *Journal of Personality and Social Psychology* 80, 814–833.

Cheng, C., Kogan, A., & Chio, J. H. (2012). The effectiveness of a new, coping flexibility intervention as compared with a cognitive-behavioural intervention in managing work stress. *Work and Stress* 26, 272–288.

Cheng, G. H-L., & Chan, D. K-S. (2008). Who suffers more from job insecurity? A meta-analytic review. *Applied Psychology: An International Review* 57, 272–303.

Chiang, I-P., & Su, Y-H. (2012). Measuring and analyzing the causes of problematic internet use. *Cyberpsychology, Behavior and Social Networking* 11, 591–596.

Chua, S. L., Chen, D-R., & Wong, A. F. L. (1999). Computer anxiety and its correlates: A meta-analysis. *Computers in Human Behavior* 15, 609–623.

Chun, S., Lee, Y., Kim, B., & Heo, J. (2012). The contribution of leisure participation and leisure satisfaction to stress-related growth. *Leisure Sciences* 34, 436–449.

Chung, H. (2012). Measuring flexicurity: Precautionary notes, a new framework, and an empirical example. *Social Indicators Research* 106, 153–171.

Clark, A. (2010). Farewell to Wall Street. *The Guardian* 7 October.

Coats, D. (2009). Good work in recessionary times. In D. Coats (Ed.). *Advancing opportunity: The future of good work.* (pp. 6–12). London: The Smith Institute.

Coats, D., & Lekhi, R. (2008). '*Good work': Job quality in a changing economy.* London: The Work Foundation.

Coget, J-F. (2011). Technophobe vs. techno-enthusiast: Does the internet help or hinder the balance between work and home life? *Academy of Management Perspective* 25, 95–96.

Coghlan, D., & Brannick, T. (2003). Kurt Lewin: The 'practical theorist' for the 21st century. *Irish Journal of Management* 24, 31–37.

Cogin, J. (2012). Are generational differences in work values fact or fiction? Multi-country evidence and implications. *The International Journal of Human Resource Management* 23, 2268–2294.

Colbert, A., Yee, N., & George, G. (2016). The digital workforce and the workplace of the future. *Academy of Management Journal* 59, 731–739.

Coleman, D., & Iso-Ahola, S. E. (1993). Leisure and health: The role of social support and self-determination. *Journal of Leisure Research* 25, 11–28.

Commission of the European Communities (2009). *GDP and beyond: Measuring progress in a changing world.* Brussels: Commission of the European Communities.

Confederation of British Industry (2007). *Employment trends survey 2007: Fit for business.* London.

Connor-Smith, J. K., & Flachsbart, C. (2007) Relations between personality and coping: A meta-analysis. *Journal of Personality and Social Psychology* 93, 1080-1107.

Constable, S., Coats, D., Bevan, S., & Mahdon, M. (2009). *Good jobs.* London: The Work Foundation.

Cooper, C. (2009). The transition from the quality of working life to organizational behavior: The first two decades. *Journal of Organizational Behavior* 30, 3–8.

Cooper, C., & Dewe, P. (2004). *Stress: A brief history.* Oxford: Blackwell.

Cooper C., & Finkelstein, S. (2016). *Advances in mergers and acquisitions.* Bingley: Emerald.

Cooper, C. L., & Marshall, J. (1976). Occupational sources of stress: A review of the literature relating to coronary heart disease and mental ill health. *Journal of Occupational Psychology* 49, 11–28.

Cooper, C., & Marshall, J. (1980). Sources of managerial and white collar stress. In C. L. Cooper & R. Payne (Eds.). *Stress at Work.* (pp. 81–105). Chichester: John Wiley & Sons.

Cooper, C. L., & Robertson, I. (2013). *Management and happiness.* Cheltenham: Edward Elgar Publishers.

Cooper, C., Dewe, P., & O'Driscoll, M. (2001). *Organizational stress: A review and critique of theory, research and applications.* London: Sage.

Cooper, C., Field, J., Goswani, U., Jenkins, R., & Sahakian, B. (2009). *Mental capital and wellbeing.* Oxford: Wiley & Sons.

Cooper, C., Flint-Taylor, J., & Pearn, M. (2013). *Building resilience at work.* London: Palgrave Macmillan.

Coovert, M. D., & Foster Thompson, L. L. (2003). Technology and workplace health. In J. C. Quick & L. Tetrick (Eds.). *Handbook of occupational health psychology.* (pp. 221–242). Washington, DC: American Psychological Association.

Coovert, M. D., Thompson, L. F., & Craiger, J. P. (2005). Technology. In J. Barling, E. K. Kelloway & M. R. Frone (Eds.). *Handbook of work stress.* (pp. 299–324). Thousand Oaks, CA: Sage.

Corley, K. G., & Gioia, D. A. (2011). Building theory about theory building: What constitutes a theoretical contribution? *Academy of Management Review* 36, 12–32.

Cortina, L. M., Magley, V. J., Williams, J. H., Langhout, R. D. (2001) Incivility in the workplace: Incidence and impact. *Journal of Occupational Heath Psychology* 6, 64–80.

Costa, P. T., & McCrae, R.R. (1990) Personality: Another 'hidden factor' in stress research. *Psychological Inquiry* 1, 22–24.

Cox, T. (1978). *Stress.* New York: Macmillan.

Cox, T., Karanika, M., Griffiths, A., & Houdmont, J. (2007). Evaluating organizational-level work stress interventions: Beyond traditional methods. *Work & Stress* 21, 348–362.

Cox, T., Taris, T. W. & Nielsen, K. (2010). Editorial: Organizational interventions: Issues and challenges. *Work & Stress* 24, 217–218.

Coyle, D., & Quah, D. (2002). *Getting the measure of the new economy*. London: The Work Foundation.

Coyne, J. C. (1997). Improving coping research: Raze the slum before any more building! *Journal of Health Psychology* 2, 153–155.

Coyne, J. C., & Gottlieb, B. H. (1996). The mismeasure by coping checklist. *Journal of Personality* 64, 959–991.

Coyne, J. C., & Racioppo, M. (2000). Never the twain shall meet? Closing the gap between coping research and clinical intervention research. *American Psychologist* 55, 655–664.

Crawford, E. R., LePine, J. A., & Rich, B. C. (2010) Linking job demands to employee engagement and burnout: A theoretical extension and meta-analytic test. *Journal of Applied Psychology* 95, 834–848.

Cronin, M. A. & Klimoski, R. (2011). Broadening the view of what constitutes 'evidence'. *Industrial and Organizational Psychology* 4, 57–61.

Cropanzano, R., Goldman, B. M., & Benson, L. (2005). Organizational justice. In J. Barling, E. K. Kelloway & M. R. Frone (Eds.). *Handbook of work stress.* (pp. 63–87). Thousand Oaks, CA: Sage.

Cross, R., Rebele, R., & Grant, A. (2016). Collaborative overload. *Harvard Business Review*, January-February.

Csikszentmihalyi, M. (2003). Legs or wings? A reply to Richard Lazarus. *Psychological Inquiry* 14, 113–115.

Csikszentmihalyi, M. (2009). The promise of positive psychology. *Psychological Topics* 18, 203–211.

Cubbon, A. (1969). Hawthorne talk in context. *Occupational Psychology* 43, 111–128.

Daniels, K., & Guppy, A. (1994). Occupational stress, social support, job control, and psychological well-being. *Human Relations* 47, 1523–1544.

Daniels, K., & Harris, C. (2005). A daily diary study of coping in the context of the job demands-control-support model. *Journal of Vocational Behavior* 66, 219–237.

Daniels, K., Beesley, N., Cheyne, A., & Wimalasiri, V. (2008). Coping processes linking the demands-control-support model, affect and risky decisions at work. *Human Relations* 61, 845–874.

Daniels, K., Boocock, G., Glover, J., Hartley, R., & Holland, J. (2009). An experience sampling study of learning, affect and the demands control support model. *Journal of Applied Psychology* 94, 1003–1017.

Davis, C. G., Nolen-Hoeksema, S., & Larson J. (1998). Making sense of loss and benefiting from the experience: Two construals of meaning. *Journal of Personality and Social Personality* 75, 561–574.

Davis, K. (1967) *Human relations at work: the dynamics of organizational behaviour* (3rd edition). New York: McGraw-Hill.

Davis, R. A. (2001). A cognitive-behavioral model of pathological internet use. *Computers in Human Behavior* 17, 187–195.

Day, A., Scott, N., & Kelloway, E. K. (2010). Information and communication technology: Implications for job stress and employee well-being. In P. L. Perrewé & D. C. Ganster (Eds.). *New developments in theoretical and conceptual approaches to job stress.* Vol 8 (pp. 317–350). Bingley: Emerald Publishing Group.

Day, V. D., Fleenor, J. W., Atwater, L. E., Sturm, R. E., & McKee, R. A. (2014). Advances in leader and leadership development: A review of 25 years of research and theory. *The Leadership Quarterly* 25, 63–82.

D'Cruz, P., & Noronha, E. (2013). Navigating the extended reach: Target experiences of cyberbullying at work. *Information & Organization* 23, 324–343.

De Cuyper, N., & De Witte, H. (2010). Temporary employment and perceived employability: Mediation by impression management. *Journal of Career Development* 37, 635–652.

De Cuyper, N., Bernhard-Oettel, C., Berntson, E., De Witte, H., & Alarco, B. (2008). Employability and employees' well-being: Mediation by job insecurity. *Applied Psychology: An International Review* 57, 488–509.

De Cuyper, N., Makikangas, A., Kinnunen, U., Mauno, S., & De Witte, H. (2012). Cross-lagged associations between perceived external employability, job insecurity, and exhaustion: Testing gain and loss spirals according to the conservation of resources theory. *Journal of Organizational Behavior* 33, 770-788.

de Jonge, J., Dollard, M. F., Dormann, C., le Blanc, P. M., & Houtman, I. L. D. (2000). The demand-control model: Specific demands, specific control and well-defined groups. *International Journal of Stress Management* 7, 269–287.

de Lange, A. H., Taris, T. W., Kompier, M. A. J., Houtman, I. L. D., & Bongers, P. M. (2003). 'The *very* best of the millennium': Longitudinal research and the demand-control (support) model. *Journal of Occupational Health Psychology* 8, 282–305.

Demerouti, E., & Bakker, A. B. (2011). The job demands-resources model: Challenges for future research. *SA Journal of Industrial Psychology* 37, 1–9.

Demerouti, E., Bakker, A. B., Nachreiner, F., & Schaufeli, W. B. (2001). The job demands-resources model of burnout. *Journal of Applied Psychology* 86, 499–512.

Dent, E., Higgins, M., & Wharf, D. (2005). Spirituality and leadership: An empirical review of definitions, distinctions, and embedded assumptions. *The Leadership Quarterly* 16, 625–653.

Dewe, P. (2003) A closer examination of the patterns when coping with work related stress: Implications for measurement. *Journal of Occupational and Organizational Psychology* 76, 517–524.

Dewe, P. (2017). Demand, resources, and their relationship with coping. In C. L. Cooper & James Campbell Quick (Eds.). *The handbook of stress and health: A guide to research and practice.* (pp. 427–442). London: John Wiley & Sons.

Dewe, P. J. & Brook, R. (2000) Sequential tree analysis of work stressors: Exploring score profiles in the context of the stressor-stress relationship. *International Journal of Stress Management* 7, 1–18.

Dewe, P., & Cooper, C. (2007). Coping research and measurement in the context of work related stress. In G. Hodgkinson & J. Kevin Ford (Eds.). *International Review of Industrial and Organizational Psychology* 22, 141–191.

Dewe, P., & Cooper, C. (2012). *Well-being and work: Towards a balanced agenda.* Basingstoke: Palgrave Macmillan.

Dewe, P., & Cooper, C. (2014). Occupational stress and work: From theory to intervention. In R. Gomes, R. Resende & A. Albuquerque (Eds.). *Positive human functioning from a multidimensional perspective.* (pp.5–35). New York: Nova Science Publications Inc.

Dewe, P., O'Driscoll, M., & Cooper, C. (2010). *Coping with work stress: A review and critique.* Chichester: Wiley-Blackwell.

De Witte, H. (1999). Job insecurity and psychological well-being: Review of the literature and exploration of some unresolved issues. *European Journal of Work and Organizational Psychology* 8, 155–177.

De Witte, H. (2005). Job insecurity: Review of the international literature on definitions, prevalence, antecedents and consequences. *SA Journal of Industrial Psychology* 31, 1–6.

De Witte, H., De Cuyper, N., Handaja, Y., Sverke, M., Näswall, K., & Hellgren, J. (2010). Association between quantitative and qualitative job insecurity and well-being: A test in Belgian banks. *International Studies of Management and Organizations* 40, 40-56.

Diener, E., & Seligman, M. E. P. (2004). Beyond money: Toward an economy of well-being. *Psychological Science in the Public Interest* 5, 1–31.

Dinh, J. E., Lord, R. G., Gardner, W. L., Meuser, J. D., Liden, R. C., & Hu, J. (2014). Leadership theory and research in the new millennium: Current theoretical trends and changing perspectives. *The Leadership Quarterly* 25, 36–62.

Direnzo, M. S., & Greenhaus, J. H. (2011). Job search and voluntary turnover in a boundaryless world: A control theory perspective. *Academy of Management Review* 36, 567–589.

DiRomualdo, T. (2006). Geezers, grungers, genXers, and geeks: A look at workplace generational conflicts. *Journal of Financial Planning* 19, 18–21.

Dohrenwend, B.S., & Dohrenwend, B. P. (1974). *Stressful life effects: Their nature and effects.* New York: John Wiley & Sons.

Dohrenwend, B. P., & Shrout, P. E. (1985). 'Hassles' in the conceptualization and measurement of life stress variables. *American Psychologist* 40, 780-785.

Dolan, P., Layard, R., & Metcalfe, R. (2011). *Measuring subjective well-being for public policy: Recommendations on measures.* Centre for Economic Performance: Special Paper 23: March.

Donaldson, L. (2005). For positive management theories while retaining science: Reply to Ghoshal. *Academy of Management Learning and Education* 4, 109–113.

Donaldson, S. I., & Ko, I. (2010). Positive organizational psychology, behavior, and scholarship: A review of the emerging literature and evidence base. *Journal of Positive Psychology* 5, 177–191.

Donkin, R. (2010). *The future of work.* Basingstoke: Palgrave Macmillan.

Douglas, A. C., Mills, J. E., Niang, M., Stepchenkova, S., Byun, S., Ruffini, C., Lee, S.K., Loutfi, J., Lee, J-K., Atallah, M., & Blanton, M. (2008). Internet addiction: Meta-analysis of qualitative research for the decade 1996-2006. *Computers in Human Behavior* 24, 3027–3044.

Drach-Zahavy, A. (2008). Workplace health friendliness: A cross-level model for predicting workers' health. *Journal of Occupational Health Psychology* 13, 197–213.

Dumay, J. C. (2009). Intellectual capital measurement: A critical approach. *Journal of Intellectual Capital* 10, 190-210.

Easterby-Smith, M. (1994). *Evaluating management development.* London: Gower.

Easterlin, R.A. (2007). The escalation of material goals: Fingering the wrong culprit. *Psychological Inquiry* 18, 31–33.

Edwards, J. (1991). Person-job fit: A conceptual integration, literature review and methodological critique. In C. Cooper & I. T. Robertson (Eds.). *International Review of Industrial and Organizational Psychology.* Vol 6. (pp. 283–357). New York: John Wiley & Sons.

Edwards, J. (1996). An examination of competing versions of the person-environment fit approach to stress. *Academy of Management Journal* 39, 292–339.

Edwards, J. (2008a). A person-environment fit in organizations: An assessment of theoretical progress. *Academy of Management Annals* 2:1, 167–230.

Edwards, J.R. (2008b). To prosper organizational psychology should ... overcome methodological barriers to progress. *Journal of Organizational Behavior* 29, 469–491.

Edwards, J., & Billsberry, J. (2010). Testing a multidimensional theory of person-environment fit. *Journal of Management Issues* 4, 476–493.

Edwards, J., & Cooper, C. (1990). The person-environment fit approach to stress: Recurring problems and some suggested solutions. *Journal of Organizational Behavior* 11, 293–307.

Edwards, J. R., & Rothbard, N. P. (1999). Work and family stress and well-being: An examination of person-environment fit in the work and family domains. *Organizational Behavior and Human Decision Processes* 77, 85–129.

Edwards, J. R., Caplan, R. D., & Van Harrison, R. (2000). Person-environment fit theory. In C. L. Cooper (Ed.). *Theories of organizational stress.* (pp. 28–67). Oxford: Oxford University Press.

Edwards, P. (2001). Making history: New directions in computer historiography. *IEEE Annals of the History of Computing* 23, 86–88.

Edwards, P. D., Franco-Watkins, A. M., Cullen, K. L., Howell, J. A., & Acuff, R. E. Jr (2014). Unifying the challenge: Hindrance and sociocognitive models of stress. *International Journal of Stress* 21, 162–185.

Elfenbein, H. A. (2007). Emotions in organizations: A review and theoretical integration. *The Academy of Management Annals* 1, 1315–1386.

Elst, T.V., De Witte, H., & De Cuyper, N. (2014). The job insecurity scale: A psychometric evaluation across five European countries. *European Journal of Work and Organizational Psychology* 23, 384–380.

Emery, F. E., & Trist, E. L. (1965). The causal texture of organizational environments. *Human Relations* 18, 21–32.

Emmons, R. A. (1999). Religion in the psychology of personality: An introduction. *Journal of Personality* 67, 873–888.

European Commission: Business Innovation Observatory (2013). *The sharing economy: Accessibility based business model of peer-to-peer markets.* Case study 12: September.

Fay, W. B. (1993). Understanding Generation X. *Marketing Research* 5, 54–55.

Fehr, R., Gelfand, M. J., & Nag, M. (2010). The road to forgiveness: A meta-analytic synthesis of its situational and dispositional correlates. *Psychological Bulletin* 136, 894–914.

Fernandez-Ballesteros, R. (2002). Challenges of applied psychology for the third millennium: Introduction to the special issue. *Applied Psychology: An International Review* 51, 1–4.

Field, J., Burke, R., & Cooper, C. L. (2015). *SAGE handbook of aging, work and society.* London: Sage.

Fincham, R., & Roslender, R. (2003). Intellectual capital accounting as management fashion: A review and critique. *European Accounting Review* 12, 781–795.

Fincham, R., & Roslender, R. (2004). Rethinking the dissemination of management fashion. *Management Learning* 35, 321–336.

Fineman, S. (2001). Emotions and organizational control. In R. L. Payne & C. L. Cooper (Eds.). *Emotions at work: Theory, research and applications for management.* (pp. 219–237). Chichester: John Wiley & Sons.

Fineman, S. (2004). Getting the measure of emotion – and the cautionary tale of emotional intelligence. *Human Relations* 57, 719–740.

Fineman, S. (2006). On being positive: Concerns and counterpoints. *Academy of Management Review* 31, 270-291.

Fisher, C. D., & Ashkanasy, N. M. (2000). The emerging role of emotions in work life: An introduction. *Journal of Organizational Behavior* 21, 123–129.

Fisher, G. G. (2001). *Work/personal life balance: A construct development study.* Unpublished doctoral dissertation, Bowling Green State University.

Folkman, S. (1982). An approach to the measurement of coping. *Journal of Occupational Behaviour* 3, 95–107.

Folkman, S. (1997). Positive psychological states and coping with severe stress. *Social Science and Medicine* 45, 1207–1221.

Folkman, S. (2009). Questions, answers, issues, and next steps in stress and coping research. *European Psychologist* 14, 72–77.

Folkman, S. (2011). Stress, health, and coping synthesis, commentary and future directions. In S. Folkman (Ed.). *The Oxford handbook of stress, health and coping.* (pp. 453–462). Oxford: Oxford University Press.

Folkman, S., & Lazarus, R. (1984). *Stress, appraisal and coping.* New York: Springer.

Folkman, S., & Lazarus R. (1991). Coping and emotion. In A. Monet and R.S. Lazarus (Eds). *Stress and coping: An anthology* (pp. 207–227). New York: Springer.

Folkman, S., & Moskowitz, J. T. (2003). Positive psychology from a coping perspective. *Psychological Inquiry* 14, 121–125.

Folkman, S., & Moskowitz, J. T. (2004). Coping: Pitfalls and progress. *Annual Review of Psychology* 55, 745–774.

Forrier, A., & Sels, L. (2003). The concept of employability: A complex mosaic. *International Journal of Human Resources Development and Management* 3, 102–124.

Fotinatos-Ventouratos, R., & Cooper, C. L. (2015). *The economic crisis and occupational stress.* Cheltenham: Edward Elgar Publishing.

Fox, S., & Spector, P. E. (2002). Emotions in the workplace: The neglected side of organizational life introduction. *Human Resource Management Review* 12, 167–171.

Francis, L., Holmvall, C. M., & O'Brien, L. E. (2015). The influence of workload and civility of treatment in the perpetration of email incivility. *Computers in Human Behavior* 46, 191–201.

Fredrickson, B. L. (1998). What good are positive emotions? *Review of General Psychology* 2, 300–319.

Fredrickson, B. L. (2001). The role of positive emotions in positive psychology: The broaden-and-build theory of positive emotions. *American Psychologist* 56, 218–226.

Fredrickson, B. L. (2003). The value of positive emotions. *American Scientist* 91, 330–335.

Fredrickson, B. L. (2005). Positive emotions. In C. R. Snyder & S. J. Lopez (Eds.). *Handbook of positive psychology.* (pp.120–134). Oxford: Oxford University Press.

Fredrickson, B. L. (2010). *Positivity.* Oxford: Oneworld Publications.

Freeman, R. E., Martin, K., & Parmar, B. (2007). Stakeholder capitalism. *Journal of Business Ethics* 74, 303–314.

French, R. P., Rogers, W. L., & Cobb, S. (1974). Adjustment as person-environment fit. In G. Coelho, D. Hamburg & J. Adams (Eds.). *Coping and adaption.* (pp. 316–333). New York: Basic Books.

French, R. P., Caplan, R. D., & Van Harrison, R. (1982). *The mechanisms of job strain and stress.* Chichester: John Wiley & Sons.

Frese, M., & Zapf, D. (1999). On the importance of the objective environment in stress and attribution theory. Counterpoint to Perrewé and Zellars. *Journal of Organizational Behavior* 20, 761–765.

Freund, A. M., & Riediger, M. (2001). What I have and what I do – The role of resource loss and gain throughout life. *Applied Psychology: An International Review* 50, 370–380.

Frey, B. S., & Stutzer, A. (2002). What can economists learn from happiness research? *Journal of Economic Literature* 40, 402–435.

Frey, B. S., & Stutzer, A. (2005). Happiness research: State and prospects. *Review of Social Economy* 63, 207–228.

Friedman, R. A., & Currall, S. C. (2003). Conflict escalation: Dispute exacerbating elements of e-mail communication. *Human Relations* 56, 1325–1347.

Fry, L. W. (1976). The maligned F. W. Taylor: A reply to many of his critics. *Academy of Management Review* 1, 124–129.

Fry, L. W. (2005). Toward a theory of ethical and spiritual well-being, and corporate social responsibility through spiritual leadership. In R. A. Giacalone, C. L. Jurkiewicz & C. Dunn (Eds.). *Positive psychology in business ethics and corporate responsibility.* (pp. 47–83). New York: Information Age Publishing.

Frydenberg, E. (Ed.). (2002). *Beyond coping: Meeting goals, visions, and challenges.* Oxford: Oxford University Press.

Fugate, M., & Kinicki, A. J. (2008). A dispositional approach to employability: Development of a measure and test of implications for employee reactions to organizational change. *Journal of Occupational and Organizational Psychology* 81, 503–527.

Fugate, M., Kinicki, A. J., & Ashforth, B. E. (2004). Employability: A psycho-social construct, its dimensions, and applications. *Journal of Vocational Behavior* 65, 14–38.

Fuglseth, A. M., & Sorebo, O. (2014). The effects of technostress within the context of employee use of ICT. *Computers in Human Behavior* 40, 161–170.

Fullagar, C., & Kelloway, E. K. (2012). New directions in positive psychology: Implications for a healthy workplace. In J. Houdmont, S. Leka & R. Sinclair (Eds.). *Contemporary occupational health psychology: Global perspectives on research and practice.* (pp. 146–161). Chichester: Wiley-Blackwell.

Fulmer, R. M. (2004). The challenge of ethical leadership. *Organizational Dynamics* 33, 307–317.

Furnham, A. (2001). Vocational preference and P-O fit: Reflections on Holland's theory of vocational choice. *Applied Psychology: An International Review* 50, 5–29.

Gable, S. L., & Haidt, J. (2005). What (and why) is positive psychology? *Review of General Psychology* 9, 102–110.

Gable, S. L., Reis, H. T., Impett, E. A., & Asher, E. R. (2004). What do you do when things go right? The intrapersonal and interpersonal benefits of sharing positive events. *Journal of Personality and Social Psychology* 87, 228–245.

Gabrielsson, M., & Kirpalani, V. (2004). Born globals: How to reach new business space rapidly. *International Business Review* 13, 555–571.

Gapper, J. (2005). Comment on Sumantra Ghoshal's 'Bad management theories are destroying good management practices.' *Academy of Management Learning and Education* 4, 101–103.

Gardner, W. L., & Schermerhorn, J. R. (2004). Performance gains through positive organizational behavior and authentic leadership. *Organizational Dynamics* 33, 270-281.

Gardner, W. L., Avolio, B. J., Luthans, F., May, D. R., & Walumbwa, F. (2005). 'Can you see the real me?' A self-based model of authentic leader and follower development. *The Leadership Quarterly* 16, 343–372.

Gardner, W. L., Lowe, K. B., Moss, T. W., Mahoney, K. T., & Cogliser, C. C. (2010). Scholarly leadership of the study of leadership: A review of *The Leadership Quarterly's* second decade, 2000-2009. *The Leadership Quarterly* 21, 922–958.

Gelade, G.A. (2006). But what does it mean to practice? The Journal of Occupational and Organizational Psychology from a practitioner perspective. *Journal of Occupational and Organizational Psychology* 79, 153–160.

Gelfand, M. J., Erez, M., & Aycan, Z. (2007). Cross-cultural organizational behavior. *Annual Review of Psychology* 58, 479–314.

Gelfand, M. J., Leslie, L. M., & Fehr, R. (2008). To prosper organizational psychology should … adopt a global perspective. *Journal of Organizational Behavior* 29, 493–517.

Gephart, R. P. (2002). Introduction to the brave new workplace: Organizational behavior in the electronic age. *Journal of Organizational Behavior* 23, 327–344.

Ghoshal, S. (2005). Bad management theories are destroying good management practices. *Academy of Management Learning and Education* 4, 75–91.

Giancola, F. (2006). The generation gap: More myth than reality. *Human Resource Planning* 29, 32–37.

Giannantonio, C. M., & Hurley-Hanson, A. E. (2011). Frederick Winslow Taylor: Reflections on the relevance of *The Principles of Scientific Management* 100 years later. *Journal of Business and Management* 17, 7–10.

Giumetti, G., Hatfield. A., Scisco, J., Schroeder, A., Muth, E., & Kowalski, R. (2013). What a rude E-mail! Examining the differential effects of incivility versus support on mood, energy, engagement, and performance in an online context. *Journal of Occupational Health Psychology* 18, 297–309.

Gooty, J., Gavin, M., & Ashkanasy, N. M. (2009). Emotions research in OB: The challenges that lie ahead. *Journal of Organizational Behavior* 30, 833–838.

Gore, C. (2010). The global recession of 2009 in a long-term development perspective. *Journal of International Development* 22, 714–738.

Gowdy, J. (2007). Can economic theory stop being a cheerleader for corporate capitalism? *Psychological Inquiry* 18, 33–35.

Grandey, A. A. (2008). Emotions at work: A review and research agenda. In J. Barling & C.L. Cooper (Eds.). *The SAGE handbook of organizational behavior.* (pp. 235-261). Los Angeles, CA: Sage.

Grant, A. M. (2008a). Does intrinsic motivation fuel the prosocial fire? Motivational synergy in predicting persistence, performance, and productivity. *Journal of Applied Psychology* 93, 48–58.

Grant, A. M. (2008b). Designing jobs to do good: Dimensions and psychological consequences of prosocial job characteristics. *The Journal of Positive Psychology* 3, 19–39.

Gratton, L. (2014). *The shift: The future of work is already here.* London: William Collins.

Grawitch, M. J., Barber, L. K., & Justice, L. (2010). Rethinking the work-life interface: It's not about balance, it's about resource allocation. *Applied Psychology: Health and Well-being* 2, 127–159.

Grayson, D., & McLaren, M. (2012). Re-booting capitalism: The action agenda for business. *Harvard Business Review* 90, 40-43.

Greenberg, J. (2008). Introduction to the special issue: To prosper, organizational psychology should... *Journal of Organizational Psychology*, 29, 435–438.

Greenhalgh, L., & Rosenblatt, Z. (1984). Job insecurity: Toward conceptual clarity. *Academy of Management Review* 9, 438–448.

Greenhalgh, L., & Rosenblatt, Z. (2010). Evolution of research on job security. *International Studies of Management and Organizations* 40, 6–19.

Gregory, A., & Milner, S. (2009). Editorial: Work-life balance: A matter of choice? *Gender, Work and Organization* 16, 1–12.

Gregory-Smith, I., Main, B. G. M., & O'Reilly III, C. A. (2014). Appointments, pay and performance in UK boardrooms by gender. *The Economic Journal* 124, F109–F128.

Griffin, R. W., & Lopez, Y. P. (2005). 'Bad behavior' in organizations: A review and typology for future research. *Journal of Management* 31, 988–1005.

Griffiths, M. D. (1995). Technological addictions. *Clinical Psychology Forum,* 76, 14–19.

Griffiths, M. (2010). Internet abuse and internet addiction. *The Journal of Workplace Learning* 22, 463–472.

Guest, D. (2002). Perspectives on the study of work-life balance. *Social Science Information,* 41, 255–279.

Gruys, M. L., & Sackett, P. R. (2003). Investigating the dimensionality of counter-productive work behavior. *International Journal of Selection and Assessment* 11, 30-42.

Gulati, R. (2007). Tent poles, tribalism, and boundary spanning: The rigor-relevance debate in management research. *Academy of Management Journal* 50, 775–782.

Gupta, A., Sharda, R., Ducheneaut, N., Zhao, J. L., & Weber, R. (2006). E-mail management: A techno-managerial research perspective. *Communications of AIS* 17, Article 43, 2–39.

Hackman, J. R. (2009). The perils of positivity. *Journal of Organizational Behavior* 30, 309–319.

Haigh, N., & Hoffman, A. J. (2012). Hybrid organizations: The next chapter of sustainable business. *Organizational Dynamics,* 41, 126–134.

Hair, M., Renaud, K. V., & Ramsay, J. (2007). The influence of self-esteem and locus of control on perceived email-related stress. *Computers in Human Behavior* 23, 2791–2803.

Hall, D. T. (2004). The protean career: A quarter-century journey. *Journal of Vocational Behavior* 65, 1–13.

Hambrick, D. C. (2005). Just how bad are our theories? A response to Ghoshal. *Academy of Management Learning and Education* 4, 104–107.

Hargrove, M. B., Quick, J. C., Nelson, D. L., & Quick, J. D. (2011). The theory of preventive stress management: A 33-year review and evaluation. *Stress and Health* 27, 182–193.

Harris, J. (1991). The utility of the transactional approach for occupational stress research. In P. Perrewé (Ed.). *Handbook on job stress* [Special Issue]. *Journal of Social Behavior and Personality* 6, 21–29.

Harris, K., & Kacmar, K. M. (2005). Organizational politics. In J. Barling, E. K. Kelloway & M. R. Frone (Eds.). *Handbook of work stress.* (pp. 353–374). Thousand Oaks, CA: Sage.

Hart, K. E., & Sasso, T. (2011). Mapping the contours of contemporary positive psychology. *Canadian Psychology* 52, 82–92.

Harvey, J. H., & Pauwels, B. G. (2003). The ironies of positive psychology. *Psychological Inquiry* 14, 153–159.

Hassard, J. S. (2012). Rethinking the Hawthorne studies: The Western Electric research in its social, political and historical context. *Human Relations* 65, 1431–1461.

Health and Safety Executive (2014). *Stress related and psychological disorders in Great Britain.* London: HSE.

Heintzman, P., & Mannell, R. C. (2003). Spiritual functions of leisure and spiritual well-being: Coping with time pressures. *Leisure Sciences* 25, 207–230.

Held, B. S. (2004). The negative side of positive psychology. *Journal of Humanistic Psychology* 44, 9–46.

Helgeson, V. S. (2011). Gender, stress and coping. In S. Folkman (Ed.). *The Oxford handbook of stress, health, and coping.* (pp. 63–85). Oxford: Oxford University Press.

Hellgren, J., Sverke, M., & Isaksson, K. (1999). A two-dimensional approach to job insecurity: Consequences for employee attitudes and well-being. *European Journal of Work and Organizational Psychology* 8, 179–195.

Hellgren, J., Sverke, M., & Näswall, K. (2008). Changing work roles: New demands and challenges. In K. Näswall, J. Hellgren & M. Sverke (Eds.). *The individual in the changing working life.* (pp. 46–66). Cambridge: Cambridge University Press.

Henle, C. A., & Blanchard, A. L. (2008). The interaction of work stressors and organizational sanctioning on cyberloafing. *Journal of Managerial Issues* 20, 383–400.

Hershman, I. (1992) *Commercialization of the internet.* COMPSAC: Proceedings of the 16th Annual Conference, 21–25 September, Chicago, IEEE.

Herzberg, F. (1959). *The motivation to work.* New York: John Wiley & Sons.

Hesselink, D. J. K., & van Vuuren, T. (1999). Job flexibility and job insecurity: The Dutch case. *European Journal of Work and Organizational Psychology* 8, 273–293.

Hetzel-Riggin, M. D., & Prichard, J. R. (2011). Predicting problematic internet use in men and women: The contributions of psychological distress, coping style, and body esteem. *Cyberpsychology, Behavior and Social Networking* 14, 519–525.

Hirsch, D. (2005). *Sustaining working lives: A framework for policy and practice.* York: Joseph Rowntree Foundation.

Hobfoll, S. E. (1989). Conservation of resources: A new attempt at conceptualizing stress. *American Psychologist* 44, 513–524.

Hobfoll, S. E. (2001). The influence of culture, community, and the nested-self in the stress process: Advancing conservation of resources theory. *Applied Psychology: An International Review* 50, 337–421.

Hobfoll, S. E. (2002). Social and psychological resources and adaption. *Review of General Psychology* 6, 307–324.

Hobfoll, S. E. (2011). Conservation of resources theory: Its implications for stress, health, and resilience. In S. Folkman (Ed.). *The Oxford handbook of stress, health, and coping.* (pp. 127–147). Oxford: Oxford University Press.

Hodgkinson, G. P. (2006). The role of JOOP (and other scientific journals) in bridging the practitioner-researcher divide in industrial, work and organizational (IWO) psychology. *Journal of Occupational and Organizational Psychology* 79, 173–178.

Hodgkinson, G. P., & Rousseau, D. M. (2009). Bridging the rigour-relevance gap in management research: It's already happening! *Journal of Management Studies* 46, 534–546.

Hodgkinson, G. P. (2011). Why evidence-based practice in I-O psychology is not there yet: Going beyond systematic reviews. *Industrial and Organizational Psychology* 4, 49–53.

Holman, D. J., & Wall, T. W. (2002). Work characteristics, learning-related outcomes, and strain: A test of competing direct effects, mediated, and moderated models. *Journal of Occupational Health Psychology* 7, 283–301.

Holmes, T. H., & Masuda, M. (1974). Life change and illness susceptibility. In B. S. Dohrenwend & B. P. Dohrenwend (Eds.). *Stressful life events: Their nature and effects.* (pp. 45–72). New York: John Wiley & Sons.

Holmes, T. H., & Rahe, R. H. (1967). The social readjustment scale. *Journal of Psychosomatic Research* 11, 213–218.

Holton, E. F. III (1996). The flawed four-level evaluation model. *Human Resource Development Quarterly* 7, 5–21.

Howard-Grenville, J., Buckle, S. J., Hoskins, B. J., & George, G. (2014). Climate change and management. *Academy of Management Journal* 57, 615–623.

Huang, C. (2010). Internet use and psychological well-being: A meta-analysis. *Cyberpsychology, Behavior and Social Networking* 3, 241–249.

Huang, G-H., Lee, C., Ashford, S., Chen, Z., & Ren, X. (2010). Affective job insecurity: A mediator of cognitive job insecurity and employee outcomes relationships. *International Studies of Management and Organizations* 40, 20–39.

Huang, G-H., Niu, X., Lee, C., & Ashford, S. J. (2012). Differentiating cognitive and affective job insecurity: Antecedents and outcomes. *Journal of Organizational Behavior* 33, 752–769.

Hughes, T., Bence, D., Grisoni, L., O'Regan, N., & Wornham, D. (2011). Scholarship that matters: Academic-practitioner engagement in business and management. *Academy of Management Learning and Education* 10, 40-57.

Huq, M., & Tribe, M. (2004). Economic development in a changing globalized economy. *Journal of International Development* 16, 911–923.

Ingvaldsen, J. A., & Rolfsen, M. (2012). Autonomous work groups and the challenge of inter-group coordination. *Human Relations* 65, 861–881.

Inness, M., & Barling, J. (2005). Terrorism. In J. Barling, E. K. Kelloway & M. R. Frone (Eds.). *Handbook of work stress.* (pp. 375–397). Thousand Oaks, CA: Sage.

International Telecommunications Union (2014). *ICT facts and figures. The world in 2014.* Geneva: ITU.

Isles, N. (2008). *Greening Work.* Provocation Series 4 (1). London: The Work Foundation.

Ito, J. K., & Brotheridge, C. M. (2003). Resources, coping strategies, and emotional exhaustion: A conservation of resources perspective. *Journal of Vocational Behavior* 63, 490-509.

Ito, J. K., & Brotheridge, C. M. (2007). Exploring the predictors and consequences of job insecurity's components. *Journal of Managerial Psychology* 22, 40-64.

Ivancevich, J. M., & Matteson, M. T. (1980). *Stress and work: A managerial perspective.* Glenview, IL: Scott Foresman and Co.

Iwasaki, Y. (2003). Examining rival models of leisure mechanisms. *Leisure Sciences* 25, 183–206.

Iwasaki, Y., & Mannell, R. C. (2000). Hierarchical dimensions of leisure stress coping. *Leisure Sciences* 22, 163–181.

Iwasaki, Y., & Schneider, I. E. (2003). Leisure, stress, and coping: An evolving area of inquiry. *Leisure Sciences* 25, 107–113.

Iwasaki, Y., MacKay, K., & Mactavish, J. (2005a). Gender-based analysis of coping with stress among professional managers: Leisure coping and non-leisure coping. *Journal of Leisure Research* 37, 1–28.

Iwasaki, Y., Mactavish, J., & MacKay, K. (2005b). Building on strengths and resilience: Leisure as a stress survival strategy. *British Journal of Guidance and Counselling* 33, 81–100.

Iwasaki, Y., MacKay, K. J., Mactavish, J. B., Ristock, J., & Bartlett, J. (2006). Voices from the margins: Stress, active living, and leisure as a contributor to coping with stress. *Leisure Sciences* 28, 162–180.

Jacobson, D. (1987). A personological study of the job insecurity experience. *Social Behavior* 2, 143–155.

Jacobson, D., & Hartley, J. (1991). Mapping the context. In J. Hartley, D. Jacobson, B. Klandermans & T. van Vuuren (Eds.). *Job insecurity: Coping with jobs at risk.* (pp. 1–22). London: Sage.

Jané-Llopis, E., Anderson, P., & Cooper, C. (2012). Well-being in the global agenda. *Stress & Health* 28, 89–90.

Jenkins, R. (2004). Globalization, production, employment and poverty: Debates and evidence. *Journal of International Development* 16, 1–12.

Jennings, S. E., Blount, J. R., & Weatherly, M. G. (2014). Social media – a virtual Pandora's box: Prevalence, possible legal liabilities and policies. *Business and Professional Communication Quarterly* 77, 96–113.

Jerejian, A. C. M., Reid, C., & Rees, C. S. (2013). The contribution of email volume, email management strategies and propensity to worry in predicting email stress among academics. *Computers in Human Business* 29, 991–996.

Jex, S. M., & Yankelevich, M. (2008). Work stress. In J. Barling & C. L. Cooper (Eds.). *The SAGE Handbook of Organizational Behavior.* (pp. 498–518). Los Angeles, CA: Sage.

Johnson, J. V., & Hall, E. M. (1988). Job strain, work place social support, and cardio-vascular disease: A cross-sectional study of a random sample of the Swedish population. *American Journal of Public Health* 78, 1336–1342.

Jones, F., & Bright, J. (2001). *Stress: Myth, theory and research.* Harlow: Prentice-Hall.

Jones, F., & Kinman, G. (2001). Approaches to studying stress. In F. Jones & J. Bright (Eds.). *Stress: Myth, theory and research.* (pp. 17–45). Harlow: Prentice-Hall.

Jurkiewicz, C. L. (2000). Generation X and the public employee. *Public Personnel Management* 29, 55–74.

Kahn, H., Stevenson, J. E., & Roslender, R. (2010). Workforce health and intellectual capital: A comparative study of UK accounting and finance and human resource directors. *Journal of Human Resource Costing & Accounting* 14, 227–250.

Kahn, R. L., Wolfe, D. M., Quinn, R. P., Snoek, J. D., & Rosenthal, R. A. (1964). *Organizational stress: Studies in role conflict and ambiguity.* New York: John Wiley & Sons.

Kalliath, T., & Brough, P. (2008). Work–life balance: A review of the meaning of the balance construct. *Journal of Management & Organization* 14, 323–327.

Kanner, A. D., Coyne, J. C., Schaefer, C., & Lazarus, R. S. (1981). Comparison of two modes of stress measurement: Daily hassles and uplifts versus major life events. *Journal of Behavioral Medicine* 4, 1–39.

Kanter, R. M. (2005). What theories do audiences want? Exploring the demand side. *Academy of Management Learning and Education* 4, 93–95.

Karasek, R. A. (1979). Job demands, job decision latitude, and mental strain: Implications for job redesign. *Administrative Science Quarterly* 24, 285–308.

Karasek, R. A. (1998). Demand/control model: A social, emotional, and physiologi-cal approach to stress risk and active behaviour development. In S. M. Stellman (Ed.). *Encyclopaedia of occupational health psychology.* (pp. 34.6–34.14). Geneva: ILO.

Karr-Wisniewski, P., & Lu, Y. (2010). When more is too much: Operationalizing technology overload and exploring its impact on knowledge worker productivity. *Computers in Human Behavior* 26, 1061–1072.

Karren, R. (2012). Introduction to the special issue on job loss. *Journal of Managerial Psychology* 27, 772–779.

Kasser, T., Cohn, S., Kanner, A. D., & Ryan, R. M. (2007a). Some costs of American corporate capitalism: A psychological exploration of values and goal conflicts. *Psychological Inquiry* 18, 1–22.

Kasser, T., Kanner, A. D., Cohn, S., & Ryan, R. M. (2007b). Psychology and American corporate capitalism: Further reflections and future directions. *Psychological Inquiry* 16, 60-71.

Kast, F. E., & Rosenzweig, J. E. (1972). General systems theory: Applications for organizations and management. *Academy of Management Journal* 15, 447–465.

Kato.T. (2012). Development of the Coping Flexibility Scale: Evidence for the coping flexibility hypothesis. *Journal of Counselling Psychology* 59, 262–273.

Katz, D., & Kahn, R. (1966). *The social psychology of organizations*. New York: Wiley.

Kelloway, E.K., & Barling, J. (2010). Leadership development as an intervention in occupational health psychology. *Work & Stress* 24, 260-279.

Kelloway, E. K., Barling, J., & Hurrell, J. J. (2006). *Handbook of workplace violence*. Thousand Oaks, CA: Sage.

Kelloway, E. K., Sivanathan, N., Francis, L., & Barling, J. (2005). Poor leadership. In J. Barling, E. K. Kelloway & M. R. Frone (Eds.). *Handbook of work stress*. (pp. 89–112). Thousand Oaks, CA: Sage.

Kelly, K. J., & Gruber, E. M. (2010). Psychometric properties of the problematic internet use questionnaire. *Computers in Human Behavior* 26, 1838–1845.

Kim, H-K., & Davis, K. E. (2009). Toward a comprehensive theory of problematic internet use: Evaluating the role of self-esteem, anxiety, flow, and the self-rated importance of internet activities. *Computers in Human Behavior* 25, 490-500.

Kinnunen, U., Mauno, S., Natti, J., & Happonen, M. (1999). Perceived job insecurity: A longitudinal study among Finnish employees. *European Journal of Work and Organizational Psychology* 8, 243–260.

Kirkpatrick, D. L. (1994). *Evaluating training programs: The four levels*. San Francisco, CA: Berrett-Koehler.

Kirkwood, T., & Cooper, C.(Eds.) (2014). *A complete reference guide, Volume IV: Wellbeing in later life*. Oxford: Wiley-Blackwell.

Klandermans, B., & van Vuuren, T. (1999). Job insecurity: Introduction. *European Journal of Work and Organizational Psychology* 8, 145–153.

Klehe, U-T., Van Vianen, A.E.M., & Zikic, J. (2012). Coping with economic stress: Introduction to the special issue. *Journal of Organizational Behavior* 33, 745–751.

Kleinrock, L. (2008). History of the internet and its flexible future. *IEEE Wireless Communication*. 15 February, 8–18.

Kleinrock, L. (2010). An early history of the internet. *IEEE Communications Magazine*. August, 26–36.

Kluytmans, F., & Ott, M. (1999). Management of employability in the Netherlands. *European Journal of Work and Organizational Psychology* 8, 261–272.

Koltko-Rivera, M. K. (2006). Rediscovering the later version of Maslow's hierarchy of needs: Self-transcendence and opportunities for theory, research, and unification. *Review of General Psychology* 10, 302–317.

Krägeloh, C. U., Chai, P. P. N., Shepherd, D., & Billington, R. (2012). How religious coping is used relative to other coping strategies depends on the individual's level of religiosity and spirituality. *Journal of Religious Health* 51, 1137–1151.

Kraut, R., Patterson, M., Lundmark, V., Kiesler, S., Mukopadhyay, T., & Scherlis, W. (1998). A social technology that reduces social involvement and psychological well-being. *American Psychologist* 53, 1017–1031.

Kreiner, G. E. (2006). Consequences of work-home segmentation or integration: A person-environment fit perspective. *Journal of Organizational Behavior* 27, 485–507.

Kreiner, G. E., Hollensbe, E. C., & Sheep, M. L. (2009). Balancing borders and bridges: Negotiating the work-home interface via boundary work tactics. *Academy of Management Review* 52, 704–730.

Kristof, A. L. (1996). Person-organization fit: An integrative review of its conceptualizations, measurement and implications. *Personnel Psychology* 49, 1–49.

Kruger, J., Epley, N., Parker, J., & Ng, Z-W. (2005). Egocentrism over E-mail: Can we communicate as well as we think? *Journal of Personality and Social Psychology* 89, 925–936.

Kuo, B. C. H. (2013). Collectivism and coping: Current theories, evidence, and measurements of collective coping. *International Journal of Psychology* 48, 374–388.

Kushlev, K., & Dunn, E. W. (2015). Checking email less frequently reduces stress. *Computers in Human Behavior* 43, 220-228.

Kusstatscher, V. (2006). Cultivating positive emotions in mergers and in acquisitions. In S. Finkelstein & C. Cooper (Eds.). *Advances in mergers and acquisitions.* (Vol 5). (pp. 91–103). New York: JAI.

Kyriazis, D., & Varvarigou, T. (2013). Smart, autonomous and reliable internet of things. *Procedia Computer Science* 21, 442–448.

Langan-Fox, J., & Cooper, C. L. (2014). *Boundary spanning in organizations.* New York and Abingdon: Routledge.

Law, D. M., Shapka, J. D., Hymel, S., Olson, B. F., & Waterhouse, T. (2012). The changing face of bullying: An empirical comparison between traditional and internet bullying and victimization. *Computers in Human Behavior* 28, 226–232.

Lawler, E. E. (1982). Strategies for improving the quality of working life. *American Psychologist* 37, 486–498.

Lawrence, P. R., & Lorsch, J. W. (1967). Differentiation and integration in complex organizations. *Administrative Science Quarterly* 12, 1–47.

Lazarus, R. S. (1966). *Psychological stress and the coping process.* New York: McGraw-Hill.

Lazarus, R. S. (1993). Coping theory and research: Past, present and future. *Psychosomatic Medicine* 55, 234–247.

Lazarus, R.S. (1997). Hurrah for a systems approach. *Journal of Health Psychology* 2, 158–160.

Lazarus, R. S. (1999) *Stress and emotion: A new synthesis.* London: Free Association.

Lazarus, R. S. (2000). Toward better research on stress and coping. *American Psychologist* 55, 665–673.

Lazarus, R. S. (2001). Relational meaning and discrete emotions. In K. Scherer, A. Schorr and T. Johnstone (Eds.). *Appraisal processes in emotion: Theory, methods, research.* (pp. 37–67). New York: Oxford University Press.

Lazarus, R. S. (2003). Does the positive psychology movement have legs? *Psychological Inquiry* 14, 93–109.

Lazarus, R. S., & Cohen-Charash, Y. (2001). Discrete emotions in organizational life. In R. Payne & C. Cooper (Ed.). *Emotions at work: Theory, research and applications for management.* (pp. 45–81). Chichester: John Wiley & Sons.

Lazarus, R. S., DeLongis, A., Folkman S., & Gruen, R. (1985). Stress and adaptational outcomes: The problems of confounded measures. *American Psychologist* 40, 770-779.

Lazarus, R. S., & Folkman, S. (1991). The concept of coping. In A. Monet & R. S. Lazarus (Eds.). *Stress and coping: An anthology.* (pp. 189–206). New York: Columbia University Press.

LeBlanc, M. M., & Kelloway, E. K. (2002). Predictors and outcomes of workplace violence and aggression. *Journal of Applied Psychology* 87, 444–453.

Lee, C., Bobko, P., & Chen, Z. X. (2006). Investigation of the multidimensional model of job insecurity in China and the USA. *Applied Psychology: An International Review* 55, 512–540.

Lee, Y-K., Chang, C-T., Lin, Y., & Cheng, Z-H. (2014). The dark side of smartphone usage: Psychological traits, compulsive behavior and technostress. *Computers in Human Behavior* 31, 373–383.

Lefkowitz, J. (2008). To prosper organizational psychology should … expand the values of organizational psychology to match the quality of its ethics. *Journal of Organizational Behavior* 29, 439–453.

LePine, J. A., LePine, M. A., & Jackson, C. L. (2004). Challenge and hindrance stress: Relationships with exhaustion, motivation to learn, and learning performance. *Journal of Applied Psychology* 89, 883–891.

LePine, J. A., Podsakoff, N. P., & LePine M. A. (2005). A meta-analytic test of the challenge stressor-hindrance stressor framework: An explanation for inconsistent relationships among stressors and performance. *Academy of Management Journal* 48, 764–775.

Lewin, K. (1952). Field theory and learning. In D. Cartwright (Ed.). *Field theory in social science: Selected theoretical papers by Kurt Lewin.* (pp. 60-86). London: Social Science Paperbacks.

Lim, V. K. (2002). The IT way of loafing on the job: Cyberloafing, neutralizing and organizational justice. *Journal of Organizational Behavior* 23, 675–694.

Lim, V. K. G., & Chen, D. J. Q. (2012). Cyberloafing at the workplace: Gain or drain on work. *Behaviour & Information Technology* 31, 343–353.

Lim, V. K. G., Teo, S. H., & Loo, G. L. (2002). How do I loaf here? Let me count the ways. *Communication of the ACM* 45, 66–70.

Linley, P. A., Joseph, S., Harrington, S., & Wood, A. M. (2006). Positive psychology: Past, present, and (possible) future. *Journal of Positive Psychology* 1, 3–16.

Loewenthal, K. M., Cinnirella, M., Evdoka, G., & Murphy, P. (2001). Faith conquers all? Beliefs about the role of religious factors in coping with depression among different cultural-religious groups in the UK. *British Journal of Medical Psychology* 74, 293–303.

Logsdon, J. M., & Young, J. E. (2005). Executive influence on ethical culture. In R. A. Giacalone, C. L. Jurkiewicz & C. Dunn, (Eds.). *Positive psychology in business ethics and corporate responsibility*. (pp. 103–122). New York: IAP Information Age Publishing.

Lopez, S. J., Magyar-Moe, J. L., Petersen, S. E., Ryder, J. A., Krieshok, T. S., O'Byrne, K. K., Lichtenberg, J. W., & Fry, N. A. (2006). Counselling psychology's focus on positive aspects of human functioning. *The Counseling Psychologist* 43, 205–227.

Lorenzi, P. (2004). Managing for the common good: Prosocial leadership. *Organizational Dynamics* 33, 282–291.

Losavio, S. T., Cohen, L. H., Laurenceau, J-P., Dasch, K. B., & Parrish, B. P. (2011). Reports of stress-related growth from daily negative events. *Journal of Social and Clinical Psychology* 30, 760-785.

Lowe, K. B., & Gardner, W. L. (2001). Ten years of *The Leadership Quarterly*: Contributions and challenges for the future. *Leadership Quarterly* 11, 459–514.

Luthans, F. (2002a). The need for and meaning of positive organizational behavior. *Journal of Organizational Behavior* 23, 695–706.

Luthans, F. (2002b). Positive organizational behavior: Developing and managing psychological strengths. *Academy of Management Executive* 16, 57–72.

Luthans, F., & Avolio, B. J. (2009). The 'point' of positive organizational behavior. *Journal of Organizational Behavior* 30, 291–307.

Luthans, F., & Youssef, C. M. (2007). Emerging positive organizational behavior. *Journal of Management* 33, 321–349.

Luthans, F., Youssef, C. M., & Avolio, B. J. (2007a). *Psychological capital: Developing the human edge*. Oxford: Oxford University Press.

Luthans, F., Youssef, C. M., & Avolio, B. J. (2007b) Psychological capital: Investing and developing positive organizational behavior. In D. L. Nelson & C. Cooper (Eds.). *Positive Organizational Behavior*. (pp. 9–24). London: Sage.

Lyons, S., & Kuron, L. (2014). Generational differences in the workplace: A review of the evidence and directions for future research. *Journal of Organizational Behavior* 35, S139–S157.

Lyubomirsky, S. & Abbe, A. (2003). Positive psychology's legs. *Psychological Inquiry* 14, 132–136.

Macik-Frey, M., Quick, J. C., & Nelson, D. L. (2007). Advances in occupational health: From a stressful beginning to a positive future. *Journal of Management* 33, 809–840.

Mackey, J. D., & Perrewé, P. L. (2014). The AAA (appraisals, attributions, adaption) model of job stress: The critical role of self-regulations. *Organizational Psychological Review* 4, 258–278.

MacLane, C. N., & Walmsley, P. T. (2010). Reducing counterproductive work through employee selection. *Human Resource Management Review* 20, 62–72.

Mahoney, M. S. (1988). The history of computing in the history of technology. *Annals of the History of Computing* 10, 113–125.

Maitland, A. (2010). *Working better: The over 50s, the new work generation.* London: Equality and Human Rights Commission.

Maitland, A., & Thomson, P. (2011). *Future work: How businesses can adapt and thrive in the new world of work.* Basingstoke: Palgrave Macmillan.

Martens, P., & Zywietz, D. (2006). Rethinking globalization: A modified globalization index. *Journal of International Development* 16, 331–350.

Martinko, M. J., Gundlach, M. J., & Douglas, S. C. (2002). Toward an integrative theory of counterproductive workplace behavior: A causal reasoning perspective. *International Journal of Selection and Assessment* 10, 36–50.

Maslow, A. H. (1943). A theory of human motivation. *Psychological Review* 50, 370-396.

Maslow, A. H. (1968). *Toward a psychology of being.* New York: D. Van Nostrand Company.

Maslow, A. H. (1969). Toward a humanistic biology. *American Psychologist* 24, 724–735.

Mauno, S., & Kinnunen, U. (2002). Perceived job insecurity among dual-earner couples. Do its antecedents vary according to gender, economic sector and the measure itself? *Journal of Occupational and Organizational Psychology* 75, 295–314.

McCrae, R. R. (1999). Mainstream personality psychology and the study of religion. *Journal of Personality* 67, 1209–1218.

McCullough, M. E., & Worthington, E. L. (1999). Religion and the forgiving personality. *Journal of Personality* 67, 1141–1164.

McGrath, J. E. (ed.) (1970). *Social and psychological factors in stress.* New York: Holt, Rinehart and Winston.

McGregor, D. (1960). *The human side of enterprise.* New York: McGraw-Hill Book Company.

McLafferty, C. L., & Kirylo, J. D. (2001). Prior positive psychologists proposed personality and spiritual growth. *American Psychologist* 56, 84–85.

McMillan, L. H. W., & O'Driscoll, M. P. (2004). Workaholism and health: Implications for organizations. *Journal of Organizational Change Management* 17, 509–519.

Meurs, J. A. & Perrewé, P. L. (2011). Cognitive activation theory of stress: An integrative theoretical approach to work stress. *Journal of Management* 37, 1043–1068.

Meyers, M. C., van Woerkom, M., & Bakker, A. B. (2013). A literature review of positive psychology interventions in organizations. *European Journal of Work and Organizational Psychology* 22, 618–632.

Mills, M. J., Fleck, C. R., & Kozikowski, A. (2013). Positive psychology at work: A conceptual review, state-of-practice assessment and a look ahead. *Journal of Positive Psychology* 8, 153–164.

Misa, T. J. (2007). Understanding how computing has changed the world. *IEEE Annals of the History of Computing* 29, 52–63.

Mohr, G. B. (2000). The challenging significance of different stressors after the announcement of bankruptcy: A longitudinal investigation with special emphasis on job insecurity. *Journal of Organizational Behavior* 21, 337–359.

Moldasch, M., & Weber, W. G. (1998). The 'three waves' of industrial group work: Historical reflections on current research on group work. *Human Relations* 51, 347–388.

Moody, E. J. (2001). Internet use and its relationship to loneliness. *CyberPsychology & Behavior* 4, 393–401.

Muchinsky, P. M. (2000). Emotions in the workplace: The neglect of organizational behavior. *Journal of Organizational Behavior* 21, 801–805.

Muchinsky, P. M., & Monahan, C. J. (1987). What is person-environment congruence? Supplementary versus complementary models of fit. *Journal of Vocational Behavior* 31, 268–277.

Mullins, L. (2002). *Management and organizational behaviour.* Harlow: Financial Times/ Prentice-Hall.

Myers, D. G. (2007). Cost and benefits of American corporate capitalism. *Psychological Inquiry* 18, 43–47.

Naughton, J. (2014). The internet of things really is a big deal. Seriously. *The Observer, News Review* 15 June.

Nelson, D. L., & Cooper, C. L. (2007). Positive organizational behaviour: An exclusive view. In D. L. Nelson & C. L Cooper (Eds.). *Positive Organizational Behaviour* (pp. 3–8). London: Sage.

Newman, A., Ucbasaran, D., Zhu, F., & Hirst, G. (2014). Psychological capital: A review and synthesis. *Journal of Organizational Behavior* 35, S120-S138.

Nguyen, H., & Kleiner, B. H. (2003). The effective management of mergers. *Leadership & Organizational Development* 24, 447–454.

Nielsen, K. (2013). How can we make organizational interventions work? Employees and line managers as actively crafting interventions. *Human Relations* 66, 1029–1050.

Nielsen, K., & Randall, R. (2013). Opening the black box: Presenting a model for evaluating organizational level interventions. *European Journal of Work and Organizational Psychology* 22, 601–617.

Nielsen, K., Taris, T. W., & Cox, T. (2010). The future of organizational interventions: Addressing the challenges of today's organizations. *Work & Stress* 24, 219–233.

Nolen-Hoeksema, S., & Davis, C. G. (2004). Theoretical and methodological issues in the assessment and interpretation of posttraumatic growth. *Psychological Inquiry* 15, 60-64.

Noon, M., Blyton, P., & Morrell, K. (2013). *The realities of work: Experiencing work and employment in contemporary society.* Basingstoke: Palgrave Macmillan.

Norberg, A. L. (1984). Another impact of the computer – The history of the computer. *IEEE Transactions on Education* E-27, 197–203.

Nord, W. (2005). Treats and some treatments: Responses by Kanter, Pfeffer, Gapper, Hambrick, Mintzberg, and Donaldson to Ghoshal's 'Bad management theories are destroying good management practices.' *Academy of Management Learning and Education* 4, 92.

Nykodym, N., Ariss, S., & Kurtz, K. (2008). Computer addiction and cyber-crime. *Journal of Leadership, Accountability and Ethics* 6, 78–85.

Oakland, S., & Ostell, A. (1996). Measuring coping: A review and critique. *Human Relations* 49, 133–155.

O'Bannon, G. (2001). Managing our future: The generation X factor. *Public Service Management* 30, 95–109.

O'Brien, D., & Torres, A. M. (2012). Social networking and online privacy: Facebook users' perceptions. *Irish Journal of Management* 31, 63–97.

O'Brien, T., & DeLongis, A. (1996). The interactional context of problem-emotion- and relationship-focused coping: The role of the big-five personality factors. *Journal of Personality* 64, 775–813.

O'Donnell, D., Henriksen, L. B., & Voelpel, S. C. (2006). Guest editorial: Becoming critical on intellectual capital. *Journal of Intellectual Capital* 7, 5–11.

O'Donnell, G., Deaton, A., Durand, M., Halpern, D., & Layard, R. (2014). *Wellbeing and policy*. London: Legatum Institute.

O'Driscoll, M. (2013). Coping with stress: A challenge for theory, research and practice. *Stress and Health* 29, 89–90.

O'Driscoll, M., Brough, P., Timms, C., & Sawang, S. (2010). Engagement with information and communication technology and psychological well-being. In P. L. Perrewé & D. C. Ganster (Eds.). *New developments in theoretical and conceptual approaches to job stress,* Vol 8 (pp. 269–316). Bingley: Emerald Publishing Group.

O'Driscoll, M., Biron, C., & Cooper, C. (2009). Work-related technological change and psychological well-being. In Y. Amichai-Hamburger (Ed.). *Technology and psychological well-being.* (pp. 106–130). Cambridge: Cambridge University Press.

Office for National Statistics (2013). *Labour market statistics.* June. London: ONS.

Oravec, J. A. (2002). Constructive approaches to internet recreation in the workplace. *Communication of the AGM,* 45–63.

Organization for Economic Cooperation and Development (2012). *Measuring wellbeing and progress: Better life perspective.* Paris: OECD Statistics Directorate.

Organization for Economic Cooperation and Development (2013). *Measuring wellbeing and progress: Better life perspective.* Paris: OECD Statistics Directorate.

O'Rourke, K., & Williamson, J. (2002). When did globalization begin? *European Journal of Economic History* 6, 23–50.

Overall, S. (2008). *Inwardness: The rise of meaningful work.* London: The Work Foundation.

Pardey, D. (2013). ILM Research Paper 1: *Flexible working: A selective summary of recent research.* Institute of Leadership and Management (ILM), London.

Pargament, K. I. (2002). Is religion nothing but …? Explaining religion versus explaining religion away. *Psychological Inquiry* 13, 239–244.

Pargament, K. I., Koenig, H. G., & Perez, L. M. (2000). The many ways of religious coping: Development and initial validation of the RCOPE. *Journal of Clinical Psychology* 56, 519–543.

Park, C. L. (2004). The notion of growth following stressful life experiences: Problems and prospects. *Psychological Inquiry* 15, 69–76.

Park, C. L. (2005). Religion as a meaning-making framework in coping with life stress. *Journal of Social Issues* 61, 707–730.

Park, C. L. (2011). Meaning, coping, and health and well-being. In S. Folkman (Ed.). *The Oxford handbook of stress, health, and coping* (pp. 227–241). Oxford: Oxford University Press.

Park, C. L., & Folkman, S. (1997) Meaning in the context of stress and coping. *Review of General Psychology* 1, 115–144.

Park, C. L., & Helgeson, V. S. (2006). Growth following from highly stressful life events. Current status and future directions. *Journal of Consulting and Clinical Psychology* 74, 791–796.

Park, C. L., Cohen, L. H., & Murch, R. (1996). Assessment and prediction of stress related growth. *Journal of Personality* 64, 71–105.

Parker, L., & Bevan, S. (2011). *Good work and our times*. Report of the Good Work Commission. July. London: The Work Foundation.

Parker, S. K., & Ohly, S. (2008). Designing motivating jobs: An expanded framework for linking work characteristics and motivation. In R. Kanfer, G. Chen, & R. D. Pritchard (Eds.). *Work motivation: Past, present, and future.* (pp. 233–284). Abingdon: Routledge/Taylor & Francis.

Passmore, W. A. (1995). Social science transformed: The socio-technical perspective. *Human Relations* 48, 1–21.

Patel, A. S., Bowler, M. C., Bowler, J. L., & Methe, S. A. (2012). A meta-analysis of workaholism. *International Journal of Business and Management* 7, 2–17.

Pawelski, J. O., & Prilleltensky, I. (2005). 'That at which all things aim.' Happiness, wellness, and the ethics of organizational life. In R. A. Giacalone, C. L. Jurkiewicz & C. Dunn (Eds.). *Positive psychology in business ethics and corporate responsibility.* (pp. 191–208). New York: Information Age Publishing.

Pawson, R., & Tilley, N. (1997). *Realistic evaluation.* London: Sage.

Pekrun, R., & Frese, M. (1992). Emotions in work and achievement. In C. Cooper & I. Robertson (Eds.). *International Review of Industrial and Organizational Psychology* 7. (pp. 153–200). Chichester: John Wiley & Sons.

Perry, J. L. (2012). How can we improve our science to generate more usable knowledge for public professionals? *Public Administration Review* 72, 473–482.

Peterson, C., & Park, N. (2003). Positive psychology as the even handed positive psychologist views it. *Psychological Inquiry* 14, 143–147.

Peterson, C., Park, N., Hall, N., & Seligman, M. E. P. (2009). Zest at work. *Journal of Organizational Behavior* 30, 161–172.

Pfeffer, J. (2005). Why do bad management theories persist? A comment on Ghoshal. *Academy of Management Learning and Education* 4, 96–100.

Pfeffer, J. (2009). *Building sustainable organizations: The human factor.* Stanford Graduate School of Business: Research Paper Series No 2017. February, 1–27.

Pfeffer, J. (2010). Building sustainable organizations: The human factor. *Academy of Management Perspectives* 24, 34–45.

Pienaar, J., De Witte, H., Hellgren, J., & Sverke, M. (2013). The cognitive/affective distinction of job insecurity: Validation and differential relations. *Southern African Business Review* 17, 1–22.

Podolny, J. M., Khurana, R., & Hill-Popper, M. (2005). Revisiting the meaning of leadership. *Research in Organizational Behavior* 26, 1–36.

Popovich, P. M. (2010). Introduction to special issue on 'counterproductive behaviors in organizations'. *Human Resource Management Review* 20, 1–3.

Porter, L. W. (2008). Organizational psychology: A look backward, outward, and forward. *Journal of Organizational Behavior* 29, 519–526.

Porter, L. W., & Schneider, B. (2014). What was, what is, and what may be in OP/OB. *Annual Review of Organizational Psychology and Organizational Behavior* 1, 1–21.

Porter, M. E., & Kramer, M. R. (2011). Creating shared value. *Harvard Business Review* 89, 62–77.

Powell, A. L. (2013). Computer anxiety: Comparison of research from the 1990s and 2000s. *Computers in Behavior* 29, 2337–2381.

Powell, G. N., Francesco, A. M., & Ling, Y. (2009). Toward culture-sensitive theories of the work-family interface. *Journal of Organizational Behavior* 30, 597–616.

Prensky, M. (2001). Digital natives, digital immigrants. *On The Horizon* 9, 1–6.

Price, T. L. (2003). The ethics of authentic transformational leadership. *The Leadership Quarterly* 14, 67–81.

Privitera, C., & Campbell, M. A. (2009). Cyberbullying: The new face of workplace bullying? *CyberPsychology & Behavior* 12, 395–400.

Probst, T. M. (2005). Economic stressors. In J. Barling, E. K. Kelloway, & M. R. Frone (Eds.). *Handbook of work stress* (pp. 267–297). Thousand Oaks, CA: Sage

Puranam, P., Alexy, O., & Reitzig, M. (2014). What's 'new' about new forms of organizing? *Academy of Management Review* 39, 162–180.

Quick, J. C., & Gavin, J. H. (2001). Four perspectives on conservation of resources theory: A commentary. *Applied Psychology: An International Review* 50, 392–400.

Quick, J. C., & Macik-Frey, M. (2007). Healthy productive work: Strength through communication, competence and interpersonal interdependence. In D. L. Nelson & C. L. Cooper (Eds.). *Positive Organizational Behavior* (pp. 25–39). London: Sage.

Quick, J. C., & Quick, J. D. (1979). Reducing stress through preventive management. *Human Resource Management* 18, 15–22.

Quick, J. C., & Quick, J. D. (1984). *Organizational stress and preventive management.* McGraw-Hill: New York.

Quick, J. C., Cooper, C. L., Gibbs, P. C., Little, L. M., & Nelson, D. L. (2010). Positive organizational behavior at work. In G. P. Hodgkinson & J. K. Ford (Eds.). *International Review of Industrial and Organizational Psychology* 25. (pp. 253–291). Chichester: John Wiley & Sons.

Ragu-Nathan, T., Tarafdar, M., & Ragu-Nathan, B. (2008). The consequences of technostress for end users in organizations: Conceptual development and empirical validation. *Information Systems Research* 19, 417–433.

Rainie, L., & Wellman, B. (2014). *Networked: The new social operating system.* Cambridge, MA: The MIT Press.

Ramarajan, L., & Reid, E. (2013). Shattering the myth of separate worlds: Negotiating nonwork identities at work. *Academy of Management Review* 38, 621–644.

Rand, K. L., & Snyder, C. R. (2003). A reply to Dr Lazarus, the evocator emeritus. *Psychological Inquiry* 14, 148–153.

Rathunde, K. (2001). Towards a psychology of optimal human functioning: What positive psychology can learn from the 'experiential turns' of James, Dewey and Maslow. *Journal of Humanistic Psychology* 41, 135–153.

Rayner, C., Hoel, H., & Cooper, C. L. (2001). *Workplace bullying: What we know. Who is to blame and what we can do.* London: Taylor & Francis.

Reichard, R. J., Avey, J. B., Lopez, S., & Dollwet, M. (2013). Having the will and finding the way: A review and meta-analysis of hope at work. *The Journal of Positive Psychology* 8, 292–304.

Reinke, K., & Chamorro-Premuzic, T. (2014). When email use gets out of control. Understanding the relationship between personality and email overload and their impact on burnout and work engagement. *Computers in Human Behavior* 36, 502–509.

Reisel, W. D., & Probst, T. M. (2010). Twenty-five years of studies of job insecurity. *International Studies of Management and Organizations* 40, 3–5.

Resnick, S., Warmoth, A., & Serlin, I. A. (2001). The humanistic psychology and positive psychology connection: Implications for psychotherapy. *Journal of Humanistic Psychology* 41, 73–101.

Rich, G. J. (2001). Positive psychology: An introduction. *Journal of Humanistic Psychology* 41, 8–12.

Ritzer, G. (2011). *Globalization: The essentials.* Chichester: John Wiley & Sons Ltd.

Roberts, Y. (2014). Britain is an ageing country – so maybe it's time we started to cater seriously for people's needs. *The Observer, In focus: Society.* 9 November, 30.

Robertson, I., & Cooper, C. (2011). *Wellbeing: Productivity and happiness at work.* London: Palgrave Macmillan.

Robertson, J. L., & Barling, J. (2013). Greening organizations through leaders' influence on employees' pro-environmental behaviors. *Journal of Organizational Behavior* 34, 176–194.

Robinson, S. L. (2008). Dysfunctional workplace behavior. In J. Barling & C. L. Cooper (Eds.). *The SAGE handbook of Organizational Behavior* (pp. 141–159). Los Angeles, CA: Sage.

Rodriguez-Munoz, A., & Sanz-Vergel, A. I. (2013). Happiness and well-being at work: A special issue introduction. *Journal of Work and Organizational Psychology* 29, 95–97.

Rose, M. (1978). *Industrial behaviour: Theoretical developments since Taylor.* London: Penguin Business.

Rose, M. (1988). *Industrial behaviour.* London: Penguin.

Rosenblatt, Z., Talmud, I., & Ruvio, A. (1999). A gender-based framework of the experience of job insecurity and its effects on work attitudes. *European Journal of Work and Organizational Psychology* 8, 197–217.

Roskies, E., & Louis-Guerin, C. (1990). Job insecurity in managers: Antecedents and consequences. *Journal of Organizational Behavior* 11, 345–359.

Roskies, E., Louis-Guerin, C., & Fournier, C. (1993). Coping with job insecurity: How does personality make a difference? *Journal of Organizational Behavior* 14, 617–630.

Roslender, R. (2009a). So tell me again … why do you want to account for people? *Journal of Human Resource Costing & Accounting* 13, 143–153.

Roslender, R. (2009b). The prospects for satisfactorily measuring and reporting intangibles. *Journal of Human Resource Costing & Accounting* 13, 338–359.

Roslender, R., & Fincham, R. (2001). Thinking critically about intellectual capital accounting. *Accounting, Auditing & Accountability Journal* 14, 383–398.

Roslender, R., Stevenson, J., & Kahn, H. (2006). Employee wellness as intellectual capital: An accounting perspective. *Journal of Human Resource Costing & Accounting* 10, 48–64.

Rothbard, N. P., Dumas, T. L., & Phillips, K. W. (2001). The long arm of the organization: Work-family policies, employee preferences for segmentation and satisfaction and commitment. *Academy of Management Proceedings* GDO: A1–A6.

Rothbard, N. P., Phillips, K. W., & Dumas, T. L. (2005). Managing multiple roles: Work-family policies and individuals' desires for segmentation. *Organization Science* 16, 243–258.

Rothwell, A., & Arnold, J. (2007). Self-perceived employability: Development and validation of a scale. *Personnel Review* 36, 23–41.

Rousseau, D. M., & Fried, Y. (2001). Location, location, location: Contextualizing organizational research. *Journal of Organizational Behavior* 22, 1–13.

Rubin, G. J., Cleare, A. J., & Wessely, C. S. (2008). Psychological factors associated with self-reported sensitivity to mobile phones. *Journal of Psychosomatic Research* 64, 1–9.

Rumens, N. (2005). Extended review: Emotions in work organizations. *Management Learning* 36, 117–128.

Rusk, R. D., & Waters, L. E. (2013). Tracing the size, reach, impact, and breadth of positive psychology. *Journal of Positive Psychology* 8, 207–221.

Ryff, C. D. (2003). Corners of myopia in the positive psychology parade. *Psychological Inquiry* 14, 153–159.

Rynes, S. L. (2007a). *Academy of Management Journal* editors' forum: AMJ turns 50! Looking back and looking ahead. *Academy of Management Journal* 50, 1277–1279.

Rynes, S. L. (2007b). Afterword: To the next 50 years. *Academy of Management Journal* 50, 1379–1383.

Sabella, R. A., Patchin, J. W., & Hinduja, S. (2013). Cyberbullying myths and realities. *Computers in Human Behavior* 29, 2703–2711.

Sackett, P. R. (2002). The structure of counterproductive work behaviors: Dimensionality and relationships with facets of job performance. *International Journal of Selection and Assessment* 10, 5–11.

Salanova, M., Llorens, S., & Cifre, E. (2013). The dark side of technologies: Technostress among users of information and communication technologies. *International Journal of Psychology* 48, 422–436.

Samnani, A-K., & Singh, P. (2012). 20 years of workplace bullying research: A review of the antecedents and consequences of bullying in the workplace. *Aggression and Violent Behavior* 17, 581–589.

Sarachek, B. (1968). Elton Mayo's social psychology and human relations. *Academy of Management Journal* 11, 189–197.

Saridikis, G., & Cooper, C. L. (2013). *How can HR drive growth?* Cheltenham: Edward Elgar Publishers.

Saunders, P. L., & Chester, A. (2008). Shyness and the internet: Social problem or panacea. *Computers in Human Behavior* 24, 2649–2658.

Schaubroeck, J. (1999). Should the subjective be the objective? On studying mental processes, coping behavior, and actual exposures in organizational stress research. *Journal of Organizational Behavior* 20, 753–760.

Schaufeli, W. B. (2004). The future of occupational health psychology. *Applied Psychology: An International Journal* 53, 502–517.

Schaufeli, W. B., & Taris, T. W. (2014). A critical review of the job demands-resources model: Implications for improving work and health. In G. F. Bauer & O. Hammig (Eds.). *Bridging occupational, organizational and public health: A transdisciplinary approach.* (pp. 43–68). Dordrecht: Springer Science+Business Media.

Schmidt, C. K., Raque-Bogdan, T. L., Piontkowski, S., & Schaefer, K. L. (2011). Putting the positive in health psychology: A content analysis in three journals. *Journal of Health Psychology* 16, 607–620.

Schneider, B. (1987). E=f(P,B): The road to a radical approach to person-environment fit. *Journal of Vocational Behavior* 31, 353–361.

Schneider, B. (2001). Fits about fit. *Applied Psychology: An International Review* 50, 141–152.

Schneider, I. E., & Iwasaki, Y. (2003). Reflections on leisure, stress, and coping research. *Leisure Sciences* 25, 301–305.

Schwartz, B. (2007). There must be an alternative. *Psychological Inquiry* 18, 48–51.

Schwartz, S. H. (2007). Cultural and individual value correlates of capitalism: A comparative analysis. *Psychological Inquiry* 18, 52–57.

Schwarzer, R., & Taubert, S. (2002). Tenacious goal pursuits and striving toward personal growth: Proactive coping. In E. Frydenberg (Ed.). *Beyond coping: Meeting goals, visions, and challenges.* (pp. 19–35). Oxford: Oxford University Press.

Scoble, R., & Israel, S. (2014). *Age of context: Mobile, sensors, data and the future of privacy.* Lexington Patrick Brewster Press.

Selenko, E., & Batinic, B. (2013). Job insecurity and the benefits of work. *European Journal of Work and Organizational Psychology* 32, 725–736.

Seligman, M. E. P. (2005). Positive psychology, positive prevention and positive therapy. In C. R. Snyder & S. J. Lopez (Eds.). *Handbook of positive psychology.* (pp. 3–9). Oxford: Oxford University Press.

Seligman, M. E. P., & Csikszentmihalyi, M. (2000). Positive psychology: An introduction. *American Psychologist* 55, 5–14.

Seligman, M. E. P., & Csikszentmihalyi, M. (2001). Reply to comments. *American Psychologist* 56, 89–90.

Seligman, M. E. P., Steen, T. A., Park, N., & Peterson, C. (2005). Positive psychology progress: Empirical validation of interventions. *American Psychologist* 60, 410–421.

Shaw, L. H., & Gant, L. M. (2002). In defence of the internet: The relationship between internet communication and depression, loneliness, self-esteem and perceived social support. *CyberPsychology & Behavior* 5, 157–171.

Sheel, A. (2008). A brief history of globalization. *The Economist* 25 July.

Sheldon, K. M., & King, L. (2001). Why positive psychology is necessary. *American Psychologist* 56, 216–217.

Shin, D. (2014). A socio-technical framework for internet-of-things design: A human-centred design for the internet of things. *Telematics and Informatics* 31, 519–531.

Shorey, H. S., Rand, K. L., & Snyder, C. R. (2005). The ethics of hope: A guide for social responsibility in contemporary business. In R. A. Giacalone, C. L. Jurkiewicz & C., Dunn (Eds.). *Positive psychology in business ethics and corporate responsibility.* (pp. 249–264). New York: Information Age Publishing.

Shu, Q., Tu, Q., & Wang, K.. (2011). The impact of computer self-efficacy and technology dependence on computer-related technostress: A social cognitive theory perspective. *International Journal of Human-Computer Interaction* 27, 923–939.

Simonton, D. K., & Baumeister, R. F. (2005). Positive psychology at the summit. *Review of General Psychology* 9, 99–102.

Sine, W. D., Mitsuhashi, H., & Kirsch, D. A. (2006). Revisiting Burns and Stalker: Formal structure and new venture performance in emerging economic sectors. *Academy of Management Journal* 49, 121–132.

Singelis, T. M. (2000). Some thoughts on the future of cross-cultural psychology. *Journal of Cross-Cultural Psychology* 31, 76–91.

Sissons, P., & Jones, K. (2012). *Lost in transition: The changing labour market and young people not in employment, education or training.* London: The Work Foundation.

Smith, J. H. (1974). Elton Mayo revisited. *British Journal of Industrial Relations* 12, 282–291.

Smith, J. H. (1998). The enduring legacy of Elton Mayo. *Human Relations* 51, 221–249.

Smola, K. W., & Sutton, C. D. (2002). Generational differences: Revisiting generational work values for the new millennium. *Journal of Organizational Behavior* 23, 363–382.

Snir, R., Harpaz, I., & Burke, R. (2006). Workaholism in organizations: New research directions. *Career Development International* 11, 369–373.

Snyder, C. R. (1999). *Coping: The psychology of what works.* New York: Oxford University Press.

Snyder, C. R., & Lopez, S. J. (2005). The future of positive psychology: A declaration of independence. In C. R., Synder & S. J., Lopez (Eds.). *Handbook of positive psychology.* (pp. 751–767). Oxford: Oxford University Press.

Snyder, C. R., & Lopez, S. J. (2007). *Positive psychology: The scientific and practical explorations of human strengths.* Thousand Oaks, CA: Sage.

Snyder, M. (2009). In the footsteps of Kurt Lewin: Practical theorizing, action research, and the psychology of social action. *Journal of Social Issues* 65, 225–245.

Somerfield, M. R., & McCrae, R. R. (2000). Stress and coping research: Methodological challenges, theoretical advances. *American Psychologist* 55, 620-625.

Sparrow, P., Hird, M., & Cooper, C. (2015). *Do we need HR?* London: Palgrave Macmillan.

Spence, J. T., & Robbins, A. S. (1992). Workaholism: Definition, measurement and preliminary results. *Journal of Personality Assessment* 58, 160-178.

Spira, J. B., & Feintuch, J. B. (2005). *The cost of not paying attention: How interruptions impact knowledge worker productivity.* September: Basex Inc.

Spreitzer, G., & Porath, C. (2012). Creating sustainable performance. *Harvard Business Review* 90, 92–99.

Spreitzer, G., Porath, C. L. & Gibson, C. B. (2012). Toward human sustainability: How to enable more thriving at work. *Organizational Dynamics* 41, 155–162.

Sproull, L., & Kiesler, S. (1986). Reducing social context cues: Electronic mail in organizational communication. *Management Science* 32, 1492–1512.

Stanton, A. L., Kirk, S. B. Cameron, C. L., & Danoff-Burg, S. (2000). Coping through emotional approach: Scale construction and validation. *Journal of Personality and Social Psychology* 78, 1150-1169.

Stanton, J. M. (2002). Company profile of the frequent internet user. *Communications of the ACH* 45, 55–59.

Staufenbiel, T., & Konig, C. J. (2011). An evaluation of Borg's cognitive and affective-job insecurity scales. *International Journal of Business and Social Science* 2, 1–7.

Stears, M., & Parker, I. (2012). *Responsible capitalism and behavioural change: Evaluating the Social Business Trust and planning for the future.* London: Institute for Public Policy Research

Stewart, T. (2012). Computers are everywhere. *Behavior & Information Technology* 31, 325–327.

Stich, J., Farley, S., Cooper C. L., & Tarafdar, M. (2015) Information and communication technology demands: Outcomes and interventions. *Journal of Organizational Effectiveness* 2, 327–345.

Stiglitz, J. E., Sen, A., & Fitoussi, J. P. (2009). *Report by the Commission on the measurement of economic performance and social progress*. Paris: OECD.

Strazdins, L., D'Souza, R. M., Lim, L. L-Y., Broom, D. H., & Rodgers, B. (2004). Job strain, job insecurity, and health: Rethinking the relationship. *Journal of Occupational Health Psychology* 9, 296–305.

Suler, J. (2004). The online disinhibition effect. *CyberPsychology & Behavior* 7, 321–326.

Suls, J., David, J. P., & Harvey, J. H. (1996). Personality and coping: Three generations of research. *Journal of Personality* 64, 711–735.

Sulsky, L., & Smith, C. (2005). *Workstress*. Belmont, CA: Thomson Wadsworth.

Sumner, A. (2004). Why are we still arguing about globalization? *Journal of International Development* 16, 1015–1022.

Sutherland, V. J., & Cooper, C. L. (1988). Sources of work stress. In J. J. Hurrell, L. R. Murphy, S. L. Sauter & C. L. Cooper (Eds.). *Occupational stress: Issues and developments in research*. (pp. 3–40). New York: Taylor & Francis.

Sverke, M., & Hellgren, J. (2002). The nature of job insecurity: Understanding employment uncertainty on the brink of a new millennium. *Applied Psychology: An International Review* 51, 23–42.

Sverke, M., De Witte, H., Näswall, K., & Hellgren, J. (2010). European perspectives on job insecurity: Editorial introduction. *Economic and Industrial Democracy* 31, 175–178.

Sverke, M., Hellgren, J., & Näswall, K. (2002). No security: A meta-analysis and review of job insecurity and its consequences. *Journal of Occupational Health Psychology* 7, 242–264.

Sverke, M., Hellgren, J., & Näswall, K. (2006). *Job insecurity: A literature review.* (Report No 1). Stockholm: National Institute for Working Life.

Swedish Council for Working Life & Social Research (2009). *Conference Report: Sustainable work – a challenge in times of economic crisis*. 27–28 October. Stockholm.

Symon, G. (2006). Academics, practitioners and the *Journal of Occupational and Organizational Psychology*: Reflecting on issues. *Journal of Occupational and Organizational Psychology* 79, 167–171.

Tamres, L. K., Janicki, D., & Helgeson, V. S. (2002). Sex differences in coping behavior: A meta-analytic review and an examination of relative coping. *Personality and Social Psychology Review* 6, 2–30.

Tan, L., & Wang, N. (2010). Future internet: The internet of things. 3rd International Conference on Advanced Computer Theory and Engineering (ICACTE): V5-376-V5-380.

Tarafdar, M., Ragu-Nathan, B. S., Ragu-Nathan, T.S., & Tu, Q. (2005). Exploring the impact of technostress on productivity. *Proceedings of the 36th Annual Meeting of the Decision Sciences Institute*, November 19–22. (pp. 13771–13776). San Francisco, California.

Tarafdar, M., Tu, Q., Ragu-Nathan, B., & Ragu-Nathan, T. (2007). The impact of technostress on role stress and productivity. *Journal of Management Information Systems* 24, 301–328.

Tarafdar, M., Tu, Q., & Ragu-Nathan, T. (2010). Impact of technostress on end-user satisfaction and performance. *Journal of Management Information Systems* 27, 303–334.

Tarafdar, M., Tu, Q., Ragu-Nathan, B., & Ragu-Nathan, T. (2011). Crossing to the dark side: Examining creators, outcomes, and inhibitors of technostress. *Communications of the ACM* 54, 113–120.

Taris, T. W., Kompier, M. A. J., de Lange, A. H., Schaufeli, W. B., & Schreurs, P. J. G. (2003). Learning new behaviour patterns: A longitudinal test of Karasek's active learning hypothesis among Dutch teachers. *Work & Stress* 17, 1–20.

Taris, T. W., Kompier, M. A. J., Geurts, S. A. E., Houtman, I. L. D., & van den Heuvel, F. F. M. (2010). Professional efficacy, exhaustion, and work characteristics among police officers: A longitudinal test of the learning-related predictions of the demand-control model. *Journal of Occupational and Organizational Psychology* 83, 455–474.

Taylor, E. (2001). Positive psychology and humanistic psychology: A reply to Seligman. *Journal of Humanistic Psychology* 41, 13–29.

Taylor, R. (2005). *Britain's world of work-myths and realities.* An ESRC Future of Work Programme Seminar Series. Swindon: ESRC.

Tedeschi, R. G., & Calhoun, L. G. (2004). Posttraumatic growth: Conceptual foundations and empirical evidence. *Psychological Inquiry* 15, 1–18.

Teivainen, T. (2002). The World Social Forum and global democratisation: Learning from Porto Alegre. *Third World Quarterly* 23, 621–632.

Tennen, H., & Affleck, G. (2003). While accentuating the positive, don't forget the negative or Mr. In-between. *Psychological Inquiry* 14, 163–169.

Tennen, H., & Affleck, G. (2005). Benefit-finding and benefit-reminding. In C. R. Snyder & S. J. Lopez (Eds.). *Handbook of positive psychology.* (pp. 584–597). Oxford: Oxford University Press.

Tennen, H., Affleck, G., Armeli, S., & Carney, M. (2000). A daily process approach to coping. *American Psychologist* 55, 626–636.

Tetrick, L. (2006). Editorial. *Journal of Occupational Health Psychology* 11, 1–2.

Thayer, A. L., Wildman, J. L., & Salas, E. (2011). I-O Psychology: We have the evidence; we just don't use it (or care to). *Industrial and Organizational Psychology* 4, 32–35.

Thayer, F. (1972). General System(s) Theory: The promise that could not be kept. *Academy of Management Journal* 15, 481–493.

The Economist (2013a). The rise of the sharing economy: On the internet everything is for hire. 9 March.

The Economist (2013b). All eyes on the sharing economy. Technology Quarterly Q1.

The Economist (2013c). When did globalization start? 23 September.

The Economist (2014). Home, hacked home: The internet of things. 12 July: SS14–SS15.

The Guardian (2015). Wearable technology 'will be key to healthcare'. Tuesday 20 January, 8.

The Observer (2014). 80 landmarks in 80 years: The people and events that shaped our world. 23 November, 37.

The Observer (2015). Delivering pizza, making films ... now safety fears grow over surge in use of drones. 15 February, 9.

Theorell, T., & Karasek, R. A. (1996). Current issues relating to psychosocial job strain and cardiovascular disease research. *Journal of Occupational Health Psychology* 1, 9–26.

The Press (2015). Roll on robots: Automation's here. 29 December, A10.

Therborn, G. (2000). Globalizations: Dimensions, historical waves, regional effects, normative governance. *International Sociology* 15, 151–179.

The Work Foundation (2016). *Working Anywhere: A Winning Formula for Good Work.* Lancaster University: The Work Foundation.

Thoits, P. A. (1995). Stress, coping and social support processes. Where are we? What next? *Journal of Health and Social Behavior* (Special Number), 53–70.

Thomée, S., Eklöf, M., Gustafsson, E., Nilsson, R., & Hagberg, M. (2007) Prevalence of perceived stress, symptoms of depression and sleep disturbances in relation to information and communication technology (ICT) use among young adults – an exploratory prospective study. *Computers in Behavior* 23, 1300-1321.

Thorpe, S. J., & Brosnan, M. J. (2007). Does computer anxiety reach levels which conform to DSM IV criteria for specific phobia? *Computers in Human Behavior* 23, 1258–1272.

Tokunaga, R. S. (2010). Following you home from school: A critical review and synthesis of research on cyberbullying victimization. *Computers in Human Behavior* 26, 277–287.

Trenberth, L., & Dewe, P. (2006). Understanding the experience of stressors: The use of sequential tree analysis for exploring the patterns between various work stressors and strain. *Work & Stress* 20, 191–209.

Trist, E. L., & Bamforth, K. (1951). Some social and psychological consequences of the longwall method of coal getting. *Human Relations* 4, 3–38.

Tsikerdekis, M., & Zeadally, S. (2014). Online deception in social media. *Communication of the ACM* 57, 72–80.

Turel, O., & Serenko, A. (2012). The benefits and dangers of enjoyment with social networking websites. *European Journal of Information Systems* 21, 512–528.

Turner, N., & Williams, L. (2005). *The aging workforce.* Corporate Partners Research Programme. London: The Work Foundation.

Turner, N., Barling, J., & Zacharatos, A. (2005). Positive psychology at work. In C. R. Snyder & S. J. Lopez (Eds.). *Handbook of positive psychology.* (pp. 715–728). Oxford: Oxford University Press.

Tushman, M., & O'Reilly, C. A. III (2007). Research and relevance: Implications of Pasteur's quadrant for doctoral programs and faculty development. *Academy of Management Journal* 50, 769–774.

Uhi-Bien, M., Riggio, R. E., Lowe, K. B., & Carsten, M. K. (2014). Followership theory: A review and research agenda. *The Leadership Quarterly* 25, 83–104.

Unsworth, K. L., Dmitrieva, A., & Adriasola, E. (2013). Changing behavior: Increasing the effectiveness of workplace interventions in creating pro-environmental behavior change. *Journal of Organizational Behavior* 34, 211–229.

van Dam, K., & van den Berg, P. T. (2004). Challenges for research in work and organizational psychology: Introduction to the special issue. *Applied Psychology: An International Review* 53, 481–486.

Van den Broeck, A., de Cuyper, N., De Witte, H., & Vansteenkiste, M. (2010). Not all job demands are equal: Differentiating job hindrances and job challenges in the job demands-resources model. *European Journal of Work and Organizational Psychology* 19, 735–759.

van Dick, R., Ullrich, J., & Tissington, P. A. (2006). Working under a black cloud: How to sustain organizational identification after a merger. *British Journal of Management* 17, S69–S79.

Van Harrison, R. (1978). Person-environment fit and job stress. In C. Cooper & R. Payne (Eds.). *Stress at work.* (pp.175–205). Chichester: John Wiley & Sons.

van Maanen, J. (1979). Reclaiming qualitative methods for organizational research: A preface. *Administrative Science Quarterly* 24, 520-526.

van Osch, W., & Coursaris, C. (2013). Organizational social media: A comprehensive framework and research agenda. *46th Hawaii International Conference on Systems Sciences* (IEEE), 700-707.

van Vianen, A. E. M. (2001). Person-organizational fit: The match between theory and methodology: Introduction to the special issue. *Applied Psychology: An International Review* 50, 1–4.

Vermeulen, F. (2007). 'I shall not remain insignificant': Adding a second loop to matter more. *Academy of Management Journal* 50, 754–761.

Viney, W. (1993). *A history of psychology: ideas and context.* Boston, MA: Allyn and Bacon.

Voydanoff, P. (1990). Economic distress and family relations: A review of the eighties. *Journal of Marriage and the Family* 52, 1099–1115.

Waddock, S. (2005). Positive psychology of leading corporate citizenship. In R. A. Giacalone, C. L. Jurkiewicz & C., Dunn (Eds.). *Positive psychology in business ethics and corporate responsibility.* (pp. 23–45). New York: Information Age Publishing.

Wall, T. (2006). Is JOOP of only academic interest? *Journal of Occupational and Organizational Psychology* 79, 161–165.

Wallis, D. (1986). Book review. *Journal of Occupational Psychology* 59, 158–159.

Wang, K., Shu, Q., & Tu, Q. (2008). Technostress under different organizational environments: An empirical investigation. *Computers in Human Behavior* 24, 3002–3013.

Warner, M. (1994). Organizational behaviour revisited. *Human Relations* 47, 1151–1166.

Waterson, P. (2014). The design and use of work technology. In M.C. W. Peeters, J. De Jonge & T. W. Taris (Eds.). *An introduction to contemporary work psychology.* (pp. 220-239). Chichester: John Wiley & Sons

Watson, D., David, J. P., & Suls, J. (1999) Personality, affectivity and coping. In C. R. Snyder (Ed.). *Coping: The psychology that works.* (pp. 119–140). New York: Oxford University Press.

Weatherbee, T. G. (2010). Counterproductive use of technology at work: Information & communications technology and cyberdeviancy. *Human Resource Management Review* 20, 35–44.

Webster, J. R., Beehr, T. A., & Christiansen, N. D. (2010). Towards a better understanding of the effects hindrance and challenge stressors on work behavior. *Journal of Vocational Behavior* 76, 68–77.

Webster, J. R., Beehr, T. A., & Love, K. (2011). Extending the challenge-hindrance model of occupational stress: The role of appraisal. *Journal of Vocational Behavior* 79, 505–516.

Weinberg, A., & Cooper, C. (2012). *Stress in turbulent times.* Basingstoke: Palgrave Macmillan.

Weiser, E. B. (2001). The functions of internet use and their social and psychological consequences. *CyberPsychology & Behavior* 6, 723–743.

Weiss, H. M. (2002). Deconstructing job satisfaction: Separating evaluations, beliefs and affective experiences. *Human Resource Management Review* 12, 173–194.

Weiss, H., & Brief, A. (2001). Affect at work: a historical perspective. In R. L. Payne & C. L. Cooper (Eds.). *Emotions at work: theory, research and applications for management.* (pp. 133–171). Chichester: John Wiley & Sons.

Weiss, H. M., & Cropanzano, R. (1996). Affective events theory: A theoretical discussion of the structure, causes and consequences of affective experiences at work. In B. M. Staw & L. L. Cummings (Eds.). *Research in Organizational Behavior* 18. (pp. 1–74). Stamford, CT: JAI Press.

Westman, M., Brough, P., & Kalliath, T. (2009). Expert commentary on work-life balance and crossover of emotions and experiences: Theoretical and practice advancements. *Journal of Organizational Behavior* 30, 587–595.

Whang, L. S-M., Lee, S., & Chang, G. (2003). Internet over-users' psychological profiles: A behavior sampling analysis on internet addiction. *CyberPsychology* 6, 143–150.

White, S., Gaines, S., & Jha, S. (2012). Beyond subjective well-being: A critical review of the Stiglitz report approach to subjective perspectives on quality of life. *Journal of International Development* 24, 763–776.

Whittaker, S., Bellotti, V., & Moody, P. (2005). Introduction to this special issue on revisiting and reinventing e-mail. *Human-Computer Interaction* 20, 1–9.

Whittington, J. L. (2004). Corporate executives as beleaguered rulers: The leader's motive matters. *Problems and Perspectives in Management* 3, 163–169.

Whybrow, P. C. (2007). Adam Smith's American dream: Time to take stock. *Psychological Inquiry* 18, 57–59.

Williams, L., & Jones, A. (2005). *Changing demographics.* London: The Work Foundation.

Wong, P. T. P. (2011). Positive psychology 2.0: Towards a balanced interactive model of the good life. *Canadian Psychology* 52, 69–81.

World Economic Forum (2012a). *Global agenda: Well-being and global success*. Geneva: World Economic Forum.

World Economic Forum (2012b). *Industry agenda: The workplace alliance: Investing in a sustainable workforce*. Geneva: World Economic Forum.

Worrall, L., & Cooper, C. (2016). *Quality of working life survey*. London: Chartered Management Institute.

Worthington, E. L. Jr & Scherer, M. (2004). Forgiveness is an emotion-focused coping strategy that can reduce health risks and promote health resilience: Theory, review, and hypothesis. *Psychology and Health* 19, 385–405.

Wortman, C. B. (2004). Posttraumatic growth: Progress and problems. *Psychological Inquiry* 15, 81–90.

Wren, D. A. (2011). The centennial of F. W. Taylor's *The Principles of Scientific Management*: A retrospective commentary. *Journal of Business and Management* 17, 11–22.

Wright, T. A. & Quick, J. C. (2009). The emerging positive agenda in organizations: Greater than a trickle, but not yet a deluge. *Journal of Organizational Behavior* 30, 147–159.

Yang, L. Q., Che, H., & Spector, P. E. (2008). Job stress and well-being: An examination from the view of person-environment fit. *Journal of Occupational and Organizational Psychology* 81, 567–587.

Yen, J. (2010). Authorising happiness: Rhetorical demarcation of science and society in historical narratives of positive psychology. *Journal of Theoretical and Philosophical Psychology* 30, 67–78.

Young, K. S. (1996). *Internet addiction: The emergence of a new clinical disorder*. Paper presented at the 104th Annual Meeting of the American Psychological Association (February). Toronto, Canada.

Young, K. S. (2004). Internet addition: A new clinical phenomenon and its consequences. *The American Behavioral Scientist* 48, 402–415.

Youssef, C. M., & Luthans, F. (2005). A positive organizational behavior approach to ethical performance. In R. A. Giacalone, C. L. Jurkiewicz & C., Dunn (Eds.). *Positive psychology in business ethics and corporate responsibility*. (pp. 1–22). New York: Information Age Publishing.

Zeidner, M., & Saklofske, D. (1996). Adaptive and maladaptive coping. In M. Zeidner & N. Endler (Eds.). *Handbook of coping: Theory, research, applications*. (pp. 505–531). New York: John Wiley.

Zinnbauer, B. J., Pargament, K. L., & Scott, A. B. (1999). The emerging meanings of religioness and spirituality: Problems and prospects. *Journal of Personality* 67, 889–919.

Zuffo, R. G. (2011). Taylor is dead, hurray Taylor! The 'human factor' in scientific management: Between ethics, scientific psychology and common sense. *Journal of Business and Management* 17, 23–41.

INDEX

descriptive knowledge 3, 194, 98, 199, 201
  and context 3, 11, 108, 199
  and coping research 9, 161, 169
development
  and context 12, 38–9, 197–8
  new millennium 7–8, 67–94
Dewe, P. 3, 107
digital natives 196
diversity *see* workface change

economic and human crisis (2008) 7, 67,
  68, 77–8, 86, 87, 195
  and globalization 15–16
economic globalization 17
economic recession (1980s) 1, 107, 110–11
economic stress 98, 110–11
economic systems, psychology of 78–9
economics
  and happiness research 82
  infiltration into management theory 7,
    78, 83–4
  new broader interests 79–80
economy *see* knowledge economy; shared
  economy; silver economy; weightless
  economy
Edwards, J. 6, 50, 51–2, 57, 58, 59
Einstein, Albert 1
electronic performance monitoring 123
Ellison, N. B. 23
email overload 129
emails 2, 23, 102
  cyber-incivility 26, 127–9
  cyberbullying 130
emotion approach coping 155, 159
emotion-focused coping 143, 144
  cyberloafing as 26, 127
  religious coping as 145
emotions
  affective characteristics of job insecurity
    114–15
  and preventive stress management 174–5
  see also affective revolution; positive
    emotions
empathy 134, 135
employability 8, 117–19, 120, 172

'environmental uncertainty' 48
Equality and Human Rights Commission
  research on older workers (2010) 30
European Union 32, 81
evaluative coping 161–2
exchange theory 127

Facebook 21, 23
field theory 50
Fincham, R. 190
flexibility/flexible working 2, 102, 110,
  119, 120
flexicurity 8, 119, 120
Folkman, S. 9, 143–4, 144–5, 148, 149,
  150, 151, 154, 155, 159, 160, 165–6,
  168–9
forces of change 3, 4–5, 12–39, 94, 194, 195
  changing nature and character 10–11,
    195–8
  and intervention research 171
  and religious coping 145
  reshaping organizational psychology 171
  reshaping work 8, 95–7
  and work–life balance 132–3
Fredrickson, B. L. 155
French, R. P. 59
Frey, B. S. 82, 83
Fried, Y. 167–8, 200
Fry, L. W. 83

GDP *see* GNP/GDP
gender
  and coping 163–4, 165
  and problematic internet use 126
  and work–life balance 134, 135
  and workforce changes 33
'gender bias' 33
gender schematicity 164
general systems theory 6, 46–7, 49
Generation X 31
Generation Y 31–2
Generation Z 32
Ghoshal, S. 83–5
Gibran, Kahil 2
Gioia, D. A. 88, 176